# Round
## the
# Turnstiles

# Round
## the
# Turnstiles

## Football Travels

by
## Mick Escott

### Illustrations by Alex Bunn

## 119 Grounds in 45 Years

Pomegranate
BOOKS

First published in 2008
2nd Edition 2009

Copyright © Mick Escott 2008

ISBN 978-1-84289-013-4

Cover illustration by John Holder

Printed by the MPG Books Group in the UK

Pomegranate
BOOKS
www.pomegranatebooks.co.uk

Thanks to: Pip Comper, Mrs. Beddows, Graham Godfrey,
Dave Johnson, Milly O'Neill, Holly Newlyn, Ken Picdyn,
Stephen Lamb, Mike Gobbett, Oscar Harrison,
Christopher Knowles, Nicky Dove, the Unsworths,
and to other writers from whom I have borrowed,
all of whom are identified in the text...

and to the Cast of Characters for their performances...

and to Alex Bunn for tennis therapy.

And finally to party chief Nick Clegg for making my mind up to vote Liberal
Democrat in the General Election many months in advance. I read that he
was to urge the reintroduction of standing areas at Premiership grounds.

## MICK ESCOTT

When he is not travelling to the furthermost reaches of England, battling with turnstiles, Mick Escott is a freelance arts administrator. Born in Devon, he grew up in Sussex, spent time in London and started his career at the Victoria Theatre, Stoke-on-Trent. From his base in Bristol he is able to pursue a range of interests, which include pints (a life member of CAMRA, he is co-ordinator of the Stedders Football and Real Ale Guide), performances, purple prose and, of course, penalties.

# Contents

Maps Of League Grounds In England And Wales:

# Foreword
## by Attila the Stockbroker

By the early 90s I had visited all 92 league grounds. This was not an anally retentive exercise (I have lots of friends, I don't possess an anorak and I HATE Coldplay); it happened organically. I'm a Brighton fan, and have been a professional poet/musician since 1980. I have followed the Seagulls up and down the divisions, as often as possible co-ordinating our away fixtures with out-of-town gigs – and when that simply wasn't possible, I've gone to watch the local team. I am not a member of the 92 Club. Or the Cammell Laird Social Club. Though I most certainly am a big fan of Half Man Half Biscuit.

Since my heady achievement (!) an awful lot of clubs have got new grounds. I haven't been to some of them, and this does not cause me the slightest problems with my self esteem or make me itch in awkward places. I may well get to them one day following the Seagulls: if I don't, it doesn't matter. One thing does matter, though.

FOR ELEVEN YEARS BRIGHTON & HOVE ALBION HAVEN'T HAD A PROPER GROUND AT ALL.

Finally, on 4 September 2007, more than ten years since the last game at the Goldstone Ground, we got the irrefutable go-ahead from the Government for our new stadium at Falmer. Which means that 13 years after our home was sold behind our backs to moneymen, we'll have a decent ground again.

And I hope that the people responsible for all of this – who know very well who they are – will one day rot in the Northwich Victoria salt mines, with loop tapes of Phil Collins's greatest hits and endless slow-motion videos of Crystal Palace reserve games as their only respite.

I wish Mick all the best with his book.

Cheers,

*Attila the Stockbroker*

Attila the Stockbroker
PA Announcer at BHAFC
*www.attilathestockbroker.com*
*email: myspace.com/attilastockbroker*

# Illustrations
## by Alex Bunn

# Cast of Characters
## and their affiliations

**Alice**

'I was born in gert Brizzle Children's Hospital (and proud of it) within the sounds of Ashton Gate…I was sharing a flat in Clifton – right posh that was – then I got a place in Bedminster, up the hill from the ground – I could hear 'ooogherghh' when they missed and the cheering when they scored.' She was initiated when City lost 1-2 to Derby in the last game of some season. 'We had awfully funny weather that day….'

**Attila**

See the Foreword, which says it all, except for food preferences. I did witness him scoffing in an Indian restaurant in Bradford before a gig.

**Bob**

Although he has lived in Charlton for a while, he has always supported Forest. It amused him as a boy that the Forest ground was in the county and County in the town – on opposite sides of the Trent. He remembers "Yer daft pyclet" as a 1940s term of abuse. Not like today's language!

**Bogs**

Of Irish origins, but started out at an Ipswich game. He retains affection for the Town, also adopting a certain North London team as he lived close to their former home in N5. He was a regular participant for oval-balled Wasps when they played in Sudbury and before they were transported to a sequence of football league grounds.

**Botha**

Born and bred in grey, drab Huddersfield (his words – how disloyal), his eyes were opened to the glories of colour, music and excitement at the Hawthorns in 1967. He was visiting his grandparents (West Brom beat Chelsea 4-3, he recalls). Immediately hooked, he returned the next day for a reserve match. It was a velvet phenomenon. His affections have remained with the Albion ever since.

**Clemmie**

Developed a soft spot for Newcastle, all because of Alan Shearer, throb, throb. However, she felt sorry for Sunderland when we suffered their sad failure against Birmingham City during the Countdown. The balti pie was good, though. Her sister Katie had a more humble introduction to football - a soggy afternoon in Exeter, enjoying a 2-1 cup win over Eastwood Town.

**Drudge**

A native of the Suffolk/Norfolk border, he didn't develop an interest in Norwich City, but 40 years later admits to a preference in his adopted Bristol for the City, as they do best. Meanwhile he likes basic English food (not my attempt at chicken) including a pie at an occasional football game, like that one at Swindon.

### Foxy
He's here because of our mutual exposure to England on the night of the penalty shoot-out fiasco in 1966. He hasn't been seen since to develop the topic. Let us guess he's a fan of Leicester, whence he came.

### Fredders
A Worthing lad, he followed Brighton, God's team. More recently he settled in Derbyshire and awaits opportunities for Seagulls away games.

### Frumps
Port Vale because they awakened an interest at a time when they played in yellow as well as black and white. She also had a bit of a crush on Peter Shilton, guarding the net for their neighbours.

### Fuckin' Dave
Introduced to Manchester City by his father, and so it stayed, as a season ticket holder. He also went to Stockport games (they used to play on Friday evenings); even the Traffs, on occasion, on alternate fortnights, not being able to keep away from the beautiful game.

### Goatwoman
Lapsed Leeds, latterly rampant Rovers (Donny that is, who appeared at the Millennium Stadium in 2007). A bit of a gloryhunter, then.

### Graham
Millwall. Yet to drive a vehicle to a game. Could there be a connection? He's a telling proof reader, corrections mostly in Millwall's favour.

### Jacquie
A former Pompey girl, her interest in Cheltenham was inspired by a total enthusiast of a friend at the time when they shot from below the Vauxhall Conference right up to the Third Division.

### JCB
As a country girl from Norfolk, she's more attuned to tractor events than football, but she did enjoy that man's embrace at Villa Park. So the Villa it is.

### Jersey
A pin in the donkey's arse for Worcester City, as he enjoyed a kip there, on the concrete in August, to the amusement of surrounding fans. A pint full of local hop nectar has been raised to his memory, many times.

### Karen and Jol
They moved to Walkley, which was in Sheffield's Hillsborough constituency. In addition Jol's political comrades were all heavy duty SWFCers, and he went to the odd game back in the mid-80s. It grew from there. He had been a Chelsea supporter but recognized quality when he saw it, and so the breakdown of that

relationship was not hard. Karen went to the ground just the once.

## Landy
Cardiff, as a Taff, and on a working career over the border has beterraced many a club, including Dover Athletic (when at their peak), Tonbridge Angels (now, there's a name), Leyton Orient (and there), latterly alighting upon West Bromwich Albion. Enjoyed the Millennium Stadium for one of Wales's lesser RU international efforts (Italy were good value for their draw and the other lot were exposed – player power or arrogance?).

## Loz
Of Stoke and West Ham lineage. Adopted Coventry as an esoteric option. Claim to fame: played with future Villa captain Gareth Barry for Brighton Boys.

## Marilyn
A County Fermanagh girl, she followed Lisbellaw Wanderers for a while because her boyfriend played for them – everyone did. Prefers rugby.

## Mickey G
Blackburn Rovers as a son of that city and a perennial season ticket holder, but avoiding Halifax Town. Violent, that lot, and from Yorkshire.

## Mickser
Manchester United, but as a Mancunian – Heaton Chapel (more Stockport really) perhaps just about qualifies.

## Mike
With a school friend developed an interest in Stoke, in parallel with their improving fortunes. The reverse happened, too, but not a further volte face in 2008 when the Potters joined the Premier fray.

## Neil
Exeter born and bred but bizarrely hadn't supported Exeter or really any football team prior to moving away from the area with his family at the age of 13½ to live in Kent. His home town team then became more and more important. Because friends from Exeter went to England matches at Wembley and then also to Exeter away games, he went along to meet up with them and the affection was born.

## Nelson
The Florida Gators always, Sunderland in 2004-05 (Americans like winners). Since then he's had to endure score draws, not a concept familiar to Americans.

## Nice Lady
Under F' Dave's influence Man City, having been dragged there for so many matches; acclimatized through Nottingham Forest – born thereabouts; also has a liking for Arsenal for (perceived) quality of manhood.

## Peter
With an early career involving ten different schools, he eventually adapted his

professional assimilation with Stoke City into admiration of the game's complexities and of Stanley Matthews in particular. His attachment to the club burgeoned, as a means of contact with his daughter after his marriage broke down. He took to distant days out in support of the Potters' quest for renewed success.

### Pom

Can claim a rich Staffordshire background, with her antecedents terracing at Molineux and managing in the Potteries. However, she was born and bred in Bristol. Her cousins were involved with the Rovers so she feels at one with them.

### Priv

He has developed an active interest in a number of clubs: Shelbourne (Dublin), Halifax Town, AFC Wimbledon and, most of all, Stockport County. He tours the country, as an Away Match Travel Organiser (thus called 'Amto' too), exercising a discerning palate for pies and curries. In Stedders's pub it was steak and red wine, but that was after the Accrington visit and was followed by our doubles triumph at pool.

### Rand

Birmingham City from childhood, but can't quite recall visiting St Andrews. Next Newcastle United whom he followed along with colleagues at a distance on Teesside in the early 70s. Newcastle were in Div I, Middlesbrough in Div II. Then he shifted to Stoke City. More recently spotted at Exmoor Rangers, but has actually been to Priestfield Stadium (ten minutes from his house) a couple of times and noted the Gills' floodlight pylons 'like a praying mantis'.

### Rickles

A genuine Traff, of local origins. He was a brave boy: when his classmates at secondary school in Ilkley expressed mass support for the local team, one Leeds United, who happened to be in the ascendancy at the time, he stuck up for Manchester.

### Robin

West Bromwich Albion, inspired by Jeff Astle in his heyday. He did enjoy John Gregory's Villa debut from the rafters, the boys embarrassing Liverpool (2-1).

### Rouge

Liverpool – she's a red-blooded woman. Involved through her spouse, an active supporter; loves John Aldridge.

### Ruthie

Moved to Edinburgh at three years old and became aware of Hearts, but now profoundly anti-football: the sound of the crowd, with associated anger and fear. Even so, survived the game at the National Hockey Stadium.

**Rutz**

Her grandfather played for Crystal Palace, and she formed a modest attachment to them – likes red and blue too. She brews a great posset and is a bagatelle champion.

**Seep**

No interest whatsoever, but concerned about brain damage from all that head use. She did show interest in Ambrosia creamed rice, however, rather a throwaway for one committed to organic cooking materials.

**Stedders**

From Severn Beach, unique in my experience. His love of Bristol Rovers began with their home game against Exeter in 1965. University days saw a diversion to Southampton and Birmingham City. 'After my Rugby-playing days it was back to the Gas and real ale' (to the extent of his own guides recommending five pubs per footy town) with, as a consequence, football-related depression.

**Steve (Bramley)**

Leeds: born, and died, there, far too young, but he was around at the time of their 1970s supremacy.

**Steve (Conisbrough)**

A Bolshevik by inclination and psychiatric nurse by trade, his affiliations are to red wine and malt whisky. He does, however, harbour a desire to elope with Ronaldo and has a soft spot for Preston North End, originating from his college days there.

**Tallulah**

Her first experience of the Glorious Game was when her Dad took her to Stoke City v Manchester City match a few days before her 11-plus exam. In an important gesture of rebellion against an elitist method of educational testing (or was it a response to what she'd just seen?) she stuck her finger into the in-car cigarette lighter on the way home and had to take the exam with a heavily bandaged finger. She's been a Stoke fan ever since. She enjoyed Sellafield, as a tourist.

**Taylor and Ben**

Ben was introduced to football through Stockport County by his dad, Taylor. The ground was easy to get to from where they lived at the time, so an affiliation blossomed. It was family friendly, too, with free tickets to encourage youngsters to attend. After the move to Edinburgh Ben admitted to hitching a lift to Murrayfield. By the way, Ben's mum Lizzie was from Luton.

**The Dude**

Derby County, through his father, a member of Derbyshire Constabulary; since, Aston Villa, starting with the impact of a thrilling (European) evening game, and continuing with occasional floodlit visits.

**The Mad One**

Wolves through and through a few boozers on the way.

## The Mine

After dabbling with Brighton, as another Worthing-born, and Tottenham (for his profession, and Danny Blanchflower and Jimmy Greaves were good at theirs at the time), he moved to saintly Southampton, duly reaffixing his affiliation.

## The Toff

Tranmere from the start, sometimes solitarily cycling to Prenton Park in his early teens. The name alludes to a fog-bound game (Tranmere 3 Norwich 1), not having been able to observe any of the goals (even the keeper didn't see much), he persisted loudly in calling for it to be abandoned. What a sense of fair play! On Radio 5 Live, following his eloquent contribution, he was dubbed "Tranmere's poshest fan".

## Tiptoes

'Suffers' Aston Villa in the course of good parenting. Can't be all negative as he watched the Villa v Blues game on Sky in Ireland. The generous chap does willingly limber up to the Villa Village for acquisition of tickets for friends.

## Tom

A surfing man, he touched upon the Villa while at Brum Uni, later taking them on through his annual charabanc service up the M5 for tempting evening games.

## Turky

His football affiliations, like his ego, are MODEST (his words). For what they are, you might say Hilal Football club Riyadh, from where hailed Sami Jaber of Wolverhampton, though we once spent a great weekend there, with Jersey.

P.S. His soubriquet is in no way related to Exeter fans' appellation for their neighbours Torquay, though we had a great weekend there once.

## Wakey

Manchester City, derived from the maternal side, and Doncaster Rovers. Named after Wakefield and Emley. Allegedly displayed great bidding skills for a turnstile at the Belle Vue auction.

## Warner

Likes The Big Event but not the game, for example Wembley (old) – for the record witnessing the Euro 96 Final. Preferred Prague Xmas Market to Czech Republic FC. He alleges that his great (x4?) grandmother jumped over the top of the Wellington Monument. That was way before professional football was even a seedling.

## Wully

Nowt. As a son of the Metropolitan Borough of Wigan, really should try harder.

# Introduction

I seem to be an inveterate collector. Following in the footsteps of my dear old mother, father, grandparents, I fear it's a serious hereditary matter, perhaps a genetic disorder. From a common preoccupation with family photos – I'm encumbered with a mass of them which still have to be sorted out (can't chuck them yet) – grew a need to accumulate particular things, the small Observer's Books for instance, from no.1, Birds, to 96, Gardens. This eventually sparked off a search for the gaps, which include numbers 38 and 39, dedicated to aircraft, civil and military, issues strangely missing from the list on the back of subsequent volumes. The search continues. I will take it to my grave, or to eBay.

On an excursion late in the odyssey, I happened upon a publicly displayed exposition on 'Collecting' in Manchester Art Gallery, which opened as follows: 'Collecting is a passionate pastime. The thrill of the hunt to find a particular object or to seek out the best example of its kind can send the collector on a never-ending quest. By its very nature collecting is highly personal and people collect for many different reasons: some may be inspired by a particular type of object, or even a specific subject they are interested in.'

Football was destined to join my fray of collections, from April 1959. Aged 11 and three quarters, I was already vaguely intrigued by the long list of League teams since my father 'did the pools'. At 5 o'clock every Saturday the wireless was ritually tuned into the dulcet tones of, I reckon, the forerunner of James Alexander Gordon. This was an absolute routine in our household, along with lunch at half past twelve and tea – with cake – at half past four, all cast in stone. There the ubiquitous punter, pen in hand, crouched over his coupon hoping to win a fortune. It was a ritual, universal right through to the introduction of the Lottery. The re-enactment of it is one of my abiding memories. My father never won much with Vernons Treble Chance ('Littlewoods', famously providing Viv Nicholson with a jackpot in 1961, and 'Vernons' survived as 'brands' until renamed in 2008 by Sportech, the gambling firm) but something of the drama and excitement communicated itself to me. I was later to join him on the pools caper and remember one week being helped by a late result – thank you Queens Park Rangers for managing a draw – to a prize small but to be treasured and remembered (6s 8d I think).

I listened in awe to the teatime delivery of the names, far-flung and exotic: Tottenham Hotspur, Port Vale, Crystal Palace in the League; Heart of Midlothian, Third Lanark, Queen of the South, to name but a few Scottish clubs to await in the last stages of the reading. And the long lost Workington, Southport, Barrow and Gateshead, inducing a strange curiosity. What and where were they? An early book purchase was to be the Geographia Great Britain Commercial Gazetteer, an atlas supported by statistical entries for each settlement. I was now collecting places, too, unaware then of such equations as between Birkenhead and Tranmere.

My father never took me to a football game – race meetings more like; he was a Lester Piggott devotee and, later, Desert Orchid (he joined the fan club). Because I had never seen a professional match I was unaware of its magic. When I did experience it, I was overwhelmed. The bustling streets around the ground, the din of the crowd, the singing, the chanting, the banter, the shouting, the ebb and flow of excitement, the disappointments

and the thrills of the event were to stir my emotions as nothing had done before. Instantly I fell in love with this phenomenon, and the affair has lasted ever since.

The eventual initiation at a football ground didn't happen until Boxing Day 1963: a visit to the Goldstone Ground, Hove, to see Exeter triumph. I recall the naïve thrill of anticipation of all those other grounds, if they were anything like this haven of bliss. Unfortunately a win for your team away was to prove quite a hard act to follow – it wasn't long before I was exposed to the other side of the coin: the suffering and disappointment, yes torment, endured habitually by soccer-goers.

Easter holidays 1959, when my fate was determined by a football transmission on the wireless: it surrounded the First Division tussle between Aston Villa and Manchester City to avoid the drop to the Second Division with Portsmouth, already down. Villa, for whom I had already developed a soft spot, eventually suffered the drop. I was surprised at how upset I was. My devotion to the Football League had been born, reinforced the following November, when they thrashed Charlton Athletic 11-1 down in the Second Division. The prospect of following a team capable of such excitement was irresistible.

In the late summer came the unavoidable purchase of my first ever football annual, of modest dimensions and design, but standing out above all the bigger, glossier merchandise on some newsagent's stall. It was the ever-reliable, so it proved, football annual produced by *Racing and Football Outlook* that first caught my interest late that August, to endure the final First Division table with the notional dotted relegation line above Villa's entry and to anticipate fixtures at their depressed level. From then on it became a habit to look forward to the volume's appearance every year. From the pocket-sized (4.75" x 3.5") edition costing 6d, from 1953-54 to 1962-63, it has blossomed into a 7.5" x 5" glossy volume which in 2007, by then called *Football Guide*, was priced at £5.99, the same by mail order, which is pretty good. My copies for 1959-60 to 1961-62 must have spent considerable time in pockets as they are somewhat tatty. The contents of the annual even now provide the basics, for my purpose the tables, results and fixtures: the standard statistics. In the new century editions a whole page of opinion became devoted to each Premiership club, two to a page for the other divisions; as well as the Scottish Premier League (Celtic and Rangers have also been allocated their own full pages).

Back in 1959-60 the entire League Division I was crammed into six pages, comprising squads and comments. The teams have gone but we are now provided with websites, nicknames and Outlook forecasts. The opinions and forecasts have made amusing reading after the end of the season. In 2004-05 Wolves and Leicester were tipped for the Championship automatic promotion places, which went to Sunderland and Wigan, who were predicted to finish eighth and fourth respectively. On the other hand I haven't been too concerned with the extensive betting information, reserving flutters for quixotic fancies. Other annuals have been dipped into over the years, notably the *Playfair Football Annual* whose special feature was complete grids of League positions over many seasons; and a few *Official FA Year Books* carrying a review of various strands of the English game. And we mustn't forget *Rothman's* for its wealth of statistics.

At some stage at a car boot sale I happened upon a collection of annuals going back to 1935-36. Such events can produce fortuitous surprises. These comprised *Littlewoods, Daily Worker, Sunday Chronicle, Daily Mail, Empire News, News Chronicle & Daily Dispatch* and *News of the World*, a treasure trove which enhanced the collection dramatically. Also all over the country, once the new season was underway, there was likely to be a local volume on the subject. There was quite a range – I have found that annuals have always proliferated. Examples are *Wee Red Books* from Scotland and the *Sentinel Football Annual* from Stoke-on-Trent. Once you embark upon collecting, it develops its own dynamic.

From football annuals it was inevitable that actual clubs and grounds would follow. Placed alongside the general was particular loyalty. You follow the team/s of your choice.

Within my family mention had been made from time to time of the intriguing name 'Aston Villa'. At the time – I was in short trousers and had never been north of London – it was saddening to be informed that they played in the 'West Midlands', sounding even grimmer than 'Birmingham'. But the deed had been done in 1959 and I was hooked. Perhaps there was an element of supporting the underdog. After all, they had been relegated for only the second time in their history.

As I deem myself valid in my affections, this takes me to the matter of 'gloryhunters', the category of supporters illustrated so well by Tone Ov Voice in the Wolves fanzine *A Load of Bull* (Issue 129): 'There are three blokes I've met recently who really sum up gloryhunters. First, I bought a car in Birmingham from Tom. As we were completing the paperwork I asked our thick-Brummie-accented Tom whether he was a Blues or a Villa fan. "Neither" he says, "oim a Man Utd fan". I always laugh at people like this and once I'd settled back down, asked him why. "Well," he says "I was born in Manchester weren't oi." I didn't give up this easily. "Which part of Oldham was that then?" I ventured. His answer to this question said it all – "My dad's a Man Utd fan too". Ah, there we have it then, his Dad was a gloryhunter as well. Yet, is the son of a gloryhunter necessarily a gloryhunter too? The joke is that if our Brummie Tom had been born in Cleethorpes, would he still have paid homage to his natal town and supported Grimsby Town? Yeah, right.

'Next comes Dick who I met at a dinner dance recently. When conversation turned to the day's football I asked Dick where he was from. It was Luton. "Ah" says I, "you'll be a Luton Town fan then." His response was yes and I thought, oh good. But then there was this rider to his reply. "But my second team is Man Utd." "Why's that?" I ask in dismay. "I don't know" Dick continues, "but I always look out for their score." There are proud Luton fans out there but I'm afraid Dick isn't one of them.

'Then there's Harry. This was the best one. I'd made a presentation at one of my customers and had been invited to dinner afterwards. Everything was going fine and then the conversation turned to football. From his accent I knew that Harry was from the North West somewhere. So when he announced that his favourite team was Chelsea it did make me laugh. I turned to him and said "you'd better have a bloody good reason for this." "Well," says Harry, "I'm from Barrow but they don't have a team anymore so I picked a team who play in the same colours." My god, what an answer, and as he'd so particularly set himself up, I had to have a tilt. "First," I told him, "Barrow *do* still have a team, it's just that they're not in the League anymore. Second, there's quite a choice of teams who play in blue and white I think." Strange, isn't it, that given the variety of teams from which to choose like Southend, Colchester, Carlisle (and the last is just up the road from Barrow, after all, if you must have a league club), Millwall… Harry actually fell on Chelsea. What chance, eh!.

'Apart from Tom, Dick and Harry, there are other out and out gloryhunters. Like those who live in a town with no league team, say Tipton, and struggle to decide who to support. Let's call this one Steve. Let's see, 92 league clubs, who shall it be? I know, Liverpool! What a lucky choice. Later when poked fun at by his Wolves and Albion mates, Steve retorts: "how can I be a gloryhunter when they haven't won the league for years?" Absolutely no comment. Let's reflect on some Liverpool fans' sense that theirs is the club of the underdog however tangible the achievements, expensive the merchandise and elusive the access. A breakdown of Anfield attenders would be interesting.'

More recently a refreshing new movement has been developing: the second team, a notion derided by some purists. Some League clubs were realizing that they now had no answer to worship of the top Premier teams. Every Premiership tussle was available to the public: in bars, on their home screen, and for a mere mean average of about 60k per game inside a major stadium. A lesser entity had to become resourceful: encourage the younger generations to adopt a club, theirs preferably, as a place to visit for live games, in the second, third, fourth, even fifth divisions. This meant going to Fourth Division games at Brentford as well as following the glorious Chelsea on the telly. Why not? This in turn could burgeon into community activity. There was also the possibility of the concept linking up with members of the squad, cultivating senses of loyalty, belonging and commitment to their contractees, XFC, for that season, or some period. Negotiation was often at arm's length between the club and the individual's agent. Players, for long in need of nurture as an element of their employment, being valuable and vulnerable, could get involved with the world outside for training, performance and parade; fans could meet them, as an ingredient of the gradual identification with their (second) team. They could even play, in teams established by the professional club. Déjà vu – to the old world of accessible professional football clubs? Well, why not? Everyone would benefit from this piece of apparent original thinking, in the new commercial world.

In 2007-08 Barrow, seen above as the unwitting victim of a gloryhunting fan, who might eventually find himself able to follow Chelsea in the media and turn up for his/her local team in action, were one level below Exeter City and still playing at Holker Street. The latter was from the very beginning my personal team to adopt, being born nearby. We had moved away from Devon, but I eventually sought to attend one of their games each season, sometimes more, whether at St James' Park or on bleak away terraces somewhere around the country. This was the origin of an ambition to visit far-flung grounds.

Gradually as my life took me to different parts of the country, I searched out the local teams, mostly for the football but not exclusively so, as I developed an interest making a football game a feature of a trip, growing into a vague aim of seeing one or two new clubs each season.

This gathered pace when individual friends admitted to a parallel interest, leading to experiences which would include the essential element: footy. This developed into Saturdays of greasy spoon fodder, wanders, pints of ale, football on a terrace in the afternoon, followed by theatre/music etc, as the arts also held a fascination for me. Lots of either/or, all most fulfilling. Lots of action, much noise.

From the start I had kept a diary of erratic content, but always recording events, such as a football fixture (as well as lists of films and plays seen – I always enjoyed my obsessions), absorbing a mental list of grounds visited. So, when the time came for precise tabulation, I was able to wade through each diary to list them all and so confirm those remaining to be visited. Often an entry lacked the status of the game, like which division, or the result, or anything much, but these could be ascertained easily enough. The combined offerings of diaries and annuals (current for fixtures, subsequent for results and tables) began to flesh out a story of life at the time. Where the chosen game lay in a grander scheme, e.g. Leyton Orient v Scunthorpe United in May 1989, at a time when I was living in the capital, it was because the encounter was crucial to the destinies of both teams. The ethos of a top of the table clash between Cinderella teams on the last day of the season turned it into a great advertisement for live football. The five goals helped, of course. However, poring over old diaries isn't always good for your peace of mind, sometimes serving to unearth long-suppressed negativities.

An idea gradually materialized to visit all League club grounds, qualified by the need for a formal basis for the fixture. Some of the best days have been invalid for the quest – seeing a lower league club entertain one with higher status in a friendly was often entertaining, a red letter day, like Kidderminster Harriers 1 Leicester City 1 (21/7/03), a harmonious pre-season affair in the name of an obscure Cup (though it's often evident that not much love is lost on occasions termed "pre-season friendlies", especially between local rivals). In May 1972 Notts County beat Nottingham Forest 3-0, a thrilling encounter, in the Nottinghamshire FA County Cup. My only visit to Ayresome Park, Middlesbrough, was for the excellent, widely promoted and thoroughly indulgent, Cleveland Jazz Festival (late July 1978). The inn my companion (from Poole but I don't recall where his loyalties lay) and I chose for the weekend was within walking distance. It provided prodigious breakfasts. I can hear the fried egg sizzling to perfection even now! We feasted on the stark northernness of the ground, which took the tour de force projections of George Melly into new realms of bliss. At least that's how I remember it. I first made it to Edgar Street, Hereford (19/5/85) as the passenger of the referee for an amateur game. Pegasus were playing and the low-key event allowed an extensive backstage examination. Considering the relative humility of the home team Bulls, the infrastructure seemed surprisingly, well, professional. The size of the pitch was striking, not to mention the massive floodlight pylons. This was a great day out with a drive through gorgeous countryside. This is an emotive matter: a wistful feeling even surfaces with the memory of Paulton Rovers v Clevedon Town in a foggy Western League fixture (2-2, 29/11/86).

The dim prospect of entering all the 92 grounds was jeopardized somewhat with a trend, accelerated by Lord Taylor's Report on the 1989 Hillsborough Stadium disaster, of clubs moving to new grounds, as it did not feel right to count the former ground of a club - every club had to be seen in its up-to-date residence, of recent origins if necessary. The reduction of the list began to seem unachievable in the mid-Nineties as more clubs were moving to new grounds than the number of turnstiles negotiated year by year. On top of this I was finding, to my dismay, that the new grounds were less interesting and the experience less enjoyable, than going to antiquated ones, often erected in the nineteenth century. Although it was exciting seeing a contemporary stadium come into view, too often it would flatter to deceive when venturing through the portals. More about that later.

The need to accumulate eventually filtered into that esoteric symbol of the workings of soccer: the turnstile. After caressing a few traditional examples at games in the mid-Noughties, there cropped up a chance to acquire my own. Doncaster Rovers were widely publicized to be leaving Belle Vue, where they had opened for business on 26 August 1922. Eighty-four years on, after a final display against those pretenders to the second flight, Nottingham Forest (how things change), which Rovers duly won 2-0, the club proceeded to dispose of the contents by auction, scheduled for a few Sundays hence, in January 2007. To join the fray was not easy. The contact number on the advertising flyer turned out to be unobtainable, the staff in the town centre Donny shop hadn't been told anything. Wakey, yielding to my entreaties to pose as my proxy as I was otherwise engaged in the South West that day, at least lived locally. After persistent enquiry to anyone who might have some knowledge, culminating on the day itself, he gleaned details from the club office, obtaining the programme, the passport to bidding privileges. But the hardware was all still in situ. The 18 turnstiles listed in the catalogue were difficult to link to the lot numbers, both as to location and dimension. What exactly would a proud new owner be getting? This was most unorthodox for an auction. It was guesswork. Imbuing my representative with authority to commit up to £200 for one turnstile, notwithstanding removal (extraction), conveyance (weight) and position (bulk) considerations, he secured lot 106 'in the Main Stand' for £170, with VAT, making the total £199.95, a perfect match to the budget. The acquisition was somewhat challenging to comprehend when he told me of his success in staggered mobile messages. I'd just bought a turnstile!

A few days later The Dude and I arrived at the sad, scarred ground (the site perhaps to become a car park for the new Keepmoat Stadium, unofficially of course) in a Berlingo van hired for the day. Fortune smiled: by what I esteem as sheer chance 'Ken and Ricky' emerged from the dereliction. Wakey had communicated by text "..ok

2 collect turnstile and ask 4 Ken or Ricky the groundsmen". "Bonanza" I thought as the place had seemed deserted on arrival, surviving doors locked and no one in sight. Ken said their contract was to be there for a few days of extraction – willingly but for another £20 (each) – and I was happy too, as they did the job without demur. There emerged a problem of identity. 'Lot 106' there was not and there was nothing left in the Main Stand. The three residual turnstiles were fine, notwithstanding, and in excellent condition. There wasn't much else we could do in the circumstances. We agreed on one to fit the situation best. K and R dug it out from its well-rooted setting, somewhat close to the harshly exposed away

terrace, in clear view of a sodden pitch, scarred by lines of brown where turf purchases had been excised. We bumped into a rueful lifelong supporter who was there to collect his particular square yardage of hallowed turf, where one of Donny's long-lost sons had performed heroics, he recounted. The lads humped the ominously massive item into the van, which seemed to be shrinking. It was accompanied by the counter grill, together with another barred handful, the upright bum barrier, normally sited between two turnstiles, in Rovers red, suggestive of medieval torture. It might serve as a runner bean training frame. More good fortune: it all fitted snugly, just. I had stopped myself from pondering upon the consequences of the van, hired for the day, proving too small. We left with a van full of metal, to manoeuvre the high wind southwestwards.

The initiative had already developed into the salvage of a precious artefact. Other bits of old Belle Vue, turnstiles included, must by now have been melted down for new use. This was a contemporary example of unthinking loss of football history, industrial heritage. I was empathizing with my plaything, an elaborate vermilion construct, seductively angled and shaped. Its crowning glory was a counter showing '08013', with a number of noughts off the register I'm sure. And, being a collector, would I be able to resist the future temptation of souvenirs from doomed grounds Gay Meadow, Saltergate, Anfield...?

By August 2003 the goal of completing the project had begun to seem attainable in the foreseeable future. That year six grounds came off the list (five from scratch plus Walsall's identikit Bescot Stadium as a repeat trip to the Saddlers) and in 2004-05 six original, two replacements. The aim to place games in the diary was helped by having companions empathic to it. The spirit of a football game is so much better as a shared experience. After all it was a quest, a one-off. Even so I couldn't resist the occasional diversion – other places, different sports like a Sunday cricket match, a point-to-point or perhaps pétanque in a country pub, though that has still eluded me, as such facilities have betimes been converted into a kiddies' playground tendency.

I developed a self-propelling momentum in furthering the strategy, which towards the end of 2003-04 was growing into a proper two-season plan, at last drawing up a list to facilitate a final season schedule as being as varied as possible and with maximum satisfaction potential. This meant a lot more than merely attending games. There would be several blueprints – league/cup games; weekend/midweek; combining more than one ground in a trip; weekends away/theatres/exhibitions; bars/stand-up comedy; people permutations. The two-year project did mean reducing Villa visits, but it was to be hoped that by 2006-07, with the project complete and time to spare, they would have become an entertaining, purposeful and successful side. No way would I forfeit my annual minimum Exeter trip.

In August 2004 a dispiriting aspect of the outstanding destinations was the heavy bias towards new as opposed to original grounds, something yielding a dull but chronic sinking feeling. This was exacerbated by the bulletin, emanating from a neighbouring conversation in a pub, that Coventry City were committed to a move. In fact all the grounds eventually visited in 2004-05 were new edifices. The one hitherto untouched club was Hull City, the project a New Year fixture at their Kingston Communications Stadium. I had missed out on Boothferry Park, though maybe the floodlights could be saluted on the journey, or, more likely, two fingers for its failure to withstand its usurpation. Ultimately five of the new stadia were visited and by May 2005 the list was down to Transfers 5 Virgin 4, a tantalizingly disparate group.

I was aware of the inherent obsessiveness of this and I fear that I have wearied friends, indeed probably boring anyone who would submit to audience status. This was all the more reason to reach a conclusion in minimum time, i.e. one more season. No added time allowed.

Another nagging influence was the grief associated with the process of obtaining match tickets. It used to be a simple thing to do, and still seems to be at more modest levels in the hierarchy, but increasingly had become a serious hindrance, involving such barriers as 'membership required' and stated loyalty to at least one of the teams involved – prohibitive when it was by definition a single visit. We have to turn to the advent of the Premier League, which soon came to mean higher ticket prices, in a way similar to what happened to many products after decimalization. But in football prices were not rounded up but seemingly multiplied. Young football enthusiasts could no longer afford to attend games. Alongside that grew the opportunity to see them on big screens. Findings of a Premier League supporters' survey in 2007 included the telling statistic that only 9% were under 24. This compares with 22% aged 16 to 20 at Coventry City in 1983 and 25% at Aston Villa in 1992. In 2005-06 the average age of attenders was 43, and there are enough of them, willing or conditioned to pay exorbitant prices, to preclude a neutral punter from buying Premiership tickets at many grounds. There is a social issue here, that formerly football was a catalyst for the maturing process. Yes, there was hooliganism, which can partly be explained by the sheer numbers of younger supporters on what were then terraces. For the majority of young people attending games, which was then affordable, there was an element of acquiring bonding and loyalty values. And even in 2007 you could watch league matches in Germany for a mere £6.

The final straw came from Arsenal Football Club, for whom I have sustained a lifelong antipathy. It's perplexing how they have attracted 'girlie' interest. Nice Lady likes them (her excuse: some players' high quality bodies, and friends of hers concur), as did a couple of Manchester-based models in a newspaper report, favourite players cited as Thierry Henry and Freddie Ljungberg. At least this is a reversal of the usual Manure support from afar, like North London. It seemed portentous that the latter's leading team's much heralded move to Ashburton Grove, going on Emirates Stadium, was scheduled for Summer 2006. This provoked the fearful challenge, reminiscent of a Greek mythic quest, of actually gaining admission to this temple. It was essential to complete the tabulated sojourns before that came to pass. I might of course relent with the Gunners (or 'ASNL' as Sky and the BBC euphemistically head their scores up on live transmissions. The standard is to identify a team by its first few letters. At least Harry Enfield was graphic in his Stavros persona. I refer to 'the Arse'; ARS to ITV, bless them) if offered a visit as by someone else doing the organizing, as the plans and reports of the stadium revealed an elaborate palace reaching to the sky.

You have to experience these things, even if just once. I have readily admitted being an addictive ground and turnstile collector. Any discipline will do, from cricket to American football, to Ashburton Grove to Wembley (new). Anyway, to mitigate the unpleasantness of having to admire Thierry Henry's smug supremacy on new home territory, and pay for it, their version of 'red' in 2005-06 was most appealing, evocative of the beauteous burgundy – or was it plum? – hue of the pride of Edinburgh, Heart of Midlothian, a far cry from the vermilion or cherry of so many 'red' teams. Unfortunately they reverted to a standard hue the next August. Yes, I'm preoccupied with footy colour display. And why do goalkeepers so often wear garb utterly unconnected with the other ten?

The basis of this volume is therefore visits to the grounds of all the 92 clubs in the English Football League. The criterion is attendance at any time at the current addresses of each member for an official game, chosen from FA Barclaycard Premier League, Coca Cola Championship and Leagues One and Two fixtures (or under their previous identities – see Appendix 2), or home cup ties in the FA Cup and the League Cup (current label 'Carling'). The season chosen to conclude the quest was 2005-06, for the reasons above.

There had emerged a complication. In constructing the final list, certain additional terrace exposures clearly needed reporting, beyond the strict complement of 92 League members. How can you omit your own team, which was then residing in the fifth division, in around 100th place overall? What about Wembley(s) – do a chapter on London without them? Unthinkable. And Bristol Rovers' latterday residences, so many, so compelling? And I've already mentioned Ayresome Park, Edgar Street (out of the League and back again) and Roker Park further up. Some old grounds, sadly recycled in unpalatable ways, turned out to be worth greater observation: see Donny triumphant at soon-to-be-turnstile-free Belle Vue, the Keepmoat experience should be shared, if only for the self-deprecating Huddersfield chants. This was after date. Some are mentioned in passing, e.g. Millwall's Den for access problems (and fear of egress). Then there's a total non-sequitur: Castleford RFC – the story must be told! Arsenal are beloved of so many outside London claiming some connection, usually displaying hints of considerable education and disposable income (well, notoriously expensive and highly rated Islington is within walking distance of their base). They refer to them as the 'Gooners', somewhat faux-familiar I feel. So, in the end I felt obliged to pay the Emirates a visit, as objectively as I could manage. See Appendix 1 for the full list.

The sum total of these tangents produces another magic number: 119. There are 150 'Psalms of David' in the Old Testament (Authorized Version taken here), as Gentiles have it (or Holy Scriptures, which has more of a ring, to the people from whom it sprang). The 119th (CXIX) is massively long – 176 verses and goes on a bit, like extending 92 to 119 in this tome (curiously the 117th psalm has only two verses). "This psalm, the most comprehensive of all the psalms, is a particularly artificial product of religious poetry. It (has)… the formal feature of the alphabetic acrostic…The psalm is a many-coloured mosaic of thoughts which are often repeated in a wearisome fashion…" (Artur Weiser). 'Acrostic' is: "a number of lines of writing, especially a poem or word puzzle, in which particular letters, for example, the first, in each line spell a word or phrase." There you are.

"Testimonies, judgements, statutes, commandments, law, evil ways, wondrous works, pilgrimage, rebuke, righteousness" abound in Ps. CXIX. Of course, it evokes aspects of football and its infrastructure. Better practice was encouraged among the Jews, just like the purveyors of football. This is the point at which to raise the moral tone, but the confounding of the 119th is a bit relentless. Instead I shall insert Psalm 58 – all of it – the subject being judgement of the wicked and much more fun. Perhaps football could learn something from the psalmist. Please indulge me – my grandfather was a vicar, after all.

*1. Are your minds set upon righteousness, O ye congregation: and do ye judge the thing that is right, O ye sons of men?*
*2. Yea, ye imagine mischief in your heart upon the earth: and your hands deal with wickedness.*
*3. The ungodly are froward, even from their mother's womb: as soon as they are born, they go astray, and speak lies.*
*4. They are as venomous as the poison of a serpent: even like the deaf adder that stoppeth her ears;*
*5. Which refuseth to hear the voice of the charmer: charm he never so wisely.*
*6. Break their teeth, O God, in their mouth; smite the jaw-bones of the lions, O Lord: let them fall away like water that runneth apace; and when they shoot their*

*arrows let them be rooted out.*

*7. Let them consume away like a snail, and be like the untimely fruit of a woman: and let them not see the sun.*

*8. Or ever your pots be made with thorns: so let indignation vex him, even as a thing that is raw.*

*9. The righteousness shall rejoice when he seeth the vengeance: he shall wash his footsteps in the blood of the ungodly.*

*10. So that a man shall say, Verily there is a reward for the righteous: doubtless there is a God that judgeth the earth.*

Penalty! Red Card!!

Meanwhile Paul Cookson, Poet-in-Residence at the National Football Museum in Preston, gave us:

> *'The Footballer's Prayer'*
> *Our team*
> *Which art eleven*
> *Hallowed be thy game*
> *Our match be won*
> *Their score be none*
> *On turf as we score at least seven*
> *Give us today no daily red…card*
> *And forgive us our lost passes*
> *As we forgive those who lose passes against us*
> *Lead us not into retaliation*
> *And deliver us from all fouls*
> *For three is the kick off*
> *The power and scorer*
> *For ever and ever*
> *Full time.*

Now is the time to confess to a deliberate mistake. Those readers with an anorak-like tendency will count 120, not 119, grounds on the list. Blame Doncaster Rovers, the pride of South Yorkshire. I couldn't resist trying out their new turnstiles. Think of it as a bonus. Anyway, altogether there are 124 grounds, as Castleford RFC, Kidderminster Harriers and Wembley (old and new) are here for spurious reasons. I look to Psalm 124 for justification:

*They had swallowed us up quick: when they were so wrathfully displeased at us.*

"They" refers to "men", who "rose up against us". This is marvellous as "wrath" is my favourite word, even if comprising only half of "wrathfully".

After the 2004-05 season, awaiting publication of the fixture list, I was hoping that the final few would not to be augmented by any other clubs moving, unbeknownst. As well as football annuals, an essential new season purchase would be a football grounds guide, for planning and navigation.

The thoughts at that stage were:

1) The best of the bunch was likely to be Bloomfield Road, one of two old grounds not yet visited (in any way) and a thought to culminate the quest with a weekend in Blackpool (League 1).

2) Bolton Wanderers (Premiership). Do a one-off hotel package at the Reebok, already the subject of enquiry, which included a stadium tour to transform it into a treat, thus overcoming the obstacles of Premiership tickets and out-of-town location.

3) Try to endure this least attractive prospect in a sleek, anonymous fashion. The earlier attempt to tackle the newish fortress Deva Stadium (Chester City, League 2), had been thwarted, arriving for a 1998 Bank Holiday game in what seemed at the time a wasteland, in the remotest recess of an industrial estate, to find the game had been rearranged for the following evening – and not even all of the place was in England.

4) Coventry City (Championship). Having been made aware of their forthcoming move, to an address so far unidentified, at least they were languishing in the Championship, after so long among the elite. This suggested comparative ease of ticket acquisition. They had narrowly avoided accompanying Nottingham Forest in a second, ignominious, relegation, in a few years. I had enjoyed, and endured, Highfield Road several times as a Villa fan. It should not be difficult to fix a date at some stage.

5) Hartlepool United (League 1), the other untouched club. The ideal was that Victoria Park (formerly 'Ground') could be enjoyed with the Stadium of Light in a single north-east feast of fun. Please let fixture schedules allow, as I heard a carload from Wellington, Somerset did one Easter: games in the afternoon and evening. They chose the Pools to support permanently, just for fun – an example of inverted gloryhunting? Never mind the daunting distance.

6) Revisit Lincoln City (League 2), to tie in with the Christmas market, the subject of coach tours from all over the country (I had noted in a window in Devon). The previous attempt, as part of a Bank Holiday weekend tour of the region, had elicited utter frustration as Fuckin' Dave and I actually tried a pub on the way to Sincil Bank in April '98, drooling with anticipation of the indulgence in store. The barmaid informed us, without much discernible sympathy, that the game had been called off that morning. Watching the results in the room in our pub/hotel later on the fixture (v Exeter City, I'm afraid) was the only one postponed in the entire League, following extensive flooding in the preceding days. Indeed it had been curious that the streets were uncluttered by game-goers. They knew something we didn't. Wandering to the

ground, post quaff, we peered through the gates and the pitch looked lush, green and quite playable, in fact totally tantalizing. As it transpired we spent the afternoon enjoying historical Lincoln and saw the film *Jackie Brown* in the evening. In one of the pubs I practised left-handed writing on the quick crossword.

The game was re-scheduled not long after, in midweek, and the Imps duly won 2-0.

7) Plough Lane had been experienced early on with my London buddy, Bogs. Having missed out on the Dons' interim residences, the recently reinvented Milton Keynes Dons (League 1) now had to be faced. Also they had narrowly avoided relegation, suggesting a struggle in '05-06. I'd rather see teams near the top than bottom for a greater likelihood of confidence and enthusiasm. Likely means: a day-trip with some friend I hadn't seen for a long time, so there would be a lot of catching up to do, that is to say diverting chitchat; alternatively assemble a bunch of enthusiasts for a cathartic/masochistic experience. There would probably need to be inducements – a carrot of opportunity in MK Centre for evening culture perhaps.

8) Sunderland (Premiership), by whom I had been transported during a confident (old) Div 1 period at the superlative Roker Park. It was my model football day out. Jostling, friendly pub, the Roker Pie Shop, whose offerings I failed to test, hitting the Albion instead, though I've still got the snap I took of the pie shop's eye-catching red and white striped awning; the best fish and chips, (salt and vinegar essential, like ice and lemon in gin and tonic, as Annie Walker once pronounced in Coronation Street) and of course the Roker Roar. The facts: Sunderland 1 Nottingham Forest 1, Div I, 18/2/84. A big potential challenge, however: gaining access to the Stadium of Light, as they'd just been promoted comfortably as Championship champions: a League Cup game, perhaps.

9) A similar difficulty presented itself with Wigan Athletic (Premiership), Championship runners-up in 2004-05 and Premiership members for the first time in their 27-year League history. They hadn't established much following in the JJB Stadium – but the Premiership? And with local derbies with Bolton and Blackburn in prospect, alongside the Mancunia and Scouseland representation they could be set to display house-full signs. I hoped they would. Again it looked like a cup game might be needed.

What would the computer throw up in the fixture list? What would be the effect of televised games? Would cup draws help or hinder? And the vagaries of the weather and effects of global warming? The turnstile quest was on.

# Chapter One
# Floodlit Fun

## Evening Games

Evening games are imbued with a special quality, with the sound waves cutting and wafting through the night air. This excitement intensifies after the clocks go back in October, floodlights in dark skies making a major contribution to the atmosphere of a ground. We really should be grateful to have been around to enjoy the age of the pylon floodlights, introduced in the 1950s. Wolves gave an early demonstration of the success of this latest innovation, which stunned and delighted their fans – they cost about £10k. Wolves beat South Africa 3-1 in their first game (30/9/53). Confidence grew and the Hungarians came to Molineux on 13 December 1954, fielding five of the players who had humiliated England. Of the Wolves team, only Billy Wright, the captain, had been on the receiving end of those two heavy international defeats.

Wolves wore a special satin version of the old gold shirt which they believed would look better under the floodlights.

"The game started and building quick, controlled attacks Honved were 2-0 up after 14 minutes, to the despair of a crowd that was just a couple short of being the 10th of 55,000 at Molineux since the war. Wolves finally opened their account with a Hancocks penalty just after half-time, and from then on the atmosphere was electric. Only 15 minutes remained when Swinbourne got his head to a Wilshaw lob to give Wolves a deserved equaliser. Within 100 seconds Shorthouse, Smith and Wilshaw combined beautifully to set up Swinbourne, who conjured up a fine hooked shot to put Wolves in front as a crescendo of noise filled the stadium. Even the legendary Puskas could not save Honved with the score staying at 3-2, a result that made front page headlines in at least one national newspaper as Wolves were proclaimed champions of the world!" (Wolves website)

By the way it's interesting how, at a friendly, the paying public drift in and out as if it were a Roman Catholic mass. Of course it is holiday time and admission is cheap, £10 the going rate in 2007 (£5 concessions and children).

Man-made pitch improvements, like under-soil heating, chemicals and covers, have reduced the number of postponed matches – still surely the biggest disappointment for the fan already condemned to seven days' wait for another 'fix' and now gloomily contemplating an even longer wait. Football has not always embraced change so readily, as the artificial pitch fiasco of the 1980s showed, but we can now enjoy international matches under floodlights on showcase pitches, conducive to camera relays, not the sandy quagmires of yore.

Ever since their inception, floodlights have been a boon to the game. The only qualification to this resounding success story surrounds the funding of ground improvements at the lower end of the game. Should the League/government subsidize the stragglers and the strugglers? If not, why not? The money's in the coffers from taxes and turnstiles.

A different enthusiasm continues to be generated in the early, hazy summer weeks of the season through the anticipation of all those glorious months of football with the quickly changing League tables, sports fans inclined towards football having been forced to make do for far too long with Wimbledon tennis, athletics championships, Test Match cricket, not to mention Masters golf. Or national team failure in a World or European tournament.

Now that the Premiership schedules so few midweek evening games, it has become a problem catching any at all – the one in August and the other a month after Christmas have become something to make a beeline for in the fixture list, being a means of visiting a new ground seldom possible at the weekend, formerly known as Saturday afternoon.

Retiming of league games has become so dictated by broadcasting bodies that on Saturday 10/11/07 Derby County v West Ham United was the only Premiership game to kick off at 3pm. For Villa games, for reasons of work and availability a midweek evening has become a carload venture, such as the 1-0 League Cup Round 3 victory over Burnley (25/10/05). This was so good. A carload of hedonists on a motorway for a hike: The Dude on a rare venture away from Bristol Rugby and Alice experimenting tentatively with a foray into unfamiliar territory, a supremely easy journey courtesy of Tom, the surfer (he favours surf, turf, spuds, puds but mainly conversation in a restaurant, and above all chicken casserole), though his cd machine only took one at a time. But this was only the VW. This was superfluous due to the constant banter in the back. We soon reached, on this occasion, a convenient and jug-adorned pub, Villa inclined, for bowls of Irish coddle and a quart of East Anglian ale.

Hard on those heels was the smooth final lap to identify a prized parking space, with the vehicle negotiated 180 degrees round the block, primed for the return journey; then the urgent march to the stage. It was a visual feast under the lights, Burnley wearing blue, claret and white in a close reversal of Villa's colours. The decorative display was completed by the burly black referee (Uriah Rennie, 'South Yorkshire', commanding respect) kitted out in egg yolk yellow. Alice, a Bemmy girl (Bedminster, the Bristol equivalent of 'Essex', where a local culinary choice, pony club plops, based on meringues, may have been introduced by her), threatened to do a streak, but it really wasn't warm enough, and she was kitted out like something from *Dr Zhivago*. I was heeding the advice of my dear old mother (the one from whom I inherited my tendency to hoard): wrap up well. The Dude, who dons shorts for most of the year, was also buried under an assemblage of garments. He'd been "knocked over" by his first evening game at Villa Park, in the UEFA Cup 'the sheer size, like an amphitheatre, grass a shade of green heightened by the floodlights' (plus curry and beer before and more beer after). Unfortunately that time Villa beat 'Atletico de Madrid' (it said on the ticket) 2-1 (17/3/98), only to lose overall on the away goals rule, 2-2 on aggregate. But the experience had a profound effect as he now counts himself a Villa supporter, entirely consistent with a Bristol Rugby season ticket and a love of oxtail. But then so does Nigel Kennedy, termed 'the music world's most famous Aston Villa supporter – now domiciled in Cracow'.

Back to the weather: on the other hand two days after this game, with the clocks ready to fall back for winter, swimmers were witnessed in the sea at North Berwick. (North Berwick doesn't readily suggest itself for immersion even in high summer, such is the climate up there.) Finally our favourite lads squeezed past the lower-division team to reach the last 16. I was gratified that the stalwart Kevin Phillips, coveted while at Sunderland and Southampton, and in 2007-08 to enjoy striking prowess for the Baggies, scored the only goal with a punishing shot. Why couldn't Juan Pablo Angel show any penetration, let alone score, game after game? Even so the Villa faithful found occasional opportunities to shout 'There's only one (Juan) Pablo Angel'. He was also responsible for the winning chant, from the pen of Jonny Hurst, from East London, who was awarded a £10k bursary as Chant Laureate in 2004-05. With the proper Poet Laureate Andrew Motion in the chair and judges who included Barnsley FC poet-in-residence Ian McMillan and Radio 1 presenter Chris Moyles, the Premiership sponsored the initiative with the aim of unearthing "fans who could capture the humour and emotion of football", chants being "the lifeblood of our stadia, typifying the spirit, the passion and the wit of the beautiful game". So far I am in complete accord. Here are the winning lyrics (to the tune of *Copacabana*):

*His name is Angel,*
*And he's a show boy,*
*An Alice Band keeps up his hair,*
*Juan Pablo from Colombi-air,*

*He came to Villa,*
*To be a winner,*
*He succeeded overnight,*
*Our very own Angel Delight,*

*Just to hear the Villa roar,*
*With each Juan Pablo score,*
*We've got him on a four-year deal,*
*But we still want more,*

*At the Villa, at Aston Villa,*
*The greatest club west of Manila,*

*At the Villa, at Aston Villa,*
*Football and passion,*
*All ranges of fashion,*
*At the Villa, we have it all,*
*La la, Aston Vil la la,*
*Aston Vil la la la,*
*Vil la la la.*

But the guy just didn't score enough goals, at last in summer 2007 becoming the subject of a free transfer to New York.

'Premiership la la la' wafted from the away section of the North Stand, which looked like a sell out, 'Championship la la la' retorted the Holte End, almost full, despite a poor attendance of 26,872. Leaving the ground, 'Chim chiminee chim chiminee chim chim cheroo, we are the bastards in claret and blue' a batch of blokes chanted. It could have been either side.

It is salutary to note that the same round a year before had produced the result Burnley 3 Villa 1. We returned to the pub for a warming recovery, relieved rather than thrilled. With the temptations of such a retreat, Villa-inclined, or alternatively a respite in a family-run Asian restaurant, in Birmingham's Balti Triangle, a full vehicle isn't difficult to achieve for a half-day (evening) trip.

Another variation on this is a thumping thrill in driving rain, viz Villa's eclipse of the behemothic Arsenal 5-1 on 25/4/79 (Tiptoes and I celebrated in the nearby Upper Grounds). This had been postponed owing to the Gooners' FA Cup involvement – they made it to Wembley to beat Manchester United 3-2. It was a Wednesday evening bonanza at a time when Villa Park was still adorned with its traditional floodlights. These, traced out to make 'A' and 'V', were a beacon for the M6 and a true football landmark. In addition to the evident purpose of actually illuminating the ground effectively, the odd dark patch adding perversely to the experience, floodlights serve further benefits. There is an immediate association with the subject, a football ground with all that implies. This eyeful is important. They are landmarks, the star in the sky, leading to the shrine. The image is the first link of anticipation to reality as you progress down the streets towards the ground.

So often Victorian grounds are located down labyrinthine backstreets. The stark, blurred-edged lights enhance the treasure hunt. You will be trundling groundwards amid the crowd jostle if on foot, recumbent bodies in doorways and the debris of corner shops and lurking black bags notwithstanding. Arriving by car many is the time the floodlights have assisted in orienteering. The immediate task is to judge where to search for a parking space, then to achieve that small thing, possibly paying a local boy a coin to 'look after your car for you, sir' (or return to discover damage or theft). The torrential conditions lifted this game to a fine sensation of fulfilment, the best result I have witnessed against the Gunners, and Villa's biggest home win for some time before and after. They could produce dynamics on rare occasions. They scored four at Wolves and Spurs that season; the Arse finished seventh, the Villa eighth.

P.S. I just wanted to include the word 'behemoth' for fun (oh, now I've repeated it), though Arsenal at that time were 'boring' rather than forbiddingly animalistic.

By contrast it has been disappointing to arrive at grounds with fairy-type stadium lights, the banks of smaller lights dotted along the stand tops, no doubt cost-efficient but providing less atmosphere, and localized, not seen from a distance. Subtle lighting has its place, e.g. Clifton Suspension Bridge in Bristol, a static monument straddling the Avon Gorge, where the lights were designed to trace its outline against a black sky. At football grounds they make scant contribution to the ethos of a live game.

The League Cup (by turns in the names of its sponsors: Milk, Littlewoods, Rumbelows, Coca-Cola, Worthington and, since 2003-04, Carling offers a unique facet, being played only in midweek until the late winter final in a national stadium, now back to the new Wembley). It is notoriously less popular with mainstream fans, derided widely in the press, whose allegiance is unsurprisingly to higher-profile games. Several of the games below were typical of this. There was plenty of full-throated heartiness in the first round at Walsall and Shrewsbury, a holiday atmosphere, many fans straight from the pools and bars of Iberia, no doubt. Attending such a game is an essentially thrilling experience as these days there is always a result, even though you sometimes have to suffer the ultimate process of the penalty shootout and – horrifying possibility – miss out on a pint after the game. I have to report that this has actually happened – see Kidderminster below. Also, for a Villa fan, the League Cup may assume the role of line of least resistance. When they join the fray, more than likely the opposition will be from the lower orders. The expectation is to witness a win, especially if they are favoured with a home draw. In the long-gone years when they qualified for the UEFA Cup competition, they received the reward of byes until the third round, when there were a mere 32 clubs remaining. And in each round in all cups there is the tantalizing factor: which of those numbered spheres in the 'hat' will Fate toss out? Here is an example of the cruelty of fate: Villa drew Manchester United at the first hurdle in 2007 and again in 2008, as well as in 2002 and 2004 – Villa lost the lot. I had better luck at Gloucester City (0-2 to Braintree Town): My raffle ticket (blue 319) won me the Christmas cake.

## Chesterfield 0 Aston Villa 4
## Division III, 19/4/72

I was studying in Nottingham. Mickey G, with whom I was in a group of seven blighting the noble science/art called Geography (and other unwitting subjects), was an avid football, that is Blackburn Rovers, enthusiast. An evening bus through parts of Nottinghamshire and Derbyshire took us through varied land use which we had been studying. We eventually marvelled at one of Derbyshire's most famous sights, the twisted spire of St Mary and All Saints – how does it stay up, vicar? *Treasures of Britain* states that it's 228 feet high (ToB was published in 1968 therefore pretty new on this bus trip and long before metres were invented). And I've since ventured into the church, a fine resting place among a few old streets and pubs. Recommendation: the Rutland Arms, worth a mention above the ale and aspect (of the church) because players sometimes patronize it and it has been known to involve itself with the Spireites financially, contributing to a match. It welcomes away supporters too.

'The Recreation Ground', Saltergate, has been home to the club since 1884. It is at the top of my list of terminally old, doomed to be replaced by a committee-bespoke out-of-town horror. It is therefore utterly desirable. The club's League membership dates honourably back to two centuries ago. Formed in 1866, Chesterfield are also the fourth oldest club. From 1900-01, their second Second Division season, to 1908-09 (when they finished penultimate and sank into oblivion until the Third Division North was invented) they enjoyed Derbyshire derby games with Glossop, League Division II members from 1900 to 1915.

There was a splendid sandwich shop within spitting distance, clutching whose products you get occasional sightings of the rusty corrugated iron frame on the short walk up a terraced street to the Main Stand, further embellished with ivy here and there. Venturing further on the same block which runs the whole length of the long, eastern side, you might find yourself enveloped among away fans electing to sit in what is termed the 'Wing Stand' (doubling up on the numbering system which would confuse were it not for the immensely friendly and wise stewards, apparently there for the fun of it, stationed at judicious intervals. There are two lots of numbers in the same stand: the sagacious henchmen must have been used to patrons' queries for generations).

Alternatively be traditional while you can and stand/huddle on the open terracing of the Cross Street End, cruelly exposed to the elements, which can prove malevolent when the distant view changes from alluring purple Peak to threatening skies over the boggy moors. The Main/Wing Stand is fetchingly creaky – and leaky, much of it threatening to collapse over the wooden-seated attenders, or at least sprinkle them with damp, crumbly bits from any number of nineteenth-century technology metals. There is a strange paradox in the ever-lengthening prospect of a move to a former glassworks, when that is what's in such short supply in the ground – the gents has some glass extant in the gaping, discoloured windows, but the abiding impression is of metal, wood and paint merging and mouldering. And I also loved the proud, comfortable turnstiles, painted a very long-life weather-proof Chesterfield blue, and, by default, on display through red metal fencing between the urinal section and the small vending booths. This is a Bovril-and-chicken-and-mushroom-pie place. I don't relish empirical testing in the new Glass House stadium when the time comes. As it is, for me the clincher is the floodlight pylons, a magnificent piece of overkill (like the blue, fetchingly rotund, turnstiles), proud, tall and bearing a curious paucity of actual lamps. This quartet could have rivalled the church spire as a landmark had the M1 been built on the western, not eastern-side of the town.

The game at Saltergate was at the time when Villa were running away with the Third Division championship. The atmosphere in the ground was electric, not least because away supporters were in the majority with their team triumphant. There did not appear to be any restriction on numbers of away fans. It was a good example of the thrilling spectacle provided by live sport incorporating a thoroughly satisfying experience in itself, a confident display by Villa and amazing vocal support – chants, shouting, enthusiasm. Unsurprisingly I don't recall anything from the Chesterfield Spireites. Vic Crowe's Claret and Blue Army did their lads proud. And Mickey G willingly became a Villa fan for the evening. It was lager and crisps for him afterwards. My diary entry for Villa was 'superb', an unique adjective over the aeons since.

## Mansfield Town 1 Blackburn Rovers 0
## Division III, 12/2/72

> We travelled just north, an excuse
> To see Mickey's Rovers make news,
> But Field Mill saw defeat –
> For the Stags a rare treat,
> As down went the 'Amber and Blues'.

Mickey's favourite went by the name of Metcalfe, a special Rovers attraction at the time. In the Yorker in Nottingham afterwards he had his lager and crisps, cheese and onion I think. My order was Guinness and peanuts as we relived a dreary evening with Rovers losing again.

Meanwhile the Stags had achieved their record attendance as recently as 10/1/53, predictably to see neighbours Nottingham Forest beat them 0-1 in the Third Round of the FA Cup. However, they were comparative League novices, replacing Nelson in 1931. This shows a perversity of the system: Nelson had been in the old Third Division (North), Mansfield were placed in TD(S), Walsall being moved from (S) to (N), Reading and Cardiff having been relegated. (The Saddlers finished 17th both years.) Mansfield were switched to TD(N) the next year, 1932-33, where they played Walsall. Barnsley and Bristol City had gone down. To extend the excitement, Thames were out and Aldershot and Newport County in, all in TD(S), so the complement was restored to 22 clubs in all four leagues. An away programme note in the current century had it that regional transfers were to rescue marginal clubs from some of the tremendous travel produced by their spot on the atlas. But surely the old Third Division was a pragmatic affair, someone having fun scouring maps in an annual summer test to minimize the 48 members' travel depending on each year's distribution, and in time to determine the fixtures. This phenomenon was before motorway dominance and computer introduction. At least the AA and RAC were there to lend a hand, in the days of provision of that level of service.

The 1953 Cup game against Forest was TD(N) (lower reaches) against Second Division. Drawn away in both the earlier rounds, Town had destroyed Scarborough 0-8, followed by a 0-2 win at Accrington, the latter finishing bottom of the League. (Mansfield Town were Mansfield Wesleyans from 1897 to 1905, incidentally.)

Field Mill is one of many grounds in the North East Midlands/South Yorkshire zone still to be with us. Only Derby (1997) and Donny (2006) have upped and outed from their old grounds; and Rotherham, exiled in 2008 from Millmoor. Meanwhile the late Eighties saw substantial onsite redevelopment. There is a counterpart in the brewing trade. I recall Mansfield Brewery mainly as the source of keg beers in clubs, no alternative, and pubs – I'd probably have gone for Guinness, if those were the only option. That's because Mansfield produced no real ales during my years of ale apprenticeship (early 70s). However, it eventually moved with the times and started producing lowish gravity Dark Mild and Cask bitter. Changing times do not always produce improvements.

1999 saw the purchase of the brewery by Bank's and Hanson's of Wolverhampton. There followed the complete loss of the company by Mansfield, company and town as the concern joined the combine's remit. It was still to bear the name 'Mansfield' (evidently the Marketing Department considered the name carried enough appeal to subsist). Meanwhile a sequence of family-run brewing companies sold out to the giants (for loads of money) rather than contemplate a management/employees, in fact community, purchase. It is rare to be able to cite a practice in the world of football as a model for the commercial world to follow, but 'community' is a concept common to breweries and football clubs. Several professional clubs are now owned and run by their supporters. In the case of Lincoln the long trail from administration to solvency was achieved thus and Chesterfield has turned round from a £2m deficit to a black balance sheet. The national Supporters Direct comprises groups interested in running their football clubs. The idea is to develop partnerships with local authorities. We enjoy the brews on offer in association with football games. Micro breweries are springing up all over the place. Good! It would be even better if established smaller brewing companies could stay in business in their own locale, often also served by a football team, say Mansfield Town. Another thing which improved most belatedly was Field Mill. In the new millennium it boasts stands on all four sides, one proclaiming 'Stags', and one 'M.T.F.C.'. And from August 2008, somewhere: 'Blue Square Premier' and 'Setanta'. But the town can take solace from the simultaneous Olympic achievements of its daughter, Rebecca Adlington, in Beijing's showpiece swimming pool.

## Shrewsbury Town 1 Plymouth Argyle 1
## League Cup Round 1 First Leg, 20/8/91

This was a solo effort, pigging out over several days on culture and indulgence, having left friends behind in Brecon (jazz festival), the Long Mynd (wedding) and Machynlleth (arts festival).

Shrewsbury followed, county town of Shropshire (for a while 'Salop' until it was realized that the word had untoward connotations in the vernacular of la belle France – so what?), the occasion a League (Coca Cola) Cup game in the lost era of two-legged ties, on a sun blessed evening. And indeed the citizens of Plymouth were fated to look forward to their turn as hosts to the Shrews. Gay Meadow was a sociable place, my terrace neighbours chatting away, so I was almost able to overlook the excruciatingly feeble tea, dotted with a congealed film of (powdered?) milk.

STFC joined the League in 1950 and were another example of the eccentricities of the regionalized Third Division. They spent one season in the northern section and the remaining seven in the southern, before becoming founder members of the Fourth Division in 1958-59, which probably made little difference to their team-travel budget, unlike Carlisle and Gateshead (at the time), Torquay or Exeter. They achieved their first promotion that season, or rather after it, clinching fourth position in a very late rearranged game.

Gay Meadow (so named because a fairground once occupied the space) lay beside the slimy east bank of the River Severn, into which many a ball was projected over the years, on occasion to be rescued by a retainer with an ancient vessel, a coracle, and from which floods were not unknown. It did boast seriously old turnstiles, something I discovered too late for the initial visit. But just before the expungement of the Meadow in 2007, there they were at the away end, a subtle green and period-frilly, but obscured from view by the terrace leaning bars. The turnstiles in the areas of home traffic, like the Wakeman Stand, were a disappointing rusty black, vertically double-barrelled and in no way enticing should they be destined to become lots in the June auction. The old ones were hallowed, having experienced Cup Final traffic c/o the erstwhile Crystal Palace ground prior to the Great War. It is certainly credible that the club had been trying to move to a new home, for several years already, aiming for a green-field site on the periphery of town. This was much lamented by traditionalist ground lovers all over the country, as much as anything for the location of Gay Meadow, central and sited most aesthetically. What price the housing destined to replace it, with elegant aspect of proud former hospitals and, in spring, a bank of daffodils captioned 'Britain in Bloom'? A tidy sum I surmise. Still, on a further visit on 9/4/07, the Shrews overcame a derisory 0-1 half time shortfall against W(MKD) in a League 2 fixture to earn punters 10p off pints at the Prince of Wales (would have been 20p had the 2-1 result surmounted another notch up to 3-1). The new century aspect included such worthiness as 'Shrewsbury Homes supports the future of the town'. Was this the organization whose imminent task was to destroy the edifice for housing? You might be driven to something else writ large: 'Wood's Shropshire Beer – with a kick'. Well

I would, as I love the stuff, among all the other gorgeous Shropshire brews. I came fully expecting to hate the new almost-built stadium two miles away. But the doomed Gay Meadow was not, alas, blessed with much of merit (acid test the turnstiles, though the floodlight pylons were brilliant) and when I braved the 'new-stadium' as it was held pre-name-deal, I would probably shed tears over the loss. Local opinion from a straw poll of sensible/itive burghers (car park attendant, blokes in pubs with good beer) was solidly pro 'new-stadium'. Lifts were included in the specification, and 'Ladies' loos', a world away from the single bowl at one end of the old ground (one apparently full-blooded male told me). As for the n-s, it was discovered to be more convenient than those at, say, Bolton, and with the benefit of watering holes crawlable from the town centre. The railway ran right past the site. The bulletin that those in authority had decided against introducing a station stop was sinking-feeling material. It would have provided an expedient service from the town station and other points. The worst thing is that you don't register surprise, only resignation. How bloody stupid!

The club's coat of arms features three golden lions with projected red tongues with the motto 'Floreat Semper' and indeed the town was renowned for floral exhibition.

Shrewsbury's citadel was blessed with so many good things: that August evening in 1991 friendly Salopians in the pubs, notably the Three Fishes, and the aged guest house on a hill in the old town. The next morning I enjoyed a leisurely wander round the maze of streets. It's got most things but lacks a cathedral, an exception among the major towns with long traditions on the western side of central England. Hence 'Town' I suppose, though it is perhaps odd to emphasize that it is not a city. Some of the buildings date back to the thirteenth century, the castle from around 1300. Charles Darwin was born there. So was Admiral John Benbow (1653-1702), born the son of a tanner, who died of wounds suffered in the War of Spanish Succession. Thank you, Steve (Conisbrough), Wikipedia and The Admiral Benbow (my God, that 7.5% Gwatkin cider). And he inspired the inn in *Treasure Island* – the Admiral, not Steve.

The next evening, Wednesday the 21st I think, not wishing to overdo it, I met my bucolic friend, The Mad One, for Villa v Man U, a frustrating 0-1 outcome modified by alcohol before the game in the Upper Grounds and somewhere in Wolverhampton afterwards. I'm surprised I can remember as much as I do of this mini-trip. The Mad One went the way of Foxy (after the Wembley (old) England failure) to disappear in an alcoholic haze. Those benders were always impressive, but I couldn't and can't remember much.

## Shrewsbury Town 0 Wycombe Wanderers 1
## League 2 (4), 29/12/07

In the *Big Issue* the week before this fixture, Mark Metcalf pointed out the poverty of provision for disabled supporters in new stadia. Alas, Shrewsbury's 'new 10,000 all-seater stadium' was an example. 'A glorious new chapter in the Shropshire side's history ended its association with the quaint Gay Meadow ground close to the town centre that offered little in the way of comforts for disabled supporters,' he stated. The Disability

Discrimination Act, twelve years old when the stadium opened, contained provisions not met in the specifications. The ladies' loos may be good (no obvious user around to ask) but of the required 100 wheelchair spaces, only 25 were elevated instead of the 75 required. The article also drew attention to a basic error at the Emirates Stadium, which may cost Arsenal £2m to make good – at present carers have to sit apart from their charges, there being insufficient space. Imagine that.

The new place was actually called the 'New Stadium' (but 'New Meadow' on the website – they're run as a speciality, with the address simply 'Oteley Road' with no name ascribed to it) as, just like Swansea before 'Liberty' in 2005-06, there was at this time no sponsor whose name to apply. The faithful called it New Meadow (like Swansea fans clinging to their Vetch after the move). The fun was in the approach to it, having enjoyed a brief sneak preview the previous April, when we had also noticed the enterprising shuttle service (a 57-seater coach) run by Ian Price, landlord of the Prince of Wales. At around 2.30 we duly joined the short trail round the corner and over a bridge to transfer from the lush-beer venue to the plastic blue seats. This represented a move from Ansells Mild and St Austell Tribute – the local Salopian was off – to wash down gammon, egg and chips or bangers and mash to instant Bovril (no pies: no appetite). The epicurean Tiptoes gave the Bovril "a good 8" out of 10, but was seldom to be seen with a hot meat drink so that may indicate a rarity aspect; Wakey awarded 7, later downgraded to 6 and a half. "It's got an oily tang" he said, adding that he particularly remembered the one at Boston as being better – "a hot and crisp flavour". The boy in front shared the unidentified contents of a a thermos with his older chaperon. He sported a scarf with the legend 'Pride of Shropshire'. The next best team in the county was Telford United, three leagues down. They won 0-3, we were to hear. Telford's manager was phlegmatic on the coach radio.

Ian was a Shrews season ticket holder, also arranging trips to away fixtures. Next was to be Peterborough. I was relieved to have phoned for three places on the Friday (£3 to us, £2 for regulars, together with the significant benefit of match programmes, which Ian had obtained – £2.50). Had the trip not been booked, we would have been asking directions for the short cut by foot, as the charabanc was to carry all of 58 on the outward journey. It had to be tried in any event for novelty value, and because by then we were foot-weary following the trudge from the station. What a pity about the railway line. You could have trained it from Stockport direct to 'Stadium Halt', should there have been such a phenomenon. Someone said 900 Edgeley Park enthusiasts had attended their team's recent 3-1 defeat. We were told, more than once, that parking space was inadequate, the location reminding me of Darlington: out by the ring road with limited hard shoulder opportunities. Park and Ride there was, also other pubs, in the town and outside it, offering a conveyance similar to Ian's.

The final bonus at the Prince of Wales was to be shown memorabilia from the old ground acquired at the June auction – seats and signs, both practical and ornamental by the bowling green at the back. I was assured by a Prince loyal that the old Crystal Palace turnstiles were safe – somewhere – and not the object of a meltdown.

The stadium had a welcome open feeling. The four stands, named for the points of the compass, were of separate construction and similar appearance owing to the uniform roof levels and lamps on short pylons at regular intervals. Kick-off was delayed by 14 minutes because those on the East Stand were reluctant to illuminate. Balls didn't often fly over the stands towards or onto the railway track, as had been their wont into the river in times of yore. Perhaps old habits die hard, as ballboys and fresh balls were produced for the ready just as they used to be when one was lost to coracle retrieval whenever it assumed a skyward and outward trajectory. Play was speeded up as a result. Reminiscent of Wimbledon – tennis championships, not Plough Lane. No waiting around for someone to retrieve balls settling into a blank space on a terrace.

It's telling that at Gay Meadow average attendances had been 3,997 (2005-06) and 4,730 (2006-07), the latter perhaps inflated as it was the last season before demolition, and how sad it had been to pass the pylonless site a few hours earlier. (Back in August 1991, I saw from the programme that the only League game thus far, against Wigan, had attracted 3,875, and that was in the old Third Division.) Town's average gate over the first half of 2007-08 was 5,422. Compare the official capacities: Gay Meadow 8,000, New Stadium 10,000. Impressive, but I did wonder whether it wouldn't have proved more economical to build bigger? It was good at this game: 6,208 turned out to see the poor display against the Chairboys, for whom striker John Sutton scored the only goal in the eighth minute. Wakey commented: 'Bluddy 'ell, they seem afraid of the ball.' 'Pretty dismal' said Tiptoes. 'That's what they should have been doing - have a pop at it' added Wakey. Tiptoes' son, Henry, was simultaneously at the Kassam Stadium, Oxford for Kidderminster, down in the Conference.

The programme provided the table for attendance statistics, as well it might as the figures showed the Blues'/Shrews' New Stadium in a good light. Attendances in the basement ranged from Bradford City's 13,566, MKD's 8,358 (another virgin ground and the team saw the year out with breathing space in pole position), our venue this day third, right down to 1,637 at Accrington in 24th and bottom. The next three up were also comparative ingénues: Dag/Red 1,935, Barnet 1,994 and Macclesfield 2,275. Interesting if nothing else. And I picked up on the long awaited Morecambe mistake. 'O' not 'a' in the programme. There was a piece of invention with the surname of Leon Crooks, the Wycombe no.26, spelt 'Croo9ks'.

The game was dreary, we all agreed. We were subjected to individual fans' opinions on Radio Shropshire on the transit return journey. Had they seen the same game, conveying the "we wuz robbed" syndrome? Guys, your lads were crap, and Wycombe just deserved a happy return journey. Having learned about the beer discount for a victory, Tiptoes wondered, sotto voce, if the prices would now be increased by 10p.

I gleaned from the programme the 'Biggest League win at Shrewsbury for each team: 29/01/94 Shrewsbury 1-0 Wycombe; 29/01/05 Shrewsbury 0-1 Wycombe'. My goodness – we witnessed the equalling of the record! No wonder the only sparkle was the rain bouncing in the floodlights. I have to add that the brash red and white quartered shirts of the visitors were distinctly more dramatic than the muted blue and amber home strip. The cohorts of the Wanderers were also much noisier (377 I guessed, actually 417 on the website as visitors, in the North Stand) with 'Wycombe Barmy Army' (WBA?) vocals and drum for much of the latter stages of the encounter while their lads dreared to an away win. And below was that often-observed strange presence of flags of the United Kingdom and St George. To be fair to the home supporters, they did muster an occasional 'Come on you Blues.'

On manoeuvring egress from the South Stand we were greeted with the benefit of the tardiness of the start: the day's results were on display aloft. Villa had overhauled Wigan to record their first-ever League win against them. Exeter had performed identically against Conference part-timers Histon. No goals at Oxford, though reports were to claim that the Harriers should have done better. The other WBA had trounced Scunthorpe 5-0 to return to the top of the Championship – two from Kevin Phillips. Why couldn't he have found a similar golden touch during his time at Villa Park? Then we joined the throng for the pubward journey.

We later heard of the fatal heart attack of the Motherwell captain Phil O'Donnell during their 5-3 defeat of Dundee United. It was eerie that footballs themselves, the spherical objects, seemed to be constructed in the 'Well's amber and claret. This was the case both at this match and at Villa Park on New Year's Day, when the entire full house clapped to his memory for a minute. We were then treated to Martin O'Neill's newly magisterial Villa overcoming Tottenham 2-1.

Here is a contemporary scoreboard comparison: The New Stadium had a narrow panel above the aforementioned WBA with admirably minimal information, e.g. at one point:

| 23 (time remaining) | SHREWSBURY | 0 |
| | WYCOMBE | 1 |

Unfortunately this all seemed to be in yellow and became difficult to discern against the background. Rather like the team.

Meanwhile at Villa Park information had at last been refined, on the massive displays aloft on opposite corners of the ground, to list both teams, with names in number order in white, transformed into yellow upon receipt of a similar coloured card, and the number of goals scored appended to the appropriate player. The whole thing was interrupted whenever a happening was deemed worthy of a replay. Very good, and even more satisfying as Villa were top in both respects – goals and yellow cards. Three days later, it was Villa 2 Spurs 1, to celebrate the new year.

The Villa game was so far away from the dearth we had witnessed this afternoon, and double the price (£16, £32), but the masochist in a football fan commits him relentlessly to the prospect of satisfaction. We still had plenty of that in the day out, progressing from a sunny train trip via the working, and derelict, Black Country through mouth-watering rural landscapes to floodlit fun and ultimately a standard-priced pint (£2.40).

# Newcastle United 6 Barnsley 0
## Division I (2), 7/4/93

The Magpies were five points clear at the top of the table with seven games to go, and only a month left. On a good day Barnsley were a competitive team, but were overwhelmed on this Wednesday evening. Andy Cole scored a hat trick and a huge crowd grew ecstatic on the swelling open terrace where I was sardined. This would be hard to beat anytime, anywhere: football for the travelling fan. Having survived the initial assault course challenge of mounting the East Stand, described by Simon Inglis as 'a tall, exposed cantilever, without screen walls and therefore forming a dark silhouette of angled concrete standing out against the sky. Nowhere else is the wonder of cantilever technology more stunning than here. The roof has no right to defy gravity and stay up, but it does.' I emerged battered from the vertical effects of all sizes of boots and the buffets and embraces which followed each netting to the zenith of Cole's third, and United's sixth, goals. We were all utterly exhilarated. No threat, just boisterousness. The Toon Army, indeed. I was beginning to empathize with the concept and its intensity.

The ground had the vital merit of proximity to the city centre, which was awash with black and white to the extent of bunches of balloons in said colours, festooning multitudinous hostelries. Access and retreat were a lot less painful than the crush in St James' Park. I had lifts from my hostess in leafy Gosforth, a stone's throw from the defunct home of the erstwhile Rugby Union supremos of the same name. Mind you, listening to Marilyn, from Northern Ireland (try her colcannon – exquisite), and Warner – Somerset/Devon borders (local cider with a slice of lemon, but the best is the porridge cooked with salt – banned from many kitchens now I fear – topped with soft brown sugar or golden syrup and laced with a modicum of whisky, not bad for a virtual teetotaller) – communicating could be as difficult to comprehend as some of the quothings emanating from the terraces and streets. Access to a stadium has not always been easy and reaching the safety of the ground can prove hazardous, as in the approach roads to the former Highfield Road, Coventry, as an away fan, and getting to Millwall. It proved easy to find a pub nearby for aperitifs, and I derived vicarious joy from the vibrant buoyancy of anticipation. It was self-contained – in this establishment pied cliques - which precluded admission of a new person. Chelsea in 1999 was similar in this respect, but downtown Newcastle is a far cry from Parsons Green and I emerged invigorated.

The ground was undergoing improvement – a new £5.6m stand (the 'Sir John Hall' – Leazes End) was to open the following August. It was salutary to note that a mere twelve months before this Newcastle had won a reprieve from relegation to the Third Division at the last minute in tandem with a narrow escape from bankruptcy.

The previous Saturday had produced an almost equal goalfest in this protracted tour of the north: in the Premier Division Blackburn 4 Liverpool 1, boosting Rovers' goal difference, which culminated at 22. They were fourth and Liverpool sixth in the final table, while a glance further up the list revealed Villa at their most recent top two finish as runners-up to 'ManUre'. It can't only be Wolves fans who call them that, which is where I discovered it. For light relief, *Sherlock Holmes the Musical* was on at the theatre, in stark contrast to the savage, and rewarding, *Decadence*, involving extensive character assassination, by Steven Berkoff (Joan Collins was in the movie version). 1993 was clearly a year of varied stimuli as we also fitted in a return trip on the 'North Yorkshire Moors Railway' (it said on the brochure). As well as a bottle of Theakston's Owd Peculier (delightful for elevenses) watching the steam waft by, we enjoyed a respite in a pub at the terminus, Pickering. On the return journey I espied Fuckin' Dave. He was just 'David' then in the days before he developed the habit of arriving late for arrangements, including all-too-brief timed squash courts; then he was 'Granville' for a while, but we won't go into that now. But I will say that he survived the packet of scratchings upon which I lost part of a tooth. F' and his kids were mounting an outward bound carriage. The vehicle was emitting shrieks and smoke and the windows proved admirably impenetrable, so contact was denied. But since then we've made a habit of sending each other holiday postcards bearing a train illustration, which is often a challenge.

## Sheffield Wednesday 0 Norwich City 0
## Premier League, 31/8/94

I was on my own on a tour of the Midlands and Yorkshire catching up with friends. I'd found a guest house in Owlerton/Hillsborough itself, though the weather was dreadful, raining throughout the game. No score draw notwithstanding,

Hillsborough Stadium was a model 40k capacity emporium – reported a dozen years later as being blessed with the largest female support in the league. In 2006 'At some of the biggest Championship (where the Owls resided) clubs more than one in five season ticket holders are now women'. In the Premiership 'the number of female football fans attending top-flight games this season is now 18% of the total – up from 13% in 2004-05'. This is extrapolated to a total 'in the region of 2.33 million'. An explanation was 'as football moves closer to the music and entertainment worlds.'

Wednesday's manager was Trevor Francis who celebrated the recent win at Wimbledon, the Crazy Gang at Selhurst Park, in the programme. The team photo made a colourful triple centre-page extension. The blue and white vertical striped shirts were adorned with four items: 'Sanderson' across the torso with the club's owl outlined in yellow. There was an attempt at subtlety in the sleeves, the solid azure blue of the front broken up into several small stripes over the same width. Très chic. The trend was against the Norwich game producing home goals, however, as Wednesday had scored three in their first game (lost 3-4 to Spurs), two in their second (lost 3-2 at QPR), then the single goal to beat the Dons, so the opposition's net was clearly destined to remain untouched in this game.

Two women behind me described the niceties: 'Brilliant ground i'n't it?' Then 'Bet they don't like it so wet.' And on identifying a player through the dazzling gloom: 'Observant aren't I!' 't's still a man's game,' she added at half-time.

Friends of someone? They were in a small minority in 1994, perhaps an early symptom of change to come. And from up the road in Huddersfield, a female fan was

heard to comment: 'Ooooh he's got a lovely arse.' To which the writer responded: 'Yes love, but what about his sliding tackle? Oh stop it this instant' (*A Slice of Kilner Pie* fanzine, 1996). *Strictly Come Dancing* judge Len Goodman might not agree that it's a real man's game, claiming in the *Stage* magazine: 'Those footballers score a goal, they kiss and cuddle each other and then go into the showers and compare each other's willies,' he says. 'In dance you have a beautiful girl and you are holding her close. Which one is the more sissy? – I don't know.' Boys will be boys, Len. What about rugby players in the scrummage? He didn't touch on homophobia, as such, the football world perhaps being rather less conducive to gayness than that of the celebrity ballroom.

In April 2006 30k enthusiasts saw Wednesday go one better, literally, by beating Norwich 1-0 in their battle against relegation back to the third level, whence they had scrambled up via the play-offs the previous year. The Canaries' winger, Darren Huckaby, was closed down by defender Frank Simek (USA), thus almost assuring safety. My cousin Karen finally yielded to persistent persuasion by her season ticket-holding (male) family members to attend her first ever football game – they'd lived in the steel city for years. Yes, she enjoyed it very much (the crowd even more than the match). Everyone should try a game once – many are pleasantly surprised and they gain a lifelong memory.

When the Owls travelled to Brighton a few days later they won 0-2. 7,573 attended, which of itself is testimony to the urgent need for of a bigger stadium for the Seagulls – how many were turned away that day, or were resigned to preclusion? The result consigned a whole batch to the gloom of doom: Brighton, Crewe and Millwall. A final note about attendances: Wednesday's best in 2005-06 was 33,439 in February 2006, to see them lose to their neighbours from Bramall Lane, who went on to secure promotion as runners-up to Reading. In turn Wednesday held them to a 1-1 draw away after the trip to the South Coast. 27,307 went to that game.

I liked the ground as it was in 1994 and enjoyed a few days of Englishness as this was soon after returning from a hot and intensively cultural trip to Egypt. Cats and dogs – how refreshing! Animals are so scraggy in Egypt. I remember the Beehive Inn and found that the game ticket, purchased at the time, was £12.50, such an issue being rare for a cash turnstile transaction. The programme was £1.60. We need these details.

On my next visit (Sheffield Wednesday 0 Leicester City 2 – Championship, 6/10/07), 11 years after the ground was one of the chosen few elected for Euro 96 use, it still impressed. Faded and seductive, with curves connecting the top of each stand and sundry weeds proliferating in the spaces between the angular and tortuous steps up from the Bovril dispensary (and reassuringly putrid gents) below the vast 'ASD Lighting Kop'. It was my kind of ground. The home team were atrocious, provoking impassioned articulations, at least from cousin-in-law Jol, along the lines of 'Laws must go'. (By the way Karen's lamb shank, and the gin, had converted my mood from well-pissed-off to benign after the five and a half hour drive. The AA Route Finder said less than three and a half. The train next time. Grrr!). In fact Leicester's manager was the one to depart, three weeks later, to join the ailing Bolton Wanderers. Woeful but a division more elevated. So we caught him in mid-contract – he was only there from 13 September to 24 October. 699 *Bolton Evening News* readers responded to a poll about whom they wanted as the next manager at the Reebok. Twelve voted for Gary Megson (more than half voting for AN Other, not impressed by anyone of the list). The paltry dozen was not surprising considering the guy's Premiership record – seven wins from 48 matches at West Bromwich Albion, and indeed his cynical attitude to his new employers at Leicester. The decision seems to have been an exercise of power on the part of chairman Phil Gartside. Bolton were bottom of the League when Megson took over, even sad Derby being a point better off. He did take them up to a safe 16th.

The programme (a standard £2.50, the ticket the going rate of £21 for the second division and 20,010 was the turnstile total) dedicated a full page for 'Wall of Fame…The Brian Laws Gallery…Purchase yourself a brick and cement yourself into the heart of your club!' Not if the man is ejected, you won't. This time in daylight, the rich blue and white stripes of the home shirts, by then advertising 'plusnet Broadband', together with smart black shorts, were somewhat sharper than the team or the stadium. There was a sharply contrasting image wafting around the goalmouth: a purposeful lilac twin suit, which adorned goalkeeper Lee Grant, he who let in two unnecessary goals, an Owl with a whole page, for the 'one to eleven' questions in this issue. His favourite holiday destination was 'Dubai because it's not too far to fly and the service is great'. Well, I liked it too as the best hotel I've ever set foot in was there, the Jumeirah Beach, the snorkelling was ace and the water warm (at the cusp of the year). 'Who is the most famous person you have ever met, Lee?' 'I was once in a lift with David Beckham.' Time to move on.

## Wycombe Wanderers 0 Bury 1
## Division II (3), 27/8/96

I still think of Wycombe, and perhaps always will, as League newcomers. I'm afraid I remember them in the Isthmian League. They were members for many years, translated to the Vauxhall Opel League where they finished champions in 1987 (the programme listed all their triumphs as 'Isthmian'), with 32 wins from 42 games, and a massive 101 points, nine ahead of Yeovil Town who were undergoing a brief respite down in the feeder leagues.

Their nickname is the Chairboys, High Wycombe being a furniture production hotspot, you understand, though some have replaced the 'a' with 'o' to connect the club, anomalously, with high-pitched youths in surplices. Wanderers won League status as Conference champions in 1994, and were promoted to Endsleigh League Division II in their first season. They finished sixth in 1995 and 12th in 1996, on this occasion meeting a side just promoted. Bury were old school, having joined the League in 1895 and been destined to hover between the second and third levels for most of their history, though it's reassuring to note that they have achieved as many as 22 years in the top flight, even if most recently in 1928-29.

On the day, Fuckin' Dave was the driver, proud owner of a car most suitable for a journey such as this; we found a pub, the Hour Glass, at the start of the final drag into the industrial estate – the ground was at the far end. At that time it was 'Adams Park'. There was time for a snack and some liquid there. Home fans were in good spirits, despite witnessing their team's failure on the night. For some it might have been something to do with the 'park'. Having endured the long, dreary approach the site of the ground was a welcome surprise. It was in the countryside, more or less. In fact rather more than less given the industry surrounding the approach road. So beauteous were the surroundings that, for an aerial snap thereof, I scrambled up to the top of the car park, on the way passing through open iron gates bearing the name 'Loakes Park', sensitively transported from the club's old ground. Excellent: a vestige of heritage. This was a Chiltern hillside such as where you might expect an ice cream van to turn up with mivvies and twisters. Some local punters do a double whammy: quaff in a watering hole over the chalk ridge in West Wycombe, of Hell Fire Club Caves fame, before the hike, dropping down to the pristine green park for their entertainment .

We stood close to the action under the succinctly named Buckinghamshire Chilterns University College Stand. The website employed initials, a boon for anyone with a tendency towards repetitive stress syndrome on their keyboard. Wanderers seemed in complacent mood afterwards too, when we resumed our bar station with one for the road. It's reassuring to note that almost always these days it's possible to find a pub in reasonable distance from the ground with at least one real ale on tap. The Campaign for Real Ale has done a good job over the years.

On my return visit (Wycombe 0 Bristol Rovers 3 – League 2, 1/4/06) the away bogs failed to accommodate the needs of 1,500 travellers. For some, relief was sought in the dustbins as well as the somewhat curtailed trough. "Bin there" shouted one wag. It was pissing down outside too, but then the effect of the sound of running water on a bloke's bladder is well known.

Hotly tipped for promotion that season, they tailed off badly – this was their third defeat in a row. It was Rovers who made it up to League 1 the next season.

## Wolverhampton Wanderers 2 Charlton Athletic 3
## Division I (2), 11/1/00

This was an encouraging opener to the new century (if you believe a century can begin with a zero) fixture at Molineux. We saw Wolves eclipsed by a Charlton side destined for the top flight. The score flattered the home team. The Addicks had been relegated narrowly the year before and were on the way to becoming a stable Premiership side after the forthcoming promotion, essentially through the guidance of manager Alan Curbishley, still holding the reins right up to 2006, signalling the end of their top 20 membership. The £17 ticket had been obtained in advance, but we noticed there was plenty of cash turnstile admission.

Molineux, offering sport and leisure before the football club moved in 1889, used to have a 'Cowshed' like Exeter and others, even MK Dons' National Hockey Stadium where there may just have been a modicum of intention to intimidate the opposition, faced with concrete cows. The Wolverhampton version was knocked down in the 1930s for the creation of the North Bank terrace. Fifty years on in 1986 Wolves were in a parlous state, the team in the bottom division and half the ground closed, including the North Bank. This was a local authority decision following the Bradford fire the previous year. With patronage, as it might be termed, and purpose from the same local authority, championed by the leader, John Bird, independent funder Sir Jack Hayward and Gallaghers, developers, the club and ground were rescued to herald the modern era. It would be churlish to carp at the ASDA store built nearby as part of the process – good locations aren't only for footy fans. Approaching the stadium is a pleasure as you survey it from above, and it occupies a central spot in the City of Wolverhampton (status conferred in celebration of the Millennium), on the list of touristic destinations. Molineux attracts substantial female support, like Sheffield Wednesday, thoughtfully catered for through enlightened toilet provision, one hears.

One such fan, back in the Thirties, was my friend Pom's mother, Frances, who went to games with her boyfriend at the time Major Frank Buckley was the manager. She remembers there to be 48,000 in the ground for a game against Manchester United. It was so packed that they couldn't even get their sandwiches out. When extricated later they were squashed. They used to get lifts on a lorry at her workplace, three miles away in industrial Bilston, her boss being a Wolves fan. "Of course you could always tell the result from the menfolk's expressions on returning home after a game…They would get the *Pink'un*, Saturday evening football rag", the equivalent of which was to be found up and down the country, e.g. the *Green'un* in Bristol. Then the *News of the World*, among several Sunday papers, before the weekly church service. They would often go to weekly rep performances at the Grand Theatre, since modernized and presenting touring productions.

Meanwhile, in this diversity- and minority-aware age, disabled attenders are easily accommodated at good sightline positions, given the gradient upon which the ground is built. In 2000 Landy and I had a fulfilling evening out in a fine modern stadium, 'The Custard Bowl' to some of a Throstle persuasion (*The Football Rivalries Report 2008*, produced by the New Football Pools, had WBA and Wolves as the top of The 10 best derby disputes – *Western Daily Press*), even if the away eleven won. Our spot was in the Billy Wright Stand (Upper) but close enough for plentiful atmosphere. Wolves have achieved plenty indeed, mainly during the post war years (champions the year I first became interested in football – 1958-59 – for one, and Cup winners the next, thumping Blackburn 3-0). This is held in eternal memory, in identifying with the place as it used to be. Sid Green reflected in *We Are Wolves*: 'I miss the atmosphere of the old terraces, when you stood in the same place and got to know the people around you. A bag of sherbet lemons would be handed round and a full packet of fags would disappear in a flash. I fear the arrival of a new generation of fair weather fans. Perhaps they should get some practice in first on a cold and wintry night at Tranmere or Grimsby. Our type of inherent support comes from a degree of adversity and endeavour, not courtesy of an American Express card and a fluffy cushion.' (*We Are Wolves*, edited by Charles Ross, *Juma* 1997.) But: 'as much as I miss the old Molineux, I have to admit that in truth it was a dump – albeit loved by us 'Bankers'. And the phoenix that rose from the ashes of the decaying old stadium – in fact two of them, in Bully (the free scoring Steve Bull) on the pitch and Sir Jack (Hayward) off it – was long overdue…'

There was surely a contribution from the uniqueness of their insistent colours, old gold (and related shades) and a solid black. This is reinforced in the brick Wolf image, impressively inset in a wall near Molineux's front entrance, a quick turn away from Billy Wright's effigy, though perhaps a bit dated by the mid-Noughties.

In Y2K Wolves were going through a period of lassitude during which you felt they were in danger of collapse just as much as of attaining one of the top positions. They did survive that season to become a yo-yo side, starting with the unfortunate eclipse by the Baggies, who overhauled them for promotion in 2002 after they had seemed uncatchable at Christmas.

We recovered after the final whistle with a fine pint at the Posada in the town, while traffic subsided. We enjoyed this ground, a far cry from its state on my previous visits in the Seventies. No doubt they have updated player needs in keeping with new millennium practice. Meeting a self-confessed WAG, in fact the ex-wife of a noted Wolves player in the eighties, the effects of recruitment of that talented but impressionable teenager into the squad of a professional football club were very mixed. Any success in his career was somewhat muted by personal immaturity, marked by aggression and irresponsibility. She blamed the club for lack of support.

Postscript. The Millwall visit had been courtesy of the generosity of the Molineux ticket office, in January 2005. On 24.12.07 at 11.15.10 (it read) I received this text message on my mobile phone: 'Merry Christmas Mick and a happy New Year from everyone at Wolves – thank you for your support!' They must have a mightily long list. Thank you, Molineux.

## Kidderminster Harriers 1 Cardiff City 1, Cardiff won 5-4 on penalties League Cup Round 1, 24/8/04

Kiddy are intruders in these scribblings, as they performed even worse than the impecunious Rushed and Dire Ones in 2004-05, and were relegated to the Conference six points worse off, with bottom club Cambridge. After a mere five years in the bottom division, having achieved tenth at their zenith, the Aggborough outfit has to be included for its balmiest offering: the scrumptious Aggborough Stew, made especially or the fans over the years, upon which Landy and I feasted at this unfortunate game.

My companion, Taff Landy, a Cardiff City supporter, considered the Bluebirds fans' notorious bad behaviour reprehensible. There was no aggression at Aggborough that evening, though, which was a very protracted affair with extra time and 11 penalty kicks (and no pints afterwards, licensing laws not by then relaxed) to send the Welsh lot to Milton Keynes in the second round, where they triumphed 1-4, followed by an identical penalty outcome at Bournemouth. In the last eight they lost 0-2 to Premiership outfit Portsmouth, to end an impressive run. And we had witnessed them struggle past an ailing bottom division club in the first round. Ah, the drama of cup ties!

The Harriers brought a short-lived new dimension to League football in the Midlands, as neighbours of Wolves and West Brom, and sported one of the most inventive names, relief from the 'Towns' and 'Uniteds' which abound.

It's strange (and trivial) that the same three – in full, Wolverhampton Wanderers, Kidderminster Harriers and West Bromwich Albion, have among the longest names, with 22, 21 and 18 letters respectively. The only others in competition are Brighton and Hove Albion (20) and Rushden and Diamonds (18) – though shouldn't conjunctions be disallowed? Moreover the Diamonds' precursor, Irthlingborough, sported 23 letters, and Bournemouth and Boscombe Athletic a mighty 30, before they converted to AFC Bournemouth, a flagrant attempt to leap to the top of fixture lists, universally presented in alphabetical order. Indeed the 2005-06 *Racing & Football Outlook Guide* had them them ahead of Barnsley and Blackpool, but only in the narrative; they sank to their proper level in the fixtures. By the way, in 1999 Kidderminster was the site of the first ever senior football match conducted by three women officials, led by Wendy Toms. 3,125 turned up to see Nuneaton Borough win 1-2. By the way part two: north of the border Hamilton Academical in becoming singular dropped from 19 to 18 letters, well eclipsed by Inverness Caledonian Thistle at 26. Heart of Midlothian, perhaps most evocative of all, adds up to a mere 17. It must be pointed out that Inv Cal This is seriously spurious in the letter count contest, as a hybrid deriving from days of yore. I remember doing a ground-tour-reccie of Inverness in 1962, when the teams trying to outdo Elgin City were Caley, Clachnacuddin and Thistle. Clach are still there but the triple-barrelled combo has turned out to be an effective concoction, still in 2008-09 in the top flight north of the Border.

## Southampton 3 Colchester United 2
## League Cup Round 3, 27/10/04

The afternoon had been spent at Windsor Castle, mainly because there did not appear to be anything else easily available for culture vultures to patronize in the general area.

Please be aware that National Trust properties (at least) appear to close down for the winter when the clocks go back. Note further that many are closed on Fridays, thus thwarting long weekends earmarked for indulgence in multiple NT properties. So two of Her Majesty's abodes were experienced in a short time. I just wish the customers had been allowed to see more of both buildings. As so often with stately home trips, you emerge weary and replete on one level, there always being plenty to admire before the well-earned plastic seat for a pot of tea and slice of lemon drizzle cake.

Supporting displays seem to be improving all the time as the Heritage Industry pursues its exponential skyward trajectory. However, neither of these wallet-drainers was a truly satisfying experience, because of the residual feeling of short shrift. In both cases the extensive grounds had a liberating effect. At Sandringham that weekend we admired autumn floral displays, buying a plant or two in the shop, stretching legs on historical turf under multi-centenarian trees, and catching leaves, before they touched the ground – to do so earns you a year's good luck. I'm sure it was fulfilled, not least by all the football grounds subsequently enjoyed. Positive thinking – eh?

I had attended the Dell for a League game (Southampton 1 Watford 2, Div I, 26/12/84, a good year for both, finishing fifth and 11th respectively), that cherished, cramped old ground one of whose abandoned turnstiles was acquired by a fan at an auction, it's been reported.

This was the token visit to St. Mary's (Friends Provident i'faith, capacity 32,689), in the rain and under the floodlights. We never saw the (even wetter) River Itchen which maps reveal to be adjacent, reminiscent of Shrewsbury, should your imagination be fertile. The Mine, who lived in the area but wasn't free for this visit, told me that it was impossible to get tickets for a Saturday League game, so here we were squeezing one in on a Wednesday as part of an oblique tour crossing the map like a drunken spider. We were staying in a convenient, and pre-booked, Travel Inn for the event and had allowed time for what developed as an unsatisfying, wet wander round part of the city, where we tried a down-at-heel Wetherspoons pub and the Anchor, near the market: pints, relief because we were harbouring from the rain, and with a tableful of away fans scoffing pies elsewhere in the bar.

The Saints scrambled a narrow victory, though we were rooting for Colchester who took the game to their betters. I liked the new ground – compact and atmospheric, in fact cosy; best to be there in the dark and wet, I reckoned. Oh yes, I felt like that at Hillsborough. Ergo, rain is good for ground appreciation. We didn't bother with half-time nourishment, for which you would certainly have to absent yourself for the final minutes of the first half to avoid the irritation of waiting for an interminable queue to be served in a game which always seemed likely to produce goals. This was a cup game. Anyway the cold and damp had got to us. Best to be rooted to the red plastic spot, we concurred.

We happened upon a few more pubs afterwards, albeit of little worth, the need for refreshment and shelter being more acute than the pursuit of quality: big screens everywhere, featuring games from afar.

Evening games will always uplift and excite. Something about them takes the experience out of the ordinary into the theatrical. The senses are exaggerated. The players on the stage move in sharp relief. So many of the best experiences have been taken even further away from the Saturday afternoon norm by the climatic context: rain, snow, setting sun and darkness itself convert the endeavour into something artificial, unreal, elusive.

Senses have been stimulated by the stew at Kiddy, the downpour at Hillsborough, the visual delight of descending upon Molineux and a comprehensive feast at Gay Meadow, all accentuated, I'm sure, by their placement at the end of the day. Of course the benefit is extended by indulgence in the sequel – there's a sense of calming wellbeing in ruminating over a pint after an evening game.

Let's call it therapeutic.

## Chapter Two
# Roads to Gloom

## Away Games

**A**way games: a phrase weighed down with the likelihood of failure and frustration. On the other hand, if your glass is half full, the benefits of adventure, change or experiment win the day. The pilgrimages undertaken over the decades have become a complex phenomenon to maximize the chance of a prevailing good memory. You admit implicitly that your team will probably lose, especially if your team is the Villa or Exeter, but sometimes extend yourself to unbelievable lengths to contrive a worthwhile trip. This is notwithstanding attendant challenges to be faced each time, to do with the journey, locating desired sites, problems with the ground and, finally, after the encounter, car, bus or train logistics for escape, often in delay and confusion in the dark.

Several football grounds have served the multiple benefit of, in ascending order:

- an interesting cultural experience (least likely of all, see Luton),
- success on the field of play (rarely, but note such gems as Exeter's League Cup triumph at St Andrews),
- pursuit of the 92 (almost always but note disappointment at the gates of Boscombe).

These foolhardy ventures have fallen into three categories: the Villa, the Grecians and on behalf of others, where the project has involved a preference for the away team: Millwall at Plymouth (as the parlance goes in American football) for Graham, an exiled Lions fan; Bristol Rovers at Wrexham (sneaking affection for good old Gas); at Scunthorpe for anyone, in this case Rochdale; finally Sunderland, heirs apparent to the Championship throne, at Gresty Road.

## 1. Villa on Tour

### Manchester United 4 Aston Villa 1
### Division I, 6/2/82

It was just as well that this was sandwiched between provisions at the Carters Arms, Sale, and Yates's Wine Lodge, Manchester city centre, which in those days was largely patronized by hardened older solitary drinkers. The Yates's motto, inscribed on a t-shirt I wore for years, was 'Moderation is True Temperance'. I thought it an appealing sentiment, begging to be disproved. My customary tipple when patronizing Yates's was Leading Port. Perhaps in the Carters Arms we might have observed:

*On the breasts of a barmaid in Sale*
*Were tattooed the prices of ale.*
*For the sake of the blind,*
*Upon her behind,*
*Was the same information in Braille.*

To the game. Villa were largely invisible, overcome by Ray Wilkins, Gordon McQueen, Bryan Robson and top goal-scorers Frank Stapleton and Garry Birtles, names cloaked in romantic mists of memory. Many of the 1980-81 Championship-

winning stars were on show, but lacking. Jimmy Rimmer and Kenny Swain struggled at the back, the team captained by the sterling Dennis Mortimer, whose best was now proving not to be good enough. They had found it difficult to find form in the League, perhaps exacerbated by preoccupation with the European Cup, which I have to mention they went on to win, praise the Lord!

United were that week in second place behind Southampton (who were to finish seventh). It was not yet Manchester's era. The Red Devils, belying their nickname, had been knocked out of both domestic cups at the first hurdle, so had only the League to concern them at this time: difficult to conceive of a quarter of a century later.

*The Football Grounds of England and Wales* by Simon Inglis was published the year after this game, so I shall quote some of his comments of the time, the book arranged in a regional format, the very first entry being this ground:

'Bobby Charlton called Old Trafford "a theatre of dreams"...

'When the Stretford End roars the noise is equivalent to a modern jet airliner taking off. United fanatics from all over the world come to tour Old Trafford with all the reverence and awe normally reserved for stately homes and cathedrals [just so in visiting the citadels of the 21st Century – see the report on the Emirates]...

'Soon after the War, Old Trafford witnessed two very different record attendances. On 27 December 1920 United's largest ever League attendance, 70,504, watched a match v. Aston Villa [the record audience of 76,962 witnessed the removal of Grimsby by Wolves to the tune of 5-0 in the FA Cup semi final on 25/3/39, though Pompey upstaged them in the final: 4-1. And another 4-1 marked the establishing of the record gate in the new all-seated high volume Old Trafford. 76,098 saw United entertain Blackburn on 31/3/07.]

'In May the following year, only 13 people bothered to pay for a Second Division fixture between Stockport County and Leicester City. Edgeley Park had been closed following crowd disturbances. County were also doomed to relegation, so the fans decided to boycott proceedings. In fact there were about 2,000 at Old Trafford to see the game, but the majority had stayed on after United's afternoon match v. Derby County to see two games for the price of one! [And I have been consistently foiled in my latterday attempt to see two games in a day, though quite willing to pay for both!] ...

'Inside the ground is like a huge red cavern, with two sides of modern cantilever stands and two sides of older constructions...

'An all-enclosed stadium is all very well in a hot country, but in rainy Manchester it has presented problems for the Old Trafford pitch, which does not get enough natural ventilation [some lessons are never learned – the Reebok Stadium is one example of a later design which turned out to suffer the same problem]...

'Old Trafford is not apparently impregnable as Anfield, or as grand as Villa Park or Highbury [a lot has changed], yet its more uniform design and three covered corners make it a sound trap of red and white aggression [with the loss of immediacy if you sit up in the upper tiers of the modern stadium].'

As a comparison and contrast to the sad piece of suffering of this encounter, almost exactly a year earlier I had beheld the Villa confident and victorious at Highfield Road, to record yet another win (17/1/81, 1-2) over Coventry City. Villa rarely lost to the Sky Blues. Before the game Turky, Jersey and I were enjoying our periodical reunion in a great big hostelry with separate bars for each persuasion. We were correctly in the Claret and Blue bit. A misguided Sky Blue enthusiast ventured in, only to be straddled over the pool table, beaten up and ejected gutterwards. He did provoke it, though. Continuing on this tangent of Coventry, Highfield Road was pleasant enough, in a walkable residential area, and as away fans in the Mitchell and Butler Stand a good view was afforded. M&B churned out crap beer, ubiquitous in the West Midlands at that time. We did get some lush Robinsons on this Manchester visit, perhaps more by luck than judgement.

An universal problem at that time was to get League and Cup games played, many being postponed due to harsh weather, as pitch protection methods were in their infancy. The Pools Panel had come into its own. The League table was something of a mockery as a guide to form and achievement, as the programme showed the numbers of games played varied from 19 to 23. Coventry were a point behind and a place below West Brom, but had played four games more.

My memory of Old Trafford is primarily from Euro 96. Back in 1982 there was all the atmosphere associated with the red and white army, which had been green and gold and white and blue in various stages up to the club's conversion from Newton Heath to Manchester United in 1902. Their gates 80 seasons later had varied between 38k and nearly 57k (for the League Cup second leg v Spurs). The local derby at Maine Road attracted 52k, but as a whole Man U's support was well ahead of the rest. Heads and, often, feet.

Also from a different age were the Churchman's Cigarettes cards which depicted 'Association Footballers' in the '2nd series of 50'. Well, 48, actually, in the Woodbine Tipped 10 pack, picked up at a car boot sale. There was no. 1 Andrew Beattie, Preston North End, a former quarryman sporting fulsome white, black and black and white (long socks rigid with shinpads), then no. 31, Thomas Manley, Brentford, formerly Manchester United, the monochromatic image on the front showing a truncated left leg, as it booted the ball out of the frame; and Stan Cullis - who he? - (no. 11), of Wolves, 'born at Ellesmere Port'; and more, until a surprisingly bulky one came up. It was no. 2, Manchester United's Beaumont Asquith. Far from the adornment of shinpads, or even a jockstrap, Beaumont was stark bollock naked and really quite demure in attitude, his eyes cast pensively down: anyone's guess what ball he was spotting. The card was well adhered to the real image beneath. From the top side it was hard to imagine the prowess of the man with the following achievement: 'In 1938/39 he settled down as a centre-forward and was a notable success, scoring 28 goals and helping Barnsley to win the championship of the northern section of the Third Division'. Then he was transferred to Man U.

## Watford 2 Aston Villa 1
## Division I, 26/2/83

The Villans here embarked upon a run of four defeats. I was introduced to Vicarage Road by local friends Tim and Michelle, supporters of the Hornets, having missed out on the 'Brewers' – Watford FC a few decades earlier, named after the ground's erstwhile owners, Benskins, whose name has miraculously resurfaced on the barrels of a modern substance, a good pint but not real Benskins to the diehards. It's called 'branding'. Let's carry on digressing to set the scene, before resurrecting the ignoble memory of the game.

I had just left my job, equipped with a Parker pen as a leaving present (you should see my handwriting now – perhaps I ought to return to fountain pen use as a discipline to improve it. It's rumoured that flowing pens, with ink replenished from a Quink bottle, can have this effect). Eventually after the send-off I saw the cult movie *Nosferatu* in a cinema, a late-night showing. I don't remember anything about it. Something for daytime viewing in retirement. I resolved in my diary not to spend money and to reduce car use, I recall, because I was moving to a local workplace with more job satisfaction (it was hoped) but less remuneration.

So Watford was the start of a week off between employments. The perambulation followed an intriguing nationwide course.

We were in the steeply terraced Vicarage Road End, affording a fine view, meaning I was a token home fan and completely exposed to the elements. The smaller, covered, Rookery was earmarked for away fans, who were thereby able to produce fulsome volume reverberating round the metal structure. In a former life it had been a cinder bank, upon which blackberry bushes flourished through the ash terracing redesignated for football observation.

The new 'South' (formerly Rookery) Stand opened for business with Bristol City's visit on 22/4/95. Saracens RFC have shared the ground since 1997, many followers choosing the Rookery, calling it 'Rover South.'

Barry Endean was valiant and Ray Lugg uniquely Man of the Match – apart from this showing, against the Villa, of course, he failed to cut the mustard in this division. Watford was the first club to introduce a Family Enclosure – part of the North End terrace. The local rag, the *Watford Observer*, was featured in a prominent stand clock carrying the pithy adage 'tells more, sells more' – a bad run by the team would on occasion involve suitably positioned camera shots with bit of slogan as backdrop.

No doubt Villa's showing in the Home Counties depressed the team, as I witnessed a sad 1-2 defeat at the feet of Juventus the next Wednesday in the European Cup Quarter

Final accompanied by former housemates Caroline and Phil. We drowned our sorrows in the Upper Grounds, something of a habit. 45,531 were present, saying something about the era – it was the Holte End terrace – and 70k turned out for the disastrous second leg, which Juve won 3-1. Villa were on a downward spiral. Arsenal had beaten them 2-0 at Highbury in the FA Cup Sixth Round just before.

They don't go in twos, but contrasts, when you play the same team in quick succession. On 19 February the Hornets had done the M1/M6 trip for a 4-1 drubbing in the Fifth Round. It was a competitive time. Watford were in the top three and Villa fifth, both with far better home than away records, so I suppose this League result was predictable. Mark Walters scored the Villans' goal. Meanwhile Gordon Cowans had been chosen by Bobby Robson for the England team. Tony Barton's 'Team Talk' in the European Cup programme (40p – that long ago?) omitted this game completely (fair enough, it was only four days before, but these days that would be enough for programme turnaround), boasting about the FA Cup victory and the consistency and form since early January. Though cup activity evaporated during this period, the Lions did sustain their League form to finish sixth, outmanoeuvred at the last by way of Tottenham's game in hand. Watford were runners-up to runaway champions Liverpool.

To round off the story of the tour, it was three grounds and games in eight days as the following Saturday featured the Barnsley visit. Outcomes notwithstanding, such a range of entertainment in most varied settings, in different company, is the kernel of live football, set in projects over the atlas. I was well satisfied by this injection of lifeblood on immersing myself in the new post back home, tied to a desk, far away from the freedom of the terraces.

## Luton Town 1 Aston Villa 0
## Division I, 1/10/83

*To Luton town centre – a first ever amble*
*I duly arrived, parked, embarked on a ramble –*
*A featureless place, little merit or thrill*
*No water to see, not a ruin, nor hill.*

*But the Bitter End beckoned, good name for an inn,*
*The Best was from Shefford, most welcome, but thin,*
*The White Hart was next – at last I got in,*
*Through footy fans to the bar, Benskins for beer,*
*(Though I really preferred Charles Wells Bombardier).*
      *The buzz was a win, yes, some goals for a treat,*
          *Not a spot kick defeat.*

*To Kenilworth Road to see Villa's demise*
*They failed to score any, perhaps as a tease.*
*No away wins so far and after this, none,*
*Iniquitous outcome – the lads should have won.*

*While back home in Brum they'd won each of the four,*
*Were Super Cup holders, were tipped for much more,*
*With Withe, Spink and Curbishley, Morley and Shaw*
*The pride of the Midlands, now facing the Hatters,*
*You'd expect them to turn the home team into tatters.*
      *And what did we get from the would-be elite?*
          *A spot kick defeat.*

In a similar vein was Villa's 1-0 defeat at Stamford Bridge a generation later in August 1999. The White Horse on Parsons Green was the first *Good Beer Guide* pub I identified, having space as blue, white and flesh-coloured patrons were spilling outside. It was a warm summer's day – men bare-chested and women revealing designer bra straps, or not. Immediately the atmosphere and body language said 'confident', 'affluent', 'untouchable' and indeed there was no one to talk to: civilized and contained as was the entire occasion. The beer was tasty, gleaming in the sun, a ploughman's lunch the going fodder, probably invented (only in the 70s, it's been said) for this kind of market. Upon reflection, is there any such thing as a ploughman? This was a very far cry from the bleak expanses of Luton's shopping centre and a scrambled pint of quasi-local beer. Which should a suffering away punter prefer: a frustrating reversal against the run of play or a narrow failure having defended throughout, as seemed to be manager John Gregory's game plan at Stamford Bridge? Despite the grievance at Luton, 'we wuz robbed', I'll go for that one – Villa showed some style at Kenilworth Road. Poet John Hegley had better luck on both goals and wit counts, as follows:

> *Luton versus Middlesbrough*
> *Five whole goals to Luton Town*
> *And Middlesbrough not one*
> *But though their team was five-nil down*
> *Their fans were up for fun*
> *And when their consolation came*
> *Before the whistle blew*
> *They echoed Luton's 'we want six'*
> *With a modest 'we want two'.*

I only made it back to Bedfordshire in 2005, for a rather small amount of work with Luton Carnival (a single day away), a massive jamboree exploding over the Whitsun Bank Holiday, but requiring all-year-round organization with overspill into the realms of training and education, and facing issues of access, diversity and inclusion, some Noughties buzzthemes. Not for profit but in acute response to the requirements of funding bodies and stakeholders. It had grown into the biggest in Britain after Notting Hill: no possible competition as that fiesta is held over the late-summer bank holiday weekend. A well-funded happening, it reflected the local population, with a substantial Afro-Caribbean element, and not a lot of football, even of a Hatters nature.

Driving in from the M1, I passed adjacent to Kenilworth Road, noting that the club really is hemmed in at that address. The plan was to move out nearer the M1 to a stadium with a 15,000 capacity, some increase on just over 10k in 2007-08. It's understandable.

## 2. Exeter Away

### Birmingham City 1 Exeter City 2
### League Cup Round 3, 26/9/79

What a total treat this was, the night after the vexation of a goalless draw between the Villa and Everton. The home team were gracious in defeat, the Grecians having provided good value. The Blues had just been relegated to Division II and Exeter, managed by rising star Brian Godfrey, had managed their best ever 9th in the Third Division, with rare aspirations for the Second Division. So there was less of a gap between the opponents than at most points in their history (let's cite 2003-08: Birmingham mostly in the Premiership, Exeter out of sight).

This League Cup run was most exciting for Exeter. In the two-legged Second Round they had overcome Doncaster 6-4 (5-1 after extra time in the second, home, leg). Their prize in the Round 4 was to be a trip to Anfield, to lose 2-0 to Liverpool, the reigning champions.

The season would see an advance for both clubs – the Blues straight back to Division I and the Grecians to another highest ever, eighth, which remains their pinnacle of achievement.

Despite being an alien (= a Villa fan) St Andrews was always an agreeable place to visit, and latterly seductively streamlined in its progressive cantilevered style. It occupied a hill in Small Heath to the south east of the city centre. There were splendid drinking opportunities just off the main drag, easily walkable from New Street Station. As a rail traveller you can admire the stadium as a landmark from a train, most likely static, aiming to enter Brum from north or east. The station is the biggest interchange in the country and the home straight nowadays would allow plenty of time to finish the sudoku, your chapter, mobile phone arrangements or sending a final email while the precise platform is arranged with someone in the Platform Designation Facility (PDF) within the station.

I have never minded the predictable mouthings from the Bluenose faithful, like: 'Shit/spit on the Villa', 'If you hate the Villa, stand up', somehow to me sporting a humorous edge, partly owing to an airing of native Brummie wit, in turn of phrase and local intonation. The wealth of resigned observation on the terraces, and in the modern age even while seated (except during spasmodic thrilling or expectant bits), kept up the entertainment despite what you've paid to see being 'crap', to quote an oft-uttered noun.

And now for a Blues joke: 'Why can't you circumcise an Aston man?' 'Because there's no end to those pricks'. Speaking of male members, it was at a sparsely attended St Andrews game, for I did habituate the place on occasion, that a well-bladdered youth (no doubt having downed copious drafts of lager in one of the pubs referred to above, or, more likely, a keg palace, without diverting his course from the main drag, and unconcerned with discretion) attracted our attention further along the terrace with a high-tenor rendition of an indeterminate song, perhaps a solo chant. This was accompanied by substantial penile exposure, issuing a strongly curved projection of pee. However, I don't remember anyone getting wet. And 'Piss on the Villa' is another frequently employed epithet. In another situation, in 2007, a related display resulted in a hearing. But this time it was a player in the Arngrove Northern League. Dunston Federation's Cain Young 'lifted his shorts to reveal his private parts'. Young was also accused of making "inappropriate" remarks to a young female Shildon [the home side] fan as he walked back on the pitch.' The result was 1-2, so there was some comfort for the Feds.

Anyway, the Villa, in every way, have enjoyed continuing status as the premier Second City club, and the poor old Blues have languished for far too much of the time outside the top flight, so you have to make allowances. It could be argued that one of their greatest achievements was Beau Brummie's (a dog) winning the first ever Mascot

Grand National in 1999, in a field of 17.

It was a happy day, seriously belated, when 'Small Heath' were promoted in 2002. Even happier was their immense achievement of finishing an elevated 10th in the 2003-04 table, celebrated with a lap of honour. Well, bless my soul! It's all comparative, one might surmise. And rather sad.

In 2002 it was double glory for the West Midlands as the Throstles edged up with them (ahead of Wolves: three West Midlands Premiership sides at once – the first time for aeons!). Before that the Claret and Blues had been forced to make do with the Sky Blues as companions, just about, for a protracted period. Cov conveniently contrived belated relegation in 2001, to let the region prepare itself for the aforementioned double elevation. Of course the greater presence didn't mean a lot apart from extended angst and much airplay on the BBC's *Match of the Day* and its competition on the subject of the relegation zone, as WBA plunged out and back again, and Wolves made it the next time round, having finished fifth, but for one season only.

Epilogue. The triumph above remains among Exeter City's proudest occasions. I occasionally bump into older Blues fans with a quiet respect for the Grecians.


## Bournemouth 1 Exeter City 3
## Division II (3), 6/3/93

Switching allegiances to my more humble team on a special deal train ticket, this was a much more organized outing. The phone call had been made earlier the same week. Recalling the Cherries v Villans admission failure in 1988, this was vindication. May I propose it as an example of catharsis. Having learned something about procedure, this time I telephoned the ticket office. The hand-piece minion affirmed that of course Exeter City supporters could gain admission on the day. We did, easily, strolling through a semi-detached zone to the ground, in Boscombe, exactly the same symbiotic relationship as sandy-beached Cleethorpes bore to Grimsby Town, though clearly more prosperous than Lincolnshire. Having imbibed with advantage on the way (featuring the Exeter Arms, no less) we enjoyed the modest away facilities of Dean Court. The programme welcomed the visitors 'to Court'.

It was also an excuse for another jovial night (already booked to avoid disappointment – lovely pink pillow cases) in one of the south coast's premier resorts. If reports are to be believed, this sleepy retirement centre has recently developed into a favoured location for Stags and Hens festivities. What with annual Party Political Conferences, I expect traditional locals wished the calendar would rewind to when Bournemouth was in Hampshire and the club was still Athletic. In 1971-72 the club was playing under its new identity of 'AFC Bournemouth', but throughout the red game programme, which I acquired from a programme shop, was referred to as 'Bournemouth and Boscombe', sort of custom and practice, with no 'Athletic' to be seen in the script. The programme, costing 10p, with decimalization also a novelty, was entitled *Head for the*

*Top with* [in black] *the Cherries* [in white]. Indeed in the published Division Three table 'Boscombe' (sic) were in second place behind the Villa after 35 games, ultimately to lose out in the promotion race to that day's guests, B&HA, who even now remain as long-winded as then. At that time Boscombe boasted the prolific Ted MacDougall, leading marksman in the Third Division with 40 goals. Next best at that stage was Wood of Shrewsbury with 29. Mention must be made of the fabulous occasion, a few months earlier, when Ted scored 9 in the 11-0 FA Cup annihilation of Margate (21/11/71). By then, April Fools' Day 1972, the back page of the programme was dedicated to a promotion of Ted MacDougall Sports Ltd. 'The "Cherries" new look shorts – the first team in the country to sport them. Styled and manufactured in West Germany by "Allround". The, presumably, tempting photo displayed the unclothed upper and elegantly attired lower parts of 14 team members, smiling sheepishly to a man. At least the garments were in no danger of inadvertently dropping, as they were all adorned with waist strings tied carefully in bows, also the latest in German technology, no doubt. When Ted went on to Old Trafford the riddle was posited, albeit orally unless spelling doesn't matter: which three postwar 'flowers' played for Manchester United? Of course the answer was 'Blanchflower (Jackie), Viollet (Dennis) and MacDougall (Ted)'.

Botha, that Huddersfield émigré, and I that day in 1993 enjoyed the Grecians turning it on. The other two in our party going mad in Dorset, Debbie and Warner, each a cream tea enthusiast from West Country heartland, i.e. not Cornwall, patronized the Russell-Cotes Museum, highly recommended to them as the next best thing after Exeter City away. Meanwhile our Grecian elbow-nudgers in the away end were in constant flux answering the dictates of their appetites with the makings of a meal. Fodder in the cattle enclosure was how it seemed. The game didn't hold out much promise, City not having won in their last eight league games. I'm sure we had a talismanic effect. Botha may have been influenced by the famous joys of this neck of the woods, as he later moved to Brighton, having first designed the hare (rabbit as he put it) logo used by Bath Ales. Good one, Both! And that was around the time that he developed a fascination with spam. We once had a Spam evening. It was in the winter.

It was a twin Devon triumph that year, as Plymouth shared this best result at Dean Court. Even better, Exeter completed an impressive double over Argyle: 2-0 at home and 0-3 away. They saved their best results for the games under review, as they finished two places above the relegation places, with Bournemouth two and Plymouth five places further up the league. You have to enjoy these pieces of inconsequential detail.


## Preston North End 0 Exeter City 1
## Division III (4), 29/10/94

Jersey and I arrived by a circuitous sequence of transport modes. Having reached the north end of the county town of Lancashire, we sampled a local Lancashire dish, parched peas, for which I must make a hearty recommendation, to which add barm cake, a local variation of a bread roll – big barm cakes are best. Matthew Brown bitter at £1 per pint ameliorated the scorched throat effect which threatened to ensue. The hostelry was most welcoming. Friendly people, Lancastrians.

City's fanzine (*Exe Directory*) preview had this, with reference to the former Astroturf playing surface: 'No ready made excuse for a City defeat this time as Plastic Preston are no more. I should quantify [sic] that statement by confirming that Preston themselves are still around (and with an average gate of over 8,000 and a £10 million pound takeover in the pipeline they're likely to be around for a fair while longer than we are), but they're not plastic anymore ("They're not pla-a-stic a-nee-moore").' Well, Exeter were victorious but weren't around anymore, for those five angst-ridden seasons. Won the battle, lost the war? We just missed the artificial pitch, which had been dug up at the end of the 1993-94 season. It had been strangely popular with community users and a survey of fans revealed 65% to favour it.

This occurs to me as being a pivotal game for both clubs, but especially for the Lilywhites. On the Saturday morning their home record was W1 D0 L3, in 16th position (out of 22, it being a year prior to divisional adjustment) to the Grecians' away tally W0 D1 L5, in 15th. Neither was a high achiever thus far. City went from indifferent to disastrous and finished bottom, yes 92nd, having been relegated the previous year. They should have swapped leagues with Macclesfield Town, but were reprieved, Macc's Moss Rose ground failing the facilities test. These days achieving clubs are permitted to assume their elevated status with the proviso that facilities must be enhanced to the appropriate level within a certain time. North End rallied after this debacle, to finish fifth, followed by the championship the next year. It was non-stop from there – three years on they were champions again, and can be said not to have looked back thereafter – they were unlucky losers in the 2005 Championship play-off final against West Ham, and beaten by Leeds in the semis in 2006. That was as good as it got for a while. It was certainly their turn for a stab at the Premiership, though in 2007 they sank below the play-off zone at the end of the season, having led the division for a while earlier on. Then, in 2008, after a protracted flirt with the relegation zone, they rallied to finish 15th.

The net progress over the recent years accords with the aspirations of David Moyes, then PNE's captain, in the excellent programme. For £1.30 the purchaser received 40 pages more or less dedicated to the game, the ground and related material. Moyes, elegantly captured in the yellow and black away strip, opined that the club would become big again, helped by new backers and the fans. There were 6,808 to observe the defeat that day in the bottom half of the bottom division, and the club does seem to have retained a consistent and enthusiastic following. As for the backers, I hope they were satisfied with the revival.

Mr Moyes blossomed brilliantly to run Everton in the Noughties, guiding them to Champions League activity in 2005-06, though the *Racing & Football Outlook* was not alone in describing the feat of the qualifying fourth position as 'over achievement' (they finished 17th and 11th in the seasons before and after).

Deepdale's crowning glory was the West Stand, elegantly pillared. And Preston was to be rewarded with representational status as original League members, the National Football Museum being erected under the main stand, subject matter including artefacts of the glorious game of soccer over the decades. Having examined and thoroughly enjoyed the display in 2008 I am still bound to gorge the palate anew with those peas and barm cake, finishing with a game at Deepdale. The idea would be to enjoy wholehearted support of Proud Preston at home. End of digression. It's a great shame that Jersey is no longer with us to share a further North End visit.

A Thai meal, all-in for £20, awaited us that evening. Jersey loved all-in deals; his fry-ups were always a selection of what was on offer (by which I mean discounted owing to the imminence of the sell-by date) at the Co-op. But he did make a fuss when given a smaller plateful of whitebait than either Turky or me in a pub on the way back from Torquay.

So many new experiences in one day in Lancashire's county town! What joy to see Exeter win in one of the country's most historic soccer settings.

## Rushden & Diamonds 1 Exeter City 0
## Division III (4), 29/3/03

A day-trip from Birmingham to witness, it transpired, the dying embers of the Grecians' 83 year-long League membership. At the time I reckoned this would prove to be the critical game as they battled with others in the nether reaches of the bottom Division (Carlisle especially, need I add). They missed many chances in the second half and were well worth a draw. What price local rivalry between the Rushed and Dire Ones and the Ploppies, sorry, the Poppies, i.e. Kettering Town, themselves almost gaining League status when runners-up in 1994?

R&D were only formed in April 1992, amalgamated from Irthlingborough Diamonds and Rushden Town, the creation of millionaire Max Griggs. In 2001 they edged into the League ahead of Yeovil Town, the cream of Somerset famed for aeons of giant-killing exploits and a parallel endless wait in the wings for League admission. Upstarts indeed were the Diamonds, sporting an impressive stadium, and on the brink of their first League promotion a month after this match as champions.

The crucial point for a deserved draw would have taken Exeter up to 49 points in the final reckoning, level with Swansea and the above-mentioned. City ended with a goal difference of −14. Swansea's was −17 and Carlisle's −26. I am still upset about it. The ignominy of being dumped from the League is acute and chronic. Being at the upper end of the Non-League family tree (and it could have got worse) was no compensation for losing the credit of League status. They had to battle for the FA Trophy – in fact often won not by a Fifth Division team, but challengers from the depths below them, viz Grays Athletic in 2004-05, and from 2007-08 the widely unwelcome Setanta Shield.

Only two clubs are conveyed from the Conference to the Football League each season, replacing those finishing 91st and 92nd in the Establishment. Diamonds were duly to taste their own medicine – bottom of the League in 2006, upstaged by

Accrington Stanley, back again as champions after 44 years. I remember the tax bill provoking Accrington's passing in February 1962. So Exeter were to have a chance of revenge in the 2006-07 Conference encounters, something they failed utterly to do, conceding the double. Rushden's sequence of final positions is fun to read, as follows, 'R&PO' being the *Racing & Football Outlook Annual*'s prediction (usually pretty close):

|         | League name             | Level | Posn | R&PO |
|---------|-------------------------|-------|------|------|
| 2000-01 | Nationwide Conference   | 5     | 1    |      |
| 2001-02 | Nationwide Division III | 4     | 6    | 11   |
| 2002-03 | Nationwide Division III | 4     | 1    | 4    |
| 2003-04 | Nationwide Division II  | 3     | 22   | 6    |
| 2004-05 | Coca-Cola League 2      | 4     | 22   | 19   |
| 2005-06 | Coca-Cola League 2      | 4     | 24   | 23   |

This day out was a comprehensive feast of exploration to an unfamiliar area. Wakey and I perused the odd couple, Higham Ferrers and Rushden, before a quick sniff at Irthlingborough on the edge of which we parked the car, ten minutes' walk from Nene Park. An oddity here is the 2001 population census figures for these settlements: Higham Ferrers/Rushden 31k (25 in R, six in HF), but if including Irthlingborough, as you obviously must, the total leaps up to 37.5k, Irth boasting a mere 93 more souls than HF. Even so, it was only beaten by Boston for modesty of immediately local potential supporters (35k).

Higham Ferrers Church, at the southern end of the town, on rising ground, was an oasis of calm after the throng of High Street and market. It sported an unique arch. We exuded prayers for the cause of Exeter. After this we perused Rushden briefly, i.e. as long as was warranted. Pubs had already been identified, the most tempting being the Rushden Historical Transport Society, or former railway station, beyond the ring road at the top end of the town. We did not need to look further as the place was a gem, full of memorabilia (though not footy stuff, there being no tradition in those parts), opening onto the flower-bedecked platform. Were there the ghosts of long-dead trains and rare travelling fans sleeping it off in one of the carriages? It was the kind of place for all-day vegetation with newspapers, engaging in social intercourse and dabbling in a huge variety of beers, as long as you could get a bus or taxi to your destination – no trains and folly to drive. The process was painless and attained an ethereal quality with the merciless stab of Exeter's anticipated downfall.

To follow up on the return journey we needed an awakening, which was provided by England FC on the overhead telly in a tavern in Northampton. The European qualifying fixture against Liechtenstein in Vaduz produced a 0-2 win for our boys. I still held affection for them at that time. Poor Wakey lives eternally in hope and for Summer 2008 decided to adopt Portugal, where he'd enjoyed the 2004 event, partly aloft upon a statue in Braga city centre.

# 3. Away for the Day

## Plymouth Argyle 3 Millwall 2
## Division II, 17/11/90

Via Exeter Services for a rather good black coffee, my squash partner, Graham, and I sped to the Oddfellows Arms in Plymouth for a run-of-the-mill refreshment surrounded by Argyle green; no Millwall presence. There was also plenty of green in the setting. Easy to reach and scenic, and the game proved competitive and dynamic. Millwall got their revenge back at the Den (4-1), and went on to play-off failure against Brighton.

The Pilgrims, the green team, came into existence in 1886 as Argyle FC. There are varied explanations for the name of the southern-most and western-most League club.

Here are three:

1. after the keen footballing Argyll (observe spelling) and Sutherland Highlanders army regiment stationed in the area
2. after a nearby pub, the Argyle Tavern
3. after Argyle Terrace, round the corner when a new green football club was the burning bar talk.

The name became official with the club's professionalism in 1903. Since so much emanates from local history, assisted by accident, I favour the last, most prosaic, option. I'm sure Plymouth's mascot, Pilgrim Pete, hailed from just such a street. Plymouth are the Pilgrims – the club's emblem is the ship which carried the Pilgrim Fathers to North America in 1620.

Home Park was bombed by Germans and blitzed for renovation, to become a convincing 'traditional' football ground, i.e. with sturdy floodlights, a seductive setting (rural aspect) and a renowned stand – the Grand/Mayflower, with a green and white balcony wall, inspired by the pre-war designs of Archibald Leitch. The top attendance, 43,596, saw Aston Villa in 1936, during their first season out of Division I; the lowest was 1,875 v Hull City in depressed 1979. Interesting, that, Hull being the largest place (11th by population) never to have the experience of top-flight football – but only up to May 2008, when 104 seasons of suppression ended on the Wembley (new) turf, as the Tigers beat Bristol City 1-0 to join the elite. Plymouth is the second largest (17th), depending on your interpretation of 2001 census figures. And in third position is Birkenhead, 22nd in the list with 200k souls. Consider for a moment the performance of Tranmere Rovers, the representative of the Wirral. Their highest ever league position was fourth in the Second Division in 1992-93; Hull's, third in Div II in 1909-10; and Plymouth's the same in 1932 and 1953. Much of a muchness and each so close to a starter year among the giants.

As the local rivals to 'Plymuff Argool' are traditionally the Grecians from Devon's county town, and vice versa, we might have heard anti-Exeter chants, but, alas, that detail eludes me. Exeter have been referred to as 'Scum City' in these parts, while Plymouth are called 'the Snot' and 'Gargoyle'. St James' Park escaped local condemnation regarding ground opinion when a 1995 survey at Home Park had Underhill and Twerton as the worst places visited in the League that year. It has been noted that Argyle adopt a patronizing attitude towards their rivals: 'the Snot seem to think that they're Barcelona to our Brechin.' So perhaps they think they can afford to humour Scum City with a tacit acknowledgement that St James' Park is all right for a lower-level club, while Barnet and Bristol Rovers deserve better. From Exeter's point of view 'we may detest Argyle, but we wouldn't want them to disappear, as the two derby matches give an intense charge to otherwise mundane seasons watching the Grecians. Equally, whilst Torquay may be perceived as little more than a minor irritation, our games against them do at least attract decent crowds and force the West Country media to acknowledge that there is life beyond the Green Slime' (*There's a Good Time Coming*, May 1996). Also every fanzine must at some produce something along the lines of a 'missing link'. Here it was '*homo argylus*, found along the Devon/Cornish border…characterized by its stooped demeanour and small thick skull…traces of what appear to be his natural habitat – green plastic seats – have been found, although there is no evidence that he was aware of how to use them, preferring instead to jump up and down in a threatening manner.'

The enunciation of 'Plymouth Argyle' must sometimes carry a forbidding ring when cup draws are made and, say, Sunderland have to journey from remote north east to distant south west. In early September 1975 a friend (Ian from Oldbury with a Baggies affiliation, but fancying a diversion while on a bucket and spade holiday in South Devon) saw newly promoted Argyle squeeze past the Rokerites. This was at a League game. The outcome was 1-0, Billy Rafferty beating keeper Jimmy Montgomery, destined to earn a (non-playing) European Cup Winners medal for Forest five years later. Pitiful was the look on the faces in an away coach, faced with the prospect of an immediate long haul back to Wear(y)side. Perhaps this should count for something in Argyle's home record – a built-in advantage to mitigate their own endless journeys to away games. Why 'Home' Park? Because 'Away' is mostly so far distant?

During our own return in 1990 my passenger promised to do the driving the next time and not spend the majority of the journey wittering on about bloody Millwall, with intermittent mouthings about the consequences of Bosman. I was obliged to annihilate him on the squash court.


## Wrexham 1 Bristol Rovers 0
## Division II (3), 3/4/99

This was the ground where, in an attempt to join the Gasheads (or any unfortunate travelling horde) on their travels, you can find yourself wading in urine from the Gents overflow. On this sunny afternoon 3,075 were present, a few of whom were in the same predicament, and it turned out to be an energetic day. It is recorded that I swam

40 lengths that morning, mostly crawl to get it done (and I prefer it). After the game I drove like the clappers to join Rutz in Brecon for Easter fun, misjudging how far away it was. Perhaps gyrating gingerly to avoid a soakage of piss was meant to be part of the grand plan from above, or a diversion from the direness displayed on the pitch.

Back in the mid-Sixties Wrexham had been in a parlous state. Finishing 92nd in 1966, they went into the red to the tune of £34k, a rather serious sum in those days. A year on, their League position had improved by 17 places. They were unbeaten at home and recorded a jump in income from £39,415 to £57,532. On the transfer front they made a profit of £21k (sales £31k, purchases £10k). The supporters club contributed £11k, leading to an overall profit of £36,810 – into the black by £3,279. Truly a world away. This was all recorded in the long defunct *Soccer Star* magazine. Returning to rock bottom 92nd in 2008, they at last succumbed to the great drop out of the league.

The Racecourse Ground was an unlikely setting for the international games hosted for the Welsh national team from time to time. The nearest real-life race course is at Bangor-on-Dee, not a million miles away, where I have spent a jovial afternoon losing 100% of my investment in ill-chosen nags. But, for those bound for the Wrexham Dragons, there was the Turf Hotel next door, spurned on this occasion in favour of the Railway Inn. It was reassuring to find all these facilities so close together. Navigating was no problem, despite the town's dubious identity as Welsh: it's on the east side of Offa's Dyke, the ancient dividing ditch originally dug in the eighth century to separate the Kingdom of Mercia (Offa was its monarch) from the marauding heathens beyond. Centuries later the settlement of Wrecsam was won back and for a sequence of 87 years was to support Wrexham AFC as one of Wales's three (English) Football League clubs. A friend from Blaenau Ffestiniog, on one occasion described as the dreariest place in the country (grey slate in the rain contributed), was a sometime Wrexham fan, his schoolmates going for the inevitable Man United and Liverpool. Good for you Max! The Racecourse Ground benefitted from its nationality, hosting occasional international games.

Pursuing the trunk road route south through the glorious Welsh Marches was a cinch, in the old century (if you chose your time right) a delight for a car with a purpose or just a sense of adventure, a mind shift from foot soldiers of yore. No doubt I'd now find it bespattered with speed cameras. Brecon Cathedral was located without difficulty. The concert was magnificent, what I saw of it, eventually arriving late. My feet squelched sotto voce towards the row Rutz had chosen, thankfully right at the back. Bach's Mass in B Minor was just right for chilling after earlier thrills, despite a woman further up the nave contriving to disrupt the show by having a fit in mid-recitative.

## Scunthorpe United 2 Rochdale 2
## Division III (4), 10/4/04

An Easter excursion. The train ride from Doncaster was the final leg to Scunthorpe, home of the Iron. However, we were on the wrong side of the tracks for furnace spotting. This vies as the ultimate in football visits, very close to the original 'grim' featured in Grim Up North parodies. The only glimmer in these parts was the Honest Lawyer on the fringes of town, and from the glass eye of the local in his personal corner with his half of stout. We had already tried the Blue Bell and the Farmer as well as suffering the abysmal town centre. There was no humour or hope anywhere in evidence that Saturday morning.

The trudge to Glanford Park sealed the depression. We got the route wrong and endured a circuitous route through what locally may be the upmarket area.

Some of this suffering was self-inflicted by Wakey and me, I admit, though there was a paucity of road signs, and it threw up other day-trips in some relief. The 'Park' was surrounded by horrid retail outlets on a ring road and was as featureless and gloomy as everything else about the place: football stuck out on a limb, the building from a kit and patronized as something away from real life, presumably exemplified by bypasses to take people anywhere else.

The ground had been the League's first new one since the 1950s, and by now was showing its age. However, Scunny's initiative did provide a template for others. The local industry was brought to punters' attention on the North Stand: 'British Steel: Scunthorpe Works, Home of Quality'. The superseded Old Show Ground was much lamented, and portrayed in song (by Chris Vaughan) thus:

> *No more shall I enter by turnstile*
> *That stadium where heroes were made*
> *To climb in anticipation*
> *The steps so long ago laid*
> *No more will United's great heroes*
> *Display their wide range of styles*
> *But Brownsword, Thomas and Cammack*
> *Will haunt the supermarket aisles!*

This may only affect the faithful, who patronize the nearby mall (more American usage, though over the Pond they pronounced it to rhyme with 'appal'). The club's current name only dates from 1956, the words 'and Lindsey' having been dropped at that point. From 1895 the Old Show Ground had hosted a new team called Brumby Hall United, an ingredient of 'Scunthorpe United' four years later. In 1910 they combined with North Lindsey United, adopting the name Scunthorpe and Lindsey United, which was to augment the Third Division (North) with Shrewsbury Town in 1950. A club good at invention when it came to their place of work, in 1958 the Old Showground erected the first cantilevered stand in the footballing world, duly destroyed 30 years later.

This game somehow produced four goals but little evident purpose, despite Scunny and Rochdale having a common need for points. Unsurprisingly they finished in 90th and 89th positions respectively (2004 being the year Carlisle at last dropped out of the League).

In fact late in the game there was an incident to lift our spirits: play being stopped by a goose alighting upon, and not budging from, the pitch. Then there was a laugh or two. Give it an England jersey, certainly not coloured Glanford (or, really, Old Show Ground) claret. A venue which produces an epitaph capturing the spirit of loss alongside wildlife interrupting play on the replacement supermarket green sward can't be all bad! Let's have a hoopoe next time.

## Crewe Alexandra 0 Sunderland 1
## Championship, 12/3/05

A feast of Englishness for Nelson, comprising the advent of spring on a country drive through Gloucestershire and Worcestershire. We paused in Bridgnorth, Shropshire, whose centre represented a wide range of architectural eras, from the half-timbered town hall to the Victorian Gothic St. Leonard's Church, producing an impressive amalgam. That and every Saturday it accommodated a bustling street market. This we sampled – local pies and cheese for souvenirs – but the evocative old funicular railway connecting High Town to Low Town and the River Severn would have to wait for another occasion.

At Wybunbury, just outside Crewe, we dropped into a worthy pub for a pint and a sandwich and snatches of some game on the overhead screen to warm us up. Ten minutes later, parking for the match was close and easy (in a street named after Dario Gradi, the top man, who also inspired the name of the fanzine: *Super Dario Land*). He was the longest standing in the League, gaffer since 1983. This was a mere two streets from Gresty Road. I had not realized that the name of the ground was actually the 'Alexandra Stadium'. It certainly looked smarter than what I recall from my previous visit in the Seventies when Harry Gregg was in charge and the ground was called 'Gresty Road' as it still is by word of mouth. For decades the team was a bottom division mainstay, in the bottom two positions four times between 1978 and 1983. By the time of this game the Railwaymen had spent seven of the previous eight seasons at the current, elevated, level. The club boasted an admired youth policy which made a considerable contribution to this achievement.

Nelson was from Florida, fan of the university institution the Gators, which excelled in American football, basketball, baseball, women's softball and soccer, men's and women's swimming and diving. The University of Florida was a flagship. As part of the recent equal rights policy, men's wrestling, a minority activity, was killed off, to be replaced by women's volleyball. The Gators were based in Gainsville, a few hours' drive from Tampa, famous on this side of the Atlantic for Malcolm Glazer, double owner of Tampa Bay Buccaneers and Manchester United FC. The Buccs won the Superbowl in 2003, against expectations, but struggled thereafter. You can understand the Glazers' attitude to Man U in terms of performance. They had achieved the ultimate goal in US sport and were desperate to repeat that on a high-profile world stage. The Traffs seemed the best chance, even aided by their mid-Noughties history, underachieving by their standards, having only managed the FA Cup trophy against a lower division team in recent memory. They could do with a boost.

Nelson, who makes a fine pureed cauliflower dish which baffles people who 'don't eat green vegetables', like Warner, was keen to see some 'soccer'. This was the best we could do, there being nothing viable anywhere closer on the appointed day. Sunderland's performance took them to second place behind free-scoring Wigan, on goal difference. We loved the winners as is the American wont. A satisfying occasion, but next time it would be incumbent upon me to go a bit upmarket in selecting a soccer game. Americans are used to the panoply provided by the modern game – perhaps Villa Park? Perhaps not, as there would be an absence of 'bleachers' in our plastic-seat-obsessed scenario, and a dearth of colourful, jolly usherettes selling burgers and beer, facilities an American might require. You're welcome. The very thought takes me back to that wonderful, and long, evening Rutz and I spent seeing Boston Redsox. We were made very welcome.

Despite the roads to away grounds presenting great doom potential, it has always been a worthwhile enterprise to brave this torment. Surprisingly often your team comes away with points or at least credit. Look at any results list or league table. The pools panel, pundit or expert judgement reconcile only fitfully with the records. Amazingly there are always a few teams with better away figures than home.

It's never good to over-anticipate in life, whether a holiday, a restaurant or theatre visit, certainly not a football game. It's a phenomenon for pessimists, or realists, getting a result in addition to enjoying all the other parts of the package being seen as a bonus. Is it perverse that the heart of these carefully wrought stratagems – the result – is the most elusive and variable element?

# Chapter 3
# Stretching the Point

## Football Weekends

The point stretched feels like a lot more than those forfeited in a drawn game. I have enjoyed many a minibreak in different parts of the country, football often being the catalyst for extending friendships and waistlines. It is the variable factor, sometimes completely out of control, the action unscripted, often the main event. Meandering round the Thames Estuary took Rand and me to Priestfield Stadium and Roots Hall in completely contrasting settings. One Kent, one Essex, two different divisions, five years apart, icing on the hedonistic cake of weekend wassailing.

It is not a deliberate mistake that the point-stretching route pursued is up the eastern side of the country. The rich diversity of footy occasions in places more noted for wind than rain is enhanced by the diversions westwards to Stockport and Macclesfield on perversely dry days.

Compare the satisfaction provided by silk at Macc with the compelling offerings of market town Darlington, a surprise treasure to many who have ventured there. Contrast the honest anachronism of Millmoor with Hull's Kingston Communications Stadium (the name says it all) and a ground which disappointed me for looking too grand for what it actually offers. Then there are the memories – take pre-conversion Bramall Lane and then cross a world to the Riverside, bearing the name 'Middlesbrough'.

## Shrimpers with Gills

### Gillingham 3 Notts County 1
### Division III, 22/11/86

Seep and Rand were long-standing friends from my Stoke days and committed (fishless) vegetarians. My brief incursion into that discipline had lapsed some time before on catching a whiff of sizzling, sputtering bacon. This often happens. Bacon has a lot to answer for. Seep had turned non-meat into an art form, nay a banquet, at least on my visits. There was preserved a plethora of platefuls, fare ranging from bean feasts of every pulse to chard and cucumber from the allotment, not forgetting lettuce pie, in fact all sorts of tart and flan. I also remember the occasional soufflé.

They were leading a quiet life, with life membership of the National Trust and occupations in puppeteering and librarianship, doting on Posy the pet cat. You can be anonymous in Gillingham, Kent's most populous settlement but not a favoured destination for those with culture or beauty in mind. Linked with Rochester and Chatham on the Medway, a score of years after the chosen match I found it boasted many rewarding pubs and eloquent landlords alongside a paucity of gas stations, for which it's expedient, but not convenient, to frequent out of town shopping parks.

During my stays in the Eighties, when petrol was cheaper and petrol stations widespread, there was some contact with Den, the neighbour (particularly over the garden fence), though whether Denise or Dennis wasn't at all certain. On this trip we had rambled round Rochester flea market in the morning and in the evening played Scrabble and rummy, flattened by the repast. In between I had eventually persuaded my hosts to face Priestfield Stadium, a stroll from their house. Seep had yielded to the suggestion after years of attrition, and having steadfastly withstood my onslaughts through all those years of residence in Stoke-on-Trent. She struck lucky in witnessing four goals at her once-in-a-lifetime football game. Both teams finished the season in the top seven, and the Gills missed promotion only on the away goals rule then used in the final deciding play-off match against Swindon.

Since their election as original members of the Third Division in 1920, the Gills' history has included the thrill of a repeat election to the League in 1950 when the Third Division was augmented from 44 to 48 clubs. They had failed re-election in 1938, competing in the Southern League (1938-44), Kent League (1944-46) and Southern League again (1946-50). They eventually flourished in the Noughties, in the second tier from 2000 to 2005, a far cry from the record of New Brompton FC, renamed 'Gillingham' in 1913.

This encounter with Notts County was at a ground which had lacked any attention for some years. At that time it boasted the Gordon Road Stand, 'probably the oldest stand still in use' (Simon Inglis). The postwar period had seen the main ground improvements, funded by large gates in the Cup and Southern League, a run which helped the club win its second spell of League membership. In the late Forties the terracing was concreted over and contemporary turnstiles were introduced. Since the late Nineties a transformation had been perpetrated – the Medway Stand and Rainham End reaching up so high that it's difficult to believe that they merited the granting of planning permission, given the tightly knit terrace housing all around. The current floodlights in a flat configuration of nine lamps across and four down were evocative of a praying mantis.

Cast your eyes down and observe the smooth roof of the old Gordon Road Stand topped by the appealing jagged edges of Victorian housing. Meanwhile the modern fan is encouraged to try the Medway Golf Centre; not so in 1986. At least play has always been enjoyed at close quarters as the bottom rows almost abut the pitch.

The game was energetic; Seep was sure all the heading would damage the players' brains, but we shared the opinion that it would probably prove to be of marginal effect as there was not likely to be much in there anyway. Indeed there was a lot of aerial play.

Our routine also embraced photography, Seep collecting old cameras (she bought one at the flea market). Rand had undergone a professional contract with Stoke-on-Trent Museums and continued to produce his own work. His Super 8 movie machine was a source of some embarrassment. (Un?)fortunately it had a faulty battery, so he had to resort to more static methods. I dabbled in single lens reflex, Canons at that time, and darkroom experimentation. One summer, when I joined them in their rented cottage in the Yorkshire Dales, we tried using Quality Street chocolate wrappers, vanilla fudge crimson, toffee finger yellow and 'the purple one', as camera filters, producing indistinct but appealing, to us, images of the ilk of impressions of a queue of cars down dale and uphill in the sun.

In Kent this was extended into black and white explorations on subjects like industrial debris on the banks of the Thames at Grain, tombstones in Boxley churchyard and contrejour effects at the ruins of Reculver Castle. Unfortunately we all forgot to take our cameras to the football game. They were in greater evidence at Rochester Cathedral and Castle, both compelling viewing along with Chatham Historic Dockyard. It was hoped that this would become a World Heritage Site, as had been mooted, assisted by better transport round the curves of the Medway with the ultimate people trap of a cable car.

Suddenly there has emerged awareness of branding and the realization of what rich resources the Medway towns can offer if tapped. This might trigger the building of hotels and investment in a new museum involving importation of artefacts from the Imperial War Museum. It would make sense of the 2001 230k+ census reading thereabouts. An urban area as populous as Southampton should truly have more recognition. In fact, since the closure of the dockyard where Portsmouth Historic Dockyard's inherited crown jewel the Victory was built, this part of Kent has displayed lethargy and a paucity of self-belief. As it is you can indulge in traction engines in Chatham, Morris dancing and the already popular Royal Engineers Museum in Brompton, betwixt Chatham and Gillingham. Follow this with a wee dram (to be selected from a range of 35 single malts), 175mm slug of wine (a ladies' wine club met until 2006), a refreshing half of cider (two very real, most tasty and STRONG to choose from) or, what it's ultimately about, a pint of ale. The venue? The King George V, formerly 'The King of Prussia' until this became inappropriate with the onset of the Great War. The place is an inn in the old meaning of the word, offering accommodation, not least a four-poster bed. For my money Gillingham is good for pubs – this is only one example. Fortunately it only needs one Football League club.

## Southend United 4 Newcastle United 0
## Division II, 1/1/92

We chose a trip treat to expel some New Year blues, following the Auld Lang Syne session in Den's local in Gillingham. This was to be Southend's biggest win of the season and the Tyneside outfit's worst defeat (along with Wolves, 6-2).

The Shrimpers of Roots Hall – what idiosyncratic names. This, the club's very own home, was named after the house previously occupying the site, replacing the Southend Stadium where they were tenants up to 1955. It is actually in Prittlewell, also providing the nearest railway station, of which Southend is the – wait for it – south end. In 2005 the half-century anniversary was celebrated by way of a pre-season friendly with Norwich City, the first ever visitors to the Hall. In 1955 it had been a Division Three (South) League fixture; in 2005 respective statuses, Coca-Cola League 1 and Coca-Cola Championship.

The blue, white and, of course, black awoke us, at odds with the quiet of the residential area where the Hall was erected. To this add the Shrimpers faithful screaming incomprehensible vituperation, which we assumed referred to the inadequacies of certain players' skill, or maybe there were Kursaal Flyers fans among their number. Speaking of which, even more lost in time than the musical combo is Kursaal Stadium, home to the Blues from 1919 to 1934. The name was an indulgence on the part of American owner Captain David De Forest Moorehouse, who in 1912 bought the seafront amusement park (called Marine Park to 1910, then Luna Park). This was the home of Southend Athletic FC up to its collapse.

Name changes were rampant thereabouts, the Captain being captivated 'by a similarly named leisure facility in Ostend. He funded additional attractions such as a scenic railway and converted the domed building into a magnificent ballroom. His vision was to own the most popular attraction in the country. However, his funds were not limitless and when he heard that local football club Southend United, who had been playing at the first incarnation of Roots Hall since their formation in 1906, were bereft of a home ground he enclosed the north-east corner of his Kursaal grounds as a football pitch. He became actively involved in the revival of Southend United following the Great War...' (*Venue Master, Groundtastic* football grounds magazine, issue G42).

Well, the date chosen for this trip was New Year's Day, after all, so a little cacophony might be allowed. I'm sure Captain Moorehouse would have taken it personally, in the best possible way.

We didn't make it to the country's longest pier, or look any jellied eels in the face, though Rand could have tried some within his mellowing terms of vegetarian interpretation. I like eels smoked, with new potatoes and a cold Chablis. There's a place in the Somerset Levels… On the other hand the way Rand delivers a slice of bread to the toaster is something to behold, a sensual phenomenon. He likes it uncooked, as well, by the loaf.

The Shrimpers hit the headlines in November 2006 by knocking the Traffs out of the League Cup. They became the 81st contemporary League team to have

met them and the only unbeaten one! The goal scorer was Freddy Eastwood, a Romany, bought from Grays Athletic for £40k (in 2004), and resided in a road which, said Basildon District Council, 'doesn't actually exist.'

Comparisons were made in the Press between 'the Romany' and 'the Rooney' (price £30m, also transferred in 2004), whose pile was a £4.25m mansion in footballer belt Cheshire (including gym and cinema), not to mention something rather choice in Florida. For the 2007-08 season Freddy was acquired for Wolves by Mick McCarthy, £1.5m his tag. He had scored 65 for Southend in 135 games, though not enough to save his team from sinking to the bottom division. Meanwhile he had become Welsh, as, though born in Epsom and living most of his life in Basildon, his maternal grandfather was born in Llanelli. Something wrong there, methinks. Mitigation can perhaps be allowed from his move to Wolverhampton, not far from the Welsh border, with wife Debbie, son Fred Jr and daughter Chardonnay, together with his undertaking to learn his new country's national anthem (in Welsh).

## Posh and Pilgrims

### Peterborough United 2 Cardiff City 0
### Division III (4), 13/4/98

Let's leap up the map to Horncastle, Lincolnshire, featured in a book of Enid Blyton's, educed from my memory, and Tattershall Castle, a stately ruin, which projected us towards Mickser's abode on the damp fringes of the Wash.

Via historic buildings, rife in the area, we arrived at Peterborough, bought toothpaste from a pharmacist and explored the massive Norman cathedral. We indulged in Old Speckled Hen, Marston's Pedigree and pork scratchings in the Cherry Tree, surrounded by good natured guys in Posh royal blue and white. The London Road crowd didn't seem to rate manager Barry Fry very highly, formerly manager/ owner, partly to do with his selling the impecunious club to a pizza magnate. The ground itself benefited from the Freeman's Stand, which had been open for two years, providing 5,700 seats and, it can be imagined, influencing the atmosphere in the ground on days when there are expanses of emptiness. The Posh, on the other hand, have not been a badly supported club. I recall their election to the League at the expense of Gateshead in 1960, mostly to do with United's supremacy at the summit of 'non league' in the preceding years. They went straight up to the Third Division in their first season. And it was so unjust for the dumped club, finishing with Oldham and the plural Hartlepools well below them on points. It has been surmised that the journey to the League's furthest outpost was, let's say, beyond the pale for travelling fans. Redheugh Park may have been geographically south of the Tyne and St. James' Park, but as well as one of the longest mainline trips it involved train changes and a walk – a thoroughly trying and unpopular venture. Attendances bore this out.

Anyway life isn't fair, otherwise Exeter City would not have lost their League place! How on earth did Hartlepools avoid inglorious dismissal with their disgraceful record in the early Sixties, seeking re-election every June from seasons 1959 to 1964 (24, 23, 22, 24, 23)? As Oxford United's 1962 invitation to join the Fourth Division only came to fill the vacancy created by Accrington's resignation, it can be concluded that the doors were closed. Not even the relentlessness of Hartlepools' ineptitude influenced the voting club chairmen away from the idée fixe of protection of the League's current members. Hartlepools' escape from the abyss was initiated by one Brian Clough, manager for the next two seasons, after which Pools ascended gloriously to the Third Division. They reduced themselves (themself?), dropping their 'S', in 1969.

The goals were both in the second half. Cardiff's curious statistic up to then was that of 41 games they had drawn 22. In their remaining five games they drew one more and lost the other four. It was the year new boys Macclesfield went straight up, behind Notts County who achieved 99 points. It could have been even more. The Magpies went off the boil, wasting into an unfortunate complacency.

The return journey made a bit more sense of the thinking behind the Lincoln v Exeter postponement. We were diverted because of flooding, extensive in the surrounding country.

That was all the football, the proceedings being broadened by our visit to Newmarket Races the next afternoon. Fuckin' Dave was the only one to show net winnings. Mickser and I? Zilch, each way. Beginner's luck as F' had arrived a racing virgin? He enjoyed it enough to join the party to Wincanton Races one Boxing Day, an event often jeopardized by the weather. We didn't make it in the turbulent conditions, settling for a more sedate session in Wells, basking in the cathedral and Crown Inn (liberal and liquid luncheon). It cost about the same, given the almost inevitable failure with the bookies. And it was good to see the Crown, name untouched, featured in a very funny 2006 film, *Hot Fuzz*.

After the day observing flat land and pitch, we repaired to Mickser's place for red wine and meat, all mellow and welcoming. He is seriously carnivorous. And footy on the telly.

The next morning we pigged out at a transport café we'd noticed on the westward-bound trunk road. Mickser had said it was highly rated. Dave wolfed down his platter in no time – he's very speedy when it comes to food. On the way back to base we mused over our next destination – an early 1998-99 enchantment? It was likely to be up to Maine Road, where he was a long-standing season ticket holder, in the pre Nice Lady era.  And so it transpired.

## Boston United 4 Cheltenham Town 1
## Division III (4), 11/10/03

After this fiesta, the only thing we felt we'd missed was a tour of the Wainfleet Brewery, which rose provocatively out of the flat Lincolnshire landscape. We did enjoy their products, though, in a number of Boston's profusion of rewarding watering holes.

It was an escape from pressurized work demands: Wakey had finished a series of night shifts and I was trying to meet deadlines in several places at once. At least I was awake for the drive from Birmingham; he was in recline most of the way, I recall. He responded to an intermission for nourishment in Melton Mowbray. We each sampled an eponymous pie (and chips) in the White Hart.

The Boston inn booked for the night was in confusion about the booking. I had discovered on a speedy website perusal of Boston's cultural offerings for the weekend that the local arts centre was presenting Mugenkyo Taiko Drummers. Forewarned, it made sense when the landlady asked us if we were there for the drumming, so I nodded assent, as we'd quickly decided to get tickets for this at the Blackfriars Arts Centre. It sounded a tempting event. However, a little knowledge is a dangerous thing, as it turned out that she was alluding to a room booking for a real life drummer, one of the company. The difficulty lay in her thinking the reservation to be for one person, not two, and there wasn't any spare accommodation as all the rooms seemed to be taken. Fortuitously the performer/guest materialized at that point. After a bit of banter the problem was solved. All was well: she discovered the slip of paper in the diary, indeed confirming a double, and duly led us up to the attic, evidently a sudden addition to the booking plan.

A cup of tea later, with Wakey safely slumbering, I was set to obtain tickets for the concert: Japanese drumming by a troupe including our neighbour, who seemed to hail from somewhere more local and familiar, judging by his demeanour and accent, was irresistible. I was already envisaging an intriguing breakfast conversation on the niceties of the form. The venue was just round the corner. Arriving at the box office I confidently awaited my turn while the matron ahead of me by degrees comprehended the pantomime ticket information being uttered, but not conveyed, by one-woman band in charge. The customer was a member of an amateur group, I learned. Tickets were eventually purchased for various permutations of her family. At length it was my turn, after a telephone enquiry during which exchange the ominous words 'sorry love, we're sold out' were uttered. I asked, tremulously, what there was for that evening. The message was that only some seats held for the company were left. If not taken up, they could be released for sale in the last half hour before the concert. She would have to wait for the company manager to tell her to instruct her to that effect. Having recorded my interest in two tickets, but with little confidence that this would materialize in an actual contract, I decided to venture to the stage door in the hope that someone, perhaps our neighbour, could help. How lucky that I bumped into the very person who always seemed to turn up on cue. I explained the situation. He responded 'No problem, mate, we don't need them.' I asked if the company manager could tell the box office. She'd gone off at the moment but there was no problem. No one else could deal with the box office. There was at this stage an ever-diminishing hour to go before the curtain went up.

I returned to the attic to find my companion seriously asleep, so decided the next duration's preoccupation had to be to make sure we could get tickets. It would now become a suicidal matter should I, he being comatose, miss the show. I returned to the box office, where there were several punters forming a queue. I had my paper, containing local events both mainstream and alternative, brought up the rear and tried to be patient. My turn came as it turned 7pm – half an hour to go, as stipulated. But the tickets hadn't been released. The salesperson placed a call to be told that the company probably didn't need them all but the company manager still wasn't back. I put in my plea with the tale of woe that we'd come all this way… and a band member had told me the tickets were surplus to requirements. She seemed a bit affected by this sad performance and comforted me that she was sure there would be space for two, but it might be at the last minute. At that moment a call came through – two would be available. 'Thank God', I screeched, quite overwhelmed. Another call enquiry interrupted us. The next emotion was agitation as Wakey was still snoring away in the attic, a few critical minutes away, but it was politic to make sure I had the tickets in hard copy form to avoid disappointment, nay a mad scene, in returning to find them sold to another. With the seconds precipitating, I ran the distance to the horizontal one and awoke him in as gentle a manner as I could muster, i.e. not. Now Wakey was not good in these situations, his natural state being in repose.

He showed a rare burst of anger as I summarized recent events thus: 'Get up now the concert starts in ten minutes!'

He retorted: 'Why couldn't you wake me up earlier? I was all warm and toasty.' Why indeed?

Managing to rally, he girded a loin or two, donning garb in disarray, and he and I sped to the foyer to the sound of the three minute bell. Our seats were in the circle, whither we bounded. But they were occupied. A mix-up at this stage? We never knew. A most beneficent maiden aunt type, who I'm sure had worked there woman and girl and carried the authority of total control in her territory (the Circle), didn't disturb the occupants but showed us to two seats which had appeared out of nowhere.

'Aren't they someone else's?' I posited.

'Don't worry about that, dear' she responded.

I concerned myself no further regarding this mystery, which may have struck deep into custom and practice of Blackfriars seat management, not to mention staff power. There was no further problem. The concert was utterly magnificent. We both expressed a wish to try out the specialized drumming techniques for ourselves, but I have to emphasize that this hasn't yet happened even after further exposure to the Mugenkyo Taiko elsewhere. I've seen courses advertized.

Afterwards we missed the performers, hoping for an exchange the next morning as already mentioned – the need for refreshment was acute, and duly satisfied in the Ship, then the King's Head, finally the Magnet, our abode, where we got into conversation with people who lived in a very old house opposite. No lock-in at the pub and the night was yet young, and Wakey still, well, awake, so we accepted the offer of malt whisky with them in their stately withdrawing room. Lovely stuff but in the morning I was suffering, a rare experience the morning after, and couldn't manage the opulent plateful of pub breakfast, downing paracetamols instead. There was no sight of our neighbour, in fact of any of the four performers, in the bar-cum-brekfast room. The quartet had somehow defied probability in the upper recesses of the pub and had all stayed overnight, in a space which had evoked memories of a forbidding Beatrix Potter incarceration setting for malevolent rats. The four materialized in the car park on our mutual exits. An exchange ensued and, given our mutual urgency to get on with the day, we decided to look out for them in future. It had been a truly spell-binding performance, the group based in Lanarkshire, the leader, Mackie, hailing from Bristol, developing Japanese drumming techniques.

Next stop: the Boston Stump, i.e. the tower of one of the largest churches in the country, St Botolph's. We scrambled up the steps to the top where Wakey was overcome by an attack of vertigo as soon as we hit the narrow parapet, which opened up a vast panorama from which there was no retreat. Alas, immediate egress was essential. Somehow we descended the shallow spirals, for him to sit quietly (or pray) in a nave pew. He recovered in the glorious, reassuring body of the church, displaying contributions from a series of architectural styles, which created a harmonious effect. The town centre, with street market, had just the character associated with a busy country town, with the same mixture of ages as in the church and a couple of showpieces – the eighteenth-century Fydell House, closed to the public but with an impressive exterior, and the Guildhall, a statement of confidence and success.

From there we repaired (by then respectively recovered from hangover and vertigo) to the King's Arms and Indian Queens, revelling in excellent Batemans products. Wakey chose XXXB, not advised for lunchtime drinking. Just as well he wasn't driving.

At last it was climax time – the sun-drenched final straight to York Street, the home of the Pilgrims. This was their fourth season in the League, and Cheltenham's seventh. A new boys clash then, with little history, with no previous meetings at this level as Cheltenham had just been relegated. They both ended up in mid-table this year, too. There being a minimum of figures to record, let's see how the *Racing & Football Outlook* predictions have done for Boston:

|         | R & F O | Final table |
|---------|---------|-------------|
| 2002-03 | 14      | 15          |
| 2003-04 | 17      | 11          |
| 2004-05 | 6       | 16          |
| 2005-06 | 7       | 11          |
| 2006-07 | 12      | 23          |

You can't expect perfection. Indeed Conference Premier members Ebbsfleet United's six-year record against their weekly opponents was completely blank in the 2007-08 annual: an omission. It's understandable, I suppose, as the name was a fresh entry, reinvented from long-term aspirers Gravesend and Northfleet. Very unpopular, too – no consultation with the supporters.

The top-half outcome in 2005-06 was a mite flattering at the end of weeks of close contest in the Fourth. On the last day that season Oxford failed to beat the Orient, thus doing a straight swap with Accrington, whose tax evaporation had let in the Us 44 years earlier. A year later there was another fortuitous swap: Boston out, Dagenham & Redbridge in. In 2002 Boston United finished champions of the Conference but had been involved in financial irregularities. Despite this they were awarded the League place, with the sanctions of a fine of £100k and the deduction of 4 points. Many considered this should have gone to the Daggers, as runners-up. On top of the matter of principle they both achieved 84 points, 14 ahead of third-placed Yeovil, and D&R had done the double over Boston.

This game was an entertaining affair as the score line suggests. It had the feeling of an uncluttered, free-flowing Saturday afternoon out – just right really. The ground held 6,643 and lent itself to positive vibes on a sunny, successful afternoon.

## Lincs with Yorks

Easter 2001 saw a few days in North-East Lincolnshire and South and West Yorkshire. Fuckin' Dave was at the controls so we could enjoy a smooth drive, our first destination Castleford to break our own Rugby League ducks and, in any case, the soccer games were on Saturday and Monday. Nowadays our providers in Sky would surely have engineered the rescheduling of a game or two to Good Friday. We could then have pigged out on three football events. Before searching out Castleford's profferings we wanted a roof over our heads, provided admirably by the Queens Hotel, rundown but with some character, on a hill on the edge of Pontefract. It was a quick decision and reasonably priced with fascinating décor which defies description, so I won't try! We had already visited the ruined castle and made the essential purchase of liquorice Pontefract cakes. Only consider the Queens now if you're thinking of the fringes of Pontefract as a place to live – it's since been converted into flats. But consider Pontefract anyway for a peculiar diversion: the annual Liquorice Festival, at which Pomfretians welcome all, offering such mouth-watering temptations as liquorice knitting. This has eluded me up to now. Not so the Wakefield Rhubarb Festival, down the road from 'Pomfret', filling a splendid weekend. Highlights were rhubarb ale, brewed by the city's own Fernandes Brewery, a rhubarb producer visit (up the road, in the heart of the Rhubarb Triangle. Wakefield's location has been described as being 'in the armpit of Leeds': it conjures up a disquieting image), followed by a meal in which all the courses featured the vegetable, yes, really. The best was the dessert – lemon and lime syllabub on a bed of stewed rhubarb. Just gorgeous.

## Castleford Tigers 22 Salford Sharks 24
## Rugby Super League, 13/4/01

Castleford was intended for food and drink but we only managed the latter, nothing appealing on the nosh front. Kentucky Fried chicken emerged as a last resort in Ponty after the game, which involved, after all, only 80 minutes of playing time plus an intermission brief by Association Football standards. It seemed so much shorter than what we were used to. We were advised to park in the town and walk to the ground where admission was by cash only at the turnstiles. We endured a pint of something smooth in a central pub (the Prince of Wales Feathers) with a potentially bellicose atmosphere, crowded with the fraternity of boisterous market stall-holders (we imagined). Joining the throng milling to the Wheldon Road (aka The Jungle) was easy. The game was a 'rumble in the jungle' between lesser luminaries of the top division, Castleford Tigers and Salford Sharks, the Lancastrian visitors featuring Martin Offiah (remember Chariots...?). The game seemed to us novices more fluent and direct than Rugby Union. Fuckin' Dave's preoccupation with Manchester City precluded many Rugby expeditions. When a player was injured – a frequent occurrence – play continued. Time added on, established as a feature in football games and at the discretion of the man in black, had no place here. It was just as likely for the game to finish before the allotted time, at the referee's discretion. The match was close and exciting, theme music piped through after each try; all curiously old-fashioned from a soccer fan's viewpoint. The only thing which seemed of the new era was the appendage 'Tigers' and associated image promotion. In days of yore most Rugby League teams were known only by the name of their location, except some we'll never forget. Rochdale Hornets, Wakefield Trinity and Bradford Northern used to be a few. But even this has been compromised, viz Wakefield Trinity Wildcats. In the world of professionalism the philosophy of names has been transformed; brands and images introduced. Old rivalries have not. The main target of the derision was not the team's Lancastrian opponents; reasonable, we thought, to expect a re-enactment of the Wars of the Roses. But no, the target of derision was the 'Whinos', i.e. Leeds Rhinos, a handful of miles to the west. The following appeared in the match programme. It is a story from Harry the Scoreboard Hamster.

> *A Whino fan gets on a bus. He pays the fare and climbs the stairs to the top deck. The only other passenger is a nun. Whino man sits behind her and as the bus pulls off, he leans forward and says*
> *'Wanna shag luv?' The nun goes very red and ignores him.*
> *'Go on – a quick one on the back seat' says the man.*
> *The nun leaps to her feet, dives down the stairs and jumps off the bus at the next stop. Two stops later the Whino is downstairs waiting to get off. The driver says to him 'What did you say to the nun to make her leave so quickly?'*
> *The Whino replies 'I asked her for a shag, not that it's any of your business!' The driver says 'If you want a God Girl you're going about it all the wrong way. Go home, get a white sheet, go to the convent at 8pm and hide in the bushes. When a nun comes along after evensong, put the sheet over your head, jump out and say you're the Holy Ghost and you'll be quids in.'*
> *Whino man gets off the bus, goes home, gets a white sheet, goes to the convent and hides in the bushes. Shortly after 8pm a lone nun starts walking up the path from the chapel. Whino with the sheet over his head jumps out.*
> *'Er, hello I'm the Holy Ghost' he stammers.*
> *The nun is startled 'Oh wow, amazing – You can do whatever you like to me.'*
> *Brilliant thinks the Whino. He bends the nun over backwards and does the deed. He's finished in ten seconds flat at which point he whips off his sheet to reveal a Leeds shirt.. 'Surprise! Leeds fan!'*
> *The nun looks back at him, whips off her cassock.. 'Surprise! Bus driver!!!!'*

Also, Harry the Hamster needed a new home as a new bar was to be built, apparently with subscribers to the '200 Club'. 'So if you want to contribute and give an alcoholic Hamster a gud 'ome leave any donations in a brown paper bag under the scoreboard. Cheers HARRY.' Bless.

## Grimsby Town 2 Watford 1
## Division I (2), 14/4/01

We left for Grimsby the next morning, visiting the fisheries which were massive but predictably quiet on a Bank Holiday Saturday. Onward to Cleethorpes for ozone inhalation from the freezing North Sea. It would have been a good frisbee setting

had we been so prepared. Instead we found a spot, Willy's Pub and Brewery, close by, electing to postpone food until we had parked for the game, aspiring towards fish and chips for obvious reasons. I did sense a caveat in that my previous visit as a student, driving a car with a slow puncture and four passengers, had yielded not even a hint of haddock or scallop. Anyway F' and I had luxuriated in an excellent breakfast in the hotel/pub in Pontefract. Why does this type of establishment seem to provide better, or more ample, fare than the average guest house? B&Bs should be specialist in this – it's their bread and butter.

Our progress went according to plan. A memorable eveningnewspaperful of nosh, the cod fondly imagined to have been caught locally. We washed it down in a strange but welcoming public house close to the ground. Both sets of supporters mixed harmoniously in a big open room which seemed like a community hall. Grimsby Town used to be the only club situated in a town different from its name. Blundell Park is in Cleethorpes. Now we have Horwich (Bolton) Wanderers, for a start. And another rarity: this was the only time I've watched ships sail past as a football spectator. I'm glad we were in the John Smith's Stand, which afforded the opportunity.

As a passing tourist I attempted to take a photograph of the view, but was apprehended by a steward.

'Why?' I queried. No reason, only

'That's the rule, mate.' This was the ground where I successfully snapped a strange sign on some corrugated iron outside instructing 'No ball games'.

We soon felt the blast from the open vista. A sunny morning had turned into hail and freezing rain. The programme, called *The Mariner*, had the unusual device of a full-length double-opening centre page spread of the player of the issue, complete with a space headed up 'Autograph' from the waist down.

This fortnight's pin-up was Richard Smith, central defender, nicknamed Smudge/r or Scrudge, posing in a total of six outfits, prevailing colours pied black and white, naturally, as well as red (chest hair on view), blue (hooped), yellow (in mid-stride), blue (plain dark) and a smart suit, receiving a 'man of the match' bubbly bottle. He was graced with the initial 'R' on the back as there was also 'D' in the squad. A central defender, the best bit was the note about R's first-ever goal for the club, against Wimbledon the previous December. That's another club where the name was different from the place of origin. That was until they donned MK (at last winning a cup in 2007-08, beating this very Grimsby in the final of the Johnston's Paint Trophy, in front of an audience of 56,618). Well done Smudge/r. Interesting that three games against the Dons had been postponed – out of a season total of five. When eventually played, both away and home matches were drawn. He professed admiration for:

1) Angelina Jolie as 'best looking woman' (before she was a really big star: 1-0 to you Smudge);

2) the unfortunate Steve Irwin 'famous person invited for dinner', subsequently eliminated by a sting ray: 1-1. This unfortunate choice was exacerbated by the biography, published not long after his demise, *Steve Irwin: The Incredible Life of the Crocodile Hunter*: author Trevor Baker's credits included Kylie Minogue and a tie-in to *I'm a Celebrity Get Me out of Here*.

3) Let's choose a final one to give the lad a break. 'What is your favourite joke?' The programme censors banned it: 2-1. Good on you Smudge. My favourite joke is the one about the young lady in Bude. Does a limerick count?

## Rotherham United 1 Northampton Town 0
## Division II (3), 16/4/01

This occasion is more prominent than many in the memory banks, as the affair was properly imbued with football stuff. We had enjoyed a four-star hotel in Sheffield, offering two-night Easter breaks, with leisure facilities, which F' Dave had organized. He was a university lecturer, thus having plenty of time and scope to achieve such boons. We enjoyed the new Millennium Galleries, also in the evening a Chinese gangster film in the arts cinema. The subsequent watering hole featured a number of females in furry boots, an university indulgence, one imagined.

On Easter Monday we took the A6178 towards Rotherham, which came across as contiguous with Sheffield on that side, offering healthsome country walking opportunities on the other. Magna had only recently opened at Templeborough, a former steel works, which had tempted us as a morning event. It was an immense industrial exhibition on the subject of nature's elements, graphically displayed on a huge scale. All was fine except the admission system which was in its infancy and extremely disorganized. It was just as well that we drove straight there after checking out of the hotel, as we certainly needed all the available time before the joys the merry Millers would provide. Afterwards – 7/10 for Magna, we reckoned – it was clear that we should go straight to Millmoor. We found the Moulder's Rest Hotel, a friendly, crowded hostelry, described in the *Good Beer Guide* as a 'traditional family local', just a stone's throw from a very congested Millmoor (8/10). I remember lots of splinter potential in the wooden structure and a queue for Eric Twigg's Pukka Pies, which were steaming and succulent. It was a terminally old-fashioned ground surrounded by dark, satanic industry. The floodlight pylons were wondrous to behold. How sensuous it would be to sample the scene in twilight, for maximum impact.

Glyn Watkins, the Bradford City man (visit www.bradwan.com) had this to say: 'with so many fine floodlight pylons lost to us, because of development that shamefully disregarded our heritage, Millmoor now has one of the highest floodlight pylon ratings of any English ground. Obsessive, back stabbing, critics from other pylon clubs may argue that Rotherham's pylons are welded, not bolted, and therefore ineligible for the highest rating. We would reply that there are four of them; they are clearly visible; and behind the ground there are two fine scotch derrick cranes in the scrap yard, and 110k supply pylons, to give extra interest. We would also add that although the pylon has brought light to millions, there are some, so called, pylon fans who choose to flounder in the darkness of their own selfish egos, rather than help spread the light.' Glyn is well-known for his obsession with pylons. For me 9/10. Perhaps the equivalent of the Weld v Bolt dilemma should be applied to turnstiles as well.

At the time of the game the Millers were challenging for promotion and the score line belied their positive play, which we thought would be a credit to Div I (2) the next season, five games after this triumph. This time they should have netted a hatful. We were witnessing one of their 16 home wins in the League. Claret Defender

John Frain made his presence felt, martialling his motley peers. After ten years' service for Birmingham City he joined the Cobblers, making a considerable mark through a telling free kick in the basement division play-off final against Swansea in 1997 (1-0). Four seasons later he was established as a popular mainstay at Northampton and this afternoon helped to keep the score down, again a single strike. In due course United were promoted in second place.

All that remained was the easy getaway to the MI, for the remainder of the weekend's 601 miles we eventually clocked up.

## A Hat Trick for Yorkshire

### Sheffield United 3 Birmingham City 0
### Division II, 17/4/71

Momentous as my first football weekend away and his one and only, he confessed 34 years later, The Mine drove us up from working London to weekend Yorkshire. We had booked the Alexandra Hotel in the city centre, and arrived there with not much evening left, though at least spring was in the air by then. We could do justice to a variety of cultural exposure, not least to early 1970s Sheffield and its rough and ready pubs.

In the morning we wandered round a sequential list of about 30 points of interest in the city centre, gleaned from a Tourist Information leaflet. After all it was something like the sixth most populous English city at the time, with plenty to see. The tour included the cathedral, valid even if upgraded, to add to another parallel collection, English cathedrals, well ahead of my peregrination round football grounds in the Seventies. Beyond Bramall Lane, southwards, was the Abbeydale Industrial Hamlet, dated another hundred years before the ground, late 18th century. We tried this out first thing on the Sunday morning.

This was the first Football League ground I'd been to outside London and Hove and presented an impressive history. It had hosted internationals in both football and cricket. Bramall Lane still boasted its Pavilion, to be removed in 1982, and, so it is said, an alien experience, with narrow turnstiles and a penlike enclosure at the away end. But the frontage, reputedly impressive with sufficient space in front to admire it, in club colours, was not erected until 1975. Cricket was still played there, after 150 years, up to 1973. There was a claim to fame, that it was 93 years old when staged the first recorded game under floodlights. The ground itself disappointed in sharing functions with Yorkshire Cricket Club and providing an unfocused atmosphere. This was somewhat compensated by the game itself, one of the Blades' 14 home wins, the best in the Second Division. They made it to runners-up position. Their stars in at that time included Trevor Hockey, whom I later enjoyed urging his way for the Birmingham

Blues; also Alan Woodward, who developed an admirable trick. Emerging from tunnel to touchline he would carefully and deliberately tap a ball with the inside of his boot to precipitate its trickle on a slow, wide curve into a goalmouth.

Neither The Mine nor I could remember what made us decide on either Sheffield or this game, but it confirmed anew that football was fun, as from then on it became a regular item on the social calendar. As light relief that evening we watched *Paint your Wagon* in the Odeon, complete with Lee Marvin's concern with a wandering star. Mine and I agreed that wandering to football clubs was a good thing. As it turned out we only reunited for footy once or twice at Stamford Bridge, with Chelsea my local team for a while, though lacking fealty. The Mine's preference during his London years was for Spurs. His support was pragmatic. He shifted his life to the Solent area and started following Southampton FC. A sojourn in Yugoslavia for a few years had failed to inspire him to follow Red Star Belgrade.

The return journey in the morning started with Rotherham, for the first time, for a cursory visit en route through impressive and surprising places, promoting parts north of Watford to two people steeped in the south. The MI would have been blissfully free of traffic in 1971, but so were Retford, Lincoln, Spalding, Huntingdon, Saffron Walden…our tortuous scenic meander.

## Leeds United 1 Sheffield United 0
## Division I, 22/1/72

*A weekend trip to Leeds to meet*
*An old school friend, but trick or treat?*
*Have we moved on, bad to repeat?*

*This student life, so much to do:*
*A Polish meal, a pub or two,*
*A club as well, one from a few.*

*Morning so soon? My head, oh dear,*
*No curtains, it's a bit rough here,*
*Strong tea to get us into gear.*

*Into the centre, for a look,*
*A mix of brash display and nook,*
*(I used my tokens for a book),*

*Pub gems down hidden alleyways*
*It's got some mystery, seems a maze*
*This, Yorkshire's grandest, biggest place.*

*The game is on, we've read the piece*
*Over a quick one in the Fleece*
*But nosh now please: fish, chips and peas*

93

*In last night's paper – uninspired –*
*And next more pints of beer required;*
*By then I didn't feel so tired.*

*Indulgence done without recourse*
*We're ready for the tour de force*
*The throng leads us straight there of course.*

*Jostled by fans each inch, yard, mile,*
*Reached Elland Road after some while,*
*Stood terraced through a tight turnstile.*

*Both sides committed to the core*
*(at Bramall Lane 3-0 the score)*
*The Blades could just have scraped a draw,*

*But Leeds were often rampant here –*
*They finished runners-up that year,*
*And Revie was top manager.*

*This place we held in good repute,*
*Our voices hoarse and all but mute,*
*Recovered quietly watching* Klute,

*A fine Jane Fonda film to see,*
*With butterkist and coke as tea,*
*A great day it turned out to be.*

*We found a pub for one last jar*
*Called Whitelock's, celebrated bar,*
*And four pints were enough by far.*

*So, Sunday papers next for us*
*And still good friends, no strain or fuss.*
*Just one more session, then my bus.*

Elland Road was a proud showpiece of a stadium, Yorkshire's best, still in the country's biggest 10 into the Noughties, fit to serve great achievements – from Don Revie's regime on the pitch through to hosting for Euro 96 qualifying stages. Good/bad boy Billy Bremner, consummate player, captain and later manager, was lauded in song:

*Little Billy Bremner is the captain of the crew*
*For the sake of Leeds United he would break himself in two;*
*His hair is red and fuzzy and his body's black and blue*
*But Leeds go marching on.*

As well as the mass of support attracted in this major one-club city, the team should have spawned a spate of more distant enthusiasts from those golden years. Tone ov Voice wrote: 'At least gloryhunters who stick with their team even when the rot has set in are worth a little admiration. They almost become real fans. Leeds is the best example here I suppose. Following their 60s/70s success they've attracted gloryhunters who may soon enjoy "Third Division" football. There's only one Peter Ridsdale.' Wolves fanzine Issue 129, 2007. Mr Ridsdale then published *United We Fall*, an unsparing account of the affair [of the man with the club]'... 'Early on in his chairmanship he and his counterpart at Aston Villa, Doug Ellis, confide they both know that Bolton will sell Alan Thompson for £3.5 million. Why not both offer £3.5 million, Ridsdale suggests, and let the player decide? They shake hands. Leeds offer £3.5 million, Villa bid £4.25 million. Thompson goes to the Midlands' (*Daily Telegraph*). As a Villa fan I remember innocently enjoying Alan Thompson's debut on the park.

A further instance of bad practice involving Villa was Leeds's manager, David O'Leary, writing *Leeds United on Trial*, which was launched in January 2002 when Leeds were top of the League. Within six months, O'Leary had been sacked (to join the unfortunate Villa), Leeds had missed out on the Champions League for a second successive season and the road to perdition had been joined. The title upset a lot of people because we had made it clear that the Bowyer-Woodgate case was not Leeds United on trial, it was two of our employees. Some of the stuff in it was frankly fiction.'

Anticipating the drop to the Third Division in 2007, United were guilty of more bad practice. They entered, legally, into a Company Voluntary Arrangement, not only suffering a, by then irrelevant, 10-point deduction in the season in its dying moments, rather than the new campaign, as Rotherham United had done in 2006, but also were able to avoid substantial debts outside the world of football. Players and clubs owed sums regarding transfer deals were a higher priority. As administrators, leading accountancy firm KPMG reported the debt at 31 March 2007 as £35m. It was good to read that the Football Association was to review the rules affecting this kind of situation.

Ultimately a 15 point deduction was imposed on the League 1 (3) new boys. They rose above that to gallop up the table, after a fabulous start to the 2007-08 campaign, coinciding with the publication of *Leeds United on Trial*.

2007 also saw the demise of a Leeds fan and (nearly) player, bodybuilder Reg Park. Born in 1928 he was the son of a gym owner. Showing early athletic promise he attracted interest from the club but 'acquired a burning desire to be the world's best developed man,' he recalled. In 1951 (Leeds were fifth in Div II) he won the Mr Universe competition, 'setting up on a career…demonstrating his bulging physique and phenomenal power – he claimed to be the first person in the world to have bench-pressed 500lb in 1953.' (*Times* obituary 27/11/07). Leeds were 10th in Div II. Seven years later saw his embarkation on a movie career, kicking off as Hercules. This was the 'sword-and sandals' era. And he was to inspire the future Governor of California, Arnold Schwarzenegger, his successor as body supreme, earning the Mr Universe accolade initially in 1967. Schwarzenegger's career mirrored Leeds's more illustrious period. Perhaps they would have benefited from the mighty Reg's presence in their ranks in the 1950s.

Moving sadly forward to the mid-Noughties, Bremner's statue, in uplifting posture, had declined to a sorry state and the stadium was showing its age. Nevertheless, heralding their debut at the third level, of their 23 forthcoming day tripping bunches of away fans, in 'the official 2007/08 Football League preview' was posited to 'the club insider': "which ground are you looking forward to visiting". 20 chose Elland Road, a typical comment coming from Leo Tyrie, Leyton Orient's press officer: "It's got to be Leeds. You don't get to play in a 40,000 capacity stadium every week.". On the other hand the Crewe nominee chose Yeovil "it's a tidy stadium with a great atmosphere and the locals are very vocal", and the Hartlepool and Millwall voters went for Doncaster's new Keepmoat Stadium.

I'm glad to remember, even if vaguely, my trip there at the time of the Whites' zenith. In 1972 they finished runners-up and won the Cup.

## Middlesbrough 4 Coventry City 0
## Premiership, 7/9/96

Football was sandwiched between tourist activities in County Durham. Beamish Museum offered immense Hereford bulls; also old-fashioned sweets in the cobbled village street. My favourite was toffee crunch, khaki-coloured in a sack shape.

Well, Boro did beat Derby 6-1 the next March, but this real-life result was an impressive margin, in a full, spanking new, Riverside Stadium (capacity 30,500). The debate in the seats around me was around the capacity question. It had been decided to restrict it to the 30k level, as a larger ground wouldn't justify the capital outlay. At that time this limit seemed misguided as the team was filling the stands. I was relieved to have made sure of a ticket, dispatched by post (almost a novelty) price £12.50. This was my first replacement ground. It felt alien from the town whose name it carried, though it was a brisk walk from the town centre, where I enjoyed the statutory lunchtime fare. There was little in the vicinity of the stadium, apparently the first stage in a development planned into the future. I had a premonition of many gruesome progeny of this idea: visually impressive but stereotyped stadia to come, all over the 92.

My neighbours, debaters and families, had come in from North York Moors villages and suburbs. The routine was already well-developed: drive to the ground, leave the car (likely to be of Land Rover ilk) in a designated, manned car park and trot or hike to the ground. No pub visit (near the town, at least), hassle-free viewing, excising some of the essence of urban football club support, when attenders were single-mindedly focused on the game. The new package had developed as a family excursion – circuitous chitchat over sandwich and thermos flask distribution. This has since hardened up as the model for practising supporters, the growing checklist applied to every new ground to provide a safe and sanitized experience. It was salutary at the time that football could become the province primarily of those with big budgets, or no need for a budget. What had happened to the local, urban Ayresome Park fans?

The home team had a superstar in Juninho, who delivered that afternoon. It was Boro's 'nearly' cup season. They were runners-up to Leicester after a replay and extra time in the League Cup (1-0), their first major Wembley Cup Final for 121 years, followed by their second and first ever FA Cup Final (Chelsea won 2-0). Middlesbrough paid the price with relegation. It was one of the seasons when Southampton and Coventry escaped by a whisker, but in the end Boro were five points short of safety. Part of this was accounted for in the deduction of three points for not appearing against Blackburn one Saturday. Some psychological knock-on could also well be attributed.

Perhaps the debaters came to modify their attitude to stadium size with the prospect of visitors the likes of Crewe and Swindon at their new level.

Boro has rejoiced in its fanzine *Fly me to the Moon* with a number of claims to fame. Since 1988, originating at Ayresome Park, a new edition, with a print run of over 2,000, has been produced for every home game. It's not surprising that it has been a prizewinner – of the best fanzine award. This kind of enterprise relies upon a committed group of core contributors including a cartoonist, valiantly supporting the club through rain and relegation. Nigel Downing, editor for much of the Nineties, had the originality to name his male offspring after revered players: Camsell and Fenton.

The original Camsell (George) scored a record 59 goals in the Division II championship season 1925-26. The team's total in the League was 122. The births were announced in the magazine. His daughter was named Hope. Nigel commented on that League Cup Final, 'we'd have gotten away with it if it hadn't been for that Heskey kid', the boy Emil being the perpetrator of the equalizer deep into injury time. Of the other debacle, Robert Nichols, *Fly me to the Moon* editor, in this, accounted by some their best-ever season, 'was honoured to be amongst a privileged band of supporters selected as the club's guests for the FA Cup Final. What other club would do that for a humble fanzine editor?'

# New Year, New Grounds

## Hull City 2 Huddersfield Town 1
## League 1 (3), 1/1/05

As the New Year dawned on the banks of the Yorkshire Ouse, one of the last (legal) fox-hunting meets was convening in Howden and I idly mused on the mere 15 football grounds comprising the remaining complement of the 92 as the year began; in fact two more were affixed later. In any case it was a happy chance to be invited to a New Year's Eve party close enough to one of the most chronically underperforming football cities to see them at home that very day. First stop Howden Minster, built in the 14th century, a ruin with a dramatic central tower. This was the best next stage in assimilating 2005. The neighbouring streets beckoned to be explored, empty between the dispersal of pink hunt enthusiasts and the New Year's Day tavern clusters later on.

We moved on to 'the King's Town on the river Hull [which] had one of the largest royal armouries in England. In 1643 Charles I came for "his" weapons, but Hull had locked the gates. Soon after the Civil War started. Kingston upon Hull's defiance is seen by some as showing independence of spirit and thought. Others claim it shows that Hull is full of untrustworthy psychos, with a liking for weapons and locking the gates against outsiders' (Glyn Watkins). It should have been the familiar quiet-day treasure hunt – follow the signs and find the ground. But there were worrying moments as, after the initial road sign to KC Stadium, there were no more. We retraced steps and tried again, eventually doing battle with the city centre, where a shrewd guess got us to the monument that is Kingston Communications Stadium. It was in Anlaby, west of downtown. What the official thinking was regarding signs to new grounds is baffling. In this case I could see the agenda item being tackled thus: 'they'll be coming from the city centre so we'll erect signs from there.' And so it was that we survived hassle in Hessle. Boom! Boom!!! However, once located, the city of K-o-H is at the end of a long road. Few come from it and if they have any sense people try to avoid driving into it. The ground is fairly convenient for enjoying what the city centre has to offer – an undemanding transfer, though you do have to find a parking space. We managed that for a couple of free 'bank holiday' hours. It's pretty obvious that visiting fans need to be helped, like anyone new to an area (e.g. that most desirable and lucrative category: tourists) and you face many quandaries if you're behind a steering wheel. I would travel to K-o-H by train next time.

Depositing the vehicle in a club car park around noon, kick off at 3pm, next was a wander round the perimeter to find the ticket office: £19 for 'DeVries Honda West Stand Corner Reserved Seating' said the passport to the pace-setting Tigers, astride with Luton at the top of the table. Next, the joy of a bit of trippery. There was a choice of venues in the *Good Beer Guide* (now justifying its '2006' appellation, though I had received it in September). In the Three John Scott's (it said), of course a Wetherspoon's pub, built opposite St Mary's Church and 'named after three past incumbents of the church'. It offered a cottage pie deal, duly executed and supplied, upon which we gorged, not having been too enthusiastic about food when we arose that morning. This was much enhanced by pints of B&T's Santa Slayer, from Bedfordshire and Shepherd Neame's Christmas Cracker ale all the way from Kent, seasonal and ambrosial but not local. A good thing, I concluded, enthused by the thought of a return visit to see museums closed that day and try some Hull-brewed Whalebone.

Time for the ground, which was entirely as expected. Two years old, it felt brand new and afforded a few predictably postcard-worthy snaps featuring white curves and the sinuous lines of the opposite stand. It didn't matter which end was which as the whole place seemed of uniform design. The home side duly dispatched Huddersfield to sustain the top-of-the-table tussle with the Luton Hatters. Hull had been promoted from Nationwide Division III (4) in 2003-04 and were on their way back to the second level for the first time since 1991. Quite a revival. Perhaps the new place helped inspire confidence.

An accolade was awarded in 1967 when they won the *Soccer Star* (magazine of that era with a green or orange cover) Programme of the Year Award. Voted on 23 counts by four pundits they amassed 84 points, Oldham got 83 and Chelsea were third with 75. At the bottom were Newport County and Scunthorpe with 23 apiece. Good, now I've mentioned the former fourth Welsh member of the League. I'm afraid I failed to visit Somerton Park, now lost forever. Newport are an example of the phoenix phenomenon along with Accrington and Aldershot (who have both made it all the way to the League).

My previous visit hereabouts, over 30 years before, predated the Humber Bridge, which we were now to cross after further problems with misleading road signs. We got to know something of the road system over the two initiatives to get to stadium and, then, bridge. I made a mental note next time to take the signs to Hessle to get immediate access (but then, I had already decided to come by train on a future visit – see above). Was it that the authorities reckon, correctly I surmise, that owing to the lack of demand on the visitor front, there was no need to bother with helpful signage? Keep them around as long as possible. The bridge was certainly a white elephant, blissfully empty, colossal and graceful against the pitch black engulfing the expanse of river.

## Darlington 3 Macclesfield Town 1
## Division III (4), 3/1/05

The 2005-06 *Racing & Football Outlook Guide* still had Darlo's ground as 'Feethams', a Freudian slip, I'm sure, two years after they moved. I shared this apparent wish to go back to the old ground, quirky and atmospheric, with footbridge and river adjacent, plus ancient almshouses. 'One of the country's most picturesque grounds, Feethams couldn't have been more English' opened the *Observer* in its 'Then and Now' series; then a snippet, lending to the checkered story of Darlington's debts: '...not all the upgrades went smoothly: floodlights were added in 1960, which immediately burned down the entire West Stand on their debut...'. It was the last ground with a cricket connection, literally; also close to the town centre, with a sense of belonging, Darlington being a lively market town. I scheduled this game at the Williamson Stadium merely to get it off the list.

From May 1999, Darlington FC was funded by one George Reynolds a total of £30m. His card carried the legend '...managing director, chairman, gentleman, entrepreneur, adventurer, maker of money and utter genius'. He has embraced gaol-serving, safecracking and the *Times* Rich List membership in his career. On assuming the Quakers mantle George embarked upon the new stadium, costing £20m, with features such as marble toilets and gold-plated taps. We did not see these. Supporters in 2005 attended not the 'Reynolds' but Williamson Motors Stadium, things having moved on and George consigned to old-news status. Being built on a ring road and necessarily driving there, the choice was to pay an exorbitant £5 to occupy the club's car park, or choose a dubious space, probably illegally, using soft shoulder for near side and the busy road itself for off side, close to a roundabout.

The ground seemed purely functional – and badly designed for the provision of refreshments. The customers joined a queue for dull, packaged fare (and offhand service from the youthful staff) and then had to queue again in an adjacent space for cans of pop from a machine: not only no fun but inefficient and aggravating, as even with the modest number of supporters in evidence that day there was a crush of bodies between the two outlets. It is salutary to bump into people who really expect a new stadium to be the perfect answer to their club's needs, like the Bristol City fan on the train to Leicester. Time will tell. It was odd that both the turnstiles, tall and regular as opposed to low and curvaceous, and the seats were all red. The team plays in black and white. At least there was one example of lightness of touch: The West Stand seats proudly presented the word 'DARLINGTON' in solid black, with 'DARLO' underneath. On the other hand, the emptiness of the place was emphasized in that we could make out the names so clearly. The North Stand was entirely void.

The visit to the town had been a pleasure in wandering round on an itinerary determined by a list of pubs whose precise locations were identified on the town map on display. This was one of the advantages of a pub-led approach to the scenario, giving the participant a bespoke town tour. We ventured up alleyways and parallel streets on an elaborate route, observed a wide range of trading outlets on the way and enjoyed two contrasting venues – the Quaker House, which featured 'Ghost Ale' (named after Ethel, the pub ghost) and Number Twenty-2 (sic) a 'classy bar on the edge of the town centre'. We had to try the bar of Darlington Cricket Club at Feethams (open to the public), from which, while enjoying a pint of a brew from Ringwood, Hampshire, we wistfully imagined Darlington FC's erstwhile pitch, cheek-by-jowl with the surviving cricket operation. Also recommended for ale was Binns Department Store. This was a town of character.

Departure was easy from our angular parking site: 55 minutes to York for an overnight stop. Alas, York City, visited in 1990 (1-2 to Scarborough, a tense local derby) were suffering their first year in the Conference, destined to finish an ignominious 17th out of 22. More than that, Bootham Crescent was to be renamed the KitKat Stadium, following sponsors' dictates, for the future. Despite these caveats, an evening in the venerable city turned out to be just right after a busy day of external stimuli in a working town and the bitter-sweet vibes of the Quakers in their new venue. All was not to be lost as years later (on 16/3/08) was held 'The Very First Bootham Crescent Beer Festival'; no mention of chocolate products, but for £7.50 you would receive 'two pints & hot food, with entertainment laid on...All proceeds to the York City Youth Development Association.' Good on you, chaps.

## And over the Map

## Stockport County 0 Ipswich Town 1
## Division I (2), 14/3/98

I've always enjoyed watching Edgeley Park looming then vanishing on train journeys to Manchester. Great floodlights and lots of corrugated iron. After the mellow Cheshire countryside you're made brutally aware that you have reached the threshold of the vastness of Greater Manchester. The Main Stand frontage proclaimed 'Stockport County' impressively.

Graham Privett (Priv), with whom I enjoyed the Accrington and Dag/Red trips at the end of this saga, rather recklessly volunteered as the Away Match Travel Organiser of the Hyde branch of the Hatters independent Supporters Club (HISC – acronyms rampant here) in 1996-97. That season turned out to be the longest in County's history (67 games). People still like to remind him about that. There were echoes of Exeter City's recent history in the message he sent me in March 2008: 'Stockport County have today launched a scheme to purchase back their ground...In 2003 Coca-Cola League Two football club Stockport County was sold by its private owners to a consortium. Due to the large debts that had been left with the club, ownership of Edgeley Park, the home of Stockport County for more than 100 years, was taken away from the football club. In 2005 the fans of Stockport County succeeded in buying back the football club to become one of a handful of football clubs owned by the fans. As part of the purchase... there is an option to buy back Edgeley Park within eight years and return the ground to its original owners. Ownership of the stadium is the only way to secure the long term future of the football club, a proud club which has existed for 125 years...It's not about who you support, it's about a real football club, with a proud history getting back its ground and surviving for another 125 years.'

The Hatters were clearly on the up. Two more examples: they beat Rochdale in the 2008 Fourth Division play-off final (an exciting 3-2 affair) and were honoured by Glossop's Howard Town Brewery. In its June 2008 issue, *What's Brewing*, the monthly organ of CAMRA, reported 'The brewery's Peter Clarke said: 'The chant of 'drink up for the lads' will be heard at the Plough pub in Heaton Moor, Stockport, because the real ale haven has launched its own specially brewed Stockport County Bitter. For every pint sold, 10p will go towards the fund to buy the League Two [sic – praise the Lord for the promotion] ground back.' Good for them. I can't wait!

The League game I attended ten years earlier was of one several episodes with Taylor and family over the weekend, in fact the least, as only he, Ben and I attended an unrewarding game – minimum exposure only, simply finding a parking space, seeing the match and escaping as efficiently as the situation permitted. Everything else we did over the two days was a group experience, frolics for five, ranging from antiques at Knutsford on the way to a performance at Wythenshawe's Forum Theatre to time out for exercise at one of several swimming pools in the Metropolitan Borough of Stockport.

Taylor and Ben were regulars at Edgeley Park for a few seasons, during which the team developed a bit of a roll, producing some exciting football. They saw some stars of the future in the making – Ben recalled one incident of an onfield fight involving a footballer later to become very well known. We can't name names as mum's the word! One of the joys for them, in a smaller crowd, was the witty comments made by the regulars who were not afraid of giving valuable advice. As well as stars of the future there were some in their twilight years. One highlight was seeing Vinnie Jones in the team – he also got into a fight, presumably practising for more violent roles in his film career.

This weekend jaunt involved return train tickets, thankfully painless on the return journey on Sunday afternoon, not bedevilled by rail repairs and cancellations. These have since become much more prevalent following the seeming proliferation of disasters on the railways. The work has to be done and was pitifully ignored for far too long, but the weekend traveller has to suffer the consequences. I therefore tend to drive, particularly if independence is needed at the destination, unless the train route is easy and regular, allowing for the odd difficulty like leaves on the line, staff problems (for so many reasons but let's limit it to sudden 'leave taking' and 'indisposition') or passenger seizure. I expect we ticket acquirers to be reidentified as 'clients' any time now, as the rail companies hone their approach to impress with their ever-aspirant customer service and proliferating 'products'. By this we have to understand the unfathomable variety of journey deals, depending on how and when you approach ticket purchase. The means justifies the end – somehow you have to achieve entitlement to the voyage – via website/telephone/station visit, as judged as most efficacious. Basically it's pot luck.

In the new century I took up National Express bus journeys to London, using the 'funfares', cheap, cheerful and effective as long as you're not afflicted by someone nearby with a predilection for mobile phone conversations, inevitably VERY LOUD, as the user has no sense of the outside world, i.e. the person adjacent. Personal stereos, the previous menace, seemed to have assumed a lower profile; we must count our blessings.

The managerial confrontation was: Gary Megson (England, born Manchester

1959) v George Burley (born Cumnock, Ayrshire 1956), the home boss destined for Stoke, West Brom, Forest, Leicester and Bolton, the daytripper for Derby, Hearts, Southampton and Scotland. Both had pursued respectable playing careers with successful conversions into jobbing managers peregrinating round the island.

The programme contained much opinion, such as Ipswich had been a 'tame outfit' when vanquished by Stockport 0-2 at Portman Road four months before. We were unlucky to see only one goal, at the wrong end as County fans for the afternoon, as the last four games had produced 3, 6 and 5 goals respectively. Since November County had occupied a handy sixth to ninth position, ready to spring into overdrive for a play-off challenge. But this day Ipswich were the form team, having overtaken the home side to reach fifth place. It was therefore something of a crunch match, alas not fulfilled in the execution.

Stockport's shirts, royal blue with some vertical fading brilliant white paint brush stripes, advertized Robinsons Best Bitter. I yearned for a draught of that. And had I met him by then I'm sure Priv the top-hatted away trips organizer would have introduced me to a suitable venue or two, as well as curry house, being a chicken balti enthusiast. Their more impressive away kit was advertised in the programme: quartered black and white, carrying the Robinsons logo more starkly in black on a white block. 'More than just another replica kit' was announced in a full-page display 'new 1997/98'. Almost time for a sale, surely, with four home games remaining. This replica shirt was none of your wishy-washy paintbrush stuff, whose subtlety cannot be seen from up the terraces anyway. It's seldom that away/change strips are intrinsically worthwhile, their role ostensibly as money-spinners, but this one might have tempted me for use on the squash court, if seriously reduced in price.

There was also a piece entitled 'Tameside Tales', showing a worthy interest in the Cheshire footy scene. While Droylsden and Ashton United were vying for promotion, the doings of Hyde United and Curzon Ashton were worth their mention. Curzon's manager had been sacked and Hyde's was under threat now that they were sliding down the table and out of all the cups. Hyde United has always been one of my favourite names, being so sonorous, for once a club's suffix making a satisfying entity, unlike the excess of Uniteds up and down the country, chosen for no apparent reason. There is mitigation in cases when the club's origins represent a union of two others, as in Carlisle whose progenitors were Carlisle Red Rose and Shaddongate United. Or when you're given the whole story, like Rye and Iden United, playing in the temptingly named Badger Ales Sussex County League. Other examples of well-chosen appendages are Wolverhampton and Wycombe Wanderers, the former so prolix and restful it might replace sheep counting as a means of achieving slumber. Try also Tiverton Town, pleasingly alliterative, while there are ubiquitous, unappealing, 'Towns'. Can't we have a few more inventions the likes of Folkestone Invicta in Kent, Racing Club (Warwick), Synthonia (Durham – Billingham Synthonia may be the only club named after an agricultural fertilizer) and Blyth Spartans (Northumberland)? I won't mention the 'AFC' issue here.

To carp further, the programme (no year printed, but the price was £1.70) committed cardinal sins on the spelling front. Middlesbrough was donated the all too frequent unwanted extra 'o' and Forest was 'Notts' not 'Nottm'. Even Tameside outfit Droylsden, above, was down as 'Droylesden'. I expect I shall become humbler when errors in this tome are identified! It may be a hangover from when Stockport County were called Heaton Norris Rovers. Permanent confusion pervades.

Back to the Hatters and the Tractorboys. Seven weeks on it was all over. County maintained their consistency to finish eighth, Ipswich fifth before losing to Charlton 1-0 both home and away in the play-offs. It is reputed that their play-off failure rate is without equal. These shortfalls may be deliberate, the argument being that it's better to be challenging near the top than suffering at the bottom. That may have become less of a consideration given the £50m estimated as lost by Sheffield United due to their new second-tier status after their relegation in 2007, amid a bitter legal process about West Ham's validity in including Carlos Tevez in late-season games, which they won to scramble out of the bottom three at the eleventh hour. Even so, not all teams are inclined towards the nightmarish financial consequences of promotion. Meanwhile Sale Sharks, oval ball people, were guest home team at Edgeley Park and doing rather better than their hosts.

## Macclesfield Town 2 Southend United 1
## Division III (4), 1/3/03

'Town' were new boys to the Cheshire/Manchester circuit and in no hurry to help the visiting fan. At Middlesbrough the ground was a landmark of the 'you can't miss it' variety, once you got to the right space. In Macclesfield it was a local secret. The delicately named Moss Rose was so inoffensive as not to be seen, until Fredders, the Seagull man, and I had reoriented by car a few times as well as on foot. No road signs, you see, and on the wrong side of the Silk Town. It's always best to find your ultimate destination first, to minimize subsequent disturbance on misguided quest failures. We were falsely confident in our allocation of time to a visit to the Silk Museum, followed by lunch in one of many taverns we passed on the way. The trouble was that the initial investigation had been troublesome and long-winded and the museum multi centred. We shall have to return for the rest of the Silk Museum, and all the other attractions in the leaflet we picked up.

Perhaps it could all have been managed in a less rewarding town, or if we hadn't stopped off in Bakewell on the way for tarts, sorry puddings – one of the most frequently committed appellation errors. Macc's White Lion, not on any list but by then necessarily convenient, was fine for a somewhat curtailed pre-match respite. It was salutary that a half day intended for getting to know a town can so unwittingly be whittled down to bits and pieces. It just goes to show one of life's truths. You can overdo the organization, or, get on with it. I have since enjoyed the prospect of examining the place further. After Stalybridge Celtic I think, another evocative and mysterious name.

The match could have gone any way. We decided to be home supporters, for me because I know more fans of Silkmen than of Shrimpers, so I was witness by proxy on

104

their behalf; just as well that they scraped a victory. Fredders considered the winning goal to 'reveal sublime skill and execution, to lift our hearts.' But I'm unsure whether he meant this.

The fans round us taunted 'all this way for nothing; you've come all this way for nothing.' It also transpired, in a subsequent conversation, that there was some parking near Moss Rose, all of fiftyish spaces following the demolition of a pub. Is there an equation to do with 'x' barrels and 'y' parking spaces?

Both teams finished the season on 54 points (Macc 16th, Sarfend 17th), six points more than poor old Exeter in 23rd position (fuck it!), but at that time they were worried. It just shows how close things are in a game, or a season.

And we returned to Derbyshire via scenic Wildboarclough – great name too. The day was counted a success. Roll on the Celtic.

But all too soon after the Moss Rose experience I was flattened by a bug. The outcome: antibiotics – no booze for a week, and no more footy until Exeter v Rochdale on the 22nd. A 1-1 draw: not good enough.

The essence of these extended trips is variety: among the football games, over different sports and through the period between sport and other happenings. This involves investment and commitment. Participants may well need time off to recover.

There are common threads to hang it all on. Inroads into Yorkshire were built up through the visits to Sheffield, Leeds and Middlesbrough. It turned out that the same could be accommodated in Cheshire.

Next, up the Scottish east coast it might be an idea to tackle Angus for Forfar, Arbroath, Montrose and Brechin City: Forfar for four (or five) goals, Arbroath for smokies, Montrose for North Sea paddling and Glebe Park, Brechin, for the 'Far Side and Hedge', apparently a real-life hedgerow on one side of the ground itself. Above all I favour Elgin City, the team from Borough Briggs, ever since their title-winning days in the Highland League long ago. Their mascot, Briggsy, a badger, says it all as a nocturnal beast, not normally bringing the side luck in daytime (Saturday afternoon).

Now we resume the eastern trail to our capital.

# Chapter Four
# Capital Challenges

## London Grounds

The capital is a hallowed soccer centre. That much is a truism. It was incumbent to tackle a final count of a baker's dozen of League clubs in London. Watford is in Hertfordshire. Barnet was but isn't, the Bees back in the League, cantering in by a few lengths in 2005, Dagenham & Redbridge, to be counted as overspill and outside the perimeter, following suit in 2007. To these has to be added, inevitably, the august (though that's the only month likely never to produce football games) Wembley Stadium. Definition of London clubs depends upon your frame of reference. The (Evening) *Standard* includes Watford and Dag/Red in its daily footy bulletin. The list provided in the *London Lite*, the evening rag you're bombarded with at every tube station, extends to Reading, Gillingham, Southend, Luton and Wycombe. That's 18 clubs linked to the capital, just under a fifth of the 92. My choice of perimeter has been the M25 loosely, without Watford and conveying the Daggers to Essex and the final chapter.

I have had the great advantage of having been a London resident in the past, and have maintained an association there, building up a confidence and enthusiasm for which I count myself lucky. I am constantly surprised by the apprehension people sometimes show at the prospect of tackling 'Town' or 'The Smoke'. Contrariwise, I have developed a need for periodical fixes of the capital, usually a few days of intense hustle and bustle on my Oystercard, and a wide choice of turnstiles for a fix of footy. We are indeed blessed to have available one of the world's great cities to enjoy. Not least among its offerings are all these soccer clubs.

In footballing terms Londinium is a microcosm of the country. Adventures round the regions of England bear this out – there is a bit of every experience in the quest to attend each London ground. The capital's cosmopolitan feel gives the visiting sports fan so much more besides. The games below, spanning 35 years, represent comprehensive diversity at the top end of grounds, a.k.a. stadia, and those elusive ones, not quite national in presence but fully equipped, aspirant modern PLC headquarters hosting Premiership games, with half an eye on qualification each May for trips over the Channel. Let's cite 'AZ' (it says on the cover – A to Z to you and me) page 66, A2–B2. It's symptomatic of the quaint old Hammers that the ground/stadium is split between two cells on the map. You can identify the location as Green Street (where it is), Barking Road (arterial, nearby), Boleyn Ground (name of ground, not on map), Upton Park (local subdivision, let us say, and nearest tube station) or even West Ham (name of club, though 'East Ham' is closer on the map, but then who can comprehend a London map). The magnificent London Underground map, beautiful with all those colours, perfectly designed by Harry Beck for practical use, bears no literal relation to the yards and spaces on the streets overhead. Not all the stations are correctly placed in terms of the compass.

The tube map certainly deserves the design awards which have come its way. Looking more closely the name East Ham is placed on a rare blank green space (Central Park, so perhaps artificially close). Supporting the setting is how you get there – the best and/or most fruitful means for each occasion all over the conglomeration; and 'other events' ranging from nothing at all (West Ham v Stoke, by coach, then back again immediately afterwards) to entire weekends presenting varied activity from top-class theatre to the purchase of provender from ethnic shops to cutting-edge exhibitions to a wander round one of several cemeteries. Suitable itineraries might be from West Ham to West End or Tottenham to Tottenham Court Road. Take your pick.

The pleasure of London is superficial, ephemeral, hedonistic – going there, doing it, leaving. Even departure is meaningful. The place is so grand that the process of escape somehow becomes significant. The capital has provided more objectivity in football ground visits than other parts of the country. You are there already and the football is simply what happens. Tottenham and Charlton, neither noted for Underground stations, have proved an easier task than many regional grounds which have necessitated meeting an intellectual challenge to determine the route.

The visits have involved many forms of transport. I drove to Barnet and was driven to Tottenham and Leyton; easy tube journeys to Arsenal and Chelsea (1999 visit), Queens Park Rangers and back from Tottenham c/o Seven Sisters; head-banging challenges for Millwall, both old and New Dens ('New' may be destined to remain part of the name of the stadium even when it assumes antiquity. There was only one 'Den'); a little research needed for West Ham, and Tottenham without a car; a bus back from Crystal Palace; overland trains for Brentford, Crystal Palace and Charlton; a walk to Chelsea back in 1970, and longer strolls from White City and Putney Bridge tube stations to Queens Park Rangers and Fulham, variously listed as 'nearest'.

As for Wembley, the Underground system was the line of least resistance in approaching the place from central London, except when using the disabled part of the car park and on another occasion in a coach party from the Midlands. The transport argument against rebuilding the stadium is critical in the knowledge that a site elsewhere, like the Birmingham area, would be more suitable for access, parking, journey time and facilities. The argument has to rest (has been lost) in view of London's status as Olympic host in 2012. So be it, but the decision, made but not fully executed with a few years still to go (and who knows what further tales of woe will be recounted before its opening?) has worsened the North/South divide. Also, Olympics showcase apart, more acute congestion will surely ensue. It was reassuring to note in 2007 that direct services were being scheduled from Birmingham stations to 'Wembley Stadium', on the way to Euston or Marylebone. This was good news to accompany the opening of the new stadium, and was enjoyed in due course in my Conference Play-off final trek.

The ground entries follow the model of the inner M25: anti-clockwise from the closest ground to a northbound point: Underhill, London Borough of Barnet. Read on.

## Barnet 1 Doncaster Rovers 1
## Division III (4), 4/11/95

At the start of the 1967-68 season in *Soccer Star* magazine appeared: 'former amateur club Barnet, the surprise packet of last season's (Southern League) Premier Division, will be one of the strongest contenders for Romford's League title crown...., most surprising addition to the staff is ex-Arsenal...wing-half Gerry Ward who was previously expected to hang up his soccer boots to concentrate on a career in banking. He will not be available for mid-week games.' So Gerry liked his footy, even at Underhill, though he was even more committed to evening classes on Wednesdays. Barnet listed some familiar names among their recruits. Barry Fry saw them through to promotion in 1993 after two seasons' League membership, itself hard-earned after finishing second in the Football Conference three times in four years. Later managers included Ray Clemence, Terry Bullivant and Tony Cottee.

However, the Bees remain in memory as a successful amateur Athenian League club. They won the championship seven times during their membership (1912-65). They retain the ground to match, the uphill Underhill. That they still reside there is partly attributable to the local authority, whose promises have failed to materialize in purpose. So they're stuck in an unappealing stadium, hardly equipped for League football. In 2006 there was even a dispute about vehicular access, involving the council I'm afraid - thankfully resolved in the end.

It is happier to note some English history in this part of Hertfordshire, a mere 10 miles north of central London.

The Battle of Barnet, in 1471, was pivotal in the Wars of the Roses. King Edward IV, of York, emerged as victor. The Yorkist tenure of the crown was soon to be consolidated at the Battle of Tewkesbury, nearest league club Cheltenham. Half a millennium later, Barnet the local football club had turned professional, just like all those fifteenth-century mercenaries, and reached the Third Round of the FA Cup, to be vanquished by Colchester United at home (0-1). The winners had a particularly good run – as far as the last eight (Everton 5 Colchester 0).

In the end High Barnet, the local tube station, Northern Line terminus, is more resonant to the world at large than the football place down the road.

'Welcome to Underhill Stadium' says the board on a stand.

> *From the Moon under Water for lunch*
> *The day's mid-table fare lukewarm punch*
> *All uphill Underhill*
> *Brace of goals, sparing thrill*
> *Low heat game, more a sample than munch.*

The hostelry produced extreme puff-pastry pies, which flossed all over the table. Bogs and I settled for the steaming bovine contents alone. And the ground didn't only boast the slope but a sizeable fee to gain admittance: all of £12 (£6 concessions), the same

as we'd paid at Chelsea the year before. We imagined the central reason was simply fiscal. They don't get many punters, so charge the paltry few an arm and a leg for the privilege.

Down in central London the fare was a lot more powerful: 'Art and Power' at the Hayward Gallery and the Royal Shakespeare Company's *A Patriot for Me*, which later won awards. These were pricey but I'd say better value than the offerings on the sloping pitch.

## Wembley Stadium (old) – England 1 Germany 1, 5-6 on penalties European Championships Semi-Final, 26/6/96

The 1976 FA Trophy Final provided my Wembley initiation (Stafford Rangers 2 Scarborough 3 – Frumps and I were there for the Rangers, a day off from Potteries interests).

Euro 96 was a world away from a coach trip from Staffordshire. I counted myself lucky to have the opportunity to buy a package of six tickets for two people for the whole tournament, through my insurance broker friend, Mike. The three group games were £35 a throw, and payment had been made nine months previously. It would be interesting to learn how much bank interest was amassed. Prices were hiked up for the knockout stages starting with £45 for the Quarter-Final at Villa Park (Portugal 0 Czech Republic 1). Having a £60 ticket to impart for the Semi-Final I took a friend, Foxy (actually partner of an ex-colleague, to put it in context) whose local tube station was Highbury & Islington, rather close to the base of a certain football club. Foxy lived there in a convenient and comfortable upper floor flat. It had the obvious benefit of proximity for a trip to Wembley Central, and he had been known to mingle at Arsenal Stadium.

In the all-pervading bluster hitting us in the face immediately on arrival at the destination, we managed to snake our way to the bar of a pub, any pub, in a mightily celebratory climate. The process continued smoothly. As it turned out the 7.30pm kick-off was scheduled a trifle late for us, as the closely-fought game endured through extra-time right through to a penalty shoot-out. Never has there been such a tense, highly-charged atmosphere. It was the climax of the whole history of England v Germany encounters, from the ultimate achievement of 1966 on this very pitch via all the disappointments for our national team alongside the dominance of the opposition in Europe for what seemed an eternity.

We were in the north terrace on aisle seats at the top of the section closest to the pitch. Alan Shearer had scored in the third minute, making 5 his final tally, the highest scorer in the Championship. It was 1-1 on 20 minutes and so it stayed to the end of extra-time. We had the best possible view of the shoot-out. After an eternity and 100% penalty success rate up to then, the tally somehow got to 5-6, inescapable on the scoreboard. Gareth Southgate, esteemed Villa captain in his day job, strode forth. He struck. Goalkeeper Kopke lunged and saved it. (Gareth's mother later asked him 'Why didn't you just belt it?') We registered the shock, faced each other, communicated prickly horror for a nano-second and tacitly agreed to run. That was a wise reaction as

we tripped up the avenue and into the first train. If the air was a strange colour within sight of the Twin Towers, it was palpably lumpen and grey in the packed tube train. Hundreds of people – both sexes, all ages, with programmes clutched as hand luggage and ornamented with every piece of merchandise the purveyors of the time could invent – were traumatized. We had no need to break the silence but telepathically, pathetically, willed the stations to fly past, motivated now by the need for relief in the bar at our destination, King's Cross. And so it was, just before closing time, a pint: a protracted intake, hardly broken by words. At last we were climbing to Foxy's flat, and fortified by essential duty-free malt whisky night caps, I needed one of the man's collection of business class eye patches to get a full night's sleep on the futon, the curtains being tastefully fine in texture. He was a jet-setter and the abode was sparsely furnished but for bottles, tiny boxes and little bags whose contents may all have been related to nocturnal needs. I don't recall much more but, when it must have been light for hours, I was nudged awake for freshly squeezed orange juice, black coffee and croissants. What else would you have in the Highbury hinterland?

The lingering feeling pervaded – of profound disappointment, pathos. Perhaps that intensity informed the fact that I have not seen him since.

The Final saw Germany reuniting with the Czechs to win 2-1 in extra time (2-0 in their Group C encounter), something of an anti-climax after the torment four evenings earlier, costing £70, a (rather rash I now think) birthday treat for Warner who muttered observations in Somerset dialect about the quality of play. Examples: he opined the Czechs to be a load of 'mumphaeds' (local pronunciation: like 'vauze' for vase) = someone daft, and in similar vein though with harsher overtones, of one or two uncommitted, clearly incompetent players 'he went in with the bread and came out with the buns.' There was a better range when he witnessed Villa v Oldham (0-1, 2/5/94) – against the run of play was my opinion.

To the eternal Wembley memory add a priceless 82-page programme (no indication on the cover but it was a worthwhile souvenir) and pricey fast food; attendance 73,611.

## Brentford 5 Exeter City 0
## Division IV, 31/10/70

This goes back almost as far as the 1963 Brighton excitement. There were pubs on each corner of the ground: the Griffin, the Royal Oak, the Princess Royal and the New Inn. We tried two and heard about the others.

On a return visit many years later, on the sun-blessed inauguration of the season (Brentford 1 Blackpool 0 – League 1 (3), 5/8/06), the Griffin proved a gem, in sight of the away turnstiles and hosting a handful of travelling supporters as well as buoyant home fans. There was also a Chelsea aficionado who was keen to display the tattoo representing his loyalty. His was a rather impressive image with fag in mouth, which was doomed to show its age following the chop for smoking in bars in July 2007. Dagger (his name? It was tattooed on his arm, or was he implying affection for the buoyant team approaching the Conference exit gate? – we have to make assumptions) might not be seriously inconvenienced as the garden provided ample provision for smokers and scoffers too (sweet-smelling burgers). Noticing my camera, he insisted I take a photo of him. Dagger's visage was framed by a backdrop of a formidable display of darts trophies (to judge by the adjacent board). The pub was almost the brewery tap for Fuller's, up the road in Chiswick. London Pride was an aptly named brew here, a mid-range session beer and worthy precursor to a game. Getting into the ground was an irritation for the travelling fan, through a most inadequate three turnstiles, jollied along by politically correctly chosen Asian officials jacketed in the kind of orange calculated to sweat up the wearer and blind those being jollied. No relation to the Seasiders' seductive tangerine, in fact a garish clash. Many missed the kick-off including Wakey and me, posing as away supporters just as I had done for the Grecians back in 1970. And then the programme, usually inspiring fresh joyousness for the first fixture, adorned with a squad photo and the contributors' prescience full of misguided optimism, failed signally in the other essential: final table for the previous season. This was the only time I can remember when it was composed entirely of noughts, and Brentford FC were fourth, in alphabetical order. This was strange as they'd actually finished a good third and bore out my argument that the play-offs are unjust. But, far from challenging in 2006-07, they finished feebly clutching the wooden spoon. The noughts approach pervades clubs' websites during the close season, and I admit to dipping into Villa's from time to time in June and July to see them in runners-up position until the awful reality of the first game of the season.

Perhaps with an eye to lifting Bee gloom (Brentford not Barnet), the New Road stand was in 2007 renamed 'the Bill Axbey Stand', uniquely after a supporter. That gentleman was born in New Road itself, abutting the ground, weeks before Griffin Park opened for business in 1904. 'Bill recalls his first memories... "When I first started watching the Bees (in 1918) I lived a few doors down from the ground in Ealing Road, so I could watch matches from my upstairs bedroom window. Unfortunately, I could only see three parts of the ground because the nearest goal was obscured!"' (*Richmond and Twickenham Times* 8/5/07). After a lifetime of devoted support up and down the country and all four divisions, he died just before his 103rd birthday. Bill had run out as mascot, in full kit, in 1995; 'The Bill Axbey Stand' seemed a most appropriate honour. That was special.

In keeping with modern times BuzzBee has become the anthropomorphic mascot, in full Brentford kit topped by a smily bee head with protuberant antennae. That's what it looked like. BuzzBee won a penalty shoot-out at the Millennium Stadium, and his highlight was meeting Graham Norton.

Let's note a few more signs of the times at the scene of our afternoon entertainment. The legend 'Bees against Racism' was displayed for all to see (viz human resources policy applied in the case of jolliers above), and having joined a less urgent, more resigned, queue at 40 minutes, all that was available to consume was a steak pie (at least it was edible, its 1970 forebear probably not to be countenanced) and sparkling water (from Malvern, Worcestershire – well, there's no League club in that county, since the sad sinking of the Harriers, so they have to compensate), Bovril being absent and tea and coffee not ready (I ask you!). At the end of the game we were requested by a tannoy announcement thus: 'Will all visiting supporters please follow the exit signs at the rear of the terrace when leaving the stadium.' Well, yes, that meant turning left, though unfortunately the gents was to the right, whither there was now no access, after all those pints and sparkling water with a tube ride to come. Oh well! And that was after six minutes added on.

Griffin Park, itself named after the brewery which had owned the land, was an inter-war construction of generous proportions (37k capacity with the record gate 39,626 v Preston, FA Cup Round 6 in March 1938, according to the *Stadium Guide*). In 1967 Queens Park Rangers had coveted it, with a view to taking it over, unsuccessfully. The capacity was eventually reduced to 12,763. A hallmark of the ground, in fact its location, was the constant air traffic. It's under the Heathrow flight path. Should you tire of the presentation below, Heaven forfend, an alternative would be plane spotting. I tried and failed to time or count planes, the unfolding drama below providing spasmodic thrills. Let alone moot the planes' identities. I wondered how many jumbo jets traced the clear blue sky during the extra minutes.

I had occasion to meet Peter Gilham, long-standing Communications Manager, who emphasized the need for outside cash in the budget, from grants and the

Sports Trust, and some of which was earned through partnerships with sponsors such as Qatar Airways, whose identity, inscribed boldly on the roof of the Bill Axbey Stand in English and Arabic, was clearly visible from the air. And the pitch was perfect. I recalled the mud and tuft scenarios of times of yore. 2006-07 was the last term for such complete celestial observation. For the 2007-08 campaign the same open terrace was covered by a low empathic structure, thus reducing the aerial aspect, and redefined as home fans' territory. Visitors were to occupy the two-tiered Brook Road Stand, as they had done in an earlier generation.

In the old days we witnessed a thrashing of the Grecians and manic approval from Bees people. At least with hindsight, comfort can be gleaned from City's 1-0 victory in the return fixture, and the season's final table: Exeter ninth, Brentford 14th.

That journey had been from nearby Ealing, where I was staying with friends lost in time. The environs were all home territory for them and Griffin Park proved a pleasant enough lower division football ground. There was a party that night, a chance to forget. But I was hooked, next stop Fulham, and I would be needing an Exeter win sometime for purposes of retrieval.

## Queens Park Rangers 0 Tranmere Rovers 0
## Division I (2), 17/1/98

Loftus Road was the Wasps fortress at the time. There was more evidence of Rugby Union at Loftus Road than at other football grounds I have attended hosting the gentlemen's game. We had South Africa Road tickets in row Q for Queens Park Rangers, who provided a performance still tinged with lethargy evocative of the recent festive season.

This was a model Capital happening, emerging from the busy cosmopolitan street turmoil, in Shepherd's Bush/White City on this occasion, conveniently the names of the closest Underground stations. There was no problem getting there, purchasing a ticket, achieving pints and, especially for Mickser, a novice more familiar with the Traffs on telly, pork scratchings (those irresistible Black Country culinary treasures upon which I have broken three teeth up to now), in the Springbok, one of an intriguing variety of pubs in the area, in between parkas and duffle coats. It was cold and overcast all day. The choice of tube stations meant we avoided much of the widely publicized negativity of nearby Thirties tower block inhabitants. There were forebodings in the spectre of broken glass pushed into cement on the top of walls near the ground.

Perhaps QPR is the ultimate polyglot club. What does the name mean now? It's not evocative of anything to link it in its setting. It's so London! And it's one of only six League clubs whose names contain a 'k' (observe many a trivia quiz). It's the one which often gets through unidentified as the word 'Park' often gets lost in articulation.

This football game was equally immersed in a series of weekend cultural activities – the Turner Prize at the Tate Gallery in the days before the exotic turbine-redundant Tate Modern inspired its new identity as 'Tate Britain', featuring the customary selection of debatable works of art; *A Delicate Balance*, a soul-searching drama far more suspenseful than the scoreless draw the next afternoon; a Sunday morning chamber music concert at the Wigmore Hall (with the drink afterwards, dry, amontillado or sweet, but just the one, and in a small sherry glass, a mere sample, thus catalyzing, as sherry does for me in any quantity, the next fixture: Turkish lunch with copious house wine). This was ideal the morning after the night before – only a swim is as good for body and soul to remedy sore heads. No time for that as well.

Play, on the stages of the Haymarket and Loftus Road, was an enigma. The £25 spent on an entertaining and demanding three hours, minds stretched by the acute writing, elevated with language, character and plot. We had a fair preconception of what we were getting, a known and seasoned product revealed in detail in broadsheet newspapers, the recipe a fusion of reliable high-quality ingredients. This show won awards.

The football cost £17, spent on live, outdoor sport, neutral in attitude though I can never help siding with one of the contenders, eventually gravitating towards Tranmere on the quiet that day. It's a facet of what football does to an enthusiast that such gravitation augmented into something quite passionate, and could have found ill-advised expression had Tranmere scored. (Rovers were near the bottom of the table, but went on to overtake Rangers in the final table.) The mixture of familiar and unknown elements are at the heart of this. It was just another football match. I don't recall much urgency. A 'goalless draw' was its certain destiny in the annals of footy statistics. But this uncertain event was shared with many thousands of expressive supporters, committed to and involved in the unpredictable fluency of the action. In the Haymarket Theatre we sat attentive and silent among a few hundred, absorbing. Chalk and Cheese Ltd had been the match sponsors.


## Fulham 0 Aston Villa 2
## Division III, 28/11/70

A month after the Brentford game, this represented a small progression into the heart of things, rewarded with a much more palatable outcome. The ground was perched on the bank of the Thames, painted in stark black and white and aspiring to Tudorness. In fact a well-earned visual reward – in London Transport Zone 2 it may be, but a trawl in any event.

The highly respected architect Archibald Leitch (1865-1939) was responsible for redesigning Craven Cottage from 1905 while Fulham was an aspiring Southern League enterprise. Perhaps they were inspired by their setting, winning the title twice to join League Division II in 1907. Archie notched up considerable credits, embarking upon Blackburn, Chelsea and Tottenham as well as Fulham at that time. All of these grounds are extant, along with Ibrox Park in his native Glasgow and many others south of the border. The sadly lost Trinity Road Stand at Villa Park, one of many victims of the post-

Taylor Report boom in all-seater stadium erection, was one of his most impressive efforts. His achievement at this riverside location embraced Craven Cottage itself, in a softer style which actually provided living accommodation. The total project cost was £15,000, record money in the Edwardian era. It's strange to realize that Leitch's football initiatives are admired now for characteristic atmospheric red-brick pomp and character, given the less amenable concepts and materials we have been forced to accept since. At the time of building they were not so popular, critics discerning a continuation of his early career on industrial projects. It's all comparative. How we pine after the extravagance and opulence prevalent up to the First World War (information paraphrased from Simon Inglis).

This game was to be held dear, not only for the recherché exposure to Villa winning away, but because of this achievement at the top of the Third Division where they were regrettably situated at the time. The home side only lost one other time at Craven Cottage, to champions-in-waiting Preston. This was the first of Villa's two seasons down below, finishing seven points behind the Cottagers, eventual runners-up.

A piece of Fulham amazement had occurred with the First Division scores on Boxing Day seven years earlier. Imagine the reader's deadpan but finely modulated delivery to convey each result, an approach to language employed by voice teachers in drama schools:

| | | | |
|---|---|---|---|
| Blackpool | 1 | Chelsea | 5 |
| Burnley | 6 | Manchester United | 1 |
| Fulham | 10 | Ipswich Town | 1 |
| Leicester City | 2 | Everton | 0 |
| Liverpool | 6 | Stoke City | 1 |
| Nottingham Forest | 3 | Sheffield United | 3 |
| Sheffield Wednesday | 3 | Bolton Wanderers | 0 |
| West Bromwich Albion | 4 | Tottenham Hotspur | 4 |
| West Ham United | 2 | Blackburn Rovers | 8 |
| Wolverhampton Wanderers | 3 | Aston Villa | 3 |

They don't make them like that nowadays: let's say weather, pitch conditions and Xmas excess were all contributory factors. My favourite was Burnley's effort.

I also like Paul Cookson's set of results:
*The football results are as follows:*

| | | | |
|---|---|---|---|
| *The game was* | 1 | *derful hope you enjoyed it* | 2 |
| *I don't know if* | 5 | *ever seen a better match be* | 4 |
| *Now I'm feelin* | 0 | *not just because of the pie I* | 8 |
| *Scoring that many's* | 7 | *but hell for them because we* | 1 |
| *At last we reached out po* | 10 | *tial with our talented first* | 11 |
| *All their supporters are* | 6 | *as parrots they just couldn't go* | 1 |
| *Playing with total* | 3 | *dom we will always domin* | 8 |
| *It was our virt* | 2 | *uoso performance they just couldn't sur* | 5 |

## Chelsea 4 Leicester City 0
## Premiership, 8/10/94

Up the road from the Cottage, Stamford Bridge before the improvements has been described as a 'right dog's dinner'. Pretty accurate when I ventured down King's Road to a football game the first time in 1970 (Chelsea 2 Everton 2).

This was an early-days venture to the gradually improving stadium, which was yet to sport elevated accoutrements: Village and Apartments and Top Ticket Prices. Yes, this was back in the time when pubs were pubs, and not eateries. The thing about the Fulham Broadwayers is that they have always enjoyed a prosperous locality with plentiful nourishment possibilities. Let's just call Chelsea the posh London club.

The goals were scored by four different players, including Gavin Peacock and John Spencer, in a team substantially home-grown, notably stalwart Dennis Wise. Glenn Hoddell was manager, welcoming a Leicester outfit headed by Brian Little, later to defect to Aston Villa.

Chelsea's season performance couldn't be more average, finishing 11th out of 22, with this home record: won 7 drawn 7 lost 7. This result was to no avail for their goal difference, which left them below Southampton on 54 points. Blame the away figures. They were playing a very poor side, in yellow and blue, duly relegated with 15 away defeats. Mind you the home Blues have themselves been responsible for some strangely coloured away strips, like grey and orange, should colours be in any way at fault. Colours, or their choice, must bear some responsibility for upsetting the fans (I speak personally) if not lending to outcomes. In the 2006 World Cup humble pie is due as the only time England donned the obvious red and white – like the flag flying out of car windows, pubs, frontages and the rest up to 1/7/06 (Portugal debacle) – was for their frustrating draw with Sweden. I'm not the only one to be vexed and perplexed by the choice of dark blue, not red. There aren't many blue roses about.

Meanwhile, a few months after the 1994 World Cup (England not in it, WAGS unheard of) Chelsea were flirting with European football, as FA Cup losers, annihilated 0-4 by Manchester United at Wembley. The Traffs had done the double and our friends were awarded admission to the European Cup Winners' Cup as losers. Losers prospering? They had just drawn Austria Memphis of Vienna in the Second Round. Austria Memphis? You may well ask. That outfit was safely removed, opening the way to a creditable European run. The manager went on to sign Ruud Gullit and Mark Hughes. There was a bright future ahead.

Many years later I happened upon a visual gem in the tranquillity of West Brompton Cemetery. On the southern horizon, suspended above the crowded, crumbling tombstones, upwards to mature trees and battered buildings, a delight as tantalizing as the Wizard of Oz's castle. It was the East Stand of Stamford Bridge. The same vista was painted on celluloid in *Eastern Promises*, when after a derby game a young Arsenal fan, complete with scarf and verbal excess, stopped to urinate on a tombstone. In midflow his throat was dramatically cut by members of the other side (a Russian faction, not Chelsea fans, who were portrayed as perfectly behaved). This was during the reign of the accolade and headline regular Special One Jose Mourinho. *BBC* and *Sunday Mirror* commentator Jonathan Pearce, 'the man the fans listen to' reviewed his tenure.

'[His] marriage to Chelsea was as splendid, lurid and ill-starred as Richard Burton's to Liz Taylor. It titillated. It enthralled. It was always going to end in a passionate split…

'For all his posing, Mourinho ended the Arsenal-Manchester United domination and he wouldn't be silenced. He was awkward, belligerent but refreshing. Ultimately, his own character contributed to the downfall. He'd become bigger than the team. Chelsea matches were more about Mourinho than the side…

'Chelsea have started the season poorly, but Mourinho would surely have dragged them around had he not criticised the quality of his squad that one last time. To imply some of the owner's multi-millions [£500m] have been wasted on rotten eggs [e.g. Michael Ballack and Andriy Shevchenko] was the last straw. Unwise? It was suicidal. He had undermined [Roman] Abramovich once too often. It was always going to end in a blaze of anger, frustration and ego.'

In the end the two Premiership titles alone, taking the Blues' grand total to three, speak for themselves as testimony to their ex-boss.


## Wimbledon 0 Manchester City 0
## Division I, 24/1/87

Plough Lane was sandwiched between the roads and immersed in the fumes of SW19, a world away from the pristine grass courts so near yet so far, where Virginia Wade had set hearts a-beating, and St George a-fluttering, a decade earlier. You really don't expect to spot a farm vehicle around here. This was the Dons' first season in the top flight. They finished sixth, their best ever during their 14 seasons among the big boys. Meanwhile the away team were destined for the drop, drawing 15 games and scoring a mere 36 goals. Bogs and I had commenced proceedings in the Windmill at Clapham Common the previous night, a fine local in those days, at a time when Young's was a purely Wandsworth enterprise. All very local. Bedford was better known for bricks than Charles Wells beers. Wells and Young's eventually became very big, finally joining forces. We celebrated the prospect of the high-flying Dons and a hatful of goals with breakfast in a Clapham café, graduating after a book case expedition to Texas Superstore to the Prince of Wales, whose *Good Beer Guide* entry stated the attraction as 'Whitbread (Marlow)'. It's hard to credit that it was actually an enticement at the time. Mind you, Sunday lunchtime saw us in the George at Southwark, that historic National Trust property, to quaff the highly regarded Brakspear bitter.

Looking at my diary for match day we also obtained tickets for *Woza Albert* at the Young Vic in Waterloo that night. I just about recall it as an entertaining piece with a West Indian theme. But then I also wrote *Temba*, a dance performance, at the Young Vic too. Let's move on, to the peach preserve, purchased in tandem with the book case, and devoured with croissants to honour the Sabbath. Messy things, I always think, though Marilyn made her own on the Newcastle visit which were actually pleasant to negotiate. Bogs always had trouble with furniture. I had to suffer his choice of inflatable mattress more than once. It took ages to pump up, a la bicyclette, and subsided in a sneaky and speedy manner soon after lights out.

We took a bus to SW19. Concerning the game, I inscribed 'somebody should have won', a portentous remark in view of the final table. Despite the paucity of penetration it remains a typical frantic and fun weekend memory. Who needs goals?


## Crystal Palace 1 Stoke City 0
## Division II, 9/5/89

Rickles and I joined forces for this visit to Selhurst Park for a kind of Stoke reunion. He had been the House Manager at the Victoria Theatre during my time there. He was now at Theatre Centre, London, and I was approaching the end of a contract with a West End theatre producer, who has since been much associated with the Stanley Park blue team. We had some comparisons to make on an evening tinged with reminiscence. For reasons obscured by time the game overran and we only just made the Flounder and Firkin, close by (relying on memory here – Rickles was just as befuddled), as a reward for the endurance suffered. My companion was a Manchester United supporter.

One Palace claim to fame is their colour change from claret and blue to red and blue, certainly what we witnessed in 1989. The ebullient Malcolm Allison is credited with this decision, arising from a loan of kits from Aston Villa in 1973. It's surprising how many clubs have changed their colours over time. Nowadays identity seems to be strongly related to the style and colour of the home strip, but only that.

The next year Crystal Palace reached no. 50 in the hit parade with their rendering of the Dave Clark Five's 'Glad all over', coupled with 'Where Eagles fly'. It only lasted two weeks in the charts. Just think: that was 139 years after the Great Exhibition at the original Crystal Palace.

Here is a case history of aspects of football in old-fashioned amateurism. A certain Edgar Elliott (Rutz's grandfather) played for 'the Glaziers' in 1907, when Palace were an average side in the Southern League. Palace Reserves ('Cardinal & Blue Jerseys, White Knickers') were playing Depot Battalion R.E. ('Red & Blue Jerseys, Blue Knickers' – Cardinal and Red sound somewhat similar, but the knickers had it, it seems) in the South Eastern League Championship.

His invitation was inscribed thus, on a postcard headed up 'Crystal Palace Football Club, Limited. Registered Office: Crystal Palace, Sydenham. S.E.:

*Dear Sir*
*You have been selected to play at Crystal Palace on Saturday next Nov 9th.*

*If unable to do so please let us know per return.*
*Yours truly*
*E F Goodman*
*Kick-off 3-0 c'*

Written in the margin was: 'bring your boots with you' – nudge nudge wink wink (for your payment). Posted at 5.30pm in Norwood, the destination, his address, was close – Thornton Heath. 'Per return' must have been understood as a seriously immediate matter, the missive having been sent 21.5 hours before kick off. The Programicard (= programme) was *No. XIII* and cost one penny (16 sepia pages 5" x 3.5"). It informed that the Upper Norwood Prize Band was to play five pieces 'before the match and during the interval', including a selection from Sullivan's *Mikado*. A page was devoted to Nevill's Turkish Baths, 'unapproachable in beauty of design, scientific ventilation, excellence in heating, comfort in dressing-rooms, capability of the shampooers, and general attention'. There aren't many such havens surviving now.

Mr Elliott was employed first by Hammond and Hussey's Builders' Merchants, then by Croydon Borough Council through to his retirement in 1937. He represented the former in many a cricket game, 'one of those stalwarts…a stylish batsman with many graceful strokes he headed the team's batting averages and was also more than a useful bowler' (local newspaper clipping) and quondam captain of Croydon Amateur CC. He was allowed considerable time off from the Borough Treasurer's Department for sporting pursuits including keeping goal, among other positions, for the Glaziers.

## Charlton Athletic 2 Bradford City 0
## Premiership, 4/11/00

Some aspects of this fixture were predictable, though in no way reducing the enjoyment of the occasion. The Addicks (compare with the Wigan and Oldham 'Latic' Athletics) retained their unbeaten home record; the Bantams had still had only one away point and a single goal. Jonatan Johansson, one of the goal scorers, was the September Internet player of the month.

Attendances were amazingly uniform – 20,043 at each of the first five home League games, tabulated the programme. It was not surprising that there have been moves to increase the capacity to around 26,000 by redeveloping the north stand. This was the modern era's latest twist of fate, with the dereliction of the Eighties still a recent memory. The Valley has only survived, thrived, as a football emporium through the determination of a few individuals. Operations have moved out and back in twice. At the time of the company's greatest woes emerged a committed, pragmatic group ultimately forming a political party. This hurt locally as Labour yielded voters to it. Bob, who joined the Dag/Red party in February 2008 (the final foray), enlightened me about the background to the resurrection of the Valley. More might have been elicited from his memory bank had I reunited with him in time for the day out in 2000, as he lived in Charlton. A fine yarn-spinner was Bob. The reunion was all too late, however.

We should try another time, though the Addicks would probably not be in the top flight, as they were for this single visit with Bogs. The local character may suggest an ingrained acceptance of the club's varied fortunes, but threatened extinction elicited the raising of hackles with fundamental effect. Surely enforced occupation of detested Selhurst, and Upton, Parks helped to drive the changes through.

It was difficult to visualize the immense bowl of the original Valley ground on this site, which hosted 75,031 against the Villa in the Fifth Round of the FA Cup in 1938. That was their golden age. The Addicks finished second, fourth and third in the First Division before the War, were runners-up and winners of the FA Cup immediately after it, and crowds averaging over 40,000 put them in an elite group. This ground was formerly the biggest in the English League, though never in competition with more exotic London stadia for presentation of high profile events, like FA Cup semi-finals. It's a mite paradoxical that its latterday capacity has turned out to be inadequate. The stadium in Y2K was neat and focussed rather than attractive. The fans made it a comfortable, relaxed environment.

A significant part of the credit for the club's continued support was due to Alan Curbishley, the energetic manager nine years into his 14-year reign at this time. The club won admirers up and down the country over this period. That is what Bogs and I experienced in this saunter to south-east London. There was no Underground service to deliver us but an easy overland trip from Waterloo East, Charlton Station being close to the ground with ample fare in a suburban area up the hill, including welcoming pub conversation. Quite up-market really. A mere £20 got us in, the game modestly reassuring as Charlton eased to the expected three points. The opposition were nearing the end of their two-season flirtation with the Premiership. This was one of 14 defeats on their travels. Their destiny was relegation in bottom place.


## Millwall 1 Wolverhampton Wanderers 2
## Championship, 22/1/05

### 1. Ticket Procurement

Three seasons' worth of false alarms were endured in respect of the New Den, caused by a chronic problem of ticket procurement.

**2002-03.** Originally Bogs and I worked out the best weekend for 48 hours of cultural indulgence hung on visiting the New Den. I made phone calls, establishing at an early stage that it might be possible to obtain tickets for the game. The designated fixture was a January comfort session against Watford. When the appointed day arrived for remaining tickets to go on sale, I telephoned. They were all gone. At that time we accepted the situation, as a) it was too late to try friends; b) we were sure we could make it the next season. We still had a great weekend (Theatres 2 Football 0), but it became an unanswered question. How?

**2003-04.** The attempt was keener. We identified a date when a number of activities were listed in London, including a game at the New Den. Rotherham were the opponents and there appeared to be an obscure kind of chemistry between two such unlikely antagonists – the last three results in this fixture had been 4-0, 1-0, 0-6. However, it was also FA Cup Round 5, and Millwall, having disposed of Telford

United in Round 4 (0-2), were drawn at home to Burnley that day, 1-0 the reckoning. In fact they were on their game all the way to their Millennium Stadium encounter with Manchester United.

One fateful and bitterly cold day Bogs trawled to the ground only to be turned away. He was told (the gist was) that we needed membership. Negative vibrations surrounding the New Den were exacerbated by a pelting of snowballs from brats. The poor chap sludged back to the station, empty-handed and soggy-gloved. We agreed it to be somewhat excessive to become official supporters for a single visit. Membership might have prompted untold mailing-list consequences. I had my own contacts who had undertaken to assist in getting home tickets. The contacts all failed. One had left his firm, so the number was no use, one (Graham) had just terminated his season ticket and the third confirmed that, actually, he was unable to get any more tickets – and naturally he wanted to attend the game. That guy also expressed surprise that the general public were, in effect, banned. Even if he offered them to us, the membership issue would have been an impediment. We surrendered, our much delayed football visit finally delayed until after Spurs in March 2005. (The rearranged fixture resulted as follows: Millwall 2 Millers 1. Well, three goals…)

**2004-05.** Bogs admitted to preferring Tottenham, as he was only inclined to see one more game in his remaining months in the capital. I still needed to experience the New Den, and I discovered an alternative means of access. I had met a Wolves season-ticket-holder and Millwall were due to host them on a convenient Saturday in the near future – this should relieve the gloom of late January. Here was a glimmer of hope. Could we prosper as away supporters? The season-ticket-holder went to every home game and a lot of away ones, but she replied to none of my messages after initial enthusiasm, admittedly over sundry pints at a Bev Bevan gig (be named and shamed, Ms Jopday – this is what happens when you rely on a woman to come up with the goods by text contact!), so I eventually tried ringing Molineux direct. It was so easy. The first phone call established the date when tickets became available; the second, on said date, saw the credit card purchase of two tickets, which duly arrived a few days later.

This was a lesson learned for the more difficult grounds. Be away. Not something you'd always choose but expedient and apparently the only way of achieving at least this goal, at some grounds. It may seem obvious with hindsight, but this was new to us.

## 2. The Adventure

The actual event emerged as a phenomenon along the lines intended above, but with Wakey – eat your heart out, Bogs! I hoped he was enjoying a Valletta team well away from all this London tribulation. His particular culinary craving was for aubergines – done by some Italian method. There should be dishes aplenty for him in the Med. Having feasted on the Whitechapel Art Gallery and pubs near the tube station including a lush and lengthy fry-up, we were lagging behind schedule. Scrutinizing the A to Z, and preferring the tube to the overland railway, we ran out of time, being forced to sprint the last leg from Surrey Quays station to the ground. On the home straight we were helped by a charming truncheon (collective noun? I know of no other) of police by the Bolina Road bridge. The last bit was easy, passing an impressive array of coaches from the West Midlands and more police, on horseback, taking a break as the game had started. Our seats were at the extremity of the away allocation nearest to deafening home fans, under a majestic scoreboard.

The New Den North Stand afforded good sightlines and the whole stadium was well balanced and compact, with a capacity of less than 20,000. Impressive but intimate, quite unlike what I recalled of the old Den. Others like it less, I've found.

Wolves scored the winning goal in the last minute. The atmosphere, electric throughout, erupted, involving appropriate sign language, chants and fervour. Shortly after that it was all over. All around us were bouncing up and down on the concrete. The home supporters bulged out of the stadium, while we Wolvos remained incarcerated. Having eventually been released we found that the dispersal system had ensured that the street, the way we'd come and the only way back, was deserted. Coaches were leaving and South Bermondsey railway station nearby, in a different direction, no doubt took a horde of residual fans. There was no police presence in our direction and we had to return to Surrey Quays under the unprepossessing bridge down the rutted lane. It was a bit worrying, given the tales of woe and aggression perpetrated about, maybe by, Millwall supporters, this route being known as the one dedicated to the North Stand – kamikaze end. Our fears were eventually allayed when we got to the police combo, still there hours later, heralding civilization and at last the tube stop. The excitement wasn't over yet. The waiting East London line conveyance, already close to capacity, was delayed because of a dog leaping to its doom further up the line. What attention seeking!

## West Ham United 3 Stoke City 1
### Division I, 20/12/75

This was a coach trip from Stoke-on-Trent to see my adopted boys on the road to Upton Park. The game was a pre-Christmas interlude down the M6 and M1, I seem to remember to avoid the alternative – shopping in Hanley. So I swapped one scrum for another.

West Ham were tending to win at home and lose away, something they reinforced this time. It was halfway through the season, QPR were top, with three other clubs on 28 points. Had three points for a win been introduced by then (not far off: 1981-82), Rangers would have been fourth, as draw specialists: 10 out of 21. Unlike my visit to Upton Park for the Villa 19 years later, we just strolled to the away turnstiles, coughed up and endured a defeat. But we were in a congregation some of whom I knew from Stoke's home games. The common factor was to get to the game having already imbibed, our reward a protected environment.

A visit to Upton Park, in a rough, aggressive area, has traditionally been a worrying experience. This deteriorated in the 1970s and 1980s when fight-promoting 'firms' prowled abroad. You didn't want to become a victim on the streets of East London. In connection with firms were the *Top Boys*, the subject of Cass Pennant, subtitled 'true stories of football's hardest men'. West Ham's Teddy Bunter firm featured a member of the eponymous family, the top boy known as 'Bunter', waxing lyrical at the memory of countrywide encounters, including fights at Old Trafford ('in the '80s') before and after a game ('the Old Bill didn't have a clue. It just kept going and going'), and of the first leg of the 1972 League Cup Semi-Final at Stoke. He suffered golf ball damage to his head ('a fucking big lump'), but the firm 'took...their end'. That tie went to four games, the Potters going on to win at Wembley. At home in 1970 Teddy Bunter would meet in East London pubs. 'We all had a go and never bottled anything...It got bigger and bigger and other people joined in...Got well known all over West Ham.'

Within the Boleyn Ground all was basic, with compressed terraces pulsating with upwards of 30k fans making an undeniable contribution to the Hammers' good home record. Near the ground Ken's café, walls plastered with local stars, did great greasy meals, seriously more expensive on match days, I've heard.

Here is a comparison. At New Year 2008 Hammers fan Russell Brand went to the Emirates:

'...I don't often attend away games and even as we approached the magnificent arena the angst of unfamiliarity was all about me. The people drinking outside the pubs on the Blackstock Road were not of my fraternity; lacking there was the bonhomie of the frequently defeated, replaced instead by a peculiar sense of assurance; men louchely swilled back booze safe in the knowledge that they were not about to witness a bout of lazy humiliation.

'It was a world away from the gallows good will of Green Street where a lunatic pervasion of detached joy prevails, revellers indifferently jig and swirl, regardless of the likelihood of 90 minutes of torture, like a gin-bleached hag merrily giving suck to a stiff blue tot.'

*I'm forever blowing bubbles*, the standard Hammers song initiating the afternoon's real proceedings, came across as light relief when you'd made it safely to your segment of terrace or stand. But not so long ago Hammers home games were notorious for racial abuse. Joining the club in 1969 Bermudan Clyde Best, a dazzling centre forward, worked his way from taunt target to crowd favourite, becoming 'a powerful role model for many black youngsters when he played up front for West Ham United' (*Black Lions* by Rodney Hinds). But he has to be seen as a rare one-off, playing

186 games and scoring 47 goals up to his departure in 1976.

A handful of years later John Barnes, son of a Jamaican army colonel, played for Watford (1981-87). 'I remember as far back as 1981 playing at places like Millwall and West Ham when you'd get the usual monkey noises and bananas thrown onto the pitch" recalls Barnes later. 'I considered those people to be ignorant so why would I show them the respect even to entertain whatever they were saying to me [e.g. 'nigger']?... It was like water off a duck's back.' He was preordained to serve the anti-racist cause as a consequence of his dazzling skills for the Hornets, then Liverpool (1987-97) and for England (79 games between 1983 and 1995). Rodney Hinds wrote of racism: "When black players represented the English national team in the 1980s they still had to endure racism from a section of England supporters. John Barnes was singled out for similar treatment both at home and abroad. In the summer of 1984 during the national team's tour of South America, he was subjected to booing and racial taunts by English fans.'

During an Everton v Liverpool game: 'Who could ever forget the image of Barnes back-heeling a banana thrown by a so-called supporter (in the late 1980's)? It was a sign of dark times for black players. The situation seems light-years away now but Barnes and the rest had to be great survivors as well as players…he is a player who still has question marks raised about his career. I believe it is fair to say that if Barnes had been white he would have been celebrated in much the same way as Gascoigne, Shearer and Lineker.'

The time was to come when West Ham appointed a black player team captain in midfielder Nigel Reo-Coker (transferred to Aston Villa in 2007), in the new-century climate where price tags and international reputations were established as paramount. Was it as recent as 1991 that '[Ron] Noades, then Chairman of Crystal Palace, suggested that black players were not able to do what white English players were able to do, especially in inclement weather?'

## Leyton Orient 4 Scunthorpe United 1
## Division IV, 13/5/89

Clapton Orient and just 'Orient' they had been, but we visited Leyton Orient at dear old Brisbane Road, deep in nether eastern Central Line territory. The ground has enjoyed a variety of name changes too: Osborne Road, Leyton Stadium and eventually Matchroom Stadium, though in common parlance it will always be Brisbane Road and was still just so in 2008-9 in the *Racing & Football Outlook Guide*. But as at Shepherd's Bush the setting and process were a routine part of life in London. The journey was by car from Islington, an easy map-reading exercise for me as passenger, maturing into an intriguing stops-and-starts matter connecting parts of London I had previously dipped into in isolation. This was dots joining and proved educational. But like the teaching process it needed repetition to bed down in memory, an elusive facility in this quest. There are locations all over the country destined to be assimilated once and forgotten soon afterwards. I was glad for the luxury of observation not concentration, with thumb on map. Match day in Leyton, not many stones' throws from White Hart Lane, Highbury and Upton Park, seemed to be just there, something going on in a mixed, busy, working community. The ground itself was unsurprising, modest and simple, overlooked by tower blocks and industry. Leyton Orient's Brisbane Road was humble but bright and welcoming. Later developments were the product of the new age of funding and building: two stands erected in a few years, paid for by residential proceeds on the sale of space on all four corners. This is in contrast to the *public* houses near each corner of Griffin Park, Brentford on the opposite side on London. The modern Matchroom Stadium offers the curious aspect (at least from row F of the stand where we were sheltering from the elements) of a balcony occupied during the game by family, friends, tabby cat, beach ball and various vessels of liquid, and much to-ing and fro-ing. I wonder what the purchase premium was for a whole pitch view. Connected with the Griffin Park phenomenon, perhaps, was the choice of Leyton Orient Supporters Club in 2006 as CAMRA's Greater London Club of the Year. Having supped excellent ale at the equivalent entity at the Millennium Stadium and the other St James' Park in the same year, I can vouch for the improving opportunities for drinking by football providers. The fans really are a civilized lot and deserve to be treated as adults. I'm sure Andrew Lloyd Webber may be counted among this number. His devotion to the Orient is such that 'he attended Elton John's 50th birthday party dressed as a Leyton Orient supporter – Madeleine Lloyd Webber dressed as a bunny girl' (*The Stage*). 'Any dream will do' you might say.

This was the last game of the season with everything to play for in the realm of automatic promotion (Scunthorpe, not Orient) and the also-rans' carrot of play-offs. Before the game the top of the table looked like this:

|  | Pld | Pts |
|---|---|---|
| Rotherham | 45 | 81 |
| Tranmere | 45 | 79 |
| Scunthorpe | 45 | 77 |
| Crewe | 45 | 77 |
| Scarborough | 45 | 74 |
| Leyton Orient | 45 | 72 |
| Wrexham | 45 | 68 |

We were treated to a thriller, featuring a hat trick from Mark Cooper. Scunthorpe arrived, portentously, with the best away record in Division IV. Though they had more to play for, they were eclipsed by the Orient turning it on, on the day. Meanwhile, through a customary fixture-list quirk, Crewe were at Tranmere, and drew 1-1. Both secured promotion. The nail-biting play-off semi-finals were to involve both the O's and the Iron. Given the table above, and my sudden affiliation to the club which had pulled out the stops for this, my sole visit, it is warming to relate that Wrexham beat Scunthorpe 5-1 over the two legs. Orient overcame Scarborough 2-1 on aggregate, going on to squeeze past the Welshmen 2-1 in the final. In those days it was a home-and-away affair (0-0, 2-1), not yet accorded the exaggerated glory of a day out at a national stadium.

## Tottenham Hotspur 2 Manchester City 1
## Premiership, 19/3/05

A day trip to White Hart Lane was Bogs's special request in his last football season in London. The following year was to see him battling with Maltese plumbing and reflecting quietly on the balcony (yet to be built) in the mid-Med sun. He had decided enough was enough of the daily grind which is a worker's lot, especially in the Capital. It's called the rat race and is, if anything, worse for someone in their fifties in a senior position, working late, and still taking papers and worries home.

On a brilliant sunny day – spring had well and truly arrived at least for this experience – we happened first upon the Beehive, Southleigh Road, where we settled down in the garden to sup ale and read the papers. Pints later we meandered up Tottenham High Road, managing a quick one at the Butcher's Arms in sight of the ground. This was a home supporters' pub with some space, but with the inimitable buzz anticipating the imminent skirmish. The mass of home colours, mainly current-year shirts, on men (and some off as it was sunbathing weather, despite the date), and women and children too, was a display in itself. Kick-off was nigh but there was, we divined, enough time to down one last pint. No problem. We sampled the 'garden at rear' (back yard), assuming positions on a wall to observe the debris of a mass match day session.

A curiosity occurred as we entered the ground. I was apprehended by an official who confiscated the lid, only, off my plastic water bottle. I was so surprised at the inanity of this that I failed to query it. Why the top and only the top? Was it not perceived that I could have waxed aggressive with the uncapped vessel?

Fuckin' Dave's double membership (with Nice Lady, naturally) had served to get us in at the away end, and very good seats they were, on the corner with a refreshing oblique line of vision. I wouldn't choose that angle on a regular basis, just as sitting in the choir behind a symphony orchestra is fun, for a change, as long as the concert doesn't involve a singer projecting in the opposite direction. After this the quest for the 92 would not need further help from Dave. I might be let off the driving. He does know the route to eastern Manchester very well by now. On the other hand he was threatening to give up the season tickets, as maintaining such loyalty was proving to be unduly draining in several ways.

White Hart Lane, belying the suggestion of quaintness in the name (like Golden Hillock Road, in an area of congested industry and housing, on an obscure route to St Andrews, Birmingham), was a smart modern stadium. It cut the mustard for that label. The look was at odds with my memory from the previous visit in 1979, when I recall a vacant look – a stand missing. My companion that time, a Spurs fan, Alan, out of Slough, suffered excessive difficulty in parking and we missed the first twenty minutes. This time was a good thing and served to expunge that memory.

Did you know that the home team, whose logo features a domestic fowl, has spawned fanzines with the entrancing titles *Cock-a-Doodle-Doo* and *The*

*Circumcised Cockerel?* Perhaps the latter was connected with the Muslim element of Spurs' following, who might prefer the term 'muslimani', a sanitized expression to use in polite society for the skinning procedure? But in fact they are better known for a Jewish fan base, exercising a similar ritual. They also used to play in dark blue.

The ground was on the busy main thoroughfare in a multicultural area with stalls on the streets purveying all manner of goodies, including a bhaji item I chose for lunch, with the water bottle, most of whose contents I had downed prior to the incident. It was tepid by then anyway.

Then the game at last: presenting typical Premiership qualities, the outcome a workmanlike home win. The programme was a shiny three-quidder, not my favourite variety, or price. I raised a smile at page 62: 'Ticket Office Match Info', conveying the impression that punters would actually be able to get tickets that way. I reckon it was justified still to smart from the failed attempts at admission. The season was three-quarters gone and both teams solidly average, with little difference between home and away form. Spurs overcame an early deficit to secure the win, not least through the efforts of England's begloved star of the future, Paul Robinson.

Here are the two teams' respective positions at the time of the match and in the final table:

| | P | HOME | | | AWAY | | | Pts | Posn |
| | | W | D | L | W | D | L | | |
|---|---|---|---|---|---|---|---|---|---|
| Tottenham Hotspur | 28 | 6 | 3 | 5 | 5 | 3 | 6 | 39 | 8 |
| | 38 | 9 | 5 | 5 | 5 | 5 | 9 | 52 | 9 |
| Manchester City | 29 | 5 | 5 | 5 | 4 | 4 | 6 | 36 | 11 |
| | 38 | 8 | 6 | 5 | 5 | 7 | 7 | 52 | 8 |

There is something and nothing to note: both teams got onto a roll at home; over 300,000 tickets were sold for standard top-level fare. There was no cup interest left, though Spurs had reached the last eight of both knock-out competitions.

Afterwards we had to find a practical way to get to the South Bank Centre. We decided upon a brisk walk to Seven Sisters Station on the comparatively efficient Victoria Line. This was very good exercise, compensating a mite for the few days without swims. Often Bogs and I had been to Clapham Baths but not this time, as the schedule was packed with more elevated delights. We now sped past the majestic face and public image of Tottenham, with a number of buildings, including the Town Hall, which stood out for their pride in a less obviously prosperous neck of the woods. The Victoria Line experience duly enjoyed, we met Ena for a pre-concert meal in a restaurant in Waterloo. Customers, seated, were duly notified, by way of a tantalizing device alerting all within bleep shot, that they should now fetch their plateful: a handset which flashed red. The chicken concoction was fine, my taste buds still registering the bhaji up until then. Ena was intrigued by the tale of our afternoon expedition and recorded interest in trying football sometime. She was to do so in Leyton - the beach ball occasion.

We relished a discreet London Philharmonic Orchestra concert. The main work was Brahms' 2nd Symphony which followed a premiere of a trombone piece by Mark Anthony Turnage. It all followed through smoothly from the football adventure. But I struggled to stay awake, such had been the excitement.

After more cultural exposure on the Sunday, Bogs and I parted, ostensibly to share his Mediterranean experience sometime. It mustn't end like Foxy after England's 1996 expiration. It didn't, and I almost got to see Hibernians FC.


## Arsenal 1 Nottingham Forest 3
## Division I, 11/3/89

The best has been left until last: my Eighties visit to Highbury to see them thumped by Forest. What joy!

To attend this thrill and Orient's display within a few weeks seems with hindsight to have been my compensation for enduring a gruelling six months' toil in London. I departed as the football season drew to a close to convert London into a place of passing delights as an eternal guest.

Arsenal Stadium, as it was termed in the programme, and they should know, was curiously cramped for an entity which so completely dominated all that surrounded it, surviving pretty well a double bombing in the War. The ground was harmonious and has boasted to be one of the best, most balanced. Unlike the Reebok or Stamford Bridge it was written that light permeates through the whole area. No pitch patches. Meanwhile it was one of the smallest, no doubt contributing to the experience. In fact the stadium became so restricted, given the massive support the club's success has generated, that they used Wembley as their venue when they could on the way to the Emirates Stadium.

Meanwhile, back in 1989, the Gunners were five points clear of Norwich at the top, having only succumbed once before at home, 2-3 in their first game, to the magical Villa. The remainder of the season was to prove a cliff-hanger, as Liverpool, at this stage with 39 points against the Arse's 55, only dropped four more points in their remaining 14 game to finish level on points, both with a goal difference of 37. At one stage the Woolwich seemed to have blown it, but memorably overcame Liverpool 2-0 in the process of winning their first title for 18 years.

Smugness prevailed for this experience, however, as the Arse bottomed out, so to speak. While we're on bottoms, Arsenal were voted the Sexiest Team by members of the Gay Football Supporters Network in 2005 and 2006, eliciting such comments as 'he can fill my Calvins anytime' of Freddie Ljungberg and, of 2006 Best Player Thierry Henry, that he had 'cock sucker lips'. At the negative end of the vote, Jose Mourinho was top hate figure in 2006, enhanced from runner-up to Alex Ferguson the previous year. Our Wayne was 'Biggest Turn-Off' both times. The aim of GFSN, established in 1989, was to link together gay and lesbian supporters of football. 'Whether you want to chat, drink, play or watch, there are members across the UK who would welcome you.' It has spawned an active league, comprising teams with such delicious names as Yorkshire Terriers (11 a side winners in 2004-05; quarter finalists in Gay World Cup in 2008'), London Leftfooters (reached the semi final of the Cup in Copenhagen in 2005; the Leftfooters are the popular favourites), Leicester Wildcats (won the 5 a side competition every year from 1999 to 2003) and Brighton Belle Ends. Unfortunately a misguided perception of decency crept in regarding the last. Fund raising considerations also played a part. They were renamed 'Bandits' – tame or what! - in competition with the Wildcats and Terriers. Around that time a controversy came to the fore surrounding the naming of a stand at the City of Manchester Stadium, after its prominent son, Colin Bell. The contributions on Radio 4's Today programme about the meaning of 'Bell end' were a welcome diversion. Ultimately it became identified as the 'West (Colin Bell) Stand'.

Man City are meanwhile to be applauded in Alex Williams, their Director of Community Affairs, speaking in favour of the Football Association's campaign against homophobia in football, following Village Manchester FC's liaison with the FA. Well-known Defender Danny Mills was pictured in a photo shoot on the subject.

And here's a chant from the Terriers to the tune of the Village People's *Go West*:

> *Together we will ride the crest*
> *Together we will stand the test*
> *Together we will play our best*
> *Together and we'll shag the rest*
> *Woof woof for the Terriers* (x4).

I shall always return to Thamesville for games, as a norm an exhilarating slot among what makes our capital great – live and artistic presentations not seen out of town. Senior football fixtures will always provide joy, despite not engaging a sense of loyalty, which resides elsewhere.

It's essential, though, to check the newspaper or *What's On/ Time Out* listing before allocating the slot to the package of 'a London football game', to avoid disappointment. It might be the Orient's turn for a Monday Sky spot. Also how about giving AFC Wimbledon or Uxbridge a whirl for a change: Wimbledon to support a virtuous and worthwhile endeavour and Uxbridge for random fun? In fact I'd like to do what I read someone did once and follow the FA Cup trail all the way through from the Preliminary Round. He chose Tividale in the West Midlands. I shall examine the draw some year.

The sum of all the events may or may not prove greater than its parts. 'At the end of the day' we'll know whether it was worth it. It generally is. You can always make good by choosing something else on offer.

# Chapter Five
# Romance and Residences

## The Notts, The Potteries, The Villa, The Bristols, The Grecians

These have formed my preoccupation and focus over the decades, so merit greater coverage. There's simply more to tell. Each has developed a different character. The Notts and the Potteries were life phases, Bristol continues, the Villa does too as a regular M5 migrant, and Exeter is for ever.

## 1. The Notts

My first visit to Nottingham was a prelude to Nottingham Forest's relegation and my own degree course, as I became a term-time resident a few weeks later. The West Ham game fitted in with a sneak preview at the end of a camping holiday in Yorkshire. Then in the first term I ended up, more by luck than judgement, occupying a bed-sit in a blind alley adjacent to the City Ground with an unhelpful view of about a quarter of it. It was enough to get the Forest ball rolling, football being something already routine with new college friends. After all, the red and white bunch was the top team in the city. Notts County were considered also-rans, or rather, not considered. They had just ascended as basement champions.

It was the first time I had been exposed to football as part of daily life. I was a Southerner, fresh from diverse and cosmopolitan London, with no experience of regional cities or a perspective assuming 'Saturday' to mean the pints and the match.

Real loyalty to a team was still in the future, Nottingham being an accommodating place, where the rivalry and passion heard of in football hotbeds were less obvious. There seemed no definable area of loyalty dedicated to either of the clubs, or, as far as I knew, pubs with strong allegiances. The Trent Navigation, the closest to Meadow Lane and convenient for the City Ground, would host supporters of each club alternately.

Notts County were originally just 'Notts' situated on the north side of the Trent – within the city. Forest's ground was in view on the south bank, nudging the wide Trent, the Borough of Rushcliffe now its local authority. Both Nottingham in character, of course, but the wrong way round for complete sense. To their friends they are 'Notts' and 'Forest' but non-cognoscenti insist on 'County' for short and for the other club sometimes the abbreviation 'Notts', not 'Nottm', Forest. It just isn't right. It's as annoying as the false apostrophes in plurals on market stalls, and 'whilst' when 'while' will do.

Notts had a claim to fame as the original Football League club, coming into being in 1862. However, Forest had the greater success over the years. In the 1970s, a century on, fortunes changed in both directions.

|         | Nottm Forest   | Notts County   |
|---------|----------------|----------------|
| 1970-71 | Div I  : 16    | Div IV :  1    |
| 1971-72 | Div I  : 21    | Div III :  4   |
| 1972-73 | Div II : 14    | Div III :  2   |
| 1973-74 | Div II :  7    | Div II  : 10   |
| 1974-75 | Div II : 16    | Div II  : 14   |
| 1975-76 | Div II :  8    | Div II  :  5   |

Those years were good to Notts, but all was to change again with the advent of Brian Clough. It was to prove to be not only the stuff of romance – Forest won the 1978 Championship immediately after promotion in third place. The *Racing and Football Outlook* comment for 1977-78 included: 'if they [Forest] have belief in their ability they should make the grade back among the top sides…Brian Clough back in the big-time…' They proceeded to win the League and back-to-back European Cups. And one effect was a sea change in football support in Nottingham.

Anticipating the phenomenon to be experienced, by turns, by Liverpool, Manchester United and Arsenal, new support was generated all over the country. People far away from the area became part of the new band of Forest fans, those who didn't know Nottingham from Notting Hill. They would be ignorant of Notts. Meadow Lane was a few hundred yards away but off the football map. The enthusiasm for Forest was palpable on my return visits to the City Ground in the period after leaving the area. And Clough may not be popular with Magpies supporters on another count.

There was an initiative by the City Council, which owned both sites, to build a 45k all-seater stadium for both clubs on the site of Wilford Power Station, just down the Trent. Who vetoed this meritorious(?) prospect? Yes, Ol' Big 'Ead. He was safeguarding Forest's interests. With hindsight it seems that the local authority's manoeuvre was a victim of bad timing. It could have become the model for shared stadia all over the country. Notts weren't averse to the idea of sharing and were later hoisted by this outcome: 'following the events of Hillsborough in April 1989, legal requirements for clubs in the top two divisions to have all-seater stadiums forced County's hand in having to redevelop Meadow Lane' (Christopher Rooney). Eventually making it to Trent Bridge for England's expungement of New Zealand in the final 2008 Test Match, the six spanking new floodlights over the cricket ground served to augment the crowdedness of the skyline when approaching from Nottingham station. The programme (£5) contained a reference to the lights at neighbouring Nottingham Forest and Notts County "which, by comparison, look like tatty old standard lamps. Just occasionally cricket can lead and football will follow." Apparently inspiration was drawn from Arsenal's Emirates Stadium. Those at Trent Bridge were undoubtedly stylish and seductive, and I heard more than one comment expressing a wish to see them when switched on at night. But I still like the traditional look - the City Ground pylons remain a fine example.

## Nottingham Forest 1 West Ham United 0
## Division I, 21/8/71

"We hate Nottingham Forest' chanted the Hammers travellers ad nauseam. It rolled off the tongue so well, even better than 'Tottenham Hotspur'. I felt an ominous surge that this was the first of many exposures to the already tedious chant. In the early 1970s, coming from the odd game at Chelsea, the City Ground became mingled with student lifestyle-inculcated interest and loyalty. I would indeed be paying the ground regular visits. Like never before I sensed the common bond of team support, mainly with other students, many of whom were already immersed in the culture from different cities. The bonding process made for ongoing camaraderie, getting acclimatized to all the trappings. It was a magical awakening.

This occasion, before I'd registered for three years in the East Midlands, was an encouraging prelude. Not so the aftermath. Bogs and I got back to the car to find its tyres slashed. And he was short-changed in a jazz pub in the city centre later on. But to kick off the crawl Yates's Wine Lodge was special – slugs of port served in the glasses of the house. The Nottingham Yates's evoked a Wyoming saloon, with swing doors and an upstairs gallery, not to mention the occasional sonorous group in the guise of a Palm Court Orchestra. I was to spend birthday evenings there, which tended to clash with end-of-year exams. I seem to remember the Augustan poets were there somewhere.

Forest were a sorry side that season, winning only five more times at home and going down with Huddersfield. But I wasn't going to mind about the paucity of good results.

Their ground was to me an appealing presence to latch onto: a predominantly red landmark on the south bank of the Trent, before the erection of the Executive Stand, startlingly tall and to be seen from the city centre, which I returned to gasp at in the next decade.

On one occasion a bunch of us were suffering from exposure at the City Ground for a postponed FA Cup Third Round tie (we chose this as reward after a punishing Geography experience), when, at 81 minutes in pea-souper fog, with Forest and West Brom locked at 1-1, the referee blew his whistle to abandon it. The handy Trent Bridge Inn glimmered marginally brighter to offer solace. The replayed game finished 0-0, the Baggies at last clinching it 3-1. They were a division higher, destined to join Forest in the Second Division that August (1973).

Nottingham Forest 2 Luton Town 1 was the first FA Cup final I remember (previous win 1898). In March 2008 the *News of the World* reported 'Pink panties given to the wives of 1959 FA Cup-winners Nottingham Forest should fetch £500 at an auction next week'. The headline: 'Undie the hammer'. A month later appeared the result Nottingham Forest 1 Luton Town 0, a third tier fixture, with the Hatters already relegated to the basement. Sad, really.

## Notts County 3 Halifax Town 1
## Div III, 12/3/72

It is curious to note that Notts, not Forest, were in the ascendancy at this time, but they only overtook the bigger club the season after it was all over for us fly-by-nights. Visits to Meadow Lane were low-key, laidback affairs and a kind of light relief. That was often necessary after a well-oiled Friday night. Mickey G didn't always manage his full share of lager the lunchtime after; I don't think I did either, though it would never have been lager. Bramley Steve was keen on football, and pints, as well. There remains the vivid memory of Sunderland's triumph over Leeds United in the 1973 Cup Final. Beer was spilt as we overemoted after Ian Porterfield's goal. The shambolic Meadow Lane ground had character and, though near to the River Trent, the impression was of traditional back-street setting. The club has seen very little violence over the years.

We must have witnessed the chant: 'I had a wheel barrow, the wheel fell off,' to the tune of *Old Smokey*, and, in the modern era, 'It's just like watching Juve', a reference to the Magpies' black and white stripes. An example of the influence of British football abroad is the choice by Juventus of a black and white striped strip, mimicking Notts County's. Mind you, 'only in Italy would a political party – the Forza Italia of Silvio Berlusconi, AC Milan owner and former PM – take its name from a soccer chant, a national team manager sprinkle holy water on pitches, or stars of a World Cup winning team [in 2006] be under investigation in a match fixing scandal.' (*Calcio: A History of Italian Football* by John Foot.)

Notts did better than Forest in the FA Cup in 1971-72, reaching the Fourth Round, not much of a claim to fame, but a straw to grasp. The following season they were set to make their debut in the League Cup semi-finals, but Chelsea beat them 3-1 in the Fifth Round.

*The Knots*

*Then Forest triumphed here, and there,*
*With Brian Clough the man.*
*Since then they've yielded to despair*
*The bank has nothing left to spare –*
*League 1 was not the plan.*

*And Notts at last were free, untied,*
*Administration taped*
*For much too long, the oldest side*
*Locked in and close to suicide,*
*They finally escaped.*

*Please now embark upon a trend*
*Much more than just survive:*
*Sound policy, no overspend,*
*Good player choice, a subtle blend,*
*The Trentside teams to thrive.*

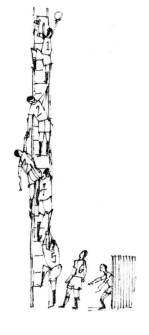

## 2. The Potteries

Life in North Staffordshire involved substantial interest in the local football clubs.
I became a regular follower of Stoke City, instigated in my very first board meeting
at work, at which a representative of Stoke-on-Trent City Council referred with
pride to 'our football team', whose base was a few hundred yards from the chambers
we occupied. They were high in the table and playing attractive football under the
management of George Eastham. It became an irresistible attraction, and I lost no time
after my first exposure in November 1974 engaging with the spirit of that pocket of
the soccer kingdom. I had spent a Saturday morning toiling over the new facility sent
from on high to bedevil administrators – Value Added Tax, not yet vernacularized as
'Vat'. Escaping into what passed for fresh air thereabouts (cars were covered in grime) I
elected to undergo my initiation at the Victoria Ground, first testing the pub/'Hotel' of
the same name.

It was easy to become immersed in the *Evening Sentinel* soccer coverage,
café chat and the rest for Stoke's day-to-day doings, reflecting my own lifestyle at
the time, focussed on matters local. The job promoted this. My workplace was the
Victoria Theatre, the building on the site of a duck pond, a former cinema, which had
fallen on hard times in the 1950s, to be succeeded as a variety venue whose displays
included a woman adorned by a snake, helping or hindering fornication in the back
row. Memorabilia included what in those days were termed 'French letters', littering
the floor for the cleaners and often the next occupants to face. In 1961, after the club's
licence was not renewed, it fell to the new, earnest, venture, the Vic, to resurrect and
convert the place for more elevated performance. Twenty-three years on operations
were moved to purpose-built premises as the 'New Vic' over the Newcastle-under-
Lyme border, and the old site was reinvented as shop units, the stage becoming a car
park. The Vic prospered as a professional repertory theatre serving the community
and funded by the local authorities – city, borough and county – along with the Arts
Council, building up a fine nationwide reputation. Football and theatre both operated
in the world of entertainment. While I was there the Vic developed working contact
with Stoke City FC.

Peter Cheeseman, the Vic's Theatre Director, had been invited by Dudley
Kernick, Stoke City's Commercial Manager, to speak at the Conference of National
Coaches at nearby Lilleshall. Having been coaxed into the theatre, Dudley had witnessed
the rigorous warm-ups actors underwent. At that time the Vic produced Road Shows
for performance in both the auditorium and in community venues around North
Staffordshire. The football team was invited to participate. The performance included
local fare: the black pudding and, above all, the Staffordshire oatcake. Players Alan
Dodd, Adrian Heath and Lee Chapman appeared at the theatre to act as celebrity judges,
featured in the *Sentinel*, for the Great Oatcake Recipe Competition. Submissions
had been sought for exotic oatcake formulae. The lads were to referee innovations
and traditional recipes. The outcome was a 2-1 final victory to cheese and bacon, an
unbeatable balance of textures and flavours, nestling in the humble oatcake. During

the competition Lee, from Lincoln, did make a case for asparagus and paprika. Clearly a man destined for more exalted turfs, such as Highbury, where he would discover provender of many culinary disciplines within easy reach.

The Potters' most famous son, Stanley Matthews, born and bred locally, had a documentary production dedicated to him at the Vic in 1994, in his 80th year. *Come on Stan!* was an artistic and commercial triumph, despite the reserve of the man, who as a retired football player and manager went as far as to avoid passing by his effigy in the city centre in Hanley. On his providing the pass for Bill Perry to score the famous winning goal in Blackpool's 4-3 FA Cup defeat of Bolton in 1953, there was uttered the pertinent comment: 'That was a great pass.' The great man responded 'It was a simple pass.' His early ambition had been to play for Port Vale, but, as recorded in the annals, he helped City into the First Division – twice. He did have a spell at Vale Park, eventually, as manager in the mid-Seventies.

Another illustrious example of the link between theatre and football was *Zigger Zagger*, the play made famous at the National Youth Theatre. Playwright Peter Terson, strongly linked to the Vic over many years, associated the football action with Stoke City, complete with red and white colours. Here is an excerpt:

> *Zigger Zagger*
> *Scene 18:*
>
> *And the ash is pressed.*
> *And you find your place amongst the fans,*
> *The real fans,*
> *The singers and chanters and rattle wavers,*
> *And a sheet of tobacco smoke hangs over the crowd.*
> *And the crowd whistles and hoots,*
> *And the policemen circling the pitch*
> *Look up and know they're in for a rough day of it,*
> *And the stadium fills up,*
> *The Open End first, then the City End,*
> *Then the paddock, then the covered seated stand,*
> *hen, last of all, the fat directors*
> *With the Lord Mayor and cigar.*
> *And the reporters are in their little glass box,*
> *And the cameramen position themselves*
> *By the goal,*
> *And there's a looking down the tunnel,*
> *Then a hush.*
> *Then out they come.*
> *The lads,*
> *Like toy footballers on a green billiard table.*
> *And the roar goes up...*

*Chorus (general roar; all sing)*

*City City, City City*
*We'll support you evermore,*
*We'll support you evermore.*
*City City, City City,*
*We'll support you evermore,*
*We'll support you evermore.*

The pity was that when performed in London in 1967, the 'City' was not identified as 'Stoke'.

## The Potters

### Stoke City 2 Wolverhampton Wanderers 2
### Division I, 20/8/75, Victoria Ground

It proved fortuitous to move to the Potteries during its senior club's best period. They had won the League Cup in 1972, their only honour (no trophy cabinet required), and finished fifth in 1974. The atmosphere at the Victoria Ground was buoyant with the likes of Jimmy Greenhoff, John Mahoney and the oatcake boys, and it became a regular wander to the Victoria Ground for me. The line-up revealed consistency from the previous season. England goalkeeper Peter Shilton, an import from Leicester City, was settling into the team. Geoff Hurst was always worth a watch, a career advance on from his 1966 World Cup exploits, as was another England forward, Alan Hudson, imported from Chelsea. But this day Hurst, who was later to transfer his skills to run a most attractive country pub just over the border in Shropshire (a better address to boot), was absent, replaced by Terry Conroy, who in turn became a Potters favourite.

Regular supporters, with some of whom I developed a nodding acquaintance, this being welcoming North Staffordshire, were to be found in the Victoria Hotel. More were convened in the Boothen End near the usual floodlight pylon, back from holidays and full of anticipation, hardly to be fulfilled.

Alas, a few months later City were forced into the awful eventuality of moving to Vale Park, home of that other club further up the Potteries (six miles and a world away), following the loss of the roof of the Butler Street Stand in a gale. Stoke beat Middlesbrough 1-0 at their borrowed venue. 'Victoria Scene' (sic) in the programme, read as follows: 'in thanking the Directors of Port Vale for their kind assistance in allowing us to use their ground this afternoon, our thoughts naturally drift back to our last league visit to Vale Park – in April, 1957, and in a mood of anti climax. The Vale were already booked for the Third Division and Stoke, after being on top of the Second Division table in mid-season, failed to sustain their bid. The game ended in a 2-2 draw...' This was 'the first Division One game ever to be staged at the ground. And what could be better in their [Vale's] Centenary year?' Indeed. It became the visiting neighbours' first home win at the ground!

Attendances are worth a perusal. 21,109 turned out, below the Potters' average. Their next few gates followed a strange sequence: 29,528 to see the FA Cup Round 3 replay v Tottenham, 38,213 FA Cup Round 4 v Manchester City, 21,001 League game v Leicester, 41,176 FA Cup Round 5 v Sunderland (they lost the replay in front of 47,583), and 17,113 League v Tottenham. Such volatile figures, and notable that FA Cup games could attract more punters than League games, in contrast to new century experience.

Back to the early-season Wolves game, there were scuffles in the streets and shops were shut, it being a sort of local derby, the clubs being separated by a mere handful of junctions on the M6. Wolves were Stoke's peer rivals, Port Vale being referred to as 'The Fail', an allusion to their '100 years of total non-achievement', though the Potters had little room to criticize. Wolves fans, whose own primary foe was their nearest neighbour, West Bromwich Albion, picked out Stoke for singular dislike. Hence the expectation of aggro.

Rand and I had met to play squash just around the corner in what resembled a tin prefab, added on to a sports centre residing in a converted red brick, originally religious, building. Then followed the Saturday Victoria venue appointments. The ground had a comfortable feel about it. Rand accompanied me to both Potteries clubs and was amazed at the huge decibel level of human vocality together with the tribal colours shining from the pitch. He found it a splendid experience, though slightly nerve-wracking and intimidating, and he was surprised at the racist taunts, of which there were a few earfuls. Basically there was just too much cacophony for a quiet lad. He has since developed more interest. On the way home, however, I sprained my ankle negotiating a fence. Just as well that I'd had my fix of sport already.

We ventured to Boothen 30 years on. The Victoria Hotel was comprehensively boarded up and the lifeless old ground-sized patch that had hosted the Potters for so long offered a selection of scruff, with the tenuous consolation of an almost-wrenched-off red gate. Nearby, Rand identified the well-established gap in the faded metal fencing which had been responsible for my injury, he alleged. Even the quiet park up in nearby Penkhull, where we had dabbled in crown green bowls and tennis, had been abandoned to nature. Our spirits were wretchedly wounded.

## Everton 3 Stoke City 0
## Division I, 11/9/76

Spaces on a supporters' coach trip were on offer from Stoke, up and over to Liverpool. The respective attractions were Goodison Park for me and Peter Shilton's legs for Frumps. She professed a preference for Port Vale, liking the yellow and black stripes of the time. In 2007 yellow was featured in the top donned by a comely young lady promoting the Vale's club shop 'sexy range of Italian ligerie [sic]'; also in the club name on the badge and the 'Port Vale Bedroom. From the floor to the ceiling and wall to wall your bedroom can be Vale through and through, just like you.'

We didn't see a lot of this game as it tipped it down all day, initially causing the coach to be late in reaching the destination. We still suffered all the goals in annihilation by the Toffees, who in 1976-77 only surpassed this in the 4-0 drubbing of Spurs. The Potters, meanwhile, continued disappointingly all season, including a sad completion of the double in a 0-1 result when Everton made the return journey to the Victoria Ground. In May 1977 City were relegated. So were Tottenham, Everton finishing ninth, their lowest position for ten seasons. Even now they can still boast the greatest current longevity after Arsenal, having most recently braved the Second Division in 1954.

Goodison Park was really the first serious football stadium, opening for business with a 4-2 victory over Bolton. These two clubs' histories have been curiously intertwined, Everton's rather more illustrious. Let me note that the building costs included £7 15s for 12 turnstiles. The ground enjoyed the presence of a church in one corner, but otherwise lacked discernible features, benefitting instead from excellent atmosphere, which was fine for the home fans that day. Had visibility been better we might have observed the five-year-old Main Stand, with three tiers, opposite the away area, costing £1m and double the size of the old one. This was Britain's biggest when built, but for three years only until Chelsea erected their East Stand. By way of compensation at 110 x 70 yds Goodison offered a rather small playing area. Perhaps this served to upset the opposition, like the overwhelming crowd-size at Old Trafford and, later on in a game, Sir Alex Ferguson's insistence on amending time added on when it suited him, so it's been reported..

There were reputedly tempting eating and drinking possibilities near Goodison, in fact abutting the bricks and mortar, but this episode was governed by expediency. On the nourishment front, I suspect we recovered in the Wheatsheaf in Stoke, a tavern that served us well on a number of occasions, including one New Year's Eve, as it were a rescue operation from a vehicle problem. Upon reflection that very expediency may be why I have undergone so few footy coach trips. It's the other side of the coin of convenience: you're tied to the driver's remit.

Everton is one of a dozen clubs inspired by the Lord, in the shape of the boys at St Domingo's Methodist Chapel, in 1878, a response in a middle-class area to the all-pervasive influence of alcohol. This is quite a contrast to the opportunistic origins of Liverpool FC, established in effect for the vacant Anfield, its occupiers, Everton by name, having moved out after disputes with landlord and sponsor. There have been moves to honour the graves of the founders by some clubs, Everton among them, having discovered it to be one Benjamin Swift Chambers.

Speaking of higher beings, mention must be made of theatre producer Bill Kenwright, for whom I worked in the late Eighties at the time when Willy Russell's stage musical *Blood Brothers* won prestigious awards. That was one of my better memories of a six-month sojourn in Shaftesbury Avenue. Bill has sustained chairmanship of Everton over an increasingly impressive period of time. Commercial theatre is a cut-and-thrust business, awash with pragmatic practices such as using the most recent week's takings, in the West End or for touring productions, to pay off creditors in pursuit of their dues.

This is alongside the rescue of the beautiful and ancient Liverpool Playhouse – in dire straits as a publicly funded producing theatre – connecting contrasting forms of entertainment in one portfolio. On the one hand Bill was able to claim in late 2006 that it was 'not an option' for Everton to stay at Goodison Park, bearing in mind that it would be deeply unpopular with the supporters to move out of town to Kirkby (New Town), a possibility being considered; on the other he is responsible for a vast array of theatre productions, of equally varying merit, in town and on tour. There are examples of football clubs at every level, all over the map, from Chelsea to Carlisle, which have survived or thrived from immense goodwill displayed, via their chequebooks, by their enthusiasts as individual entities or for perceived future glory.

## The Vale

## Port Vale 2 Lincoln City 2
## FA Cup Round 1, 23/11/74

This was my first venture to Vale Park, a complete contrast to the Victoria Ground, giving an impression of openness, abandonment, evoking occasional triumphant moments long forgotten. This was borne out by its history, at least in terms of anticipated success, as at this time it was one of only three clubs to have changed addresses since the Second World War (with Hull City and Southend United). The ambition of the chairman, Alderman Holdcroft, in 1950 had been to build the 'Wembley of the North' with a capacity of 70,000. This was especially brave as Vale was always the lesser club in the area. Stoke-on-Trent was the smallest major city sustaining two league clubs, so, like Sheffield, Bristol and Nottingham (also Bradford, too late now) in theory it has from time to time seemed obvious to pool resources and produce a single higher-quality team, but on paper only of course.

Historical timing affected what actually happened to the ground. Postwar rebuilding needs, and the Alderman's inability to continue as benefactor quite to the extent of football club patrons in more recent times, meant that it opened for business

seriously under-built, and in 1975 was still awaiting a stand or two. But I recall, with a comforting glow, the tufts of grass between the terrace paving. Vale Park had a pleasant atmosphere, open terracing with the promise of a stand on the south side, the compelling green domed Tunstall Roman Catholic church on the northern horizon.

Both the city's grounds sold succulent Bovril. Was this intrinsic hereabouts, like the creaking turnstiles and inadequate toilet facilities? With ubiquitous seating Vale Park in the Noughties lost Tunstall church as a horizon view from the Hamil Road End. (Vale

0 Brighton 1 – League 1 (3), 13/10/07, was the match.) Now the Phones 4 U/GO2/ Caudwell (Hamil Road) Stand looked out onto the home, Big AM/Sentinel/Bycars Lane End (take your pick) Stand, full of shabby, patchy peach-toned seats from somewhere. In the GO2, also out of sight for the concentration of visiting fans underneath, hung the admirably clear and simple scoreboard, carrying the name of their team in a different, not so clear, font. The fans below provided some entertainment: 'If you're 1-0 up jump around' (and many did), 'We are Brighton, super Brighton, we are Brighton from the south', and '….give a dog a bone, Crystal Palace fuck off home.'

The church could still be detected from the home end should one venture to the outside bogs, just above the eponymous Bycars Lane, I suppose, though not evident to the naked eye. There I also witnessed several blokes with a habit enjoying an illicit cigarette. Twice came admonishment from a yellow steward. For the 2007-08 season the Football League had outlawed smoking anywhere within turnstiled terrritory. Serious stuff this admonition thing – smokers were ejected from Griffin Park when I went there for a pre-season friendly. Tough line – very recently trained? But by the end of the season smokers were indulging openly by the Bristol Rovers away turnstiles at half-time, with not a murmur from stewards or policemen in the vicinity.

Back to an elbows-on-railings-above-the-toilets state of affairs. Look at the green domes, let your eye wander down to the foreground from left to right, from a clean-cut series of football pitches complete with urgent youth in designer uniforms, round to acreage devoted to age-old allotments. You could almost hear the sprouts squelching and scarecrows screaming. A joy to behold, but by then I'd acquired the taste for countless bizarre phenomena.

Good news! The Bovril was still good, but too hot to carry (too often it's tepid). I soaked my red-spotted handkerchief in the endeavour. Had that been noticed at a Bristol Rovers game I might have been admonished for displaying a link with a team not of a blue and white persuasion (it could have betrayed an affiliation to Stoke City, famous of course for red-spotted hankies) as a foolhardy and most overt Man U supporter, who was propping up the elbow rest round the Memorial Stadium pitch below, came in for some vituperation relating to inappropriate allegiance and wardrobe choice. Returning for the second half after the northward vista reverie, the more I gazed upon the pitch, the broader it grew, seeming almost square. Indeed this is one of the widest in the league (dimensions 114 x 77 yds, several yards wider than Goodison above), but it proved unhelpful to the home team, who proceeded to lose by a single goal in a very poor encounter. 'Your mum's a slag' shouted a fan desperately. Still there had been the distraction of 20 alternate white and black flags furling in the wind above the Railway Stand.

A substantial preoccupation was perpetrated by a change of managers. Martin Foyle, Vale player from 1991 and manager since 2004, had recently been dumped (26 September 2007). The palpable effect was a proliferation, as nowhere ever before for me, of fanzines for sale. *The Vale Park Beano*, ubiquitous before and after the game, upstaging the official programme *Black & White*. And *Beano* 'No.59' was in addition to the competitor *Derek I'm Gutted* ('Number Thirty Eight') which I had bought in the pub. A charming question was posed on page 22 of *Derek*: 'Would you like your udders feeled?' which pertained to the forthcoming fixture at the Galpharm Stadium. On the bottom of the same page was a regular feature on 'Former Managers'. 'Steve Bruce once won a popularity poll in *Gay News* magazine. Mainly because his face looks like an arse.' These fanzines are so rude! More to the point, one suggestion for filling the managerial vacancy was: 'Jose Mourinho (lately departed from Stamford Bridge) has said he's finished with the Premiership so clearly hasn't ruled out League One. Has suggested he might like to try a different country next, but that was before the Vale job became available. Different country, Jose? It's a different world.'

Both the mags cost £1, but *Beano* was rather better value, containing, as it did, a revival (or surplus disposal) of issue 9, dating back to January 1999, and also priced £1. The tenor throughout had been regret at the dismissal of much-loved, long-standing and successful manager John Rudge. He was Pom's cousin – she performed in the leisure sector too, as a professional singer, mezzo-soprano. When posited the conundrum:

> Q: *how many mezzo-sopranos does it take to change a light bulb?*
> A: *four, one to change it and three to look on saying 'it's far too high for her.'*
> she retorted:
> Q: *what's the difference between a soprano and a terrorist?*
> A: *you can negotiate with a terrorist.*

Unfortunately she failed to demonstrate her vocal prowess when we witnessed Exeter City beating AFC Wimbledon 2-1 to make it to the FA Cup proper (28/10/06). The crowd nearby compensated in full. She joined me in some Grecian bitter, though.

The *Beano* front cover said it all, the caption for John Rudge's photo reading 'SITUATIONS WANTED Reliable, conscientious, hard working, polite, maker of miracles, seeks skint, bottom of the league club for long term success.' The Editorial read '...recent events have shaken Port Vale supporters to their foundation with the sacking of John Rudge after 18 years' service...giving us promotion from the depths of Division 4, and leading us to unforgettable appearances, and victory at Wembley...' But '...We have looked enviously as Lee Mills has gone on to score around 20 goals for Bradford; but could John Rudge have done anything to keep him? Millsy had been offered nearly double wages, and a hefty signing fee of around £100,000, whilst John Rudge had to work in a strict wages structure. OK, Lee Mills is a greedy git but he's got no loyalty for Port Vale – he wasn't born locally and has no local connection. His priority is looking after number one, and although we might disagree with his decision, it's a fact of life that money is king in present day football...John Rudge was given money to spend, and on several occasions he agreed a price, only to be turned down by the player owing to Port Vale's strict wage structure, a wage structure that is there by necessity, due to the old problem of poor attendances. In other words it's a "Catch 22" situation in which John Rudge couldn't win.'

And John Rudge, a native of Wolverhampton (I wonder if he likes oatcakes or perhaps parsnips. Pom's speciality is crispy parsnips: not that that's ever the intention, but she shows the same generous attitude to friends as her cousin to his employers in extending breakfast invitations – if you help with her sweet peas), was soon offered the post of Director of Football at Stoke City – 8 years there to this date. This reveals something about a lot of issues. Above all the man emerges with flying colours, borne out by the release of 843 'give or take a couple' balloons by travelling Valiants during the next away game, at Ipswich, 'commemorating every one of Rudgie's matches whilst in charge'. In 2007 The Vale remained under-supported and under-funded, even with the patronage of Robbie Williams, or 'Billions' as one page in the current *Beano* had him.

*Beano: Rob, do you run a USA soccer club?*
*Robbie: Yes, I do*
*B: What's it's [sic] name?*
*R: LA Vale*
*B: What's LA stand for?*
*R: Named after Port Vale..........Lost Again! (cheeky grin).*

Port Vale had started out in 1876 at Longport, near Burslem, the second most northerly of the string of the six towns comprising the City of Stoke-on-Trent. They moved gradually south towards Hanley, the hub of the Potteries, where they were based until settling back in what had become Vale Park in Burslem. The record crowd was 49,768 in 1960 for a Cup tie with Aston Villa. In 1974 it seemed a vast expanse, though the capacity was by then reduced to 35,000. Their gates in 1974-75 had after 12 league games averaged 4,173, one of the smallest in the Third Division. By 2007 the all-seats capacity had been reduced to 18,947, according to the club's website. It seemed politic to get the capacity from the place itself as the various guides varied in their information, including a frequently quoted figure of '23,000', a little too round. Also rare was the award of 'Man of the Match' to the ne'er-do-well Adam Eckersley, who had incurred a red card.

A long time before, local author Arnold Bennett included the local teams in his best-known and most universal novel The Card (1911). Stoke City were 'Knype', (based on the district Knypersley) in the First Division and Vale 'Bursley', in the Second, neither very successful, just like real life. In fact 'Stoke' and 'Burslem Port Vale', their identities during their last League memberships, were absent from the two divisions at that time, so Bennett had conferred an elevation upon them both.

The football bit of the story hung on the acquisition of a key player by Bursley (who played in blue and red), from 'York County...quite suddenly in bankruptcy,' outbidding 'Aston Villa (£700)' and 'Blackburn Rovers (£750)' to clinch a popular deal for £800, funded by Denry Machin, the eponymous card. To provide a Roy of the Rovers conclusion, within 20 seconds the player scored the only goal of the 'opening match of the season. It was a philanthropic match, between Bursley and Axe, for the benefit of a county orphanage.'

Burslem was a comforting place with a superb, proud town hall, ornate school of art and all the features of a working community: market hall, chippies, pubs, several of them excellent. In 2007 this was still true – the Bull's Head had oatcake specials, most certainly to be devoured alongside a pint from the local Titanic Brewery. Try the wittily named Steerage and then graduate to Iceberg.

Back in 1974 the social club at Vale Park was welcoming, such as I have found in recent years at more humble grounds and another source of greater gratification. You get real ale and camaraderie between the colour strips, a concept wholly alien in the big stadia of the new century. Their remit is rather grander and more pasteurized.

And the game? Well, here are some stats: Lincoln were in the Fourth Division at that time and went on to win the replay 2-0. Not very good, Vale. 4,840 attended this game, and 6,824 the replay. In fact Lincoln's average gate was second best in the basement division: 5,794. Mansfield achieved 1,500 more than this, but they did emerge as champions with no home defeats. So it was a thorough upstaging of Third Division Vale.

I can't say that feelings of nostalgia well within me recalling the Potteries experience, as I still drop into the area from time to time, so this experience remains contemporary. It was a fabulous denouement on Sunday 4 May 2008 when, out of all the 46th-game conundrums of the Championship, Stoke City revived to the higher level they occupied when I first encountered them. Meanwhile the Vale had already been relegated to the basement. Oh that they could resurrect themselves, even developing greater support. There are plenty of people out there in the Six Towns.

## 3. The Villa

Villa Park's floodlight pylons, spelling 'AV' and clearly visible from the M6 and A38 all around Spaghetti Junction, were removed in 1990. What a loss! A further deprivation was the wooden seats and stained glass in the Trinity Road Stand, so as to facilitate improvements in quality and capacity. Such changes are gut-wrenching should you have an emotional attachment to a place. Surely some memento could have been retained to admire elsewhere in future. In this enlightened age 'heritage' considerations should count for something.

But a person's experiences of a football ground can only embrace a small part of the story as League grounds have been around for upwards of 120 years while the world has been transformed around them.

The setting remains a boon. The shrine lies below Aston Park, a green oasis in a densely populated area, with a gem to enjoy should you venture over the hill: Aston Hall, a Jacobean pile, touching the soul to the extent of presenting a candlelit carols evening at Christmastime. I recommend it. For the stadium the Trinity Road approach still provides the best visual reward – a magnificently proportioned 'classical' façade: not only the front of the building, but the surrounding gates topped by lions, 'The Lions' being a nickname of the club. This aspect, given space from which to appreciate it, lends confidence not always fulfilled by the performance within.

Meanwhile, Birmingham's reputation as a city appears to have nudged up bit by bit over a number of years, finally boosted comprehensively to match the huge investment. The crowning glory was the opening of the Bull Ring shopping centre in 2003, identified by the stunning Selfridge's building, covered in metallized dinner plates, a carbuncle if ever there was one but seductively designed and a treasure

trove for a huge public gushing out of New Street Station from which it is a short walk. It is symptomatic of the City of Birmingham's long-term enlightenment and improvement towards, at last, a favourable public-opinion rating. Selfridge's (with the spire of St Martin's Church nearby) seems to have replaced the long-standing image of the cylindrical Rotunda. When compared to major cities more popular in public estimation, like Newcastle-upon-Tyne ('NewcastleGateshead' as the twin settlements are now dispensed, formerly 'Tyneside' – that sounded better to me), really a microcosm of the something more comprehensive, like a multi-cultural, cosmopolitan, international Birmingham, the only city with upwards of a million inhabitants outside the capital.

The trouble is that its main football club has kept falling short. Distinctly 'main'. The Villa in 2006-07 was the only Premiership club, not only in the second city but the entire Midlands region. They last appeared in the second division in 1988. How good it was to see the Blues and/or the Baggies join them – yo-yo teams at the time -- in the surrounding seasons. Villa were able to pay £8.5m for West Ham's Nigel Reo-Coker in summer 2007. Birmingham City's manager of the time, Steve Bruce, told the press he wished he had the cash to afford such an investment. One year in as Villa's owner, Randy Lerner, from New York, New

York and owner of American Football team Cleveland Browns since 2002, had made those funds available, having seen potential in the club for more success than had been achieved in recent seasons. Villa had won more points, and friends, for their attractive playing style and greater success by the end of the 2007-08 season. They finished sixth, earning a place in the 2008 Intertoto Cup, from which they qualified for their first appearance in the UEFA Cup for seven years. Their team could boast more than the usual home grown players. Also more nationals on the pitch than any other Premiership club – six in the team as they ended the season (compared with three at St Andrews down the road – the Blues were relegated despite boasting more overseas players). Something to applaud, particularly as England failed to qualify for Euro 2008.

The term 'sleeping giant' has been bandied about seemingly since time immemorial as a term of abuse for underperforming football clubs, in the case of Aston Villa with complete justification. In taking up a periodical place near a floodlight pylon on the immense open Holte End terrace I wished I had become a practising aficionado earlier to match my interest from afar. There had been achievements, in the form of promotions and Cup runs. In 1979-80 four consecutive rounds saw them drawn away to be beaten by eventual winners West Ham; two years later three away draws out of three – the draws were bad luck and Spurs beat them 1-0, going on to win the Cup. All supporters have hard luck stories and to move to Birmingham in the late Seventies was good timing: something of a golden era, culminating in their momentous Championship under Ron Saunders in 1981.

They've won some things, but not enough, and over the years with each fast-turning page of the journal of football, they haven't accumulated a sufficiency to complete a story. It's obvious that they should be one of the elite, a peer to the Noughties power centres of Manchester United, Arsenal, Liverpool and Chelsea, to which add Tottenham and Newcastle who are consistently higher in any ratings list. Ron Bendall exercised a misguided iron grip on the club, and, thereafter, Doug Ellis for a quarter of a century in his second spell at the reins. 'Deadly Doug' at last pleased everybody by selling the club to Randy Lerner. I admit to schadenfreude, defined as 'malicious pleasure in the misfortunes of others', in the departure of Doug and manager David O'Leary, deeply unpopular throughout the stadium, to judge from the acerbic banners, as well as from local papers and pub chat, not to mention the fanzine *Heroes and Villains*.

Opposite the Trinity Road Stand stood the snug one on Witton Lane. When replaced as part of the long-term rebuilding programme in the mid-Nineties it was named after the chairman of whom one opinion was quoted by Simon Inglis: 'markedly acquisitive, a builder of fortunes…aggressive, obstinate and vindictive.' the Doug Ellis Stand. Apparently Deadly expressed surprise at the decision. I prefer the stand's old name myself. 'Witton' has a modest, local ring to it, and is of practical help as it leads straight down to the nearest station – Witton. Let's hope this is restored now that Deadly is consigned to history; a vain entreaty

I fear as any change is sure to reflect a new commercial thrust. To extend this I much prefer stand names not eternally tied to a benefactor's name destined to be lost in time. Keep it simple and make it supporter-friendly. If not a reflection of local geography (Trinity and Holte at Villa Park) North, South, East, West are next best, for simplicity and practicality, as expounded at Old Trafford and the newish Kingston Communications Stadium in Hull, to name but a brace. This is disavowed when renamed from something with meaning such as the Rookery at Watford. It's good to note there are still a few Cowsheds too.

The club certainly has a fine stadium, competing on the modern stage, albeit having lost the FA Cup semi-finals to Wembley (new) in 2008, though the look and facilities within the stands are no fun – relentless concrete, frightful food and gassy beer, the contemporary norm. This contrarily encourages some into pleasure-seeking at other outlets at a distance from Witton/Aston. Meanwhile I have enjoyed the more opulent hospitality as a guest in a box. It was regrettable that the Traffs contrived to equalize for a 1-1 draw (5/12/98) as the small, carefully chosen group had mostly been enjoying (those who were interested in watching, this being a corporate funday) the anticipation of a home win, washed down with red wine in coffee cups during play (to avoid detection). I have not been surprised at the number of first-time visitors who have remarked, first on the atmosphere, being something apart from what is imagined from armchair viewing; then upon the amount of organization the club achieved on match day, impressed at the quality of orchestration.

The company was floated on the Stock Exchange in 1997, Finance Director Mark Ansell being heard to say 'our shares are a good bet in the short, medium and long term'. Shares were £11, I remember as one of the gullible. In due course they were trading at a tenth of that value. It was an indulgence for a few years, being awarded exceptionally modest dividends and attending Annual General Meetings, to witness angry but articulate shareholders demanding proper management of company issues in as polite a manner as they could muster. After all it was a formal occasion, albeit held in the Holte End. The assembly was faced with the bland set-piece responses from the tableful of rehearsed authority below us beside what was destined to become the tightly whitely defined pitch perimeter. Manager of the moment Brian Little (number 10 of Doug's 13) promised much in performance and was widely believed, as in the summer it's natural to harbour hopes for the forthcoming campaign. It was special to enter the hallowed portals for this stage-managed performance (of which Birmingham Repertory Theatre would have been proud), where you felt you had a stake in the real Aston Villa. Success was part of the game plan, so to speak. Gareth Southgate, skipper, said around this time: 'We knew how close we were to being a real force, but the more we tried to make that leap, the further away we seemed to be. Alex Ferguson [well advanced in trophy accumulation in Manchester] said Villa was the team he could see coming through'. Gareth left it until 2000 to desert the sinking ship for Teesside along with George Boateng and Ugo Ehiogu, all among Villa's best players. It left a considerable gap at the back. In October 2005 it was painful to see 'Villa rejects' Gareth controlling the defence and George scoring one goal and setting up another when Middlesbrough visited Villa Park for an away win. It so often happens. Sod's Law and one of Villa's seven home League defeats that year.

You do wonder how football clubs so often seem to be above common-sense business practice – how clubs suffer from bad management and survive, accumulate massive debts, go into administration. Any normal business would fold, but something in a football club keeps it going in the Football League, with rare casualties, like Accrington Stanley, Aldershot and Maidstone United, and the odd conversion like Bristol City and Charlton Athletic. Ultimately I am glad to have been a shareholder for this time, until the waste of money it truly represented needed addressing. So the shares were sold, at a large percentage loss, the residue to be more productively applied. It had been a 'sentimental' investment.


## The Lions

### Aston Villa 2 Southampton 1
### Division I, 28/3/81

A typical Saturday Villa Park day-trip might have opened with the Cup & Saucer Café for an immense greasy breakfast, complete with a wodge of fried/mashed spud and a mug of tea in which a spoon would probably have stood up. Thus fortified, the café conveying its own character, laden with cigarette smoke and expletives, the journey to Brum allowed the ballast to settle down, the next ingestion some Ansells Mild at the charmingly betiled Red Lion, in Soho Road, Handsworth. It was a complete mismatch, blue and white tiles and wooden carvings in a Victorian hotel on Soho Road, a solidly 'ethnic' area characterized by markets and sweet shops. The beer was good, the atmosphere amenable in a snug bar sporting mirrors alongside the hunting scenes on the walls. After this it was essential to make the short transfer to the Barton's Arms in Aston, one of the outstanding showpiece pubs in the country, vying above all with the Philharmonic in Liverpool, occupying an island site topped by an impressive clock tower, i.e. you can't miss it. It's a magnificently ornate Victorian/Edwardian Grade II-listed drinking palace (1901), the show-stopper being a huge illuminated stained-glass window at the end of the biggest room.

JCB, passenger and footy novice, gasped in awe as she negotiated a bulging bap, brimming with something, who knows what (a long way from organic provender displayed at the Wednesday farmers' market, upon which I have gorged once it's translated into culinary heaven in her kitchen – her self-confessed favourite is crispy pork, with crackling, and roast potatoes). No, most of this didn't accord with the received image of the second city. She recalled that once in the ground: 'We stood at the home end with lots of people. No seats. Aston Villa players were running towards the goal and the atmosphere was really exciting. I don't know sod all about football.

There were thousands of people, electrified. It felt like something was about to happen. They scored and I leapt into the arms of the man next to me. It was completely spontaneous. I can't think of anything more important than that: you can hug a complete stranger.'

That Saturday morning the top of the table showed:

|  | P | W | D | L | P |
|---|---|---|---|---|---|
| Ipswich Town | 33 | 20 | 10 | 3 | 50 |
| Aston Villa | 34 | 21 | 7 | 6 | 49 |
| Southampton | 36 | 18 | 8 | 10 | 44 |

A critical game, therefore. The Saints had lost eight away games out of 17 and Villa had beaten them at The Dell. We go back in time for this gem, when I was living and working in Brum.

All the goals were scored in the first half, The Lions' by David Geddis and the inspiring Tony Morley, imported from the Clarets of Burnley. The season grew increasingly nail-biting, as from a good start (they'd won five of their first six fixtures, drawing the other) the possibility augmented of a real chance of the title. I was drawn into the unfolding drama. The focus on Villa, who had emerged as Ron Saunders's surprise success package, captivated Birmingham, though Ipswich were the favourites of the Press and, I suspect, neutrals. The Super Blues did lift the UEFA Cup. Come to think of it weeks later my only ever job-sacking coincided with Villa securing the Championship. Was there a connection? Everybody should be fired at least once. It's character building.

Another more literal pissing-upon was suffered on another occasion on the packed terrace. Beginning to feel strange warmth on my left calf, there grew a patch of dampness there, which I began to recognize as a trickle of urine down my leg from a bloke behind me. It occurred to me that he could have aimed better, but not in reality in that crush. I couldn't even turn round. Was there another way of looking at this? 'Friendship is like pissing your pants. Everyone can see it but only you can feel the warmth,' I heard somewhere. Somehow protest seemed inappropriate, or futile. There was lots of camaraderie following the Villa and no chance of over-exposure. And the bogs were at a distance, presenting a major challenge in this situation. Even so there was continuous disruption, by the struggle to the gents' queue or at least using a wall (or in urgent or wilful cases the sink, instead of the open depression a.k.a. urinal: these were always jam-packed with users and waiters).

I always found myself facing this battle for relief, essential at some point after several pints of the thin stuff in the tavern. This was the Upper Grounds, named after the erstwhile pleasure grounds, just up the road from the ground; the order a consistent pint of 'mixed' (mild and bitter), as close to cask-conditioned ale as was practicable in those days, with scant choice of beer and meagre quality. One of my lifetime claims to fame was, as a member of the Campaign for Real Ale, Birmingham Branch, to achieve the Upper Grounds' inclusion in the 1982 *Good Beer Guide*, for one year only, as follows:

'West Midlands; Birmingham: Aston; Upper Grounds: Mitchell & Butlers

Mild, Brew XI: Spacious Villa Park local with international clientele.'

And in 1984 the Thompson Twins would provide a quirky chart song, reaching number two – their best ever – for easy adaptation: 'You take me up to the higher [for which read 'Upper'] ground(s).' Also down memory lane, there was just one game around this era when I witnessed a scuffle at close hand. Alien supporters had somehow invaded and provoked fisticuffs, mounting to a worrying level for a short time. Her Majesty's representatives materialized and quelled the uprising. And another time, Roddums, another Villa virgin, seeking to assuage his appetite, sought to sample kiosk fare outside the ground in advance of the Holte End jostle. Alas, he was inexperienced in the ways of the saveloy, and his purchase precipitated itself wilfully from the ketchup-slithered bun to the grimy pavement below.

Ron Saunders used only 14 players in winning the title, one fewer than the famously economical Liverpool side of 1978-79 under Bob Paisley, and the regular squads of Leeds United (1973-74) and Liverpool (1987-88).

Gary Shaw and Peter Withe were Villa's main Championship strike force and a more effective partnership would be difficult to achieve, in fact it hasn't been, ever since. But it was nearly all over. They didn't cut the First Division mustard after 1980-81. It had been so good to hear the Holte Enders' 'Gary Shaw, Gary Shaw, Gary Shaw, once he gets one he gets more'. 'If you hate the Blues stand up' as well, but that is for all time. BCFC finished 13th, West Brom fourth. Southampton finally sank to sixth. It was good fortune to have been around for the seventh Championship and to have immersed myself in the prowess of Ron Saunders's Claret and Blue Army.

Twenty-five seasons on, during their apology for top flight performance in home fixtures in 2005-06, the scoreboard delicately recommended the purchase, for £16.99, of 'Champions of Europe 1982, the DVD all Villa fans have been waiting for. Grab your own copy.'

And to come: the infinite range of stimuli, from Ay to Zee, which following this club is certain to continue to provide. Come on ye Lions! John Gregory said, early on in his tenure (1998-2002), 'there's an aura about this club, a sense of history and tradition. Even the name is beautifully symmetrical, with five letters in each word. 'More pertinent was to witness Martin O'Neill's debut home game against new boys Reading in August 2006. "Martin, Martin give us a wave" shouted the Holte Enders, commonplace but uplifting. And he did. It was a moment full of promise.

All the more reason to treasure the good times. I did wish I'd been there with them in their days of sustained achievement. However, you'll always inherit history. The best time to be chosen as a Villa fan would have been the halcyon days of the late 19th century. They won the League and FA Cup double in 1896-97. That was when my grandfather caught the bug and took regular (and prompt) trains from Leamington Spa to Witton or Aston – at least that's what I imagine. It was at Witton Station that I once empathized with the throng of the claret and blue chaps awaiting the train after a match. Two comely wenches clicked past, crisp heels on the concrete, in close conversation, discussing the game, no doubt. With one accord erupted the bass bellowing 'Get your tits out, get your tits out, get your tits out for the lads.' That was good enough – by then all that was left was their unflinchingly tight buttocks.

## 4. The Bristols

If you go back in time Rovers would have been in Gloucestershire and City in Somerset, though for local government purposes the place has gone through a number of labelling amendments – in recent history as the main ingredient of the much-loathed County of Avon (Avon and Somerset Police survives as a force, perhaps to provoke animosity towards them). Before then and since, it has been the discrete 'City and County of Bristol'. Strangely, some of what is understood as 'Bristol', the place with a population of half a million in continuous urban development, is now in the district of South Gloucestershire, and more of it is in North Somerset. This is in common with other major cities, where there is a mismatch between local authority boundaries, population distribution and day-to-day interpretation of what a place means. Meanwhile many are surprised to discover that Gloucestershire County Cricket Club is based in the suburb of Ashley Down, a stone's throw from the Memorial Stadium, Rovers' long-term domicile and the home for much longer of Bristol Rugby club, subsequently to be renamed the 'Shoguns'. 'How common,' said The Dude 'we are now Bristol Rugby, plain and simple' after the club followed Bath's obvious model in 2006. Yes. Rovers had bought out Rugby in 1998. They have since shared the ground, whose conversion into a new 18,500 stadium finally got the go-ahead in early 2008, allowing the rebuilding to start after the 2007-08 season, your last chance to stand on terraces on three sides of the ground. Rugby programmes there were above the going rate, at £3. Admission was £20, but this was in Rugby Union's top tier, 2008 vintage.

The Gasheads' vitriol is focused on City, and vice versa, and no other team, exemplified in the mass reaction to half-time scores. By and large the team in fetching blue and white quartered shirts (with the odd quirk like the pink away shirt, a temporary curiosity), a standard for a few decades now, has been cast in the role of poor relations, though during my initiation to League football at the end of the 1950s, they were both members of the Second Division. Rivalry can of course be extended when the occasion demands – there have been right barneys with Plymouth and Exeter in the nature of partisan interest, and acrimony is pretty keen for Swansea and Notts County. Notts County? Nothing should surprise us in football – I know of Somerset-based footy enthusiasts who adopted Hartlepool. And Colchester and Exeter fans have harboured a weird rivalry.

The red Robins of Bristol City boast a stadium of a standard above their mid-2000s level of third tier (League 1, up to 2007) and can claim to be the best in the South West. Nevertheless there have been periodical mootings of a new stadium further out, but these have ultimately been flashes in the pan of local discourse. Ashton Gate has made its presence felt as a fine, very red, stadium, formerly a cricket ground, a landmark for a wide area. They suffered very different troubles from the long-standing poverty of Rovers, resulting from their four year membership of the First Division, for which they had waited for 54 years. 1980 saw them start plummeting right to the bottom, in 1981 accompanied by Rovers who finished at the foot of Div II. There followed insolvency and at length a new limited company arose phoenix-like from the mess. Back in Div III in 1984-85 they vied with their neighbours in the same division for something good through to 1989-90. Maybe the prospect of mediocrity continuing into the new decade was a spur, but they were both inspired that season, finishing:

|  | Played | Won | Drawn | Lost | For | Against | Points |
|---|---|---|---|---|---|---|---|
| 1. Bristol City | 46 | 26 | 15 | 5 | 71 | 35 | 93 |
| 2. Bristol Rovers | 46 | 27 | 10 | 9 | 76 | 40 | 91 |

And City reached the Fifth Round of the FA Cup. It didn't last and relegation back to the Third followed first for Rovers, renting at Twerton Park, Bath, then City. From 1995-96 to 1997-98 they were companions in the Third – then 'Second' Division, a vacuous elevation, as the modern era, marked by money, hype and the Premier thingy, had been born, making nonsense of the numbers accorded to each division. The Robins bobbed up and down in a single thrust. Then Rovers sank to the bottom in 2001, with more than cursory concerns regarding the threat of relegation to the Conference.

It might be posited that the Robins' natural level is the second tier, i.e. the Championship, to which they still aspired in 2005-06, and achieved in 2006-07, after several near misses. Their rivals, meanwhile, improved (at a snail's pace) each year of their four-year occupation of dungeon level (up to the 2004-05-06 final position of 12th – precisely halfway up, hitting the jackpot with their play-off success in 2007). They had been the last team to occupy 23rd position before the introduction of relegation of the bottom two (Exeter went out, 23rd, the next year). Lucky Gas!

Whatever the judgement on quality, Bristol has chronically underperformed in its League teams. We all hope for better when the nearest Premiership ground is in the West Midlands. It is reasonably concluded that this just isn't a football city. As compensation its rugby side battled back to the top 'Premier' League, and Bristol boasts the aforementioned cricket ground. But in 2006 and 2007 Glos were playing in the bottom division of each of the cricket leagues, as well, in 2008 being forced into the West Country shadow of supreme Somerset, who had achieved a double promotion. A curate's egg, i'faith.


## The Gas

## Bristol Rovers 1 Oxford United 1
## Division III (4), 13/9/05, Memorial Stadium

Nelson, visiting from Florida, was entertained regally to a liquid foretaste of pints at the Wellington before and 90 minutes (plus six) at the Memorial Ground on a fine Tuesday evening. Rovers' home and Oxford's away records were identical: 0-1-2, so they could both have done with a win. The guest found it a 'homey', local atmosphere. The pies (chicken and mushroom for me, a pasty, the punters' favourite, for him) in the enclave were tasty and the half-time majorettes, The Blue Flames, amusing in a gentle way.

Those were his opinions. He also remarked upon the vocal antagonism to Oxford's keeper from behind the goal following an encounter with a Rovers forward. And a curiosity, baffling many and certainly an overseas guest: the various identities of Rovers. At the end the simple rugby-style scoreboard read 'The Gas 1 1 Oxford'. During the game from time to time

it issued the variations on a rallying call: 'Come on you Blues' and 'Come on Rovers.' From the away end came 'There's only one team in Bristol' and – a reference to the proximity to the border thereabouts 'You're really Welsh.' Meanwhile the programme was called *The Pirate*. One team, four names. We all love these idiosyncrasies. Nelson was bemused. But that's not all. In earlier years they had been the Purdown Preachers, then the Black Arabs. At £2.50 a throw the 64 pages were crammed with good stuff for this, their fourth home game, with centre-page pin-up Jon Bass, no.36, in a pose backed up by Clifton Suspension Bridge.

Going back in time I had particularly enjoyed the edition opening the 1999-2000 season, worth the purchase, displaying the team in a double pull-out spread: 40 men - three in a lurid puce (goal keepers), seven in suits (backstage staff, two sporting toothsome smiles), nine in white tops (active staff), 21 in the latest, blue and white shirts promoting Cowlin Construction. Interestingly for early August at least five of these were long-sleeved. The unsmiling Jason Roberts, seen at Wigan in 2005-06, had a point of contact with me – acquaintance with his girlfriend. It was she who must carry the can for my haircut. I wonder if she accompanied Jason northwards, to create coiffures in a Wigan salon. I doubt it – such a transfer is unlikely. It was my dalliance with a recognized style, but Toni and Guy was not for me after a couple of appointments exposed to the ambience there. My prevailing memory is of long waits, loud music and raucous staff. I recommend instead Stephen Sheppard: cheaper, wider conversation and less background interference, though the girlfriend was good on the subject of Jason, his career path and style preferences. Stephen's cup of builder's tea came with a supporting saucer.

The first official blew the whistle at 7.45pm and off we wafted, absorbed into the unfolding drama. Into the game forward Richard Walker suffered scorn and, with two notional fingers erect, eventually scored the only home goal. But the crowd was fickle, honouring him with 'Richard Walker boom boom boom.' The statistics showed that he was second-highest scorer in 2004-05 with 10 in the League and four in cup games, and the best ratio, ahead of shooting star Junior Agogo. More like 'Aggro' a year later during the unhappy process of his departure to top Third Division outfit Nottingham Forest (most expensive, biggest gates by far and early pacesetters, doubtless to be further helped by the inestimable Junior). So far in 2005-06 the tally was Agogo 6 Walker 2, both having appeared in all eight games.

Rovers did extraordinarily well for away support. They took 988 to Barnet for the opening game, and 1,521 to the more convenient Torquay, with significant effect, perhaps, as they came away with a 3-2 win. But then the Gulls did sink to the bottom through to December. The first three visitors to the Memorial Stadium all brought fewer than 200. It must make a difference. The attendance for this game was 5,098.

There is a remarkable point to make about the bond between the Bristol clubs: City would prefer there not to be one, and refused to entertain the idea of a ground share when Rovers were to be exiled from the Memorial Stadium during rebuilding. The initiative was delayed and delayed again. Rovers eventually agreed terms for use of the smaller Whaddon Road ground in Cheltenham. In summer 2008 it was reported that they and CTFC were to host each other in the third tier. But these finely tuned scenarii are notoriously difficult to execute. When would building actually commence? And who would be in which division by then?

City's promotion to the Championship in 2007 had been achieved without any fuss. That Rovers also achieved promotion, the hard way, and after a superlative late season surge up the table, was apt: the two clubs have never been more than a division apart. Amazing that, but true. Richard Walker came into his own, scoring twice at Wembley and signing a new contract with Rovers.


## The Robins

## Bristol City 0 Southend United 2
## Division III, 14/11/81

My initiation at Ashton Gate was courtesy of a colleague named Ivor. I was most impressed by the ground and atmosphere; less by the team, delivering one of their ten home failures on the way to complete obscurity to the point that it's arguable that they gave the Fourth Division the best ground ever to present 92nd place football. Ivor held a season ticket (he was called, briefly, Ivor Season-Ticket) and would become a subscriber to the fund-raising initiatives surrounding the new company Bristol City (1982) Ltd. I wonder if he was the only fan(atic) to pay at the turnstile as well, so affected was he by the club's predicament.

The ground had a history as a cricket pitch. Harry Dolman, chairman of City for 30 years through to the mid-Seventies, had a stand named after him. His indulgence was bowling – see the flat greens embraced in the building plan under the Dolman Stand. In 2006 the local paper was able to report: 'The biggest conference, exhibition and banqueting hall in the South West was officially opened at Ashton Gate Stadium yesterday (5 October). Once a bowling hall, the large area under the Dolman stand has been transformed'. And there was a photo of City's chief executive, Colin Sexstone, smiling as he showed off the new hi-tech facilities. 'Among the first events to be held in the *Evening Post* [oh, now I understand] Dolman Exhibition Hall will be the Jimmy Greaves Theatre Show on November 2 – a fantastic night of sport and comedy with special guest Ron 'Chopper' Harris.' The term 'full circle' comes to mind, and I quite warmed to the idea of Chopper strutting his stuff, just like the old days. Why not? We've had Frank Bruno and Coochie Chilcott in panto at Bristol Hippodrome, despite lacking a rather important qualification, Equity membership, a telling ingredient (talent) and a significant element (drama training). On the other hand the matter did underline the link between soccer and the stage.

Mention must be made of the Robins' golden era: Second Division champions in 1905-06 and runners-up to Newcastle in 1906-07. These were the days of Small Heath, Woolwich Arsenal and New Brompton. I'm afraid I prefer all those to 'Birmingham City', 'Arsenal' and 'Gillingham'! City featured a true character in local lad, Billy Wedlock, 5'4" and thickset, a famed defender, who earned a regular place in the England team. He had remarkable ability for getting the ball, wherever it was, indefatigably. He was nicknamed 'Fatty' and 'India-rubber man' and was the essence of the City team of the time. He was known for an acute sense of fairness and only ever conceded one penalty. H. Slater Stone, 'Half-Back' in the *Bristol Evening Times*, wrote: 'It would be infinitely easier to stage Hamlet without the Prince of Denmark than to imagine Bristol City without Wedlock.' A pub opposite the ground bore the name 'Wedlocks', with a picture of Fatty together with the badges of the English Football Association and Bristol City FC.

There was another 'Wedlock' association in the area with the local (Bristol and Zummerzet) preoccupation with cider consumption, as encapsulated by Adge Cutler and The Wurzels in song, and Fred Wedlock (Billy's grandson, releasing several albums including *Out of Wedlock*). The Wurzels' signature tune remains 'I am a cider drinker, I drinks it all of the day' (that's in standard English, not at all what it sounds like in performance). Though Adge died in 1974 at the tender age of 44, The Wurzels continued on the circuit, purveying 'Scrumpy'n'Western' and showing off the wurzelphone, an industrial trumpet. I've pondered on The Wurzels' name – anything to do with the peculiar Bristol accent which adds an 'l' to final vowels? You go shopping in 'Asdal'. The Wurzels' hotbed is Nailsea (no 'l') a few miles away. In 1976 their anthem 'One for the

Bristol City' was officially adopted by the club. Suitably revised for the modern era, the song reached number 66 in the charts in September 2007.

A typical warm-up for Ashton Gate in the Noughties might comprise pies in the Merchants Arms, washed down by Bath Ales' Gem bitter (or latterly the Tobacco Factory, 'Ashton's meeting place', not requiring the perambulation to the ground). Cider was kept for summer quaffs (footy season = onset of autumn). Speaking of warm-ups this is the opportunity to mention the Robins' Championship Play-Off Final versus Hull City in May 2008. The fame of Pom (who has been noted in connection with the Potteries) as a singing teacher reached Ashton Gate following the Reds' dismissal of Crystal Palace. On Radio Bristol, following John Cleese's message of encouragement (he was less mellifluous about his birthplace, Weston-super-Mare), she gave coaching to three of the 36k Wembley-bound Robins supporters, Nick, Chris and Mike, emphasizing the need for 'articulation and projection', breathing deeply, with better use of the diaphragm, to make maximum noise right to the end of the game, plus guidance about how to stand. 'It's all about passion – for the whole game, not just to half-time.' She commented about their initial attempt: 'a bit alarming – not quite in tune.' One of them admitted that his normal preparation for a match was 'beer and a pie and walking to the ground.' With half an hour of Pom's coaching their rendition of this verse did grow a little bit more potent:

> One for the Bristol City,
> Two for the boys in red,
> Three for the fans at Ashton Gate,
> We'll follow them till we're dead, my boys
> We'll follow them till we're dead.

'There's always hope' she added, rephrasing it 'I have great hope for them.' In truth they did overachieve to get to Wembley. It was a remarkable effort the year after promotion from League 1.

The onward route hadn't changed. From the Merch, which I recalled had once been run by an Elvis aficionado, the most direct way being beside/ on a railway track, then scaling a bank to meet the challenge of a ring road, trundling over a flat green park fringed with trees, in clear sight of the former bear garden. The route survived, but as recently as 2006 the railway was rendered 'safe' by containment in a man-made covering. Just as many puddles still required negotiation on the surviving path. The quest was usually achieved with ease, though it is regretful that the game itself was not always as exciting as the introductory activities. Or indeed some of the acts performing during the halcyon cider days of the close season, like Elton John and Rod Stewart, though not together. Rod played in torrential rain in 2005, which also served to effect abandonment of the 20/20 cricket game between Glos and Yorks up the road. Traffic was gridlocked. Bristol sure can be a wet place.

But outside the ground before a home game, for a mere quid you can buy a comfort bag, whose contents include chocolate, crisps and a bottle of water, which can be emptied down your gullet in your seat (no standing here, though comment has been made with a view to restoring some areas to old-fashioned terracing: little chance, I fear). The bag, in the name of the *Evening Post*, has a subtle caption at the bottom 'YOUR CITY OUR CITY'. In 2007 this accorded with the positive spirit in the air, manager Gary Johnson, a few seasons after serving Yeovil Town a serious elevation (straight status swap with Exeter City, dammit), took City convincingly back up to the Second Division, and early halcyon days there too, all with a good grace, and for me, no trace of the arrogance to be witnessed in other managers.

Perhaps a little of that characteristic provoked this incident, which reached the daily papers: Kevin Reynolds, 43, 'admitted punching Alex Ferguson in the groin before butting and racially abusing a police community support officer. [He] pleaded guilty at Westminster Magistrates Court to assaulting the Manchester United manager at Euston Station. After the attack Reynolds, of no fixed abode, said, "I'm sorry Fergie, I did not know it was you." He then sang: "Fergie, Fergie, shut your mouth" – a Scottish football chant.' Like his Old Trafford peer, Mr Johnson was reputed to be keen on discipline, one of the differences from previous regimes at Ashton Gate. On his office wall read a slogan 'If you want to motivate players, get players that can be motivated.' Like Martin O'Neill at Villa Park he was heralded at home games, but at Ashton Gate it was 'Johnson, Johnson give us a wave,' easier to sing than 'Gary', perhaps. But surnames, mostly, yield nicknames, the wellspring of our national sports. The next piece of recognition was his being chosen by the adoring public as the 2007 BBC West Sports Personality of the Year. Just after they'd beaten table-topping Watford away. The boy done good.

At Ashton Gate you will hear the universal chant 'C'mon you Reds' – not their listed nickname 'the Robins', which is, however, the name of a nearby pub. On the other hand during the season, sometimes damp, often miserable, a modicum of wit could be salvaged from the fanzine, titled *One Team in Bristol*, making frequent reference to their rivals as 'Basement Rovers', also a succinct quip:

*Q: What is the difference between the Rovers squad and a puddle?*
*A: A puddle has more depth.*

After a game in Bristol, in fact at home anywhere, having recovered modestly in a suitable hostelry, I suggest contriving a party, hung on a DIY championship featuring the Victorian board game Bagatelle. It comprises 20 ball bearings and a cue like a drumstick, played on a wooden board, the forerunner to the sprung pinball machine. Groups of nails are framed on the board with values printed within them. Scores are built up and someone wins the 'cup' (more by luck than judgement), a charity-shop item with a label adhered announcing the achievement like 'Bagatelle champion'. Plus wooden spoons for the lowest score and other prizes as appropriate, like for most replays or best style. No prize to cost more than 50p. This is fun, but perhaps it's best to stick to football, even in Bristol.

A solution to the local strange planning decisions and oddball football clubs might be to erect a single stadium in that disappointingly empty space in the city centre, known as 'The Centre', for dual use and play there, the design perhaps also making provision for a new auditorium with commodious capacity, something else overdue for the city. Conditions might include the clubs unifying as one and naming the combined enterprise in an evocative manner.

Taking a cue from the Bay City Rollers or Heart of Midlothian imagination could flow free to embrace a reference to local history in the name. Bristol offers such a good choice: slavery, tobacco and alcohol (the wine trade). Or it could be Bristol Brunel, to honour Isambard Kingdom, the Suspension Bridge originator, as well as being satisfyingly alliterative, or employ a reference to the precise location, like 'Pierhead', Bristol being notoriously difficult to navigate. It's hardly worth remarking that none of this would ever happen, not least because of the rugby factor – given a triangle of influences, plus politics, rife in these parts.

## 5. The Grecians

'Exeter', a word which shines like a beacon in a dense passage of text. In 1904 emerged a professional football team, Exeter City AFC (A for Athletic). They became dubbed 'The Grecians' for reasons as various as their rival, the Argyle of Plymouth. Examining the ECFC website, I shall settle for an entry in the Mobiad, originally written by Andrew Brice in 1738, at the time of parliamentary elections held in the city: 'GREEKS. So we surname. I know not why, the rugged Inhabitants of St Sidwell's (the club was established as St Sidwell's Old Boys). The title seems to have arisen from their contending with the City at Foot-ball etc., they being called Greeks as making the Invasion, and the Townsmen perhaps Trojans in defending their Ground, etc...'

The point was that the Trojans were city folk, within Eastgate. The name has certainly stuck. One hundred and one years later the papers carried big coloured photos of a warlike Exeter representative in full battle gear for their appearance at Old Trafford in the FA Cup in January 2005. The warrior was a William Hill invention for their betting shops and then was adopted for a T-shirt. One or two of the big cardboard posters made their way into the hands of Exeter faithful. The 0-0 result bore out the resolve and commitment by all involved with a mere Conference side. They lost the replay 0-2, honourably and profitably.

This is a coda to the lengthy outpourings above regarding the other clubs and locations to which I have been related. Exeter City have featured widely but up to recently I have never spent much more time at St James' Park than an annual occupancy of the Popular (Big) Bank (mostly, or, when seats are required, the Cowshed, most recently in the name of 'flybe Stand'). The Big Bank boasts an open aspect of both the conflict below and the city's magnificent Norman cathedral beyond, if you choose the right spot. I am blessed, and, of course, afflicted with an emotional attachment to this red and white (and black) outfit.

Their depressed status had some association with mismanagement before they lost their League status in 2003. Leading Grecian supporter Neil Le Milliere referred to the huge role the Supporters' Trust had played in rescuing the club. This is one of several clubs with such involvement. He said in December 2007: 'of course the amazing thing about Exeter is that in the moment of crisis the supporters joined the Trust in droves and saved the club from disappearing possibly forever. From an initial dozen or so the numbers swelled up to over 2,000 and have remained in the high 2,000s since. These people have basically not only saved the club by acquiring the majority shareholding but continued to support it in what has been a very successful four seasons in the Conference culminating in a play-off final loss to Morecambe in 2007. It is an excellent example of what supporters can achieve by joining together in running a club and ensuring it is an integrated part of the community. Promotion will be the icing in the cake when it inevitably comes along.'

Neil was the man who got married on the pitch: 'Julie thought it would be a wonderful idea. However as the pitch/ground weren't sanctified for marriage we had to settle for a blessing, which duly took place after the official ceremony at the registry office. Unfortunately the day we settled on was the last home game of the season against Southend, which of course turned out to be our relegation day!

'It was a lock-out on the day (the match not the Wedding although we did have five TV crews and numerous radio crews filming and interviewing us during and after the ceremony including a Dutch crew making a documentary about the day in parallel with the day at Swansea as it was between the two of us for relegation!). And we struggled to keep all the seats we paid for for our 200 or so guests following the wedding, as the then owners continued to admit people well after all the seats and standing room had gone. Eventually they had to lock the gates on Police instructions or the Police were threatening to refuse to allow the match to go on. Disgracefully this even meant some season ticket holders were locked out.

'We did manage though and then we all got to experience the surreal atmosphere as the Exeter game kicked off 15 minutes late due to the over-crowding, which meant that for the last 15 minutes of our game the whole crowd already knew we were relegated. Steve Flack scored in this period for Exeter and it was the least celebrated game I've ever seen!

'What guests (the majority of whom were Exeter supporters) did say though was at least they had the wake, sorry wedding reception, in the evening to drown their sorrows at and forget for a while the relegation.'

At the time of their last days in the League they were on the brink of liquidation; no help coming from 'friends', including celebrities, who might have thrown a financial lifeline. Two directors ended up being investigated for fraud – a conviction was to follow – and visibly Uri Geller and Michael Jackson (the songster and 'Thriller', world-wide personality and acquitted defendant, not the erudite booze wordsmith, who died in 2007 with the huge credits *English Pub* and *Malt Whisky Companion* among others, but sadly without having produced a football book – it's our loss) had been publicity fodder at their own instigation. The Supporters' Trust, which contrived to obtain a non-executive post on the board for £5,000, worked tirelessly, in the end successfully, to save the club. There are several professional clubs run by supporters' trusts. In brief the battle was at last half-won after banking their share from this Cup tie; a financial clean sheet was eventually awarded as a Christmas present in 2005. They could have done with maximum gate money for the Third Round replay, but kept to

the usual £11 (standing) and £14 (sitting) so as not to exclude the supporters who deserved a favour. Such altruism is most welcome. Now let us turn to the chosen game.

## Exeter City 5 Rochdale 0
## Division IV, 24/3/90

This one has selected itself as the best ever Grecians win I have witnessed at 'the other' St James' Park. This was at the apex of their form on the way to their celebrated (solitary) Fourth Division Championship. It was their 14th League home win to date, having drawn the other two. This form was catching. According to the programme, dipping into their reserves, in the Captial [sic] Finance SW Counties League they had recently beaten Bristol Rovers 6-0, in the Devon and Exeter Premier Division they retained top spot beating Alphington 3-0 away. Meanwhile Desert Orchid was triumphant in a certain Gold Cup for nags. And hours (minus one) later, heralded by the triumph, British Summer Time began. And did Rickles and I espy the legendary Potteries artist Arthur Berry queuing for Bovril at half-time? His spitting image perhaps.

Terry Cooper had graced the manager's office for less than two years after unthanked service at Bristol City (sacked after Freight Rover Trophy successes and promotion) and turning the clock seriously back had been a Leeds United star during their 1970s period of prowess. An archetypical dour Yorkshireman, his programme note 'Coopers Corner' (no apostrophe) was terse and to the point. They had to work hard to beat Peterboroguh [sic]; then lost at Chesterfield. At home they accumulated 13 wins, two draws and not a single defeat. Rochdale posed a threat, with one of the best away records, in fact to finish with one more away win than Exeter's eight. Their goal difference, however, was significantly inferior, to be exacerbated at this final whistle after a hat trick from Jim McNichol and a brace from Steve Neville! In the end 'Castleford Cooper' (as a fanzine had him – he was actually born in nearby Knottingley) guided City to 20 home wins that season, the leading goal scorer being Darren Rowbotham, cruising to the pennant 10 points ahead of the Mariners of Grimsby.

Fanzines have been paramount here and in their various guises flesh out the developments up, down and out, often for the substantial band of absentee followers. Examples in the Nineties were *The Exe Directory, In Exile*, merging into *There's a Good Time Coming*, and *We'll Score Again*. In one issue of the first appeared this anecdote from the 1994 evening game at Chesterfield: 'The home supporters chanted "Get Your Tits Out for the Lads." Sexist? Nope. Weightist actually, as the said request was aimed at our very own Supporters' Club chairman Gary Nelson. Needless to say, Big Gary duly obliged, and was rewarded with bursts of "Who ate all the Pies?" from both sets of fans. Talk about making your own entertainment…' The result: Chesterfield 2 City 0.' Also committed to paper in one issue of *There's a Good Time Coming (Be it ever so far away)* was a song, whose lyrics were less clearly enunciated in the Devon air:

> *Drink up ye cider, drink up ye cider,*
> *For tonight will merry be,*
> *I'd rather have a scrubber, and roll her in clover,*
> *But there's still more cider in the jar.*

Within the hallowed portals of St James' Park there is a framed local newspaper cutting, which might bring a smile to your face. The headline recorded the visit of the 'Yorkshire Puddings' of Leeds to play the 'Devonshire Dumplings' on 12/1/29. The trophies cabinet is full, unfortunately falling short of many awards to do with their first 83 years of League status. Andy Gillard did a great ground tour.

More recently, they acquired some souvenirs from the dead Highbury Stadium – a whole row of turnstiles, tall and angular, quite unlike the rounded body-shaped ones of which there were more than 20 sited round the park. Nearby was the social club, Centre Spot, now St James' Centre, for ingestion on match day, of a bottle of ale and a pasty, or cask-conditioned ale from a handpump.

Visits to St James' Park have provided a stimulating, fraternal package. For me, following a club with such lowly status, hopes were the same, relatively – you go there with a heart primed for pumping – but expectations muted. There was less pretension and, in tandem, pressure, applied to the Fourth Division (Exeter's modal average league) than the First (Villa's). This could produce immeasurable glee on a special occasion, like the Grecians' 2005 Manchester encounters.

A City programme editor asked:

Q: *What has Old Trafford on a Saturday afternoon at 4.45pm got in common with Wormwood Scrubs Prison?*
A: *They are both full of Cockneys trying to get out.*

Football writer John Aizlewood attended the same game as me in 1997-98 in his tour of all 92 grounds (City 1 Swansea 0 – Division III (4)), opening with: 'The first thing I hear are the pan-pipes. The music of the Andes wafting up Sidwell Street, a sea of red sandstone, like most of Exeter.' This was when former 'keeper Peter Fox was manager, in mid-tenure, having spent two seasons in goal prior to that, his total stay with the Grecians being 1993-2000. I remembered him at Stoke, which now looks like the apex of his career. Exeter were in the top cluster with 20 points, but in third place on goal difference behind Peterborough and Notts County. The programme that day featured a startling cover photo of centre half Lee Baddeley 'unshaven and with the blackest eye you ever did see.' Paul Birch, with a Villa and Wolves pedigree, scored the only goal. 'Golden boy' Darren Rowbotham was also guilty of 'the worst exhibition of kicking.' After the allotted span of robust endeavour 'the crowd melts away at the final whistle. As well they might, for this Saturday is a big night in Exeter. England are playing Italy in Rome, a match to which apparently over fifty Exeter fans missed the Swansea game to attend. It's also the city's carnival. I adore carnivals, they bring families into the streets of city centres at night. For Exeter, they are reminders of times past...I adore carnivals, so long as I have nothing to do with them.' Aizlewood seemed to have enjoyed his visit to this proud and independent place.

As I have done, each year. And more in the future. Rightly regained League status in 2008 was ultimately tantalizing and I embraced the prospect of a lot more trips to Devon.

Let's finish with a trivial item. The pitch measurements at St James' Park, Exeter are listed as 114yds x 73yds and those of Villa Park as 115yds x 72yds. Rand, on observing the two for games a mere 43 hours apart, made the assumption that the latter was far bigger. Well, the stadium as a whole is massive, the Villa experience was an evening game with blinding illuminations, we were alongside the pitch, somewhat elevated - in the second tier, all contrasting with the Grecian situation. Perhaps this would be a good conundrum for optical illusion tests. A word of warning, too, particularly for afternoons in the sinking sun on a west-facing terrace: bring a cap. That day in Exeter saw a home victory, after sunset.

So ends the tale of support of teams by abode and attachment. I owe them all an unquantifiable vote of thanks.

# Chapter Six
# Generations of Style Turning

## The Eighties, The Nineties, The Noughties

Over a generation and more, I've sought out the plethora of the wide gamut of our national winter sport, as a bit of fun for an afternoon. I shall say now there are some I'd love to revisit: Fratton Park, still there after all these years and the club faring so much better in the Noughties; Prenton Park, encouraged by The Toff who doesn't waste an opportunity to muse over Tranmere's trials; Valley Parade, as it looks most impressive in clear silhouette from the A650 – in daylight can be discerned the legend 'Intersonic Stadium'. I'd welcome another South Asian experience in that pub. Also Plainmoor, Torquay, small but perfectly formed (for an indulgent outing).

A day trip in search of turnstiles can be conducted from anywhere. That's the pint glass half full, not empty.


## 1. The Eighties

### Portsmouth 2 Millwall 1
### Division III, 18/4/81

To the tune of the chimes of Portsmouth Guildhall when it strikes the hour: 'Play up Pompey, Pompey play up.' These words were the Pompey Chimes. And there was a committed fan, Pompey John, sporting bugle, bell and tattoos (an image in a manner evocative of Noddy Holder), who formally changed his name to John Mr Portsmouth Football Club Westwood; an antiquarian bookseller, too.

When the team won, the local paper carried a cartoon of a sailor with his thumbs up. When they lost it was thumbs down, with wavering hands for a draw. And: in the Navy, with a dominant presence in Portsmouth and regular rail use down to the Solent, there was a Jackspeak expression alluding to coitus interruptus: 'getting out at Fratton', being the stop before Portsmouth Harbour, which was all the way.

My own memory of Portsmouth was of the original Tamla Motown tour in Spring 1965 at the Guildhall. I'd already collected membership of the Hitsville USA Club. Mary Wells, a fabulous soul singer who recorded the original 'My Guy', the very essence of the early Motown sound, had recently left the stable to pursue a solo career, so we missed her. This was a shame. I wished she'd done 'Where did your love go?' instead of the Supremes, fronted by Diana Ross. For my money MW's voice ranks among the best, full and expressive, particularly when compared with the thin, reedy tones of Ross. Martha (with her Vandellas) were better value on the voice quality front. The Marvelettes sang 'Too many fish in the sea', the Miracles 'That's what love is made of'. Georgie Fame and the Blue Flames were in support. 'Yeh! Yeh!'

The game and ground are less clear in my mind, though I've reserved a soft spot for Pompey throughout, maybe associated with sympathy back in 1959, when they propped up the first Division I table I ever looked at. A 32-year sequence of First Division membership (literally, including WWII) was thus terminated, during which they had topped the table twice, back to back (1948-50). On this occasion in 1981, I claim a vague recollection of a Fratton male voice choir rendering 'Play up, Pompey' a few (hundred) times. Their final home record was Won 14, Drawn 5, Lost 4 in sixth position, the exact reverse of Millwall away, who finished 16th. The club has been able to boast Fratton Park as its home from the beginning, about half-way through which time it hosted the first League match under floodlights, in 1956. This also involved one of the longest journeys, from Tyneside. Newcastle completed the double over Pompey with a 0-2 win.

Having endured the wilderness for far too long – nadir reached at the end of the Seventies with a thankfully brief spell in the Fourth Division – their next promotion to the top flight was to arrive in the 2003, ensuring continuity of South Coast representation by doing a staggered swap with the Saints. Enter Harry Redknapp, under whose aegis their star was rising, two seasons after near-relegation to the Second Division in 2006. The first afternoon in October 2007 saw the brazen destruction of records with the final score: Portsmouth 7 Reading 4. The *Daily Telegraph* commented: '…ageing but atmospheric Fratton Park is steeped in legend but even old-timers were struggling to recall anything to top this. Erratic goalkeeping, lamentable defending, bizarre deflections, yes, there was all of that. But most of all it was just two teams who drove forward at every opportunity and were ready to shoot on sight. Eleven goals, true, but Reading also missed a penalty, Portsmouth had a goal ruled offside and went close on several other occasions…Glorious unpredictability still has its day, even in the highest echelons, but the most significant truth is that Portsmouth are building on their ninth placing of last term with new adventure…The previous record haul of goals in a Premier League match was nine, achieved seven times…The most goals in a top division match is 13…most recently in 1937 when Stoke beat West Brom 10-3. The most goals in any English league game is 17 – Tranmere beat Oldham 13-4 in the Third Division North in 1935.' A small detail which the Torygraph got wrong: in Bill Nicholson's first game as manager of Spurs in 1958 they beat Everton 4-10 at Goodison Park (thank you, Randall).

A good time, the 1930s, but I'd settle to have been at Pompey v the Royals for that huge hatful of goals, crap defending notwithstanding, and enjoyed the old ground, with its mock Tudor façade, before the £600m dockyard development, complete with 36k-seat stadium comes to fruition.


## Barnsley 3 Bolton Wanderers 1
## Division II, 5/3/83

Villa had been beaten 2-1 by Juventus at home on the Wednesday just after my visit to Watford, and bundled out of Europe as peremptorily as usual. I needed a change. My journey north followed for an occasional stay with a Geography mate, Bramley

Steve, stretching his not inconsiderable brain in the national P11D tax office in Leeds, I recall. He was fanatical about Leeds United and a tad defensive on the subject of Mr Revie's management during our college days, not a popular favourite outside the West Riding. But we were bound for Barnsley, who won their solitary FA Cup in 1912, shortly after the Titanic sank.

It became a Saturday of variety, targeting first the ruins of Monk Bretton Priory, within Barnsley's boundaries, and a little abject at the periphery of (much) more recent building. Having spent undue time clambering over the stained and weathered remains, Steve and I sharing an interest in the Middle Ages, we were hard pressed to find a watering hole to suit in the scant time remaining. In those days you could find a pub easily enough, but more endeavour was normally required for a draught beer of quality. In other words we were forced to drink keg bitter. Thankfully it was an exciting game. Barnsley were mid-table while Bolton finished bottom with a single away win.

Oakwell, 14 years before promotion to the Premiership, was accessible and antiquated. On returning much later (Barnsley 1 WBA 1 – Championship, 10/12/06, by which time Acorn Brewery's tasty Barnsley Bitter was being brewed nearby) the ground had been transformed into a modern all-seater stadium, where for once I was grateful to rest quietly, being suppressed by a virus at the time. It afforded a view of the last surviving old-world stand. And of Toby Tyke, a sort of bulldog who showed a misguided sense of footwear choice during the half-time entertainment in failing to make any impact upon a football. It was meant to be a penalty shoot-out for our delectation, providing a forum for the younger generation.

I never heard the crowd use the word 'Tykes', only 'Reds'. It's a long way back to the appellation 'Colliers'. Mostly they seemed to be 'Tarn'. It would have made sense if the word had been added to the club's name, but Barnsley became Tarn to its inhabitants without the need to spell it out.

In 1983 there was a hearty atmosphere, possibly boosted by Yorkshire v Lancashire rivalry; also I'm sure because support was traditional and lifelong. The ground was part of the fabric of the place itself. A 10 minute climb took you to the town centre, its crowning glory the immense ghostly town hall, dwarfing any other buildings of interest there. It's not a large centre, and it occurs to me that the club of a town of this stature has done very well to host Premiership football, simultaneously converting from a centre of coal mining to a call centre, er centre, and prompting the sometime metaphor: 'the Magaluf of Yorkshire'.

Back in Leeds for an evening of Yorkshire hospitality, Eighties style, we progressed through a number of real-ale hostelries, but were caught out by the local Saturday practice of not serving after 10.30pm 'because of the trouble' and indeed there were fights in the streets. Could this be related to that abrupt termination of beer provision? Chicken? Egg? No sports bars then, or concessionary late licensing. Just the prospect of enduring an excessively early bus queue on a cold, wet night. Why not introduce 24-hour drinking, I suggested, to pace the ingestion! (The scenario was re-enacted in Glasgow in the liberated new century. To set the scene, on a Sunday lunchtime 17/2/08, post Dumbarton 0 East Fife 3 and pre Kilmarnock 0 Rangers 2 – it's all numbers, like the anticipated two pints – alcohol was not served until 12.30pm, though the pub had been open for a while. Then, that evening, the attempt to get a pint as the clock approached the witching hour was foiled as the bar was closed to new customers. And that had happened on the Saturday night as well, come to think of it. Very Yorkshire!)

Going back in time – to the Friday in Leeds – we had enjoyed a quite different pub crawl in a suburb, towards the end of which I observed customers returning from the bar with an abundance of full pint glasses. This was the custom, with which I was unfamiliar, of double orders at closing time to 'get them in'. Not coming from those parts I had paced myself for the seven or eight already downed. Our turn was already upon us as Steve returned from the crowded bar with four pints of frothing Tetley's (the best we could do at that stage). After all 'Tetley's men are Bitter Men', proclaimed many a billboard. As were 'Ansells men', of course.

It was too much for me, overwhelmed by all those whistles blowing.


## Liverpool 2 Stoke City 0
## Division I, 23/2/85

This was a weekend with Pruney trying to cover as much as possible of what Liverpool had to offer in 48 hours. Anfield seemed a long ride from the city-centre entertainment emporia, in fact over two miles, and the ground was a magical edifice sardined among densely terraced streets. Simon Inglis noted in 1983: 'the Kop, the southern end of the ground whose patrons have made Anfield famous with their passion, wit and sportsmanship. The capacity of this enclosure is now reduced to 21,500, and although it seems physically much smaller than, for example, Villa Park's Holte End (capacity 22,600), because the terracing is covered right up to the front, it has a darker, more ominous presence. It is the Kop, more than any other part of the ground, which makes a visit to Anfield such a potentially daunting experience.' Our view was of the Kop and we were there for Stoke. The result was no surprise and a thrilling intermission between vigorous sight-seeing in the morning and classical music in the evening.

It was a season of disappointments for both teams in most contrasting ways. The Potters would be consigned to Div II with 17 points and no away wins, never since to grace the First Division in any of its identities. The Reds were reigning champions, for the third consecutive year. Their main competition was from across Stanley Park as this was the first of three seasons the local rivals were to alternate between first and second positions. The sequence continued for Liverpool, Arsenal assuming Everton's mantle. That spell was broken by Leeds United, 1991-92 champions, followed by Old Trafford domination. Liverpool's continued triumphs through the decade are all the more remarkable in hindsight.

Tragedy was only a few months away at the Heysel Stadium, Brussels, before the European Cup Final kicked off. Thirty-nine spectators died, the episode impacting on football as a whole and in England in particular. The departure of manager Joe Fagan from Anfield was imminent, after two seasons, and this one was rare, producing no honours, Juventus beating the Reds 1-0. The next gaffer was to be Kenny Dalglish.

The game provided suitable fare for thespians like Pruney and me. We had the original Spion Kop to wonder at, young, small fans on their own orange boxes personalized with red paint for their affiliation (in the days before 'Health and Safety') and Dr Fun, a former Butlins redcoat, also seaman, had provided a diversion at the ground from the 1960s. He sported a red top hat and tails and carried the greeting 'Hiya kids' on the back, accompanied by Charli, the dummy, and a horn. And the Red throng performed, vociferous, uplifting and theatrical. One little ditty carried the final three lines:

> *Walk on, walk on, with hope in your heart*
> *And you'll never walk alone*
> *You'll never walk alone*

Let's conclude with a non sequitur, that Liverpool are one of only four League teams whose name begins and ends with the same letter (along with Aston Villa, Charlton Athletic, Northampton Town, plus, I submit, Exeter Citeee, which is how it sounds on the Big Bank).

## Rochdale 1 Colchester United 0
## Division IV, 20/9/86

Wully was a Greater Manchester resident at this time. Well, he called it Derbyshire.
We enjoyed walks in the High Peak far away from football. He was happy to apply
himself to domestic chores that afternoon rather than succumb to the temptations of a
tour round the urban rim to Spotland. This was quite the lifeblood of Friday to Sunday
variety, with footy as the star turn. The routine went like clockwork: with Wully a swim
for body and soul, peerless eggs and builders' tea, the meander round outer Mancunia
(past the satellite towns like the hour marks on a massive clock), parking (yes, yes, yes),
pub (Sam Smith's, an overdue pint), pie. Then into the wasting ground, a mindshift
away from the idea of a modern stadium and before any improvements. At least on my
visit regular soccer at Spotland was still an essentially local facility, commanding small
crowds, less than 2,000 per game, but with keen vocal support.

If I were to live somewhere in the region, this would be a preferred spot to
cultivate loyalty. Allegiance could be split with Rochdale Hornets, the equally modest
Rugby League team, who shared the ground.

The Dale's only League achievement was promotion, in third position, in
1969. Over their five seasons in the Third Division they peaked at ninth. On the
other hand, despite the need for a number of re-election applications, the team has
managed to avoid the awful drop to the Conference, unlike their opponents on this
occasion. Rochdale's origins in the League were somewhat blighted. It took three
applications at a time of expansion to be awarded a place in the Third Division (N),
in 1921. Colchester, however, only entered the League in 1950 and spent 1990-92 in
exile in the Conference.

There was a moment of glory when the Dale won through to the second
League Cup final, only to suffer a two-leg 4-0 trouncing by Norwich City. The League
Cup has been a little blighted as well, by its succession of renamings after the sponsor
of the moment. This has reduced its general recognition and status as the only League-
members-only knockout competition. Meanwhile the lucky old FA Cup (invented in
1872, the Football League only being established in 1888) is graced with exemption
from mention of its sponsors – there is no reference to it in football annuals. It's always
'The FA Cup'. I feel sorry for the League Cup, which is a tangible item of silverware,
all that some clubs, like Stoke City, are able to boast, and it earns its winner a place in
Europe. Manchester United spurned it in its infancy, improving on that in 1999-2000
when they avoided the FA Cup due to big business commitments in South America
(the World Club Championship). They did condescend to join the League Cup fray.
Villa beat them 3-0 in the Third Round. Served them right!

The League Cup is notorious for inducing teams of reserves representing
clubs with big enough squads, to preserve key players, and perchance, quietly, to
reduce the fixture schedule. Rochdale's $21^{st}$ century record in the competition has been
entertaining, losing 2-4 to Wolves in 2003, 2-1 at Stoke in 2003, 0-5 to Norwich
in 2005, 3-2 at Doncaster in 2006. No wins but plenty of goals. They last reached

Round 2 in 2001-02, before their nail-biting revenge at home to Stoke in August 2007: 2-2 aet, 4-2 on penalties. They went on to more penalties at home to Norwich in the Second Round but without revenge. The result was 1-1 aet, 3-4 pens. The latter suggests some competency in execution, but how wildly that can vary. England ruined many a fan's summer by their ineptitude against Portugal in the 2006 World Cup. Surely the country's 'best' boot-wearers should do better than that. We could all see how crap they were – it wasn't just down to the quality of the goal-keeping! Meanwhile in two FA Cup Round 3 replays on 22/1/08 there were to be witnessed both extremes of penalty success. Swindon zeroed against Barnet, also of inferior status, who went through 0-2, i.e. not much better, but Bristol Rovers achieved 100% from their five spot kicks to knock out Fulham (5-3), two divisions more elevated. The Pirates went on to a rare appearance in the last eight, in a memorable March weekend of televised 6th Round Cup ties (I managed to see the lot). Man Utd lost to Portsmouth , the eventual winners, Barnsley (Champ) beat Chelsea (Prem), Middlesbrough (Prem) lost to Cardiff (Champ). The other result was Bristol Rovers 1 West Bromwich Albion 5.

Returning to the run-of-the-mill, the very modesty of Spotland and the Dale has created its own appeal. It's a popular fixture with many a travelling fan. I'd love to pay a return visit and next time gawp at the renowned Victorian town hall on the way.


## Cardiff City 1 Reading 2
## Division III, 8/10/88

Two games in two days – off to Swindon next. The Bluebirds had not started well with only Aldershot and Chesterfield below them after six games. This result extended the trend. Supporters here were abject, a noticeable number evacuating the ground before the final whistle, perhaps the expression of a national characteristic? However, as representatives of Wales in the European Cup Winners Cup, City had progressed to the Second Round at the expense of Derry City following a 4-0 second leg win three days earlier (0-0 in Derry). So they could be excused for this performance, and I should have realized that they might be hung over from the triumph. Presumably they were saving themselves for the Second Round, as they had lost 3-0 at QPR in the first leg of the League Cup, part two beckoning, three days after this episode. So many fixtures, only so much energy/talent/squad. (As it happened QPR won the second leg 1-4: 1-7 on aggregate, edging past Charlton and Wimbledon to meet comeuppance at the feet of Nottingham Forest in Round 5: 5-2 on the night.)

The ground was easy to find from the M4. Parking was achieved in due course, having realized that there was habitation, and street parking, only on one side, with main roads, football pitches and industrial use dominating otherwise. There was no need to tackle the Welsh capital itself, though the city has rewarded the effort in the past by both car and train. From the Bob (what it used to cost) or Popular Bank was a view of Cardiff Arms Park, not yet eclipsed by the Millennium Stadium. During the afternoon there appeared to be bluebirds wafting overhead, but they turned out to be seagulls, with some pigeons in support. How mundane! Equally, on seeking relief the toilets carried the alternatives 'Men' and 'Dynion'.

The ground was very blue, much faded, the steelwork for example, both vertical and horizontal. Overall it was simply drab, though an equally faded Captain Morgan Rum advert could be made out on the roof, I was made aware, relieving the monotony. The stand was massive, listing down to the pitch a seeming mile away. Meanwhile the aspect from the upper terrace was of greenery on rising ground beyond the Sloper Road Grandstand, this being on the edge of a surprisingly compact place, given that city-centre sights were in clear view. Strangely exotic was a palm tree growing in the garden of a neighbour. Tiptoes pointed it out, along with the observation that there might be a better chance of a pint after the game if we tried the seaward direction down Sloper Road. The outcome was the Cornwall – try it!

In fact Cardiff only became capital in 1955 (when Roots Hall opened for business). Bradwan remarks: 'in the mid 18th Century Cardiff was a small market town, but in less than a century it had grown to be the world's largest coal port'. Now it's outstanding for (especially Christmas) shopping and sports Cardiff Bay ('Tiger Bay' to septuagenarian Shirley Bassey), an area of regeneration and entertainment, full of epicurean delights. That is until you venture a little way into the hinterland, like so many centrally sited projects, perilously close.

Ninian Park was named after Lord Ninian Crichton Stuart, a member of a local benefactor family, the Butes, whose name crops up a lot hereabouts – the family was strongly associated with Cardiff's development, owning land and mineral rights. Indeed Lord Ninian became a Bluebirds fan. Aston Villa were the first guests, chosen as reigning League Champions – in 1910. More recent names associated with the place are fans Shakin' Stevens and Neil Kinnoch.

Ninian Park remained Cardiff City's home, capacious enough for the club's needs but falling short of a good experience. That's the nearest you get to a compliment. Does the pitch size deserve one, extremely long at 120 yds (Reading 102, Millwall 108) and 72 yds wide (Reading and Millwall both 70 yds) (*Football Grounds Factbook* by Michael Heatley and Chris Mason)? It seems anomalous that they can vary to this extent – why is there no standard in a game bedevilled by rules?

I am reminded of the oddity, thankfully shortlived, of Astroturf during its brief appearance. Those clubs who gave it a try deserve an accolade for the bravura of the idea but not the execution. Their plastic pitches arguably gave QPR, first off in 1981, Luton, Oldham and Preston an advantage (including low maintenance for several years) but didn't do much for the game as the fans knew it, with balls bouncing, players tentative and pundits giggling. Indeed players were in danger of getting their bare bits burned from contact with the surface, for which read 'carpet'. They were formally banned by the FA in 1988. The Welsh capital was mercifully at a distance from this folly over the border.

## Swindon Town 1 Chelsea 1
## Division II, 9/10/88

A squash game first, as a splurge of energy expulsion after the Ninian Park sliver of fun. Why are there so many 'Robins' about? Swindon, Bristol City and Cheltenham, close enough to each other, form a tweeting of robins, or whatever the collective noun might be.

This was the only time I managed to get Drudge, whom I had upset with imperfectly cooked chicken and I was eager to make amends, to go to a football game. He preferred all types of theatre, favouring musicals and pantomime, most of all, what was on offer at the County Ground not qualifying in his terms, though the words would fit the display we were given. In fact the game was chosen for the anticipated quality of two highflying teams.

The home team's tour of every division deserves highlighting. Relegated from the Third Division in 1982, let us tabulate the story of their league positions since:

| 1982-86 | Division IV | 8, 17, 8, 1 |
|---|---|---|
| 1986-87 | Division III | 1 |
| 1987-93 | Division II | 12, 6, 4, 21, 8, 5* |
| 1993-94 | Premier | 22, but at least they got there |
| 1994-95 | Div I (2) | 21 |
| 1995-96 | Div II (3) | 1 |
| 1996-2000 | Div I (2) | 19, 18, 17, 24 |
| 2000-06 | Div II (3)/League | 20, 13, 10, 5, 12, 23 |
| 2006-07 | League 2 (4) | 3 |
| 2007-08 | League 1 (3) | up again |

*Play-off success, scoring nine goals in the three games against Tranmere Rovers and Leicester City, whom they beat 4-3 in the final.

Meanwhile there was never really any doubt that the Blues (oh! those unimaginative nicknames again) would stride back whence they came, but their 1987-88 outcome deserves explanation. The contentious bits of the interdivisionary zones looked like this, play-offs being uniquely employed to reduce Div I to 20 clubs, while increasing Div II to 24, like the lower divisions:

| Div I (bottom) | Played | Points | Destination |
|---|---|---|---|
| 18. Chelsea | 40 | 42 | Div II via play-offs |
| 19. Portsmouth | 40 | 35 | Automatic relegation |
| 20. Watford | 40 | 32 | Automatic relegation |
| 21. Oxford United | 40 | 31 | Automatic relegation |
| Div II (top) | | | |
| 1. Millwall | 44 | 83 | Automatic promotion |
| 2. Aston Villa | 44 | 78 | Automation promotion on goals scored |
| 3. Middlesbrough | 44 | 78 | Div I via play-offs |
| 4. Bradford City | 44 | 77 | Div II via play-offs |
| 5. Blackburn Rovers | 44 | 77 | Div II via play-offs |

So the fourth team from the bottom, Chelsea, went down. It was a weird and wonderful time, with Villa squeezing into the second automatic promotion place on the last day, thanks to defeats for Middlesbrough and Bradford City. Middlesbrough were so close, with an identical record to Villa's – wins and goal difference, the latter better than champions Millwall – but Villa had scored 68 against Boro's 63. Villa did have a claim to fame to mitigate a poor home record: 13 away wins, to equal the best ever in the Division. In the play-offs Boro beat Chelsea in the each-way final, so all was well that ended well, for them at least.

This time we went by car to witness an encounter near the top of the table, the whole process proving painless. As in other cases 'County Ground' denotes an association with cricket, at Swindon dating back to 1895. It was the base of Wiltshire CCC, which still resided next door. The ground had a feeling of space, the floodlights visible from afar by road and rail. No problem finding it. Once there for a return visit, the interesting aspect was the patchwork character of the Arkells Stand, presenting myriad colours in the seats. The club has been trying to find a new site for a long time, but their present home seems serviceable enough if not very exciting. They moved several times early in their existence, settling in County Road in 1896.

These teams hadn't met since time immemorial, Chelsea's flirtations with the Second Division previously coinciding with Swindon's occupancy of the lower divisions. Chelsea emerged this year as runaway champions with 99 points, so this was a good result for the home team. The Robins conceded the fewest home goals in the division (35 for, 15 against), Chelsea's record being 50 for, 24 against, a bit more appealing. Give me goals at both ends, rather than a pre-eminence of defence.

## 2. The Nineties

### Tranmere Rovers 4 Sunderland 1
### Division I (2), 13/11/93

Jersey and I had traversed Merseyside by rail through city and under river to indulge initially in Hamilton Square, Birkenhead's showpiece, in transit to the delights of New Brighton. This precluded League football, which could have been on offer up to 1951 when its club was voted out of the League in favour of Workington. The Magazine and Pilot Inn served our needs well on a brief tour of parts of the Wirral via Birkenhead proper on the way to Prenton Park, the subdivision location in Tranmere, itself a subdivision of Birkenhead, subdivision of the Wirral, subdivision of Merseyside, if you're being technical. We had enjoyed Port Sunlight, the tourist experience, on a previous occasion, so bit by bit we were scouring the area, with the prospect of good things in Liverpool later on.

Rovers adopted a role comparable to Stockport in the Greater Manchester conurbation. It was the lesser being/poor relation on the other side of the tracks/ Mersey, sometimes employing their seniors' twilight players, yielding renewed opportunity at a lower level. This might form a kind of exit strategy for the last days of a career. Tranmere's traditional status has been lower-division, in complete contrast with this day's visitors who, up to their first relegation in 1958, were notably the club with the longest continuous membership of the First Division. In 1993 things were very different. Sunderland had avoided relegation to Division II (3) by a single point and were to finish in mid-table in 1994. The home team, meanwhile, were riding high, in fourth and fifth positions respectively, losing narrowly in the 1993 play-off semi-finals to Swindon, and to Leicester in 1994. On both occasions the winners went on to secure the last Premier League place. So poor Tranmere have never quite got there and these years were their best. In similar vein their ousting in the 1994 League Cup semi-finals by eventual winners Villa was the narrowest: (3-1, 1-3, 4-5 on penalties). Among a modest crowd of 8,497, though average for them, we caught them in their prime.

It would have been good to be around on 26 April 1958, when the race to the new Third Division reached its climax with an abundance of cliff-hanging games in Division III (N), including Tranmere v Gateshead. 'Mid-table' has never been so exciting – in the end Tranmere triumphed up to 11th, with Rochdale 10th and Wrexham 12th, all on 46 points and qualifying for the upper tier. York got 46, too, with an inferior goal average, and two teams finished with 45 (one was Gateshead) and two with 44 points. Division III (S) was tame by comparison, with 12th placed Colchester a clear three points ahead of Northampton, condemned to the initial Fourth Division in 13th.

The ground was a predictably appealing antique abode, comprising stands called the Kop (home terrace, where we hitched up), the Borough Road Stand and the Cowshed. We were in attendance just in time to enjoy these historical, dilapidated edifices, showering rust on those present should the ball hit a hard place. The very next year these three sides were replaced, the Main Stand surviving as it was. Perhaps, along with many an old ground, they were lucky here not to suffer in the Valley Parade manner. Supporters would sometimes lose a cap through the floorboards to drop into the morass of bits of paper and other debris below. A friend of mine 'The Toff', in short trousers at the time, would be designated to clamber down to rescue it.

Birkenhead's Cammell Laird FC survived, thrived even, celebrating its centenary in 2007, finishing in second place in the Unibond Division 1. Ultimately they capitulated in the play-off to Eastwood Town. The Cammell Laird Social Club, eponymous title of Half Man Half Biscuit's 2001 album, accolade by an ardent fan in the esteemed Foreword writer, Attila the Stockbroker, featured a welcome track, the 'Referee's Alphabet'. Here are a few letters:

*C is for Continual Criticism I receive from the touchline: 'Get back in your technical area'...J is for Ju Jitsu, which I quite intend to display given a dark alley and some of the narky blurts I've encountered...the P is for the Penalty shoot out – great*

173

*drama and no pressure on me...U is for the Umpire which I sometimes wish I'd been instead – you never hear a cricket crowd chanting 'who's the bastard in the hat'...the X represents the sarcastic kiss planted on my forehead by a swarthy Portuguese centre half, whom I've just dismissed...the Z could be for Zidane, Zico, Zola, Zubizaretta, Zoff, even Zondervan, but is in fact for the Zest with which we approach our work. Without this zest for the game we wouldn't become refs, and without refs, well, Zero. See also Zatopek, Zeus, Zeal Monachorum, I have a caravan there, static, naturally.*

In the game Sunderland went ahead through a goal from their record signing Don Goodman, a 'menace' spotted by Ron Saunders at West Brom. This couldn't last. We had chosen this fixture to break the Prenton duck because Rovers were riding high – second in the table, having won six of their eight home games, and netting three per game. The game promised some action. Meanwhile the Rokerites were four points off the bottom, with a fair home record (W5, D1, L2) but a solitary point away. Goodman's goal made it three so far. The men in white were in full throttle after half-time. Pat Nevin scored twice and Irish World Cup star John Aldridge once. That day leaders Leicester lost 1-0 at Stoke, so were overtaken by Rovers; Charlton went to the top after a 5-1 drubbing of Notts County.

Well satisfied, we resumed the entertainment over the water with lovely local Cains bitter in the Post House Inn. The New China City Restaurant followed with an excellent monosodium glutamate deal. Strangely prolix name, though. Why not go further and provide more options, like New and Traditional China, Formosa and Taiwan City and Surrounding Districts Restaurant/Café Bar/Takeaway. All those indulgences we took in our stride, but the next morning I cracked a tooth on Jersey's bacon, crispy, yes, and how! – a credit to the Co-op. Then we cast longing glances at the view of Blackpool, his place being helpfully located in Southport, complete with its former League club at Haig Avenue. I did once see them play Shepshed Charterhouse. They won. But I digress.


## Torquay United 1 Wigan Athletic 1
## Division III (4), 26/11/94

I'd been trying for years to get to Plainmoor. I even had a relative abiding nearby, and friends in residence, from time to time, but manifold reasons obviated the long-awaited visit: it was seaside summertime (after all, you do go there for bathing, and palm trees too) or rained off (for which Devon is well known) or an away Cup game took precedence on the day, or other commitments were more important – I won't itemize them here. Bad timing generally. Torquay is a good place to visit as such. Thus I have only ever passed Plainmoor's portals this once. I knew I would strike lucky at last as another first had just occurred – my only ever National Lottery win (all of ten quid) on the 19th. I took the hint, gave up the weekly squander, and committed a friendly weekend to the Devon Riviera. The Lottery and Plainmoor share the status of 'rare indulgence'.

The team had reached the play-offs the previous year and, now on 23 points, were substantially above Wigan in the table, who were one of four clubs on 13 points at the bottom. The fatal flaw was that the Latics were drawless – until now. And this was to be the fifth consecutive single-goal tally for the Gulls. The highlight of an illuminating programme was the League Table. This contained the rarity of two teams in bold, the second one not the opposition but local rivals Exeter, some of whose supporters in response refer to their neighbours as 'Turkey'. Normally football clubs are self-obsessed to a point. There was also a large advert for Euro 96, but its shape was irregular, indented by blocks for Rob Day Landscaping and Boots & Laces, evidently an eating house, offering Screaming Lord Sutch (small ad) and three-course meals (bigger). It did point out that it was situated next to Torquay United (in brackets). Also in the programme there was a cross word and a 'Find the hidden teams' competition comprising a 10 x 10 block of letters. Should I return to the ground, a programme would be an essential purchase to see if now Sudoku and Kakuro are now the equivalent.

Plainmoor was tiny, holding a mere 6,003 at the time, but most comfortable. This placed it at 109th in the table of ground capacities, more suited to the club's new status as a Fifth Division member in 2007. They were seriously the worst team in the League in 2006-07, still bottom after 23rd club Boston had suffered a ten-point deduction. There followed post-season shenanigans with changes in ownership and management. Leroy Rosenior, a former coach, went through a press conference as new guv'nor, only to lose the job ten minutes later following a takeover. That beats the previous record: Dave Bassett was at Crystal Palace for four days in 1984. Colin Lee, another Gulls old boy, was Rosenior's immediate successor. Thus announced the incoming eight-strong owning consortium Chairman, Cris Boyce.

It's all so pleasant getting to the ground, a bus, a drive or a walk, via charming residences, gentle hills. There were watering holes, take-aways, the trappings of a residential and touristic neighbourhood. The disconcerting thing is the Gulls' colours. Yellow and Blue seemed more like an away strip. So The Latics' blue was more characteristic of home boys' gear – role reversal. This afternoon out was one to repeat. As is this joke, which once got the biggest laugh in Torquay's Babbacombe Theatre: 'Two blondes walked into a bar. You'd have thought one of them would have seen it.'


## Northampton Town 2 Barnet 0
## Division III (4), 28/12/96

How I wished this had been at the old County Ground. On reflection, not so, because that would have meant a repeat Cobblers (very apt) visit to this ghastly eyesore later on. It was brass monkeys weather, to the extent that I wished I was a smoker to keep at least some part of my body warm, and for something to do. But smoking was banned, instructed the authoritarian notices, in a featureless concrete football ground, presumably the nanny state again, an overreaction to the Valley Parade disaster in 1985. Meanwhile, a dozen seasons on it was still commonplace to witness cigarette, and cigar, smoking during matches.

I tried Bovril and a pie to mitigate the sub-zero temperature. They proved to be predictably synthetic and unpleasant, in that order, but served to convey brief warmth and sustenance.

I think I was becoming a bit hyper myself. So cold just after Christmas and solitary for this exposure, my weekend companions preferring the cosiness of antiques shops in a quaint, but select, village in the interior of Northamptonshire. No diversions, as this was out of town and off the shelf, with treacherous, slippery country roads on the way there, almost skidding up a bank on the way. Sixfields? Intriguing name; shame they had to replace any fields with this structure.

The most interesting thing about it was the stadium's capacity: 7,653. Most odd. The club immediately attracted higher attendances at the ground, so there was some blessing, though recent attendances had been below 4,000. For this visit it was helpful that Sixfields was on the appropriate side of Northampton. Battling with late December sales traffic in the town centre would have been no fun. It remained to pay a visit to downtown Northampton years later.

In the programme, called *The Cobbler*, appeared Father Christmas – ten times – one of whom was manager Ian Atkins and a curious character with an ill-fitting white wig, pebble glasses and pouting lips had a whole page devoted to him. Readers were asked to 'Guess Who?' Presumably someone familiar to regulars as he was wearing a top in the Cobblers' mutation of claret. The players' costume has proved inventive in design over recent years. The claret – of a consistent bottomless hue suggesting vintage rather than plonk – has carried stars both singular and plural, bits of amber reminiscent of Bradford City, and stripes fading subtly up and down the torso. For this year the whole body was claretted, with a concession to white in the socks. I decided it was a device to distract your gaze from the stadium.

'Introducing Barnet', pages generously coloured Bee amber, alluded to prolific number 10 Sean Devine's debut goal against Exeter, for whom, as fate dictated, he became a mainstay later in his career. I wonder if he scored for the Grecians against the Bees. After all, following his move to Devon the song was to go:

> Sean Devine, Devine,
> He wears number 29,
> He scores every fucking time,
> Sean Devine, Devine.

Elsewhere the second line went *He wears number 10, not 9*. Aftermath: Devine, an Irishman born in Lewisham, left these shores for Auckland, New Zealand after his tme at Exeter.

The programme was the focus of my attention, being so idiosyncratic. Fixtures were on page 19, out of 48, unusually forward in the plan and a long way from the back page squad lists. There was no Div III table or note of the team's position. I worked out that they had won 8, drawn 7 and lost 8 games so were comfortably mid-table. Why conceal that? Eleven league games later the story of the season's climax was recounted by Rob Marshall for the fanzine *What a load of cobblers*. 'We went into the last Saturday in sixth place, behind Chester and Swansea. Scunthorpe were the opposition, and despite a complete sell-out in the home seats, the club refused to re-seat the visitors in a smaller area, even though everyone knew Scunny wouldn't bring more than 250 fans with them. Inevitably a few Cobblers got in the away enclosure, but fortunately there was no trouble. A first half goal by Sean Parrish eased the tension – we'd made the play-offs!

'The news got even better: Swansea and Chester had both lost, so we finished fourth, thus gaining home advantage in the second leg. Cardiff were to be our opponents and since we'd won five of our last seven games, we were the form side. The queues for tickets, especially for the home leg, were horrendous. Many regulars had a tough time getting any, as part-timers crawled out of the woodwork. What really angered me was to see the number of people in the queue wearing Man United and Liverpool shirts – some were even wearing Saints jerseys (the local Rugby Union team). Funny, I don't remember seeing them on cold windy night in Hartlepool!' They won the away leg 0-1, courtesy of 'a brilliant solo goal from Sean Parrish…For the second leg, the police were out in force: riot squads, police horses, dogs and a helicopter, but this didn't stop all sorts of fights breaking out near the ground…Although officially the gate was not a record, you could have fooled me as there appeared to be several hundred too many Cardiff fans in the away end. I guess they'd travelled without tickets and to contain them the police had let them in anyway, but if that was the case, then why did they open the gates ten minutes from the end? It just allowed the hooligan element to promptly head round to the home sections to cause more mayhem.

'The game? The atmosphere was incredible; the whole ground was singing, and when we scored, it was bedlam…In the end we ran out 4-2 winners on aggregate, prompting joyous celebrations on our part and wanton rampaging on theirs. Why do Cardiff City attract such morons? In the final it was to be Swansea. Uh-oh, we'd played them twice, lost twice (one of the games had seen new signing John Frain's debut and the inevitable last-minute goal for the oppo). Wembley. A devalued dream? Not so for an incredible 32,500 Cobblers who bought tickets. No problems for the regulars this time, so the others were more than welcome, especially if it meant some of them might come back next season. Wembley Way was a sea of claret; no Man Utd or Liverpool shirts on display here, and it was no surprise – the club shop had been devastated, you couldn't get a Cobblers shirt anywhere, they'd even sold out of replica goalkeeper's jerseys!…It was a crap game, heading for extra time…the stadium clock had been showing 90 minutes for ages, when Christian Lee, looking for an opening, was fouled on the edge of the D. John Frain stepped up to take it, and when his shot hit an onrushing Swansea defender, we figured "Oh well, extra time for sure". But hang on… The ref booked the Swansea player for encroaching and ordered the kick to be retaken. Frain stepped up a second time. He hit it oh, so sweetly, wrong-footing the 'keeper who dived in vain as the ball nestled in the bottom corner. YYEESSSSS! The feeling was incredible; we'd scored, at Wembley, in our end, in the last minute. Swansea re-started, but the final whistle blew immediately. Last minute goals, why don't we ever score them?'

The Christmas triumph I witnessed completed an unbeaten run in December.

I managed to escape easily from a venue with rather more spare space than during those May debacles. Next new (doomed to become old) ground: Elm Park, Reading.

## Ipswich Town 5 Norwich City 0
## Division I (2), 21/2/98

This was meant to be a reunion weekend on public transport, but my host Wully was committed elsewhere with little notice. He wouldn't have got much out of the game, having no interest in football – in fact I would have been a patient listener to his discoveries some distance from Portman Road, I know not what. Was this aversion connected to his origins? He was from Leigh, Lancashire, so how about Rugby League, either that lesser luminary or big boys Wigan up the road? But he didn't like that either. It is most wearisome maintaining persuasive tactics, but we should never give up the fight to recruit more enthusiasts. Some have come good after years of persuasion at least to try one football game.

I decided to try out Ipswich as a complete package and emerged feeling fairly familiar with the town, Suffolk's biggest with a population of 141k in the 2001 census, over a couple of days. This was aided by choosing a comfortable guest house, the Waverley, near the station with an omniscient landlady. For the game I was in the Cobbold Stand, an evocative dedication. The town was awash with football at Saturday lunchtime. I had difficulty gaining access to a hostelry, but mercifully achieved this in the Plough, a Town (the nickname) pub. More recently they have been called the Tractorboys, but I didn't register that on this occasion. The *Racing & Football Outlook* first records the name, as an alternative to 'Town', in 2003. It may be a contrivance but shows some imagination or flight of fancy, there being precious few farm vehicles in evidence, the character of the place being far more urban than rural.

There was reputed to be intense rivalry between the teams of East Anglia's megalopoles. I noticed fervour and business, but no undue aggression, and not really the intensity so much written about concerning local derby games; certainly this one. I've seen a quote from an Ipswich fan that the rivalry 'is a county thing, Suffolk versus Norfolk' – a touch obvious? And a Norwich opinion of Ipswich, 'the team that's going nowhere'. Well he would say that, most of the time.

This mighty victory was deeply satisfying for a neutral spectator. The Cobbold was an impressive stand on the south side of the ground and afforded excellent views, the whole thing a magnificent advertisement for making the effort to go out for a football game and not linger in the market and watering holes all afternoon. 21,858 out of a maximum of 22,559 was the turnstile tally, both teams mid-table, but after this the home team's goal difference was 15, Norwich's -19. Ipswich won 10 of their last fifteen games and clambered up to fifth position with 83 points. As was their wont they lost to Charlton (fourth – 88) in the play-offs. Both legs 0-1. Sunderland finished third with 90 points and lost out to Charlton in the Wembley 'final', 7-6 on penalties.

The remaining entertainment in Tractortown, having enjoyed the goals again on my B and B TV with a cup of tea and Bourbon biscuit, was to see Bernard Shaw's *Pygmalion* in the Wolsey Theatre, meeting up with a couple of friends involved in the production.

They were resignedly amused to have noted that a number of seats had emptied after the interval, and some patrons had left even earlier, during the first act. The ostensible reason was that it was a contemporary production, with harsh musical effects and an abstract design, i.e. not what a traditional audience might expect or wish of an interpretation of a well-made play'. They had decided what to anticipate for the whole show very quickly, and some acted accordingly. I should also point out that the Wolsey main house's capacity was 410. Compare that with 22k at Portman Road.

At a football game it is inevitable that a drift to the exits starts near the end of the game, but it would be strange to leave before seeing most of the plot unfold. A football match is not scripted, but a live encounter within an established framework, employing 22 participants, red cards notwithstanding. A theatrical production can use anything from a sole performer to a cast of thousands: a nice set of contrasts.

## Derby County 2 Leeds United 2
## Premiership, 31/10/98

£19 for a seat in the McDonald's Stand. The previous season Leeds had registered a 0-5 win in this encounter at Pride Park, so perhaps Derby were relieved to hold their own. The Rams achieved a best that year at eighth in a six-year spell in the top flight; Leeds got to third in 1999-2000 in a symmetrical sequence of 5-4-3-4-5 in the final table.

Fredders organized the trip using three modes of transport from base in a Peak village to the Rams' new home, also in an open landscape, albeit of a somewhat different character.

At that time it was an industrial desert, mitigated by the massive increase in support: the Baseball Ground's capacity had ultimately been reduced to 18k, though 41,826 had crowded in to see County play Spurs as recently as 1969. On my visit (Derby 3 Huddersfield Town 0 – Div I, 15/4/72), they were racing to the title with 16 home wins out of 21. Huddersfield were left with the wooden spoon. Baseball was actually played at the ground even after the club moved there in 1895. Several clubs played the game, including Aston Villa and Leyton Orient. The place was famously cramped and enclosed. At the time of this visit it boasted seating on all sides, along with copious standing space. At least they must have perfected the art of squeezing maximum bodies in, as at that 1969 Spurs game which was in the first couple of months of their sequence of high top-division achievement – five top four finishes in seven seasons.

A generation later, this Leeds game was during the Rams' second season in their new establishment, the first having attracted an average of 27k.

Having endured the city centre for long enough to oil us for the next phase of the journey, we discovered a most enlightened pub nearer the ground which allowed punters to bring in their lunch from the chippie next door for consumption, washed down by their beer. Fish, chips and mushy peas never tasted better, to Fredders or my hungry self. The ground design (1997 vintage) I found unsatisfying, being regular in shape and enclosed in character. Corridors were somewhat scant – the often-suffered under-provision of space and facilities. Not one for an urgent return visit, but a good trip all the same.

The East Midlands, in the form of Derbyshire, was important to me for a separate quest, having seen the stirring movie, *Dead Man's Shoes*. I saw it when released in 2004 and was intrigued to unearth the identity of a substantial, brooding, evocative ruin, in which the final, key horror took place. The leading character had become impassioned about the perpetrators of the deed at the root of the plot: 'God will forgive them, then allow them into Heaven. I can't live with that'. Hence the vengeance exacted by him. In the quest to identify the location, on journeys north I undertook diversions from the MI into pockets of hidden country. One by one they were discounted as their OS map feature didn't match the memory. I hadn't quite lost sleep over this but would soon if I couldn't track down the scene.

It eventually occurred to me to contact the arts 'media' centre where I'd seen the film. Quick as a flash came the information, identifying the independent film company concerned, indeed based in the area. Shane Meadows (director) and Paddy Considine (actor) had teamed up most tellingly. I recommending seeking out his/their subsequent efforts, like the award winning *This is England* (2006). A few emails later issued the information that the ruin was Riber Castle, a majestic hulk brooding above Matlock in the beautiful Dales. On my visit I drove past Matlock Town's ground after treading the soggy turf around the grim structure, later destined for the inevitable conversion into a modern amenity: des res. As for Matlock Town, well, why not some time?

## Colchester United 0 Millwall 0
## Division II (3), 28/11/98

Colchester is an old and new Army town, Camulodunum to the Romans, with much evidence of the military in the streets and public houses I tried, though the Layer Road ground was a haven. Wully was up against it on the work front and welcomed a chance to avoid football as well as spend a day on budgets. I meandered around vestiges of Camulodunum, spending most time in the Castle Museum; housed in the castle keep (the biggest in Europe, wrote Bradwan). In an interesting setting were displays setting out the town's more remote history. Perhaps I drifted past any bits on more recent military stuff.

He pointed out other items to fascinate:

- Jumbo – this ex-water tower has towered above Colchester for over 120 years. Decommissioned in the 1980s, there is a fight to save it as it stands.
- The Siege House – we have lots of ruins caused by bombs, but this half-timbered house is the only bullet-scarred building he knows of in England.
- Tymperleys Clock Museum – another half-timbered house. All the clocks were made in Colchester between 1640 and 1840: which suggests Colchester was chock-full of clock makers; or that the collector, Bernard Mason, was a bit obsessive.
- Finally, 'if you like shellfish then Colchester open market is a place to buy' – pots full of whelks and mussels could keep you engaged on the way to the ground. 'Most of the barracks on the long walk to Layer Road are boarded up. Soon there may be so few British Army soldiers left in Britain that Luxembourg could successfully invade.'

There was little to inspire in the ground, on or off the pitch. Both sets of Blues, the 'U's' and the Lions, were inconsequential, though I have noted the home lot from time to time as visitors, as at St Mary's, Southampton, in valiant mode.

There is an example here of how bizarre rivalries between clubs can be. According to the fanzine *The Blue Eagle* in reviewing 1995-96 encounters: '… Colchester and Exeter aren't exactly bitter rivals; after all they are on opposite sides of the country, but over the last couple of seasons there had been trouble between the fans. Mostly handbags at dawn you understand, but in these days of violence-free-footy (in the Third Division anyway), the odd broken window and punch-up merits a mention. Anyway, when the game started, there were about 60 away fans on their terrace directing chants at us, and we returned the favour. A couple of the Exeter fans seemed to get really worked up for some reason and spent the entire game volleying insults at the home fans. Granted, the game was boring, but even so someone might take the bait. They did. At half-time the away terrace struck up with that all time favourite "come and join us, come and join us…", and for the first time in a while the home fans decided to take up their offer. All but five or six of the Exeter fans immediately decided that they'd rather the Colchester fans didn't join them after all and shuffled away, but a couple stayed and for what seemed like ages, but was in fact about two minutes there was a bit of aggro. No-one seemed to get hurt fortunately, but that was more than can be said for the single Exeter flag that was liberated from the away end and brought back as a trophy, before being ceremonially burnt as an offering. Sixteen Colchester supporters ended up in court over the incident, so I doubt it wlll happen again, but the trip to Exeter won't exactly be a family day out, will it!' I wonder how the story was/would have been reported from an Exeter viewpoint.

After the Millwall game, at 16.56 hours, I espied Wully's car as preordained, a couple of streets away as there was scant parking in the area. At least this was some distance to the south of the town centre, a vehicular nightmare. You notice these things even on a day off driving, for which I was thankful. This was in those misty days before mobile phones, so we had to synchronize watches, as if on a military exercise. Quite appropriate, really.

## 3. The Noughties

### Burnley 4 Millwall 3
### Division II (3), 22/4/00

*A feast of serendipity*
*With pints and fights to play a part*
*And Burnley won 4-3.*

*The Talbot oozed such bonhomie,*
*A joyous pre-match start,*
*A feast of serendipity.*

*The goals upstaged Bertie the Bee,*
*The mascot kitted out in claret*
*And Burnley won 4-3.*

*The cops amid the grief and glee*
*Just thugged the fans apart,*
*A feast of serendipity.*

*To status Turf Moor held the key –*
*The Lions lost both game and heart*
*And Burnley won 4-3.*

*That night in Leeds, a play to see*
*Lampooning royalty and art*
*A feast of serendipity*
*And Burnley won 4-3.*

'Serendipity' is apposite in the remote cotton inclines of north-east Lancashire. Nelson FC faded, Accrington too, revivified into a 92 member in 2006. I shall decline to call them 'Stanley' as the unique suffix seems to qualify them to be fully quoted in our regular reading in fixture lists and league tables just for that reason – rarity converts their identity into the double barrel. Not so in 1958-59: I noticed a fixture list in the National Football Museum which only added suffixes if needed for identification. Sheffield United and Wednesday were entered thus, and so was the simple Accrington. The Uniteds and Towns have to live with reduced appellation. For some reason Lincoln City is an exception, usually listed in full. Strange, that. I guess it comes down to a minion setting up the names on a database to be fed through to all subscribing publications. A further pedantic observation in

2006 was the denuding of just three outfits in the depths: Macclesfield, Shrewsbury and Stockport all appeared on BBC 1 each week without any appendage and scoreman Tim Gudgin read them thus, though 'Town', 'Town' and 'County' have previously been included in the reading. Blame the minion. It was most likely only I, though, who was at all concerned.

To return to Burnley, for whom this is irrelevant, Turf Moor's capacity has gradually been reduced to 22k, more than many in a world of ubiquitous seating. It was a stadium to enjoy in its setting, which evoked the industrial heritage of the area. It was easy to imagine the place in its glory days (top attendance 54,775 in 1924). Seven goals made a fine feast on a sunny day, augmented by the associated combat in the streets.

The Turfites have won the League Championship twice, Division II twice, plus token victorships in Divs III and IV. Read on: the FA Cup in 1913-14 and the Anglo-

Scottish Cup in 1978-79. This is dazzling in view of the town's modest population, especially by comparison with the more accessible giants in other parts of Lancashire. It's surprising now to find the population argument not to be strictly valid. The even more remote Nelson (2001 census: 29k) boasted a League team from 1921 to 1931, when replaced by Chester, having tasted Second Division elevation for one season and finished rock bottom twice.

In the modern age it has become expedient to combine the upper Ribble towns into a single viable unit for census purposes, reflecting the needs of modern bureaucracy and changing economic activity. The 150k souls produced include Nelson and Colne. On the other hand Burnley and Padiham, feeling more like a unit, total 84k, still not in the lowest ten populations for League clubs. But, whatever these statistics suggest, the earlier achievements of the club were remarkable. Their average gates in the Championship in 2005-06 were 12,462 (19th out of 24), the team finishing 17th.

## Bradford City 2 Coventry City 1
## Premiership, 2/12/00

The Bantams seemed doomed. Both teams were relegated in due course, along with the Maine Road yoyos who bounced back again the next year. No such luck for Brad or Cov – less experience perhaps.

It was a welcome diversion to have the home team up with the big boys for a couple of seasons. *Racing and Football Outlook Annual* said on their arrival in August 1999: 'so City are bound to cause a few shocks (because they were free scoring in the 'First' Division) – but maybe not the biggest shock of all, which would be for them to avoid an immediate return'. They finished 17th, and down went Wimbledon after a fine extended membership of 14 seasons, Sheffield Wednesday and City's erstwhile Div I companions Watford. The forecast was better for 2000-01 after this achievement, but they plummeted, albeit valiantly. The credit for their rise and double season residence in the Premiership must go to manager Paul Jewell, 'clearly more sharp cookie than rookie' who in 2005-06 was reinventing himself at Wigan in their first year up top. Meanwhile the Sky Blues had enjoyed a most impressive 34 years in the top tier. They were also predicted for an improved League position this time, having impressed in 14th. There is a strange statistic here: in 2000 Coventry ended with 12 home wins and none away. In 2001 they went down with four at home and the same away.

This game could have produced any result. Let's say 2-1 was fair. The Paraders certainly needed it. There was an uproarious atmosphere as the claret and amber team came up with the goods – they were already well-settled in wooden spoon position in the table. It was good value for the £23 admission, in Valley Parade's new 5,000 seater CIBA Stand, replacing the cute (I was told) Midland Road Stand.

Bradford City boasted Britain's longest running fanzine 'The City Gent' (born in 1985), a preoccupation of Glyn Watkins. He has also quoted local lad J.B.Priestley hat 'nowhere in Bradford was further than a tram ride from the cry of the curlew. The trams are gone but the moors remain' in stunning contrast to the building density which has offered us glimmers of top class football, in a haven deep within. On arriving at the ground the customary quest for nourishment within walking distance was well rewarded a few streets away. The Cartwright Arms, a bit of a gastro pub (before the term was coined, I fancy), was Indian-run and both local beer and a mouth-watering dish from the Specials blackboard, even the poppadoms, were special. This was predictable as Bradford city centre is famous for curries, but this was to the north of the centre, and a pub.

In December 2000 it was difficult to visualize Valley Parade in 1985 when the Main Stand was burnt down, the ground now being substantially rebuilt, seeming well fit for top-class football, even if relegation avoidance was the central concern. The city had supported Rugby League in the form of Bradford Northern ('Bulls' for the new era) and two football clubs. Bradford FC's Park Avenue had more going for it than Valley Parade, which was surrounded by industry in the Manningham area. Park Avenue was more amenable and boasted a long lease, as well as meriting an accolade for spawning Kevin Hector in the 1960s. He went on to 'Cloughie favourite' status at Derby County, staying there from 1966 to 1978. On site were rugby (before essential elements of the local fraternity switched from Union to League and moved out) and cricket. However Bradford FC's demise was entirely predictable, when they were voted out of the League in 1970 (replaced by Cambridge). They had propped up the Fourth Division for the previous three seasons.

How much healthier now that misguided protection of League membership has eased up considerably, if not enough, with promotion and relegation from the fifth division.

Along with the trams, Park Avenue football ground was no more, just the cricket. Bradford (Park Avenue) FC's was a sad and salutary tale, featuring gross mismanagement. As a club they were no longer, ultimately expiring at Valley Parade, of all places, in 1974, when it was a ground of little distinction, just waiting for a fire to break out. Before that cataclysmic conflagration, Bradford City's ground had a tradition more associated with the Manningham area with its negative social overtones, the ultimate working-class ethos – strippers at half-time. It all had to change, and did, eventually.

It says a lot for the opposite trend that City were able to reach the heights witnessed at this game: a Premiership game at a ground for the future.


## Huddersfield Town 3 Cheltenham Town 3
## Division II (3), 15/2/03

The journey there was a West Yorkshire bargain – £1 for the train journey. First stop was the town's art gallery for an exhibition called 'Disinformation' by sound sculptor (and hi-tech electronics expert it seems) Joe Banks. We were coaxed into a huge

185

enveloping green light sensitive screen. The participant was stunned by an exceedingly brief sound, called 'Theophany' (The Voice of God), during which lightning struck, weirdly and wonderfully.

We made provocative shapes stained in the aftermath shadow. An observer might have ascribed this to boyish pranks or an enactment of parts of the Kama Sutra: one etched upon the memory.

It was time to prepare for the issue in hand. Of the several pubs in evidence in the centre, we chose the Commercial Inn for pre-match pints. Most enjoyable with an early football game on the screen above us, not always drowning out the cacophony of patrons in the snug, and a roving joint, in no way related to a Sabbath culinary experience. We were off to find a snack: chicken and mushroom pies devoured along the way. Unfortunately Wakey, a little nonchalant with a mouthful of the item, upended while attempting to mount the pavement. An old lady nearby offered to help, thankfully keeping her teeth in. He rallied, subsuming this indignity in gingerly negotiating the sidewalk, this time without mishap.

Committed ground-spotters encountered along the quest have held the Terriers' old Leeds Road ground aloft as a sad loss, its speciality the vast Popular Bank terrace holding 20k plus souls. The atmosphere in their fanatic heyday eight decades ago cannot be countenanced.

The Macalpine Stadium, as it was still named then, was a local landmark built on open ground, and seemed to have attracted more interest than many new stadia. Part of this related to the applying some Leeds Road merits: sinuous curves, a heavenward style which beckoned you up the incline to the turnstiles (a climb always yields cardiovascular benefit), and inside a well-balanced amalgam of the ingredients to satisfy the senses, even, on that day, a sunset.

This stadium can be cited as a positive exemplar for modern football management. I lament never having sampled Leeds Road. The new one was living proof that football no longer takes its audience for granted. It was a 'good' example. It must have been a difficult lesson for chairmen and directors to learn: for scores of halcyon years of blissful unconcern, when football was the main sporting attraction for the best part of the calendar, the clubs did not have to worry too much about the fans. Victorian facades were fronts for arenas regularly hosting immense crowds, suffering miserable facilities – exposed to the elements and only with difficulty making their way to bladder relief and sustenance (steaming pies and drinks) in interminable queues. From the owners' point of view it was very much a business – take the money and run, reflecting the malaise of the rest of British industry during this period. In the next generation influence shifted to the abolition of the maximum wage and the blossoming of youth culture. More disposable income, a greater incidence of disturbances, hence costly policing required; in parallel, better deals for players.

To leap to the Nineties and the new generation, the trend became well established towards modern stadium provision with basic facilities at least better than their predecessors. You could now get to the gents without hassle, though there may well be a wait, as most establishments are guilty of underprovision, viz car park arrangements. Enter the Premier League, fed and watered in its augmenting guises and deals, rife with self-interest from clubs cynical about their supporters (how much do you pay to get in?) down to fabulously remunerated players, who seem not to have been given even a hint about charitable giving.

The pies at this garden of delights were comparatively easy to queue for. Wakey duly obtained one each (with Bovril and some urgency – blame his earlier bereavement), of content different from the one destined for rodent fodder in the gutter. The game was a ding-dong affair, each team taking the lead by turns. The six goals were the most scored in any Div II game in 2002-03. Both Towns were in the relegation zone. In due course they both went down.

A further treat awaited us before the return journey – in the Station Tavern. A couple of pints there were a fitting conclusion, amid the wall decorations illustrating a bygone age when the crisp oncer spent on transport would have funded the whole day out.

## Oldham Athletic 2 Blackpool 3
## Division II (3), 23/8/03

Manchester was the venue for weekend post-conference frolics. Emerging that morning, extensive and expensive mobile phone use revealed that no way could I get into the fresh-as-a-daisy City of Manchester Stadium. For some days before and even on the day it was fixed in the diary as the destination that afternoon. Wakey and his friends, making the journey from various parts, were season ticket-holders. With hindsight it's pretty obvious that it was doomed to be a fruitless venture, being so early in a) the working life of the new attraction and b) the season. Ingress to Manchester City's hallowed temple remained one of life's more insuperable obstacles for many months until Fuckin' Dave came to the rescue.

The alternative in Greater Manchester for a League game was Boundary Park, still to be experienced and, an uniformed individual at Transport Information informed me, a 45-minute journey. Not so. Wakey and I split after a misjudged time in a convenient bar. That is, we got carried away. The instructions I had gleaned as to bus stop and number were both wrong. Or I was. As I desperately sought an official with practical knowledge, a surge of panic swept over me. Not only no joy with the 'Lazer Blues'/'The Citizens', as a football annual named Man City, but not much prospect with the Latics either. And to start with I still had to identify the right bus. Presumably all Oldham's support came from, well, Oldham, or at least North Manchester, having no need like mine that day. There was no one in Boundary blue to be seen. At last I managed to collar a bus driver, with an open door and time on his hands for a brief exchange. Nice man, he was sympathetic and accurate, and round the next corner was the very item, just as he said, scheduled to depart in one minute. It meandered around on a circuitous route including that red club's old homeland, Newton Heath. It got to Oldham in the end. It was by now nearly 3pm, but the goal, so to speak, was almost in sight. The second journey was immediate and speedy, and I followed the latest instructions, despite a throbbing brain, dismounting to find the haven of bliss round the next bend, just by a retail centre.

This was the home of the 'Blue Pride'. They were entertaining the tangerine team whose honours were pure and straightforward: Second Division Champions 1930; FA Cup winners 1953 (the rosy glow of the Stanley Matthews Final approaching England's 1966 effort for football-fervour memory); Anglo-Italian Cup winners 1971; LDV Trophy 2002.

The game was exciting, the home team letting it slip, and I think I saw all the goals, though I can't be sure. Anyway what would one have mattered in five after so many low-scoring games of late? Man City 1 Portsmouth 1 is what I missed. I was in a space standing by the perimeter, so my best view was of substitutes warming up. One of these was Blackpool striker Richard Walker, later to score quite a few for Bristol Rovers, prancing up and down the touchline. There seemed to be a plethora of track-suited persons limbering up, more than regulations laid down, I'm sure. At least a couple of them were called into action in the second half. The only snippet worth recording was Oldham's away record that season: 13 draws.

The chant 'Meat pie, sausage roll, come on Oldham give us a goal' which I have read somewhere, was not sung, unless I failed to make out the words properly. If I had heard it I might have thought of trying a pie or roll, as the immense Premier Lodge breakfast was wearing off. Speaking of Premier things, Athletic were original members of that stately body of 20 clubs in 1993-94, their second and last in the top flight. I'm not surprised to learn that the ground is built on high, exposed ground, something not observed on my bus journey. So near yet so far – the Moors murders were committed on Saddleworth above. I've also heard that being an away supporter on a bad day is extremely unpleasant.

Unfortunately, though the event developed as an early-season tempter, there was no time to do the area justice. At least we were treated to Chaddy, a sort of owl, who was available for hire at funerals and other occasions. His main claim to fame has been his exploits at the Mascot Grand National. Finishing third in 2000 and second in 2001, he claimed the crown in 2002 (breaking the course record; Ladbroke's paid out £30k on him) and 2003, only to be denied a hat trick by Graham the Gorilla in 2004. This is where the initiative diverts from Football League members. G the G represented Finedon Volta FC, based a few miles west of the venue for this event (Huntingdon Racecourse), over six fences, for which read hurdles. Chaddy put his superiority down to a vigorous training routine and the porridge diet. He said the best thing about mascot life was: 'putting smiles on people's faces…I also help the Make a Wish Foundation, Derian House Children's Hospital… Children in need and local schools to name but a few.' He was named after the (home) Chadderton Road End at Boundary Park.

## Doncaster Rovers 5 Bristol Rovers 1
## Div III (4), 2/10/03

A goalfest with Donny – on song, and the poor Pirates inept. Doncaster were a surprise package in their first season back in the League. They had finished third in the Conference, 19 points behind top team Yeovil Town and trailing Morecambe on goal difference. Then they beat Chester over two legs to conquer frequent near-misses Dag/Red in the play-off final.

Their old ground was quaintly named Belle Vue, latterly 'The Earth Stadium' (to do with mortgages). The record attendance at Belle Vue had been at a Third Division North fixture against Hull City: 37,149 in 1948. The capacity was now 10,593, curiously precise at a ground with substantial standing room. What, I wonder, was the calculation?

The town, of Roman foundation as Danum, achieved subsequent prosperity as a railway town, something recent councils have been keen to play down in 'improving' the image of the town in recent times. Dame Diana Rigg was a Donny girl. Her Medea, on the London stage, was heart-rending. She wasn't bad in that figure-hugging outfit in the 1960s ATV Avengers either.

There was a substantial building initiative afoot in the town centre. Rumours of resurrecting the long-closed 1899 Grand Theatre, which once hosted Pink Floyd, were a little difficult to countenance as the place was sandwiched deep in the development. How would you get shows in?

Apparently Doncaster was known as a butterscotch centre, bagsful often a present from the neighbouring races. That was a long time ago. I didn't notice any curiosities for sale at Belle Vue, despite its old-worldliness; only the comely 79-year-old red turnstiles.

At the time of this visit plans were afoot for the new stadium, funded by the council on a site called Lakeside Village. Apparently the lake was already there. The edifice was to house the Rovers, the Dragons Rugby League Club (the former plain Doncaster RLFC) and Doncaster Belles Ladies Football club. I hope the turf would stand up to all the studs. But on this occasion I enjoyed an old ground in its death throes; and lost a glove.

## Doncaster Rovers 2 Huddersfield Town 0
## League 1 (3), 14/10/07

This is 'Lakeside'. The ground is near the lake, not by it, and you could choose to approach it from the waterside, scaling a hillock, on whose summit opens a rare vista, an impressive stadium, surmounted by floodlights set at a jaunty angle. It was almost encouraging, though I must mutter about the unsexy black turnstiles. Black? The ultimate colour association of a football club should be through its turnstiles. Access to the furnace of endeavour. You can't ignite passion with jet black in red Donny. Thinking round the subject, it could be to do with this ground-sharing caper – Belles, Dragons etc.

Inside, the 15k and a bit Keepmoat, dreamt up as Lakeside, Stadium seemed a bit too regular in design and limited in extent – it should be bigger. There will be occasions when many will be disappointed, Donny being a set-up with ambition and promise, exhibiting considerable quality this very afternoon. Huddersfield were the very first visitors here, the outcome 3-0 on New Year's Day 2007, also setting an attendance record not since surpassed. You have to purchase tickets from the ground in advance of the game – Wakey was a bit bemused about the compass. It's admirable that the stands are named after the four winds, but the route to Lakeside and its comprehensive selection of outlets is so tortuous that, with no sun shining, it's hard to tell where you're facing. He, a local resident, not that that helps, knew not. Then the vendor managed to get our seats wrong – the party of four was needlessly placed in different rows (the tally turned out to be 6,866, it was announced, so fears would have been dispelled anyway).

The ticket experience was an exercise in officious bureaucracy, having very recently walked straight through old-fashioned turnstiles at an older Third Division ground (at Burslem, but no ticket was handed over, alas, to stick in the scrapbook). In fact good old Belle Vue came to our rescue, lost in this new construct of a desert. After the game we took up the red and white striped trail via footpaths and all manner of unidentifiable land use, ending up among a bunch of doubtful-looking youths on the jagged, derelict Town End terrace, thence a leap or two over a burgeoning wild-flower patch including verbascums of high quality (former site of the players' tunnel perhaps) into the car park, by now full of ruts but puddle free. This paradoxically had a direct view of the new stand of Doncaster Racecourse, whither an afternoon should be committed sometime soon. The alternative to joining the red and white throng would have been to employ a guiding star: the remaining Belle Vue floodlight pylon, or what's left of it, depressingly decapitated far enough up to see it all the way from the lake, as a piece of abandoned dead industry. This is my tip for parking for the Keepmoat, avoiding a soulless half-hour walk via open, most circuitous roads and enclosed footpaths to the town centre and station. Rand, who was suffering from withdrawal symptoms from a lack of tennis games, enjoyed the hike. The reward, of course, was a sojourn in one of Donny's finest market-place taverns. But his need was great – to go outside for a fix of Old Holborn.

Now for the action. The game soon came to life – Brian Stock scored in the 13th minute. 'We're just too good for you' deafened us, as we registered that we were below a hard-core bunch, of all ages and sexes. A banner proclaimed 'DR West Stand'. The seats (unlike the turnstiles) were vermilion except a block of token white ones in the North (away) Stand, which was in clear view and earshot. And Wakey and his godson Joe lent to this, muffled by this season's scarves. The programme was the, by now, standard shiny uninscribable issue (£2.50), pretty dull and unquotable, except the Team Head to Head Record (see below). With no fanzines for diversion I spent £1.50 on a copy of *Rovers World*, irresistibly tendered by a wench, in ice-cream salesperson mode. It turned out to be the 'Official Magazine', in newspaper format, aimed at football in the community I think, and very dull.

I awoke from the reverie induced by these two journals, one on quasi-toilet paper, the other standard shiny uninscribable, again, which were a good application of the axiom 'more is even less' to a raucous 'if you love the Rov'rs stand up.' And as further eye candy there grew a parade of policemen of varying degrees to judge y their hats, heights (in inverse ratio to importance) and demeanour, St Johns mbulance, Stewards, St Johns Cadets, 'EG' (what?), Liaison Officer, Press (in reen). This is what was adhered to their backs as one after another trotted past. ortunately the St J's staff were able to chat and look bored for most of the time, ere being no incidents, not even with the immense roving camera near the half-way ne.

When the bevy of Vikettes, seven of them in fact, attempted a performance t half-time, the operator seemed transfixed, or at least focused, on something in the West Stand, avoiding the pitch.

Empassioned utterances came thick and fast:
'You're not very good.'
'And you know you are, you're shit.'
'Sit down, shut up.'
'You're such shit it's unbelievable.'

The Bovril was good, considering. No-one needed to announce that, but it as a relief after so many bad experiences in new stadia.

And when Richard Wellens put the Rovers 2-0 ahead 20 minutes into he second half, 'I'm Rovers till I die' came one contribution from a substantial ongregation. The Terriers in the North Stand were self-deprecating: 'It's time to pend some money.' Rovers: 'You what, you what, you what you what,' then 'Sully ully what's the score?' (to Donny's goal-keeper Neil Sullivan, which seems odd to e – shouldn't it have been an ironical jibe at the underperforming Terriers keeper ndy Holdsworth?). This augmented into a developing theme: 'Skyman Skyman vhat's the score?' (the game kicked off at the odd time of 4pm on a Sunday for ky transmission), 'Beagrie Beagrie...' (Peter, who used to play for the visitors, ommentating on their behalf), 'Ronnie Ronnie...' (Moore, also aloft in the ommentary box, pundit for Donny and a former manager of their neighbours Rotherham United).

When invention expired we had the inventive response: 'What a load of ubbish' from the hapless North Stand away contingent. There were also some ard expletives but I didn't hear my favourite 'fuck, shit, cock,' which might have een expected given the linguistic invention experienced. It came from the central haracter in a play *Damascus* I'd seen in Edinburgh. Worth looking out for, by the vay, should it appear at your local theatre. Furthermore, I've heard Damascus is vorth a visit – must go there when I next happen upon the eastern Mediterranean.

When the whistle blew, the all-time 'Team Head to Head Record' had been narginally improved for the Rovers, to Doncaster 10 wins, Huddersfield 14 with ve draws, and Donny leapfrogged over the Terriers in the Third Division table. 11 ames had been played, almost a quarter of the season and everything to play for. The rajectory was extended to a predictable conclusion: Donny went up, overcoming eeds in the play-off final, a result well-received by neutrals far and wide.

## Yeovil Town 2 Bury 1
## Division III (4), 17/4/04

A week after the game at Scunthorpe I was joined by a merry bunch of stalwarts in pursuit of a weekend of unbridled fun. The target was Huish Park, which I had postponed for far too long a time in order to turn it into a special event. It was meant to be the long-anticipated local derby versus Exeter City, but as it turned out they swapped places in the League in 2003. That was the hard reality.

The *Good Beer Guide* offered the Mason's Arms at Odcombe, actually Lower Odcombe, a significant subtlety as it emerged. Instructions suggested it to be more convenient than Yeovil town centre, apparently in appropriate vicinity for our destination. Between the four of us the details were misread, and we were to suffer several twists and turns on our convoluted way. Fortunately, battling down the A37 we had observed signs to the ground. That much would be easy, in due course. And I had four match tickets in my pocket. Security!

The pub was dropped from the subsequent edition, which didn't really surprise me when I heard the news as it didn't do food (admittedly not strictly relevant for inclusion) and offered a paucity of ales (most pertinent), though this was belied by Stedders in the 2006-07 *Football and Real Ale Guide*: 'the home based brewery now provides 36 gallons a week of great ale exclusively to the pub'. The story is that the landlord of April 2004 did a bunk, to put it mildly. It since rejoined the listings as worth a session for ale and nutriment – to be tried on the next Huish escapade.

Back to the outing: there were a couple of Bury fans at Odcombe. We were told that footy travellers were a feature of the place (as a percentage of home attendance Bury have been the best-supported team on their travels, but they do have very modest home attendances). The pub was buried deep in the country, with a makeshift garden, somewhere in this backwater, with rampaging hens under attack from children, and extensive views, this being a beautiful, and elevated, part of Somerset.

As usual with these events, repartee and reflection turned to shaggy dog stories and we suddenly realized we were running out of time. No problem as, forearmed with images of signposts, we reached our destination easily and parked judiciously, facing out of the escape road (a Tiptoes special). A quick trundle among cohorts of green and white got us quickly to the ground. Far from a sloping pitch, for which Yeovil's old 'Huish' ground had been famous, 'Huish Park' was well-ordered and level.

This is the opportunity to mention Yeovil's age-old rivals, the pride of Dorset, (along with Bournemouth) just down the road: Weymouth, 'Weymuff' or 'the Terras', owing to their 1890s strip of terracotta and blue quarters. The point of interest was that in 1909-10 Dorset FA discovered illicit expenses payments. The club was forced to treat players as guests, thus using over 70 men. The next season there followed the introduction of a new turnstile – please note. The consideration paid by punters was interpreted as payment to the players. Their most promising time was a long way ahead. With the Glovers in League 1, the Terras at last climbed back within two levels – members of the Conference from 2006-07. No gloves in sight, in 2002 manager Gary Johnson, before his transfer to Bristol City, invented the Huish mascot Jolly Green Giant. This was symptomatic of the team's thrust to lift their debutant FA Trophy, an aim they duly fulfilled. It does sport green gloves, of course, but the eye-catching bit is the topper carrying the legend 'Yeovil Town F.C.'.

There was a selection of pies to devour at Huish, mostly by the large Bury fan singled out for that chant beloved of all football fans:

'Who ate all the pies? Who ate all the pies,

You fat bastard, you fat bastard, you ate all the pies.'

And Wakey ate one, too.

The long-awaited fodder answered our needs, washed down by a container of tea. Rouge, a chocolate brownie enthusiast, those concocted by Tiptoes being particularly lush, scoffed a pie. Strangely she seems to prefer instant to real coffee, though menthol cigarettes are her mainstay, normally accompanied by a chaser: a pint of lager and lime. I make no comment! Well, she is Piscean. The atmosphere was jovial, aided by the home side's eventual win, and it *was* their first season in the League, with further promotion hopes still alive, eventually fulfilled a season later.

We tried to battle back to base. To dwell on food, Tiptoes did the ultimate roast-pork platter for my birthday, the icing on the cake, you might say, being a separate dish full of perfect crackling. JCB would have loved it. After the final whistle he attempted full throttle with Sunday-style Somerset drivers returning from their Saturday shop, old biddies and codgers in their accustomed mode, the odd caravan and that awful prospect for efficient drivers – white vans – we made it to Bristol's Tobacco Factory for a performance of *Macbeth*, and for total overkill afterwards Rutz's famous fish pie along with samples of local beer in the Portcullis over the road to round things off. Her table manners make her a paragon for all, in particular the efficacious elegance of her squeezing of a slice of lemon, whether onto cod and chips or smoked salmon (though she hates crusts). The Scottish play, as we should refer to it, is fortunately one of Shakespeare's shortest, affording more of a continuation of the proceedings in the manner to which we had all become accustomed.

My favourite grounds over these travels were Macalpine/Galpharm, Huddersfield, for the geometry of a stylish, even enduring, construction and the trip was a comprehensive, satisfying day out; Belle Vue, Doncaster, a grotty old ground, with a sadly curtailed expectation, where in the end it felt like a time warp, and all the better for that (it's so good that a single, residual floodlight pylon remained in 2008 as a reminder, and landmark); Rochdale's Spotland, of course, for its sheer homeliness. By complete contrast the wooden spoon goes to Sixfields Stadium, Northampton – accessible but austere. It's recommended that visiting fans use taxis to get there from the station. I've been recommended the Old Black Lion to soften the blow – contribution from Chris – to be sampled should I find myself there again.

It's all serendipity: another occasion, different impulses, fresh conclusion.

## Chapter Seven
# Sufferance and Suffering

### Visits to Clubs in Old and New Grounds
### Problems with Getting Past Turnstiles and over the Physical

The first series of grounds in this grievance section felt at the time like missions on sufferance. I submitted, tacitly, to the necessity of attending games at the new homes of clubs I'd already visited. Some are presented here as double acts. With hindsight multiple visits to clubs consistently exceeded their ingredients: having gone to a ground for a game some time in the past, then bringing to fruition the self-imposed trial of a further event at the new place. An example is the first report below. Walsall FC were playing in cups each time. The first, at Fellows Park, was a needle match; the Bescot evening a treat with zephyrs wafting countless balls over the new stands; thrice into the nets. You begin to wonder about damage caused by excessive aerialism: damage to cars, unwitting headers by passers-by, even grazing to the unwitting article itself on contact with uneven or scratchy surfaces having dropped from a great height. Contrast became the binding feature of watching the Saddlers twice – I wonder if fewer balls required retrieval from outside the old ground.

Grief in many ways informs the 'suffering' in the second part. Subjects are: ticket procurement, physical endurance (bodily and climatically) and crowd crush. The first of these underwent a significant amendment in 2005-06. It actually became easier to obtain tickets. But on the occasions listed here it was very different. It remains extremely deflating and galling to recall going all the way to Bournemouth to find the doors closed with palpably plenty of space inside. The weather can drain and dispirit: at Cheltenham, where precipitation was relentless, Jacquie (a regular Whaddon Road attender – well there are a handful) and I emerged drenched to the skin after a substandard game, serving to exacerbate the experience. It was good to mollify the memory by way of a return attempt at Whaddon.

Speaking of total bleakness, I was well aware on my wet trudge to the Withdean, Brighton, that this was on account of a future foray to Falmer at BHA's permanent, and fundamentally desired, home. This is the antithesis to the Britannia, Stoke-on-Trent, which proved just as barren and unworthy as expected. Imagine treading the buddleia droppings on the barren site of the long-lost Victoria Ground in sight of that white monster.

To show how endurance is intertwined with joy for a match-goer, novelist J.B. Priestley can be quoted. In *Good Companions*, a 1929 novel since adapted into various dramatic forms, he invented Bruddersford United Association Football Club, the name an obvious amalgam of Huddersfield and Bradford, the author's stomping ground. He conveyed the essence of football support.

> *Thirty-five thousands men and boys have just seen what most of them call 't'United' play Bolton Wanderers. Many of them should never have been there at all. It would not be difficult to prove by statistics and those mournful little budgets (How a Man May live – or rather, avoid death – on Thirty-five Shillings a Week) that seem to attract some minds,*

*that these fellows could not afford the entrance fee. When some mills are only working half the week and others not at all, a shilling is a respectable sum of money.*

*To say that these men paid their shillings to watch twenty-two hirelings kick a ball is merely to say that a violin is wood and catgut, that 'Hamlet' is so much paper and ink. For a shilling the Bruddersford United A.F.C. offered you Conflict and Art, it turned you into a critic, happy in your judgment of fine points, ready in a second to estimate the worth of a well-judged pass...it turned you into a partisan, holding your breath when the ball came sailing into your own goalmouth..elated, downcast, bitter, triumphant by turns at the fortunes of your side, watching a ball shape* Iliads *and* Odysseys *for you; and what is more, it turned you into a member of a new community, all brothers together for an hour and a half, for not only had you escaped from the clanking machinery of this lesser life, from work, wages, rent, doles, sick pay, insurance cards, nagging wives, ailing children, bad bosses, idle workmen, but you had escaped with.. half the town, and there you were, cheering together, thumping each other on the shoulders, swopping judgments like lords of the earth, having pushed your way through a turnstile into another and altogether more splendid kind of life, hurtling with Conflict and yet more passionate and beautiful in its Art.*

## . Visits to Clubs in Old and New Grounds

## Walsall 1 Port Vale 1
## FA Cup Round 2, 17/12/77, Fellows Park

The cramped, creaky Fellows Park persists as a much more amenable setting than Bescot Stadium, erected close by, all of 1.65 miles away, in 1990. This game, a local

derby after all, with both teams in the Third Division, was notable for scuffles close to us. A bunch of lads were getting aggressive, in an ever-increasing patch, alerting eight or nine strapping police officers who surpassed themselves, with heavy-handed scruff-of-the-neck tactics.

The next week Walsall won the replay 3-1 at Burslem and eventually reached Round 5, going out to Arsenal who themselves proceeded to Wembley where Ipswich emerged as victors, their solitary Cup triumph.

195

## Walsall 2 Carlisle United 1
## League Cup Round 1, 12/8/03, Bescot Stadium

A number of potential takers were enjoined for this celebration of early season light-heartedness. But several dropped out, I expect in the realization that it wasn't likely to be worth the effort. My colleague Abid, whose birthday it was, wisely stayed in a Gas Street Basin bar in Brum; Tiptoes was probably in a boozer near the law courts. Landy, Wakey and I made it to Bescot (or Banks's, these days, for sponsorship purposes) Stadium by Metro, a most efficient tram service (that day), its termini Birmingham Snow Hill and Wolverhampton.

For Walsall FC, crumbling wood had been superseded by hard-edged red rail. A grey concrete stand had just been built as the newest stage in the building process. Negativity evaporated in the camaraderie of the game, surrounded by the bronzed Saddlers fraternity around us facing the dying sun, many of them seeming fresh from action at sundry Mediterranean resorts and airports, but in thoroughly good humour that evening. This is a ground where the aspect lends a hand. Choose the view of the mesmerizing M6 traffic. Unlike the other clubs where a dire reputation precedes their replacement homes (Scunthorpe, Chester…) Bescot occupies a lively situation away from its town but solidly within the conurbation, and boasts its own Metro station.

This time we were keen for a thumping home victory, Carlisle having gained the reputation of regular last-minute escapers from the drop into the Conference. They were indeed demoted the following spring. Walsall had finished 17th in the First Division, and were showing off their new acquisition, Paul Merson, ageing but still potent, and in comparatively recent memory for his stalwart exploits for Villa. He was to contribute to the Saddlers' retention of 17th position that season.

Anyway we were treated to a scrappy affair. The highlight was the performance of Swifty, the club mascot, deriving from the club's previous identity as Walsall Town Swifts. The bird paraded up and down the pitch perimeter, scaled the barrier, lay down prone and waved his/her legs in the air, to the amusement of many, including us.

After the game in our chosen hostelry we committed our predictions for the season to a scrap of paper. Landy did best as it turned out, astutely predicting the collapse of Leeds United, to be relegated along with Leicester City, and promotion for Norwich City and WBA.

## Stoke City 3 Wolverhampton Wanderers 0
## Division I (2), 8/11/97, Britannia Stadium

After extensive exposure at the Victoria Ground, where I wished they still were, and the one-off 'Potters at Vale Park' in the 1970s, at least this expression of fortitude produced a thumping home win in a derby game. What a totally different experience rom the old place. The football fans guide opined 'Stoke City moved from the much-oved Victoria Ground to the much-admired Britannia Stadium during the summer f 1997'. The location was Fenton, the next town down from Stoke-upon-Trent f the six embraced into the 'City of Stoke-on-Trent' in 1910 (when Villa won the Championship, Glossop and Gainsborough Trinity were in the League and Stoke and he Vale weren't).

The new showpiece was built on territory of the former Hem Heath Colliery nd became an immediate landmark, an impressive white castle coming into sight n the approach from Junction 15 of the M6, on high ground, whereas the Victoria Ground had been cosily tucked away within Stoke-upon-Trent (signposted 'Boothen' ight next to the ground). From the rough ground, which had been home to the Potters over (probably) 114 years, there was a clear view of the Britannia, described as esembling a crab by a friend who lived in an elevated part of Newcastle-under-Lyme, verlooking it.

It is reasonable to regret that the dead space has been left for gorse to grow, when it might have seen conversion for contemporary needs, while retaining something f the Victorian, but comfort can be drawn in observing the monstrous use put to much abandoned acreage elsewhere, formerly football hotbeds. Include among these etail therapy provision as at BHA, and characterless housing developments. A Rugby Union example of the latter: Moseley RFC's previous Birmingham home patch actually in Moseley) has been converted into uniform (desirable indeed) residences, he access road being called – wait for it – Twickenham Drive.

Past the turnstiles at the Britannia, far from admiring the white castle, we found it an impersonal wind tunnel, allayed just a bit by the excitement of the riumph. Wolves and their fans had travelled a thankfully short distance up the motorway to endure their own fiasco.

Mike, born and bred in the area, drove us without a hitch to the ample car park. He had been a keen Butler Street Paddock City fan for 20 years until 1980 when he set up his own business. It is an incongruous recipe that you gain ndependence in your livelihood and lose it on the recreation front. Gone were he carefree Saturday pilgrimages to Stoke's games. He does display the knack of Staffordshire oatcake cooking, however. He always takes this over and produces the best breakfast – it's in the blood.

Our project accomplished, evacuation was an endurance test. It took three quarters of an hour to flee the car park. This may have been a teething problem as the armac was fresh, but egress from modern stadia is a frequent frustration. It isn't good enough to allocate blame to 'pressure of traffic' when better exit design (like more roads out) could increase traffic flow and reduce road rage.

The gate was 18,490 – note the reference in Stoke's *Sentinel Football Annual* 1975-76 to the Potters' attendances as 'around the 27,000 mark' 22 years earlier. Different generations, certainly, and oceans of water under many bridges in between. The Britannia's capacity was 28k. Inside there was a slight saving grace – a sighting of he new mascot, the HippoPOTamus.

Two years later, the fanzine *Vale Park Beano* devoted a page to 'Great Cock Ups Of The 20th Century. No 2 – EXOTICA 98'. To quote verbatim the early paragraphs:

> *In early 1998 Stoke-on-Trent City Council was under fire for spending millions of pound of taxpayers' money to fund the building of the Britannia Stadium for Stoke City FC. When they agreed to spend over £3M on the stadium they pacified non Stoke City fans by promising the stadium would hold many 'community' events. At one time the stadium was even known as the Britannia 'Community' Stadium, but the word 'Community' was soon dropped. 'It's too many words to put on road signs' explained a council dim wit (and how often is the road signage to new grounds adequate, let alone full, usually referring to a nameless 'stadium' with he image of a football).*
>
> *The stadium opened in August but it soon became apparent that there were no community facilities whatsoever. What a surprise!...*

## Brighton & Hove Albion 1 Exeter City 2
## Division IV, 26/12/63, Goldstone Ground

My first-ever professional football viewing was in Hove, and my birthplace team won. I applauded under my breath on a home terrace, as the raucous Devonians made their presence felt down yonder at the 'away end', a concept then foreign to me. I was learning fast. The Grecians won promotion, too, an uncommon achievement for a club more familiar with the re-election process.

The programme was 6d in the Seagulls' (listed at the time as the 'Shrimps') oceanic colours of blue and white. Half the cover was given over to an *Evening Argus* advert and of 16 pages seven were of a commercial nature. Perhaps the complaint about excessive contemporary commercialism isn't so valid after all – it's always been pervasive. On the whole, the growing sophistication of programme production and content over the seasons seems justified – ample statistics and information alongside the preoccupation with personalities and drives to earn more cash. Never mind the ever-burgeoning laminated covers.

At the turn of the Eighties the Seagulls won the ultimate promotion and spent four years among the top 22. For a motorbike cop, like Alan Colbourne, in a five-strong team got up in yellow (aka the 'Canaries') this meant more crowds, worse attitude. Even so, notably the most difficult away fraternities over his years of service were not experienced during the Div I tenure but in the lower levels from Portsmouth, 45 miles away and just over the Hampshire border, Millwall – no surprise there – and Tottenham. This last was perhaps linked with a horrifying incident in a Second Division game between the Albion and Spurs before the latter were promoted in 1978: a desperate crowd crush, which with hindsight anticipated the Hillsborough disaster. In that drear period, the Seventies, Alan remembered the judicious use of a tunnel under the road. Supporters would bear down on the seaside on a Friday before their trip to the Goldstone. It was not unknown to use the tunnel as a lock-up, behind barred doors, for loutish fans, with release for the game on the morrow. It was not good news, despite double pay, that local derbies, e.g. BHA v Pompey, were scheduled for Boxing Day: trouble and loss of a well-earned break. Graduating from riot squad to traffic duties at the time the Seagulls lost their First Division status, he would nevertheless be dragged into the melée on match days. Coaches had to be guided through a shopping-crazy Sussex town, past the station, which, amazingly in his experience, never involved bodies under trains.

In the next generation, of football decline, you could tell police expectation by the number of yellow helmets – on cycle policemen. Skinheads would have their bootlaces removed.

## Brighton and Hove Albion 1 Darlington 1
## Division III (4), 29/1/00, Withdean Stadium

Withstanding wind-driven rain from start to finish at Withdean Stadium, suburban Brighton, established as the club's long-term temporary residence, a different kettle of fish from the late-lamented Goldstone Ground. Ironically, considering the extended, purposeful, search to find a permanent home, the club's origins were in Withdean, where as Brighton and Hove Rangers they played on a local field from 1900. On the sale of the Goldstone in 1997, cynically executed by chairman Bill Archer, they next played at Priestfield Stadium, Gillingham, Kent, well outside the club's catchment area, as tenants. They moved back into home territory at the unsympathetic athletics stadium in 1998, where in 2008-09 they remained amid protracted discussions as to a permanent future site. The basic, ultimately simple, aim was to build a 23,000 capacity stadium at Falmer on the eastern edge of Brighton.

At their current residence parking was outlawed to some distance from the ground because of strong local opposition to professional football being played in the area at all. This was exacerbated by the good support turning out for the itinerant team. Being aware of the parking restriction, I contrived a lift to the ground and endured a long, soggy walk after the final whistle.

The score line was a repeat of the fixture at Feethams in August. To the tune of 'Sailing' the faithful chanted 'from the South, we are Brighton, super Brighton' – several verses of it.

The Seagulls were 'Seaweed' to the surrounding cohorts of travelling Villa fans on my visits to the Goldstone in the 1970s and 1980s, but that's nothing compared with the vitriol verbalized at the expense of poor absent Palace, for whom I have to admit a minimal pang of sympathy. They were a modest outfit at this time, but the visitors on this occasion, Darlo, managed fourth spot in the final table, destined to lose in the play-offs.

The Withdean provender not having proved to be a temptation, I retreated to tea and cakes back in Hove – it was a bitter pill that this was courtesy of my cousins who up to 1997 could have called their house 'Goldstone View'.

This was suffering, a reluctant visit to see the team play at this venue, the need due to the club's inauspicious move from their home of 94 years. Withdean's facilities seemed minimal and the atmosphere negligible. I shall just remember their old place with a rose-tinted glow – difficult as it's on the main east/west road and Toys'r'Us beckons each time you pass.

Now a plug for Attila the Stockbroker, a big noise thereabouts and champion of the Falmer initiative. He is the hard-hitting, vitriolic, poetical bane of the bourgeois establishment, with a penchant for bluebottle descriptions of bestial decomposition (dogs, goats). I've witnessed a performance of his masterpiece *Cheryl the Rock Opera* (and boast a copy of the record), as well as in a double entertainment with that notorious pop exponent from Aylesbury, John Otway. Attila is a Brightonian, actually from Southwick, so close over the border in West Sussex it makes no difference, and a poet, whose oeuvre includes *Goldstone Ghosts*, a collection of football poems. Here is an excerpt from the eponymous poem, written at the time of the Goldstone's demise (the cataclysm of 1997):

*Goldstone Ghosts*

*As bulldozers close in upon our old, beloved home*
*And those who stand to profit rub their hands*
*So we gather here together in sad, angry disbelief*
*And for one last time our voices fill the stands.*
*This is no happy parting, but a battle-scarred farewell*
*Though victory hopes are mingled with the tears*
*And I, like you, will stand here as the final whistle blows*
*With memories which echo down the years...*

The Goldstone sold behind our backs! Enraged we rose as one
Against a stony northern businessman.
We drew a line, and said: ENOUGH! And as the nation watched
The final battle for our club began.
We fought him to a standstill. Fans United. All for one.
A nation's colours joined: a glorious sight.
And, finally, the stubborn, stony Archer moved his ground
And made his way for our own collective Knight.

The battle's only just begun, but we have won the war.
Our club, though torn asunder, will survive.
And I salute each one of you who stood up and said NO!
And fought to keep the Albion alive.
And one day, when our new home's built, and we are storming back
A bunch of happy fans without a care
We'll look back to our darkest hour and raise our glasses high
And say with satisfaction: we were there.

But first we have to face today. The hardest day of all.
Don't worry if you can't hold back the tears!
We must look to the future, in dignity and peace
As well as mourn our home of ninety years.
For me the Goldstone has an extra special memory
Of the football soulmate I so briefly had.
He christened me John Charles and taught me to love the game.
This one's for Bill. A poet. And my dad.

Attila has been 'official Poet in Residence' at the club since 2000-01 and has reinforced the point that the fan base is over 20,000, playing in a 7,000 stadium. Brighton and Hove is the 21st most populous city/town in England and Wales.

From his pen this is *Falmer Pond*:

Upon approach, the stench of foetid mud.
If, undeterred, you head towards this place
Mosquito clouds fly up into your face:
A vampire squadron, hungry for your blood.
And then you see the rats. Their gimlet eyes
Bore through you, as if sizing up their prey.
But they are full: they have a meal today.
A local dog has just met its demise.
It decomposes while they gnaw its flesh.
Diseased and dying ducks are all around

*Choking on the used condoms that they've found*
*Their scab-encrusted feet caught in a mesh*
*Of rusting supermarket trolleys. Worse!*
*A host of bats (protected species, these)*
*Each carrying a different foul disease*
*Rises on stinking wings to spread a curse*
*Across the innocent East Sussex sky.*
*A chill runs down your spine, the message clear.*
*Abandon hope, all those who enter here:*
*This is a place where creatures come to die.*
*Then, from the shadows, awful shapes lurch forth.*
*Pale, hideous forms, by putrefaction scarred:*
*With querulous moans of 'Not in My Back Yard!'*
*The zombie hordes of Falmer Village North......!*

*But, Mr. Prescott, you are stout of heart.*
*You knocked that deadly Welsh egg thrower down*
*And didn't let the crap canoeist drown.*
*We know your courage: you will play your part.*
*Outstanding Natural Beauty there will be*
*Next to that awful breeding place for flies.*
*So give the word, and we will claim our prize:*
*A Stadium for the City by the Sea.*

Come on lads, it's time to start the building programme. I want a good reason to patronize you again. So does Fredders, who would make the trip from the Peaks. It has the makings of a rare, nay unique, transformation from the present, woeful, base.

## Oxford United 2 Wolverhampton Wanderers 3
## League Cup Round 1, 5/9/00, Manor Ground

It's a shame that the compact Manor Ground had to be replaced. The Headington area was fine for an evening with good pubs and a peek at the extraordinary fibreglass shark 'Untitled 1986', inserted in the roof of a side street house. Meanwhile parking was easy in this residential neighbourhood. The ground had been left without investment for some years, affording the spectators right beside the pitch toilet-roll-chucking opportunities. There accrued an abundance on the pitch.

A League Cup game featuring a lower-division team beaten by a higher-division one via several goals was always promising - equals 'good package'. The better team, if such is drawn as in this tie, represents an improvement on the standard opposition, and the supporters have hope but not much expectation, a 'nothing to lose' feeling.

Even better as the home team, programme title *The Ox*, scored first and maintained the lead at half-time, shouting 'You're such shit it's unbelievable' towards the away cluster, and a nice one 'naughty, naughty goal keeper' at some misdemeanour. The inevitable happened, in due course, Wolves fans getting their own back with 'Bull shit aaaaaaaaaaaaghhh'!

It was at this Cup tie that I learned with a sinking feeling of the forthcoming new stadium, with a consequent repeat visit to the 'Bulls' in their new field.

## Oxford United 2 Leyton Orient 2
## League 2 (4), 28/3/05, Kassam Stadium

Ground owner Firoz Kassam produced a three-stand stadium. It was westless and a long time in construction, initiated in 1996, and four years down the line at the time of my Manor Ground exposure above. The project was dogged by problems financial, contractual, political and legal. It eventually opened for business in 2001. With a capacity of 12,450, the record gate of 12,177 was recorded for a League Cup game

in 2002 (United 0 Villa 3). This was eclipsed by a vain attempt at rallying the U's(less) by 12,243 on their very last game in the League (United 2 Leyton Orient 3) on 30 April 2006.

Too little and much too late. But they had achieved more than most during their 44-year League membership: champions of Div III twice, Div II in 1984-85, winning the League Cup the next season. Their highest-ever position was 18th in Div I (1985-6-7), when four clubs finished below them.

*Finding it proved to give me quick release,*
*With time in hand, street parking found with ease,*
*First stadium view a treat, though prospect tough –*
*Manor Ground seen before was quite enough.*
*Ticket collection next, not quite clear where*
*'That door', 'oh!' – advance sales not so dear.*

*Then found a pub, with no real beer,*
*A bap for nosh, a chat, two pints, then air,*
*Back, found my spot, good view in lower tier,*
*For Ramon Diaz' Army to appear.*
*Sparkling League 2 display from O's and U's*
*Scoring a couple each – who could refuse?*
*This three stand stadium's where the U's reside*
*And what does Kassam plan for the fourth side?*

On this three-sided stage they played in yellow and blue, evoking the Torquay Gulls, a bit too close to that awful acid tone dedicated to away strips, but at least a bit of a change from home colours norm. And in 2007-08-09 they were both out of the League. It would be neat and aesthetically pleasing if the west side could be built up to match the rest, but I was already acquiring the taste of a different look by the end of my sojourn.

It's refreshing to be able to see trees, freshly leaved, beyond during the boring bits – I was in the Oxford Mail East Stand: £12.50 for four goals, but 'no smoking in seating area'. The programme was £2.50 and I could just about mark in goal scorers Steve Basham and Tommy Mooney on the shiny surface.

## Bristol Rovers 2 Exeter City 3
## Division III, 9/2/82, Eastville Stadium

My first encounter with Bristol Rovers was through the lunchtime routine at the Fox Inn in Easton, adjacent to the M32, followed by the stroll under the motorway to Eastville Stadium, famed for being the only ground part of which was under a motorway. People used to park on the hard shoulder to watch games there. The traffic noise was unremitting, so crowd vocalism was essential. This was a mid-table game. The Grecians arrived with the highest goals-scored total in the division – 37, mostly from the boots of their star striker Tony Kellow – but had conceded 42, also the most. They were 15th in the table. It is interesting to note the fixture schedule in those days. The opening games had been on 29 August. In 2005-06 the equivalent was 6 August. By the time of this encounter less than half the League fixtures had been played. In 2006 half were completed by the New Year. This is also explained by a reduction in midweek games since and fewer weather-induced postponements. By now Rovers had played the most (25) of any of the 24 clubs. Bristol City (with a similar climate!) had got through 22 on the way to their next relegation.

The extant floodlight at Eastville remained as testament to past indulgence until into the new century, the site as a whole having since been committed to Ikea, which probably draws more crowds to Bristol than anything else. This is not an idle remark, but borne out by statistics laid down for our guidance (a free translation from Oscar Wilde). Ikea undertook to maintain the pylon, but nanny-state obsession with health and safety eventually did for it. There is still a small flight of steps, for long a part of the stadium, and evidence of the erstwhile True Blue Club at the back of the shop/tourist attraction (the next nearest branch of Ikea being at Wednesbury on the most congested part of the M6).

Bristol Rovers became known as the Gasheads because of the neighbouring gasworks. There used to be flowerbeds behind the goals too, though failing to inspire yet another nickname. The arena was primarily a greyhound stadium, the track forming a modest barrier and provideing distance from the action. The whole look of the ground said 'dogs' and 'speedway', football being a strictly functional, match-day activity.

There had been some ground-sharing with City, briefly following a fire in 1980, and plans mooted for tenancy at Ashton Gate. Even if that prospect had progressed, anathema to Pirates people, City themselves removed the issue from the equation, through their financial crash in the early Eighties. The rent required by BC (1982) was doubled and Rovers were to leave the M32 for the A4 eastwards to Bath.

## Bristol Rovers 3 Blackburn Rovers 0
## Division II, 7/3/92, Twerton Park, Bath

Four of us acquiesced in exposure to Twerton Park during Rovers' decade of residence giving rise to a temporary nickname the Twerts, though not usually uttered by the club's own supporters. The ground was a substandard, mean experience – at the outset stones had to be picked up from the pitch, walls painted and fencing erected to reduce the loss of balls into neighbouring gardens. It was also an inconvenient 14 miles away from the club's spiritual home, and a walk along the A36 from Bath city centre, quite a comedown from the soaring Georgian buildings of the central area, where you were well advised to sup up in one of the proliferation of genteel emporia before tackling the tedious Twerton hike. This continued Rovers' tradition of combating a large viaduct, not a motorway as at Eastville but the huge railway bridge which kept the riffraff of Twerton apart from picture-postcard Bath.

Mickey G had come all the way from Blackburn for this fiasco (actually also to see his son play on a school's tour on the Sunday) and Fuckin' Dave treated it as an uncommitted diversion, after all Bath isn't Bristol, though we shared some glee in the away team's upstaging. Good to see Mickey too. It was also a shock in view of the teams' respective positions and figures. Blackburn were half a division higher in the table.

The Gas remain the only outfit I have visited at three different grounds. Other enthusiasts can claim a number of nomadic clubs, and some, which have played under different names, or both, like Wimbledon/MKD.

## Reading 3 Bolton Wanderers 2
## Division I (2), 8/2/97, Elm Park

Almost extinct Elm Park was the venue, one division up from the one for the next trip below, Graham the companion, 10,739 the gate. This was a good result for the Royals, courtesy of Trevor Morley's hat trick; as Bolton went on to ascend to the top tier, losing only three away games all season. Reading had finished 19th in 1996, were 18th this year and plummeted to bottom in 1998.

That autumn the new stadium opened, funded by Chairman John Madejski to the tune of £10m. In 2000 I happened to meet a couple on holiday abroad who lived in Reading, their address Elm Park. They had heard that football had been played on the site in the past. They had noticed no sign of this piece of history. Perhaps they hadn't looked hard enough for a wall plaque. I jest, but suggest that the blue plaque system for famous dead people should be extended to celebrate former residences of football clubs. I fear Elm Park the football ground is now referred to only in football books and to children on old men's laps. It was a little fortunate to have stayed in business as long as it did, given the late Robert Maxwell's intended merger, announced in 1983, of Reading FC with his club, Oxford United, into a new super club, to be called Thames Valley Royals, paid for by the sale of both grounds. Both sets of supporters displayed their thumbs firmly down. The idea evaporated.

The comparison between these two grounds is too trite to mention: an uninteresting century-old ground, in parlous straits, but attaching sentimental value and human in scale, and a purpose-built edifice donated to the club as part of a retail development with all of a modern punter's requirements, supposedly. The Reading fanzine *Heaven 11* recorded: 'Gone will be our infamous bogs, historic terraces, inaudible tannoy system and wonderful parking facilities…there'll even be luxury quilted soft blue and white bog paper to replace the traditionalists' favourite: Izal Medicated.' The same rag had commented sagely the year before that 'basically, any team can win the division; all it takes is consistency in all aspects of the game – something Reading Football Club seems to have forgotten'. I do agree: at the end of the day there's many a slip 'twixt cup and lips. And see what hindsight can tell us about the same Reading FC after a triumphant elevation to the Premiership in 2006.

## Reading 2 Millwall 0
## Division II (3), 1/5/99, Madejski Stadium

No squash game with Graham this time, as he'd retired from the sport by now, nine years on from the last Millwall outing, and with a visit to the New Den still to come.

This time's thrill was witnessing a huge congregation of bikers at an M4 service station. Quite photogenic, as was the Madejski Stadium from the motorway. This landmark, near Junction 11, must have improved the public image of the borough of Reading as well as providing relief on a dreary journey, along with the nearby brewery, producing keg beer only. We feared the worst regarding parking, as reports identified problems, but this was not so on the day. We left the car in the chosen pub car park not far from the ground. The only requirement was to patronize the facilities. No problem. It was close to the end of the season, the result of no consequence, the teams finishing 10th (Millwall) and 11th (Reading).

And another observation about 2006: there were forebodings muttered about the Madejski's capacity to deal with the higher volume of attenders as the Royals cantered towards their debut in the Premiership, having just missed out a decade before. Again, this was a misguided apprehension. The stadium coped, just: the average attendance in 2006-07 was 23,829; the capacity 24,161.

## Leicester City 2 Bristol City 1
### Division II, 7/9/91, Filbert Street

I enjoyed a diverting evening at Coventry Belgrade Theatre the night before, indulging with Justine appearing in *The Importance of Being Earnest*, a mighty fine Gwendolen, and we wallowed in pasta and tinto afterwards. The best thing if you feel jaded the morning after is a swim and that I endured and enjoyed at the city's huge pool, which was about to host a championships. Public use was therefore curtailed. There is a serious dearth of 50-metre pools in this country.

Flattering to deceive, the visit to Filbert Street was a charming low-key affair. The team's nickname in those days was the Filberts. A filbert is a 'cultivated hazel' (*Concise Oxford Dictionary*). I found the ground easily. I can't remember how. It was a tried-and-tested routine. Back-street parking, a pub full of locals – definitely no sign of Robin Red there, unlike the Leicester v Wigan game, when the travelling fans may have infiltrated Leicester territory. On the other hand Wigan's blue is of a tasteful, subtle hue, whereas Leicester's could be called 'football club blue', a tiny bit more brash, somehow in tune with the uncomfortable man-made material shirts are made of. I'm a cotton snob, though I do wear my Villa away shirt (1991, a gift) for sport. 1991-92 was the last season of the four divisions, and both teams, average, workaday, mid-table, were miraculously enhanced to the 'League Division I' in 1992-93.

## Leicester City 0 Wigan Athletic 2
### Championship (2), 16/4/05, Walkers Stadium

23,894 watched Wigan romping towards the Premiership after a lapse in form over preceding matches, when the world at large thought they would be overhauled, in other words wouldn't believe they could hack it. Brett Ormerod scored a predictable brace (an example of hindsight) against much weaker opposition. It was a case of worst season/best season. Indeed the Latics ended up with 79 goals scored, three more than champions Sunderland. And Leicester finished 15th.

A singular aspect of the game was the persistent tossing into the fray of new balls before the one just out of touch could be retrieved. At one time there were three in view for a corner.

The Foxes, as they had become, were not impressive, nor were the road signs to the Walkers Stadium, which I was trying to approach after a tour of points west.

I saw not a single sign to the Stadium (but one to Grace Road, home to Leics CCC, afterwards, on the way to the motorway). It was only by extending my memory of Filbert Street fourteen years earlier, which I remembered hearing was nearby, visualizing the map from the cursory glance before setting out, and trying to apply a sense of direction to the south side of the city that I eventually managed to locate the ground. It was a rash assumption indeed that there would be road signs to assist.

To recount the story further, after a double take in Wilkinson's car park, where there was a charge for parking over two hours, no doubt aimed at just this, football usage and easy money. As well as the cost, drivers would face a gridlock problem at 4.55pm. I guessed at the route of most promise up and over a hill and left the vehicle in a side street by the Donkey where I enjoyed Adnam's beer in good-natured company. The Wolves press officer, Lorraine Hennessy, chose the Walkers Stadium out of all the 23 opponents to come in 2007-08: 'it's a short trip, the ground has good media facilities and they serve great cakes at half time!'. (The official 2007/08 Football League Preview magazine). But the cakes were probably not for the supporters and for Wolves for that season only: they didn't quite make the play-offs and Leicester were relegated to the third division on the last day of the season.

After the Wigan game I asked a policeman where the Filbert Street ground had been. He pointed at a block of flats a couple of hundred yards away. How about a blue plaque there?

## Manchester City 3 Everton 0
## Division I, 21/2/76, Maine Road

This was the first of several visits to Maine Road and gave us an impressive home win. The team was filled with favourite personalities from Joe Corrigan in goal through Willie Donachie and captain Mike Doyle to the thrusting strike force: Joe Royle (13 goals so far 24 games), Dennis Tueart (18) Asa Hartford (8) and Peter Barnes (four from 15 games). I once endured a pair of abrasive teenagers (female) deriding Dennis at a Stoke City game. The source cause may be lost in time, or perhaps they invented the allusion, but on every touch of the electric winger they shrilled 'Where's yer shirt, Tueart?' How rude of the girls, anyway. Warner might have responded with a variation of the aphorism: 'a whistling woman and a cackling hen ain't no good for beast nor men'. Or, on the theme of domestic beasts: 'why have a dog and bark yourself?' It was good to have seen Dennis, in shirt and tie, waxing lyrical in a programme about New York Cosmos in 2007, and hear him since on the radio in the role of pundit.

Please note that City beat United to Tampa, Florida, transactions. During 1975-76 'Rodney [Marsh] left Manchester City in 1976 and led the exodus of international footballers to play in the North American Soccer League. He signed with the Tampa Bay Rowdies in 1976 and became the fans' favourite, going on to captain his team. Rodney came back to play with Fulham alongside his good mates, George Best and Bobby Moore, which would be the last time they would all play together in England.' (Rodney Marsh website).

Maine Road had wildly varying attendances, from 49,387 for the big local derby to 27,256 for Coventry City's visit. It was a time of gate volatility, the defeated Toffees playing to a mere 20,188 v Birmingham City but attracting 55,570 for neighbours Liverpool. Not surprising, at least at the top end, as Liverpool and United led the field. It's fun to spot that Arsenal were the least popular opponents for two clubs: Liverpool (featuring strongly in statistics here) and Stoke City (also worth an occasional mention).

The ground's site had been chosen in 1922 for a club, Ardwick FC, formerly St Mark's West Gorton, whose heartland was very much East Manchester. The Moss Side/Rusholme area, where the eventual Maine Road space was located, represented a transfer to a different location, complete with public transport inconvenience. It was modelled on the then paradigm, Hampden Park, Glasgow, before the erection of Wembley. An ambitious project, it featured a car park with 500 spaces, then a novelty, and a two-phase design aimed at housing 120,000, with the prospect of hosting top-notch events such as FA Cup semi-finals. The fans were eventually persuaded to follow their club to their new domicile, and the Lazer Blues entered a new phase which subsisted into the new century.

Reference has to be made to the 1988-89 banana phenomenon. A certain Frank Newton brilliantly initiated a craze which at its zenith saw players carrying inflatable bananas onto the pitch for a third round FA Cup tie. These were projected into the crowd. Soon after, the yellow presence took off such that during a League game the scoreboard announced the attendance as '22,451 and 7,000 bananas'.

On taking a ground tour much closer to the present (before Arsenal beat City 1-5 on 22/2/03, the first four coming within 25 minutes), the trophy cabinet was most photogenic, being well stocked (compared with Bolton Wanderers), and dinky showers had replaced the fine old players' bath. 'Mr Keegan' was credited effusively by our tour guide, Pete, as the perpetrator of this further nail in the coffin of tradition, though perhaps 'health and safety', alias political correctness, played a part. Pete was certainly in awe of Mr Keegan and his enlightenment. The ground could hold up to 100,000, went an apocryphal tale; 84,569 did cram in to see City play Stoke (FA Cup 6th Round, 3/3/34, the British record for any game outside London or Glasgow) in a 1934 Cup game – and went on to win the trophy.

That was City's second FA Cup win. They won the League Cup for a second time, in 1976. The Citizens beat Newcastle 2-1, John Barnes and Dennis Tueart (torso covered, I surmise) the scorers, Alan Gowling for Newcastle from a Malcolm MacDonald cross. The full house (Wembley attendance 100,000, receipts £299,601.16p – record) marvelled at Dennis who 'with his back to goal, performed an overhead kick that bounced beyond Mike Mahoney into the bottom left corner of the net. After the match Tueart described the goal as "the greatest of my career"' (Wikipedia).

The location exchange was to be of a zigzag perambulation through back streets to Maine Road for a traipse through abandoned industrial terrain to the City of Manchester Stadium.

## Manchester City 1 Newcastle United 1
## Premier League, 2/2/05, City of Manchester Stadium

The battle to achieve admission notwithstanding, a comprehensive malt-and-hops immersion was the key to 48 hours in Manchester. This time, unlike the match, theatre tickets had proved elusive, so Wakey and I decided to tackle the entire list of pubs in the 2005 *Good Beer Guide*. There were 14 of these. We achieved 12 plus two others, unlisted, and the hotel bar. There was plenty of good stuff in Manchester. It became an odyssey to cover the city in a series of expeditions. These incorporated cultural diversions like an evocative mixed-media Zimbabwe exhibition in the City Art Gallery, and back there again later for local photojournalism. In a strange way one built on the other, though completely contrasting.

By the end of the staggered crawl, completing the tavern samples in an early lunch en route to Piccadilly Station, we felt we had a pretty good idea of the city's layout and relationships between the various bits of it. Independently we placed the 14 in order and came out with identical first and second choices and mix and match between third and fourth. So go to the Briton's Protection and the Hare and Hounds for a start. Of course it was a completely biased experiment.

The key trek was the evening foray to the City of Manchester Stadium, in 'East Manchester, the third poorest borough in Britain' and '…the inspiration for the hit Channel 4 show "Shameless", which celebrates the exploits of the unemployed Gallagher family' (per *Sunday Telegraph*). Virgin territory for me, but not for want of trying. Wakey had been a season-ticket holder the previous year, the stadium's first, but had not managed enough games to make it viable. You can only miss three at most of the 19 home League games, but 'membership', which is how it was termed, entitled you to priority booking for cup games. Here we were, courtesy of Fuckin' Dave and Nice Lady, double members whose club cards, on the model of a credit card, had been conveyed to me (don't tell) for slot insertion at the gate.

In the opaque sogginess that evening I failed to notice the colossal piece of public art, in front of the ground: 'Manchester's B of the Bang was officially launched at a memorable opening ceremony. Gold medal winning athlete Linford Christie, whose famous words inspired the sculpture's name, was joined at the event y football stars Rio Ferdinand (Manchester United) and Joey Barton (Manchester City), on 12/1/05' (source: the official project website). The very next week a television programme on the subject made riveting viewing. I wished I'd been aware of it at the time as it must be impressive and enhancing to the area, one of industrial dereliction. Further tracts of East Manchester were chosen for the national super casino, ahead of public-imagination favourite Blackpool in 2006, though the order was cancelled by Gordon Brown after a few months in office as Prime Minister, leaving the project for smaller casinos only.

The 'statue' reached to the sky, comprising inspired design and finely tuned engineering. I wondered how long it would withstand extremes of weather, like tornadoes, which we now might have to anticipate as part of predicted climate changes. I was sure the stadium would endure as it seemed rooted, a vast dome, in the hole in the ground in which it is founded. The bowl created for world athletics had been convexed upwards as a football colossus. We trudged up to the very apex via an everlasting spiral concrete corkscrew, built as a dual carriageway. When we arrived, the seats were a mixed blessing.

As new grounds go they met the prescription, but, being such a long way from the action, the effect was generalized – broad impact at the expense of detail. I wished that there was some magical means of providing the best of both worlds – the magnificent experience and atmosphere of live sport in such a stadium supported by close-ups and replays. You may retort 'electronic scoreboard' but how many of those really do the job? Not this one. Newcastle scored while I was absent from the seat. That's live sport as well! Having gyrated down to street level after the game, we tackled the return march in the merciless downpour. It's true about Manchester (and Bristol): wet. It was a surprise finding one of the pubs on our list, probably the closest to the ground, almost empty. We'd kept it just for the convivial post-match pint. I remember the landlord as a jolly chap, content to engage in discussion about local trends.

## 2. Problems with Getting Past Turnstiles and over the Physical

### Nearly Unhappy New Year

### Norwich City 2 Newcastle United 1
### Premiership, 31/12/94

I learned something that day, bright and bleak with a serious threat of snow from the north, and the fleet of coaches from Tyneside ahead of the storm, before the game at least. Arriving at Carrow Road, the anticipation of a warming, thrilling experience through which to banish the old year speedily evaporated. The ticket office had sold out. Completely. There had been some spaces but I was too late. It had been a long journey. For me this was to have been the visit's main event in a few days in an unfamiliar part of the world. I did not want to have to repeat the exercise.

With upwards of 45 minutes to kick-off, I set about unearthing a ticket, any ticket, almost any price. Yes, any price. Increasingly desperate, I enquired, beseeched and begged any potential carrier of spares. I embarked upon pestering the gamut of everyone from scarf sellers to burger vendors to programme outlets to turnstile operators, even an authoritative-looking copper. Time was running out. I had decided forlornly to assume a position in sight of the proliferating Canary enthusiasts, and adopt a mournful posture and appealing aspect to elicit a ticket; in fact more 'hang dog' I later reckoned.

Despair and urgency sometimes find a reward and my perseverance paid off with seconds almost out. A green and yellow man approached me with the words 'are you the bloke who wants a ticket?' 'Oh yes' I blabbed, and he showed me the magical passport to joy. It was mostly yellow with horizontal green stripes at the top and bottom. The top carried, in gold lettering, the words 'Norwich City Football Club' and the block capitals, black on yellow, included the information '31 DEC 1994' and '£15.00' and 'Frazer'. Praise the Lord and praise Frazer, who only wanted £10 for it. He insisted. At the bottom was inscribed 'PLEASE BE SEATED BY 11.30'. It was now dead on noon, the deal done and Frazer (if it were he) vanished from sight. I gambolled to the seat. The ticket has been firmly attached to my diary, in scrapbook mode, ever since.

It was bitterly cold in the Barclay End. The game bustled with life early on with all three goals being scored in the first half. 21,172 bodies warmed one another. At that time the Canaries were in seventh position. But they faded to sink into Division I (2) the next season. Away form was critical in this: they only gained two more points out of a possible 30. Manager John Deehan was dumped. Towards the end of the season Carrow Road suffered regular anti-chairman demonstrations. This failure was attributed to excessive budgetary constraints. Truism: you can't sustain Premiership status without investing in players. I saw that written somewhere.

This was a season after the infamous home strip – yellow and green as usual, but the green involved a palette explosion on yellow material. Widespread scorn was perpetrated.

Along with Sheffield Wednesday and Wolves, the Canaries have surely contributed to the enhancement of the feminine presence in professional football. A central role model was Delia Smith, cuisine inspirer and director. She said 'I like to sit down with my friends and have a really good bitch. And when I go to football matches I am at my most misbehaved. I sing rude songs about the opposition, such as "stand up if you hate the scum." But I don't sing the ones with swear words. I don't think they are very nice.' And no recipes please, dear.

## Sundry Suffering

The first attempt at Dean Court, Boscombe, was an ill-starred affair. We reached the gates on 5 March 1988, a wholly promising endeavour, and the coordinating element for a weekend with my friend Jersey indulging in Dorset. It turned out to be an all-ticket match, none available on the day, not even for odd home supporters who hadn't read the local paper, let alone away supporters with the supposed (I guess) benefit of a grapevine.

That was Villa's fault for being so attractive, indeed a perceived hazard, as they attracted unparalleled away support in their single-season expedition into the real Second Division. Relegated with one away win, they had a passable squad but little purpose or confidence (where have I heard that before? – yes, in respect of most Villa squads over the years). They proceeded to beat the Cherries 1-2, one of a record equalling 13 away wins in the division. We heard this on the guest house television after enjoying the weird and wonderful Russell-Cotes Museum as compensation. To quote Simon Hoggart in the *Guardian*, the museum was '…stuffed with the lifetime's haul of a wealthy couple who trawled the world for treasures. It's particularly strong on Victorian narrative paintings, such as Jephthah's Vow, three vast works by Sir Edwin Long. Now I didn't know, or had long forgotten, the story of Jephthah, who made a deal with God – if he could smite the Ammonites (not fossils, but a rival tribe) he would sacrifice the first living thing that came out of his house to greet him. He did indeed smite the enemy "with a very great slaughter", according to Judges chapter xi, but tragically it was his daughter, an only child, who was to greet him. The last painting shows him wailing over her corpse after he's sacrificed her, and you can see her soul ascending to heaven, top left. She is of course bare-breasted – these paintings were the 19th century equivalent of Page 3.'

Graham Taylor was Villa's new manager, who improved upon Villa's late record, which had included a year (1987-88) in the Second Division, to finish runners-up to the Scousers in 1990 and this game made a contribution.

Back at Villa Park let me cite another ticket problem: prior credit card bookings. The thrilling League Cup tie with Liverpool which the latter eventually won 3-4 (Round 5, December 2002) showed no sign of starting at the appointed hour, when Landy and I were settled in the Trinity Road Stand. There was no information, no announcement until, with the stadium artificially devoid of occupants for a clearly popular match, a tannoy announcement eventually informed us that kick-off would be delayed. A plot emerged of systems problems with ticket provision. Ticketmaster, or 'God' for the entertainment industry, had failed. This was the top fixture of the day. Armchair attenders listening on 909 or 693 medium wave could have told us an elaborate tale of the providers' ineptitude. Those in the ground were kept in ignorance (rather like the lack of announcements about train underperformance). Ticketmaster had simply been unprepared for the volume of people picking up their passports to pleasure at the kiosk within the gates of Villa Park. On a cold night, we were both thankfully wrapped up warm. When the filtering of credit card holders (£2.50 added to the transaction each time for 'administration' – a rip-off, which is why I send a cheque and stamped addressed envelope or the ticket office gets visited in person) amounted to a full house, well over an hour after the 7.45pm appointment, the game commenced. One consequence of the delay, augmented by extra time, was that many Scousers would have missed their last train home. At least they had the compensation of victory:

their team proceeded to add to the trophy cabinet after wins against Uniteds Sheffield and Manchester.

And then there was the sequence of attempts to penetrate White Hart Lane. This one is simple to tell. Bogs had felt the urge for White Hart Lane for several years in a mild way. On contacting the ground in the dark winter of 2004 the information was clear: no chance of tickets. We ascribed this to the lateness of the attempt and went to the Geffrye Museum (do try it), on the same side of town, instead. (Result: Tott 1 Newc 0.)

Bogs and I were determined to find a way to buck the ticket system. Parallel to the quest to do Millwall, a year on, I made my submission humbly, but desperately, to that foolhardy Manchester City season ticket holder, Fuckin' Dave. This time, only

a few weeks after the City of Manchester Stadium beseechment of February 2005, I got onto him to act as proxy to get away tickets for White Hart Lane. Unfortunately to return the favour I may be requested to drive somewhere for a football game. Up to then I had usually managed to avoid this, subtly urging that his car was of a more elevated order (too true) and I'd been awarded too many speeding points already (three with him as passenger after an Exeter victory). F', a true brick, obliged and £60 duly changed hands along with the identity kit with which (self-) important clubs furnish their investors, a captive market. Easy!

Then there was the time Bogs and I got to the gates of Villa Park to find that, 'as Leeds are the visitors', it was an all-ticket match, it being the 1980s when Leeds were big, and a (perceived) big threat. 'Sorry mate.' This was a complete novelty. Paying in advance? It was New Year's Day so we proceeded to the hair of the dog.

And another, reported by Graham the Millwall fan: during the reign of George Graham and John Fashanu, Graham, of squash and latte fame, essayed to get to a Millwall game at Bournemouth in midweek. The evening before the match the local police chief feared Armageddon should Millwall fans, barred from entry to Dean Court, go on the rampage. He relented by announcing that they *would* be admitted if they arrived at the ground. This was announced in the press (broadsheets at least) that day, and an estimated 500 gathered from all points of the compass for a rare away sighting. They were perfectly behaved, and enjoyed a 1-2 win.

And finally, at the old Den, accompanying Traff man Rickles (Millwall 0 Manchester United 0 - Div I, 8/4/89), Her Majesty's representatives strove to convey the impression that away fans were unwelcome. We were herded like cattle inside a metal-fenced pen, within an arm's length of the venom of the home horde. I didn't care about the result, which was about right all things considered (the clubs finished, rather mundanely, 10th and 11th) – you have to be politic sometimes, except in the desperate prayer heavenwards that 'our' lot wouldn't score. The mass of raging Lions could have done a Heysel with the apparently feeble metal fabric between us. The aftermath, and the prospect of Cold Blow Lane, didn't bear thinking about.

This is the opportunity to mention Springfield Park, Wigan. The occasion Wigan Athletic 1 Stoke City 0, Div III, 15/2/92. Jersey and I ingested no more than usual during the prelude to the game, featuring trains over bits of Lancashire and public houses on the way. I began to feel ill, culminating in vomitousness. This was allayed by Springfield tea (at least better than at Shrewsbury) but I was starting to feel sensitive to touch and spots began to appear on my thorax. By the morning the only course was homeward, the journey not much fun. I cancelled the evening squash game – I could hardly lift the racquet by then. Monday's verdict: chickenpox and housebound for a fortnight at least. Grown-up people aren't meant to get chickenpox. To more pleasant memories: Central Park rugby ground seemed impressive, and more, well, central. Once found, Springfield Park seemed what it was, that of a non-league club, which had done well, very well. It was still worth the day trip even if I wasn't fit for it.

## Up the Fells and Down the Terraces – 1

### Carlisle United 0 Doncaster Rovers 0
### Division III (4), 29/3/97

Much was suffered on the way to getting Brunton Park off the list, in fact a week of fell walking, during which I misjudged a slippery patch, bruising hand and leg, separately losing a pair of glasses, as a small diversion enduring England's highest point, Scafell Pike, in what the party concluded was a blizzard. The good bit was earlier in the week, when we scaled Helvellyn and marched in nonchalant fashion along the nefarious Striding Edge, narrow and not for vertigo sufferers, like Wakey in Boston. Ambleside had a quaint cinema whose offering that week was *Jerry Maguire*, a throwaway piece of fun, featuring the awful Tom Cruise. He was evidenced in a newspaper in the Noughties as an example of perfectly regular features – turn him round and he looks the same. Like his acting.

The party dispersed on the Saturday, whereat I took the northbound road to Carlisle, aiming for the municipal swimming pool, which I imagined would prove a relaxing experience for all the body parts stretched out of their normal contours over six solid days' exposure to rugged terrain. How wrong I was. I maintain the pool visit was a good decision but it was agony for my poor form. Different bits of body, it became apparent.

Outside, Eddie Stobart was in overwhelming evidence. I wish I had known then that each vehicle exhibited a girl's name, as in the comfort of my wander on flat terrain past Eddie's display patch I might have noted 'Mandragora', 'Windy Wendy' or even 'Trixie-Tallulah' . Unfortunately I later developed a habit of slowing down after overtaking one of Eddie's pantechnicons to read the names, which tend to be somewhat dull, if hybrid, like Emma Barbara, one I craned my neck to decipher.

The time was nigh for the standard gratification, duly expedited on the way to the ground, which was unusually easy to find, as well as being much more capacious than expected for a club traditionally occupying the lower divisions and so remotely placed. They were promoted in third position that year, the third of four consecutive seasons in which they went up or down, and I was unlucky not to witness a home win or at least a goal, something they achieved in 16 League games that year. I was grateful to find a bar to lean on halfway up the terrace, alleviating a modicum of physical distress. The time was nigh for United's last gasp. After the following year's relegation they ended in an average position of $22^{nd}$, i.e. $90^{th}$ from 1998 to 2004. At last they plumbed the depths, and dropped out.

In 1974-75 the Cumbrians had briefly surveyed all below them in the top Division I spot, as sure as making it to the summit of the top fell, eventually plummeting to bottom place, I would like to cite this as an example of bathos. In the next generation we have the sad tale of Carlisle in the Conference. They were always in contention in 2004-05, despite the horrors of floods in the city, affecting their pitch and requiring them to move out for several weeks. They bounced back in a single year, through the play-offs of course. Even so, a certain Jon Cartwright of Chester quite properly expressed annoyance that Carlisle came straight back and didn't do their full tour of Conference duty. Chester spent four seasons down and out (2000-04).


## Up the Fells and Down the Terraces – 2

### Bury 0 Notts County 1
### Division III, 9/4/88

Back in time, another solitary adjunct to a Holy Week group fell-walking experience with *No Way Out* as the midweek film, featuring Mr Cruise's equally imperfect peer, the irregular-faced Kevin Costner. At least it provided some of us with an enduring joke. I mean there's never an escape from those high fells in residual snow. No way out. You are committed as soon as you ascend, like the Hawthorns queue. A. Wainwright wouldn't have had it otherwise, would he?

I had an appalling cold and bursting blisters but spent a diverting lunchtime in the Trafalgar, tasting Burtonwood Bitter. I enjoyed a barm cake there as at Preston and I've heard that the area is responsible for another speciality: black pudding, which has developed widespread patronage over the years. All those times it featured on the breakfast plate and I was unaware of its Bury connection.

So, to Gigg Lane, the Shakers' home ever since 1885, when the club was conceived. One claim to fame was the floodlights, as the first in the region (Simon Inglis). They played pylon pioneers Wolves (who had entertained their own supporters at night with a luminous kit design) under their new acquisition in 1953.

The ground was used by Jimmy McGovern for the television drama on the Hillsborough disaster. This visit was before its £3m transformation initiated in 1992, and the Cemetery End subsisted as an open terrace. My memory fails on the subject of the game as I was preoccupied with my infirmities. Nevertheless Notts County were beaten by Walsall to the third promotion spot that year by one point. Their goal difference was 18, County's 33, quite substantial really. Bury finished 14th.

For a club with Bury's long history of attainment – after all they did win the Cup in 1900 and 1903, the latter establishing a record margin of victory in thrashing Derby County 6-0 (slightly better than Blackburn 6 Sheffield Wednesday 1 in 1890) – it's surprising to note their poor home support, exceeded already by the fan base of their tenants since 2005: Football Club United of Manchester. Frenetically and, from the start, successfully rising from the ashes of Red Devil support when their club acceded to the hostile purchase by Malcolm Glazer, the acquisitive Floridian, the new entity spurned the desperate take-over plea of Leigh RMI, casualties of the Conference (who had endured the lowest attendance figures of its then 22 members and bottom in 2003-04 with 18 points). 'Football Club United of Manchester' was established as an independent entity in 2005 as an 'industrial and provident society' – members contribute a minimum of one pound to secure no more than a single vote each. They lost no time in agreeing terms for sharing Gigg Lane with the Shakers. The new club's altruistic principles did not sound much like the style of its sire, the Traffs, and included:

1.  The Board (of 12) will be democratically elected by its members
3.  The club will develop strong links with the local community and strive to be accessible to all, discriminating against none
4.  The club will endeavour to make admission prices as affordable as possible, to as wide a constituency as possible
5.  The club will encourage young, local participation – playing and supporting – whenever possible
7.  The club will remain a non-profit organisation.

Unspoken was the departure from egos and corporations and the return to what the supporters wanted, e.g. immediacy and contact with the players over a pint after the game – the human element. On the other hand there is the point of view that this enterprise is misguided – why can't the aggrieved just transfer their support to a real club, like Bury FC, for example, or Rochdale?

Indeed the initial coaching staff of four all hailed from the Manchester area. In their first season, occupying one of several spare spaces in the North West Counties Football League Second Division, nine tiers below the Premiership, they ran out easy champions, registering three eight goal winning margins, including 10-2 v Castleton Gabriels. Their record defeat was a modest but repetitious 1-2 (thrice). Their attendances beat all other non-league clubs except Exeter City, including a phenomenal 6,023 against Great Harwood Town at Gigg Lane (the away fixture had been the occasion of their lowest figure: 1,028.)

Also winning the Supporters Direct Cup (missing the eligibility boat in 2005-06 for the main knock-out tournament at their level – the FA Vase – and having to wait another season to join the FA Cup qualifying fray), in 2006-07 they were to compete with the likes of Salford City, Maine Road and, yes, Trafford Football Clubs in NW Counties League Division 1. The outcome at the top of the table was as follows:

| | P | W | D | L | F | A | Pts |
|---|---|---|---|---|---|---|---|
| FC United of Manchester | 42 | 36 | 4 | 2 | 157 | 36 | 112 |
| Curzon Ashton | 42 | 31 | 6 | 5 | 116 | 38 | 99 |
| Nantwich Town | 42 | 29 | 8 | 5 | 108 | 41 | 95 |

You have to feel a bit sorry for runners-up Ashton, and Nantwich too. In a normal year their tallies would represent a stroll to the title. Our heroes had beaten Formby (bottom but one in the final table) 5-0 on the last afternoon. It was a sunny day at the end of the hottest April on record.

The initiative connected with that which had inspired AFC Wimbledon in 2002, after the perceived series of betrayals culminating in the invention of Milton Keynes Dons. Wimbledon's chairman lent an ear, and the inaugural games were at a) Leigh RMI (0-0) and b) AFC Wimbledon (0-1 to the new boys).

Meanwhile let us note that Bury's long-standing nickname owes to a local offshoot of the Society of Friends, the 'Quaking Shakers'. That's what I was told. However, a persuasive authority, Bury fan and journalist John Hudson, agrees with Wikipedia's version: 'the club's nickname, the Shakers, was bestowed upon them by club chairman JT Ingham, who at the Lancashire Cup Final on 23 April 1892 declared, "We'll give 'em a shaking. In fact, we are the Shakers"'.

At the time when that was first appended to Bury, F.C. United's parent was called Newton Heath. It's not only the football club that could do with some cash. In 1947 Bury MDC had purchased a painting, 'A Riverside' by L.S. Lowry, direct from his agents for £175 – a mere snip. In November 2006 it was sold at auction for £1.4m.

## Sodden at Whaddon

## Cheltenham Town 0 Blackpool 1
## Division III (4), 28/10/00

*To a pub for a swig and a bite,*
*Squelching off hardly knowing our plight,*
*Little atmosphere there,*
*No home goals, not much flair,*
*Whaddon Road was a sad and damp sight.*

Observing the ground from Whaddon Road itself, the most appealing aspect is of the Cheltenham Whaddon Bowling Club. Now why couldn't the name have been

conferred on the football club, when invented (as long ago as 1892)? Or think about 'Cheltenham Spa' – that's what it is and has. Jacquie thought that would be unsuitable for the football fraternity and 'Town' was nice and direct. But she's imbued by the ethos inherited from the friend who got her into the Whaddon habit. 'He spends his time moaning about the team but still enjoys it. There was all that excitement at the time they were on the up, a real sense of fans supporting them.' She was working in the town at that time. During the period of Steve Cotterill's high-achieving management she attended regularly. They were really flying. She said that eventually she couldn't come with her friends any more – they were season ticket holders and she had to sit in another part of the ground. That's not very well organized: a block for season tickets only. Not so at other grounds where as a day-tripper you find a mixture of permanent and temporary.

So her interest abated – except this time, and the next time (Reds or Robins 1 Seagulls or Albion 1 – FA Cup Round 1, 10/11/07) when Brighton dominated throughout only to concede a goal in the 78th minute. 'The Cheltenham is wonderful' screamed the In2Print (erstwhile Wymans Road) faithful. Brighton, and Hove, seemed to account for a disproportionate part of the meagre 2,984 crowd. On about 73 minutes the ball whizzed into the cavity below us for me to retrieve. It was pretty slippery. Justice was achieved on 90 minutes, with a strong, even unanswerable, move, covering acres, by the decoratively blue haired Bas Savage, converted into replay entitlement by Doug Loft. Bas was the best thing. The worst was the tepid 'beefy drink'. There was one other gem: the scoreboard, as simple as can be imagined. 'Cheltenham Town – score – minutes remaining – score - Visitors".

> *In the pub we did swig and, yes, bite*
> *And got to our seats in daylight.*
> *The Seagulls were there*
> *And the Robins? Don't care –*
> *They just can't win, try as they might.*

They lost both the subsequent games on the South Coast, still in November.

If Rushden & Diamonds were upstarts then these Robins are parvenus. They continue to attract a paucity of support and have surely over-achieved in even gaining membership of the League in 1999. Add to this the two rather impressive promotions they have achieved in a handful of seasons.

The nearest to star footballing hereabouts is:

• my rubbing shoulders with former Villa (and elsewhere) hero Dion Dublin at a Jazz Jamaica concert in the Town Hall;

• some of north Cheltenham's residents (towards Whaddon), who play top-class rugby for Gloucester RFC a few miles over the Golden Valley and under the M5.

Let's compare these neighbours:

|  | Cheltenham Town FC | Gloucester Rugby |
|---|---|---|
| League membership | League 1 (3) | Premier |
| Founded | 1892 | 1873 |
| First year in League | 1999-2000 | Always in top group |
| Cup Winners | Zero | 1971-72 (1st Knockout Cup) |
|  | Season 2007-08 | Season 2007-08 |
| Ground capacity | 7,407 | 16,500 |
| Average League gate 2007-08 | 4,310 | 14,056 |

Note that Cheltenham's average gate in 2007-08 did represent an increase of 18.1% from 2005-06, though a drop from 2006-07. They flirted intimately with relegation to finish 19th. Paying guests Bristol Rovers might or might not attract more, given the distance and intricacy of the journey from 2008-09. Rovers' average gate in their last season in the old Memorial Stadium was 6,850. At Kingsholm Glos achieved two full houses during the season: at home to Bris during the Xmas/New Year holiday and on the last day of the season against Bath. That crowd witnessed the home team's attainment of pole position. Curiously in Rugby Union such an achievement is not of any value. You have to win the subsequent knock out competition. Once again Glos failed at the first hurdle, eclipsed at the end to lose 25-26 to Leicester. 'Top of the table' meant not a jot – very mean of the authorities, I reckon, not to award a trophy for the achievement, being the best team over 22 league fixtures.

The good things, while the soccer fraternity enjoy their, I predict, handful of years of League membership, are for the visiting fans. Cheltenham is a magnificent Georgian town where you can take the sulphurous waters, feel sick and then better. Feast your eyes on the gorgeous buildings. Then try one of the friendly, welcoming pubs on the way to the ground. In other words make a day/night of it, not least because the Whaddon experience itself may serve to deflate. There is a caveat, however, if travelling by train: the station is some way out of the centre to the west while the ground is located to the north-east of the town, within hailing distance of the famed race course and beautiful Cotswold country. It's a circuitous route from Virgin Rail to limestone crescents to the ground (most worthwhile via watering holes).

Even so this is an opportunity to plug the aesthetic attractions, Cheltenham hosting upwards of 14 festivals each year, including the Screenwriters' Festival where writers, directors, producers emerge, inspired and fulfilled after four days of good stuff. This is Festival City, except that it isn't one, as the longer-in-the-tooth Gloucester, a disappointing place with some good bits, boasts a transcendent cathedral complete with astonishing fan vaulting and the tomb of Edward II, famed for his painful end in nearby Berkeley Castle.

It says something for CTFC's management over the years that it has been able to enjoy third-level status, and erect the Carlsberg, an all-seater stand in 2005-06, holding 1,100, to replace the Whaddon Road End terrace. Most generously this is the away end. It was Bristol Rovers' eventual choice to rent during the rebuilding of the Memorial Stadium sometime after 2007.

Meanwhile the rugby-playing neighbours were being forced to extend the cramped Kingsholm ground, much better placed to treat the fans – close to Gloucester city centre and affording a direct view of the cathedral, if you pick the right entrance. In the stand called 'The Shed' the crowd can be deafening – when I went it was packed to the roof with fervent supporters, some way ahead of Robins fans in production of volume. Like some soccer grounds the make-up of the Shed makes a big contribution, being low and made of tin: sonorous even on a quiet day. Glos, with working-class traditions and an eternal place among the elite, even since professionalism invaded in 1995, was also able to withstand the unpopular buffet of enforced changes in 2005 of name ('Rugby' the suffix since 2005 – at least it wasn't 'Gladiators') and colours (the traditional cherry and white hoops replaced by a predictable designer-inspired mixture).

The bottom line is that Cheltenham just doesn't have the support to justify a Football League team. It isn't a footy town, something its neighbour is, albeit the oval not round discipline.

⚽

## Suffering the Mighty Crush

## West Bromwich Albion 0  Aston Villa 0
## Division 1, 8/11/80

This is one of the original, perennial fixtures (in those seasons when WBA grace the top division or the two teams share membership at a lower level) even more a historic local derby. Both clubs were founder members of the Football League. They abide just over four miles apart, but Albion proclaim a Black Country identity, rivals being Wolves, a much further 12 miles away. Indeed cynics have called the team 'Handsworth Rangers' as part of the ground lies over the Birmingham border. It certainly feels more Brummie than Black Country, lying to the east of the M5. The Villa were invented further up the social ladder, formed from a church team, Villa Cross Wesleyan Chapel, with all the associated character improvement: courage (called 'pluck'), fair play, unselfishness and self-control. 'Football' says Peter Lupson in *Thank God for Football* 'was seen very early on as a moral agent.' The Throstles, as West Bromwich Strollers, were associated with the steel mills. One type of Them and Us?

On this day, Villa were riding high, top of the League. The Baggies (one version of the nickname's origin being from the bagmen's parade) managed by Ron Atkinson, who later moved to Villa, had just drawn at second-placed Ipswich. They were in a challenging position, sixth, with a good home record. A big crowd was on the cards for a special encounter, but what came to pass was a living nightmare.

As soon as I joined the queue at the away end it was apparent that those with claustrophobic tendencies should have avoided the Hawthorns. At once there developed a tight crush from which at once there was no escape: no way of retracing steps as the dynamic was forward and it became impossible to turn in any direction. The numbers continued to increase and formed a surging swarm behind me, while there was no perceptible progression towards the line of turnstiles, somewhere out of sight. This was certainly exacerbated by the police presence, several on horseback, towering over the hoi polloi, impotent for anything but aggravating the situation.

The Villa fans were a vast mass of upright bodies clamouring and pushing towards the hopelessly inadequate turnstile operation. We eventually heard the game start, a trigger for further passion and surging, not to say panic. The game proceeded with no goals – we would have been made unequivocally aware of any changes by those who had made it to the terraces – and little by little the turnstiles loomed. Jostling for position became the next phase as there were no barriers to separate the ticket windows into individual queues. I was able to uncover my watch at last as I fended off people behind me. That didn't provide any comfort. The clichéd maxim 'survival of the fittest' comes to mind. As did other salutary platitudes at the time. I don't know how many perished; possibly some below average height were suffocated in neighbouring armpits. But at last salvation arrived when I found myself, shaken and stirred, inside the ground. A quarter of the game had passed and I can't have been the only one to spend the rest of the first half recovering, even if within nother crush on the terrace, intent on the drama below. It was probably a benefit to s all that the result was a no-score draw. The retreat after the final whistle was treated ingerly. There was no alternative.

This Baggies v Lions occasion counts as my worst ever experience, vindicated 1st a little by Villa's championship the following May, while the Albion finished an xcellent fourth. I do love those Throstles – no end of fun! It warms my cockles to drive ast the Hawthorns on the way back from Villa Park to the M5. That day in September '007 after Villa had overcome the long-unbeaten Chelsea 2-0 ('Fuck off, Mourinho!' hanted the Holte End, as one) was so sweet. WBA, one hoped, would once again win 'remiership status in 2008. And they did.

By way of distinction I have to refer to a visit a generation later (0-1 to Charlton – Premier League, 29/1/03) for that special happening, a top-level night ame with snow on the ground, gleaming under the halogen. Within was the intimacy nd bravura of over 20,000 spectators hoping and longing, suppressed by the spectre f looming relegation. How desperate to have to make an advance booking for such n endurance. At least Landy lived only a few streets away and had worthily procured ckets. We were able to join the thrusting crowd in the trudge which featured bits of 1e Birmingham / Wolverhampton Metro line. In the event Charlton Athletic came ut on top, quite deservedly, the tally restricted to one mere goal by the desperate home am, a contribution coming from the appositely named Ronnie Wallwork battling on 1 the Throstles' defence. The futility of Albion's plight seemed of pervasive effect ,given 1e howls of derision round the ground.

Afterwards, in the Old Crown in West Brom proper, there was the comfort of armth, prime beer, scratchings and a bevy of blokes in Baggies garb resigning their am not only to relegation in May but a probable further downgrading the year after. he whole thing was a fine paradigm of evening football, a vigorous adult occasion. Vas Baggie Bird, the mascot, there to promote his/her/its team? We didn't observe him rough the ether, but since then 23rd was his best result in the Grand National. The wl also made the news for an abseiling venture at the Hawthorns.

To the tune of *Would You Like to Swing on a Star*

*Oh would you like to follow West Brom*
*Come up the Hawthorns and cheer 'em on*
*Remember Regis, Astle and Brown*
*Or would you rather be a clown?*

nd that's only the first verse. Ingestion now, work tomorrow.

The Hawthorns has become submerged in continuous West Midlands development, nd can probably stake a claim to being the original out-of-town ground built on asteland. Elevated, too, the highest Football League ground. 'I find it curiously homely, unlike those more recent erections such as the Reebok and Swansea's Liberty Stadium. Does this suggest the latter will soften over time? In many cases we may have to wait long while for Mothercare to mellow, or, preferably, vanish? What will be next?

And, thankfully not very often, there were worrying scuffles on the terraces, within danger reach. Mickey G, in his decades following Blackburn round the country considered that Halifax Town supporters had been the most scary, with bricks in and out of hand on one occasion. Exposure like that can run deep, as in the man I met who was once dangerously close to rock-chucking Chelsea maniacs on the way to Ninian Park, Cardiff. He's never been to a game since, and that was 30 years ago. My advice is to pursue your own inclinations – keep on going – and, as we've all been told, avoid eye contact should things get threatening.

## Chapter Eight
# Countdown from Ten

### The Story of the Final Grounds Visited during 2005-06

Arriving at the 2005-06 football season, the final list of grounds yet to visit eventually totalled ten:

Blackpool – Bloomfield Road
Bolton Wanderers – Reebok Stadium
Chester City – Saunders Honda Stadium
Coventry City – Ricoh Arena
Hartlepool United – Victoria Park
Lincoln City – Sincil Bank
Milton Keynes Dons – National Hockey Stadium
Sunderland – Stadium of Light
Swansea City – Liberty Stadium
Wigan Athletic – JJB Stadium

### The List

But the foreplay leading up to the ultimate cluster must be revealed. Here is the diary:

*15 July*
*In my monthly copy of the journal* What's Brewing *I had espied a reference to* The (new) Football and Real Ale Guide, *by Richard Stedman (Stedders). Just what I needed. There was a volume for each division, which would ease the task of planning the final nine, or so I thought. They duly arrived. Excellent stuff, but the pity of it: what follows leapt from the 'League Division 1' issue:*

*'Swansea*
*The Swans are on the move, to a part of town that has pubs but no real ale.'*
*All bad news. The Nine had grown to Ten and the location was unsympathetic. I contacted the club's email address, courtesy of their website.*
*Me: 'I've heard that the club is moving grounds. Is this true and, if so, when? Many thanks…'*
*Her: 'Yes we have moved to a new stadium at the end of the season, our new address is:-*
*The New Stadium, Landore, Swansea…'*

*Decided that for now I would read my new purchases no further for fear of further similar revelations.*

*I found it curiously satisfying that the new stadium was called just that for the time being, still feeling ignorant about the correct names of Hull City and Darlington's grounds as they were absent from my 2003 ground guide, when planning for early 2005 visits. Not many good guides around, were there? Also Landore was named on the map I examined and seemed fairly convenient – on the way into the city by road from the east.*

*17 July*
*Not yet summoning the will to scan more of Stedders' pages, only two days later I happened upon an article in the sports pages of the* Telegraph, *which was donated to me by a friend collecting vouchers for a country cottage (you need an excuse to read it). The article, by Jim White, was 2'3" wide x 3" tall (they hadn't yet followed the* Times *to tabloid). The title: 'Banishing the blues as Wycombe get a pre-season kick out of playing host to Chelsea and Mourinho'. As I welcome underdog opportunities and recalled the 1996 Adams Park experience with a warm glow, I settled down to the piece. The problem was that the third paragraph opened with an opinion that Wycombe's ground was a place to watch summer football. A crossbow bolt pierced the thorax as he wrote: 'The Causeway stadium has a gently bucolic feel'. Causeway Stadium? This appeared to indicate New Ground, Number 11 in the Last 9. Nine had seemed quite enough after the rush to reduce the remainder in 2004-05. Now two more?*

*6 August*
*I find all the long-awaited new-season football magazines on a station stall. Oh joy! And that was at Birmingham New Street after a day of fabulous Ashes brilliance by England at Edgbaston (the Freddie Flintoff Show). On the return journey I scoured the mags for insights. The list of 11 was confirmed – no more new addresses, thank God.*

*11 August*
*The season is underway, providing a fine Gasheads night out with Stedders, the author above, who turns out to be a Bristol Rovers regular. Football grounds cropped up in the discourse: the electric utterance from the horse's mouth, as he lives near High Wycombe, is that The Causeway is the new name for Adams Park. Thus I have suffered from a misapprehension and the last batch number is now ten again. Wonderful!*

## The Plan

Of the list, six would involve a reunion with clubs already enjoyed at their previous addresses, plus Chester and Lincoln, needing to get past the gates this time. This left Hartlepool and Blackpool as complete novelties. They should be heralded as havens of bliss. It soon became an unequivocal decision to finish with a flourish of vulgarity and ld-world values incorporating Blackpool's Bloomfield Road.

There were three Premiership grounds, Coventry in the Championship, four in 'League One' and two in 'Two'.

A schedule of games gradually emerged to produce a balanced countdown sequence. First to Bolton, being the only convenient game given the holiday route in he preceding week and the first home game of a top-division outfit.

*7 July*

*I reached for the handset, dialling the Reebok ticket number. The telephone service was efficient – I only had to redial once, and a helpful man dealt with the call. He informed me that beyond priority bookings, season ticket holders etc, remaining tickets would go on sale two weeks before the game. 'How likely is it that there will be any tickets left?' (I was thinking: if I get through on the phone.)*

*'Have you been to the Reebok before?'*

*'No.'*

*'Then it's very unlikely you'll get any tickets.'*

*To overcome the problem of admission, a state of affairs to which I was by now hardened, the only reliable option appeared to be the treat of a 'Package': the Reebok has the only stadium-abutting hotel, DeVere Whites. The Package was entitled 'Reebok Stadium Tour & Visitors Centre'. It included use of the leisure suite and free parking. This last was a real boon. We would have no intention of leaving the area, having arrived on Friday afternoon to use the leisure facilities (swimming pool, sauna, oranges). Regarding tickets, I was asked to choose 'home or away'. I chose home, having a distinct preference for the Wanderers over Everton who I felt had been overdue for relegation for many years (though you had to admire them of late, having just finished fourth, the year after Wayne Rooney was snapped up by Man U.) Anyway home support is the easier ride. This deal was sealed with a deposit, with a worrying proviso, repeated in the paperwork received two days later; 'please note that the hotel cannot confirm your match tickets until one week prior to your arrival date. In the event we cannot confirm tickets the hotel will offer a full refund. Dates & times of football fixtures may be subject to change. It is the responsibility of the hotel guest to identify any changes made to football fixtures.' Quite so, and therefore a lurking worry. I didn't want a Chester repeat and find the game rearranged for when we had to be away from Bolton, or find that the ground's capacity, perhaps insufficient for the club's popularity given their recent success (sixth place and European football qualification) meant that somehow the hotel's access to tickets would be limited at our expense. Please not, as it was to be difficult enough to facilitate visits to three Premiership grounds without the one with a hotel and a Package failing us.*

*Done!*

*The saga has commenced.*

*10 July*

*An exciting prospect suddenly came in to play for the unpromising target of Milton Keynes Dons. It could become a memorable event: as away supporters of Rotherham United on Saturday 29 October. This National Hockey Stadium fixture could be transformed by making a weekend of it and seeing Matthew Bourne's award-winning all-male production of Swan Lake at MK Theatre, which I had unearthed from the city's tourist information page on the internet. A blokes double whammy: 11 on the pitch at 3.00pm and quite a few on stage at 7.30? I decided to work on this as there could be a few takers.*

*Extract from my phone call to MKD:*

*Me: 'Can you get admission as away supporters on the day of the game?'*

*Reply: 'Of course you can, love: £15 adults, £10 concessions.'*

*There you go. Easy, innit!*

*I was now awaiting the six tickets for Swan Lake for the evening, and Ruthie had undertaken accommodation – in three rooms in a convenient chain hotel; finally there's a gallery with a recommended exhibition in Central MK (not 'Milton Keynes')! That one will be over by then but let's hope there's something interesting to see following the hotel breakfast. This project was truly launched.*

*Coventry are conveniently hosting Stoke City in a Championship fixture on 2 November, logically extending the Milton Keynes extravaganza, giving a tempting prospect of several days of varied fun in central England.*

*24 July*

*Call from DeVere Whites – at least they made the effort – to the effect that the game has been rearranged to Sunday. I've kept abreast of as many sources as possible for just this kind of revelation, and now it's happened this way. Most vexing. Yes, we can manage it, I reply, and we can keep the parking space and use hotel facilities until after the game.*

*18 August*

*Telephoned Mickey G in Blackburn, with a view to something, like a reminiscence session, while incarcerated in the Bolton hotel. He suggested getting tickets for Rovers v Fulham on Saturday. What a good idea! How propitious! Having idly pondered upon Sunderland and Hartlepool for a north-eastern single-trip staggered scenario (a bit far-fetched) the idea could be transposed to Blackburn and Bolton, over two days. Fascinating it would be to compare the experiences directly, both first home Premiership games of the season.*

# The Trawl

so as a taster for the actual list:

## Blackburn Rovers 2 Fulham 1
### Premiership, 20/8/05

On the way to inaugurate the much anticipated venture, we sampled the Crown in Horwich proper, a car ride from the stadium, featured by Stedders for a Bolton visit: Holt's of Manchester, in the sun. Lovely, and as it came to pass the only pub and pint of ale we managed in the Metropolitan Borough of Bolton.

With two season ticket holders, Mickey G., and his son, Phil, Wakey and I spent an invigorating introduction downing pints of Thwaites in a pub familiar from the past, the Gibraltar, which I mistakenly remembered as the Trafalgar. Well, the bi-centenary of said battle was imminent. Man.U. v Villa was on the box, which the former duly won 1-0. I observed the goal in mid-quaff. This happens a lot.

Parking conveniently – Mickey's territory so the ten-minute wander was a pleasant preamble - the scene was developing like a family excursion. The sun was out, we tourists were wearing shorts, well-mellowed through the pleasures of a holiday in a week of favourable weather, even venturing into the sea on the west Welsh coast, working towards the climax: footy. In reality, there was no need for reserved seats as in in Ewood Park's CIS Stand there was plenty of empty space (ground capacity 31,367, gate on the day 16,953). We chose two seats, guided by our host and became aware of being surrounded by diehard supporters, one of whom, the most loyal Mickey, pointed out that Blackburn had too small a population to fill the stadium, encouragingly improved through the benevolence of Jack Walker. His statue was in prime position outside, affording a photo session.

The fifth member of our party was Matteo, from Turin and a Torino supporter. His club's Serie A status had been in doubt owing to uncertainty regarding their finances. The Italian League had just determined to relegate Torino and Messina to Serie B. He was the boyfriend of Mickey's daughter (catching up with domestic chores that afternoon). For years she had been a member of the four-strong family season-ticket holding, . Matteo certainly liked his drink, sampling Blackburn's finest in the pub before and after, with a pint of keg something in the top bar at half-time. Some of us went for a pasty and Bovril to maintain tradition. They don't seem to do that in Italy. Wakey took a blurred photo (moral: always take more than one) of the two old college friends by the 'No alcohol in the stands' sign. Since deleted on the basis of quality control.

On the pitch the most obvious persona was that of Robbie Savage, perhaps mistaken for Tugay the Turk, and a goal scorer for Rovers, in view of their similar hairstyles. A yellow card was fair enough for Savage's general deportment.

After the game we all enjoyed the stroll back to the car and the West View, whose feature, a reward for choosing Thwaites Lancaster Bomber (4.4%), was a scratch card in the name of England's contemporary hero, Andrew the Allrounder, a Lancashire lad to boot. No prizes for us.

We returned to base via Ewood, now somnolent, on the road to Bolton. Horwich did have the mixed blessing of being more country than town, on the way to Bolton proper, good old Burnden Park having been an urban ground a world away on the other side of the borough. You could watch Bury-bound trains from your terrace spot. There was a single road to the old ground, for generations packed solid with cloth caps. On my visit there on 10/12/83, the Wanderers beat Mansfield Town 2-0 with all the thrill of the Second Round of the FA Cup. But my chief recollection is of a startling warehouse fire filling the night sky on the retreat route from the ground after their triumph, my feet excruciatingly cold. Dayglow socks had not proved fit for the purpose. This was an occasion sandwiched by 3-0 results. Mansfield had beaten Doncaster thus in the First Round and Bolton suffered a 0-3 drubbing by Sunderland in the Fourth. In 1997 the Trotters were to remove to the 28k-capacity Reebok Stadium, abandoning the old place, which had celebrated its centenary in 1995, and had hosted a record 69,912 in 1933.


And to complete the party piece:

## Bolton Wanderers 0 Everton 1
## Premiership, 21/8/05

Despite the powerful image of the stadium, both passing and approaching it, beautiful from afar, comparisons with Rovers and Ewood are not favourable to the Reebok, nor the management of the occasion.

The stadium tour was somewhat limited. It was match day, hence the immediate news that it was truncated, e.g. no 'dressing rooms', as our tour guide referred to them. On the other hand we witnessed the burgeoning production which is a Premiership game augmenting double figures of day-by-day staff to seemingly many hundreds for a few hours. The highlight for a few was a photo opportunity in passing manager Sam Allardyce office. This was the man often tipped through the season to assume the England mantle in the future. We even saw the door close, but from afar and it was hung the wrong way round for a sighting. Various subscribers posed for a snap by the name on the door. More to the point were the memorabilia, photos, programmes and framed shirts (one from the 1953 Cup Final, more renowned for Stanley Matthews' contribution) along the corridor. There were no trophies on display, but then the Trotters haven't won a lot. One they did achieve was the first Wembley Cup Final, beating West Ham (2-0) in 1923, when the ground was the 'Empire Stadium' in common parlance, being broadcast under its proper name. Fate had dictated the opposition for our game to be Everton, who over the years have met Bolton on several landmark occasions – Wanderers were Everton's first-ever League opponents, Everton the last visitors to Burnden Park and the first at the Reebok, on 1 September 1997. This was all in the tour guide's spiel.

We had espied possible lunch-break outlets from high in the ground. After the tour, with the duration of a football game to kill, we sought these out, and followed the hordes to the retail village which included a Harvester Inn. Two women in front of us in the queue (for admission to the enclave – more queues were to manifest themselves

to get inside and at the bar itself) were refused as their tickets revealed allegiance to the foes. They looked so fetching in toffee blue, too. A football fan in these circumstances is always in dire need of a pint and we elected for Guinness, there being nothing palatable. This turned out to be a misjudgement. My order was for four pints to avoid yet another claustrophobic challenge, i.e. a second visit to the bar, the queue being three deep. The callow bartender, whose eye I eventually caught, was clearly unpractised, indeed untrained, in Guinness, and ignorant of its demands. It all frothed up on the first pouring, by which time the deal was sealed, the next customer being served and me ousted. The bar congestion was such that it was impracticable to obtain a top-up from the original pouring. Wakey having managed to secure a table with two chairs, by the toilets, we fixed our gazes on the glasses with apprehension. They recovered from our earlier estimate of two-thirds full to a little more than three-quarters, and we vowed, should such an heinous instance as this occur in the future, we would pick lager instead for greater quantity and more instant gratification. Desperate measures.

Once in the ground we had a Pennine hike up to the rafters – Row NN in the top corner near the away section. There was plenty of space and a few friends of somebody in ticket control were displaying complimentary tickets. The ground had an official capacity of 28,500, the tale went, with potential for more. There were 25,608 in attendance that day, so why had I been I put off by the ticket office? Also the face value of the tickets was an unbelievable £39 (Blackburn £25). I wrote later to complain about this. No response was forthcoming.

We were flanked by a man and a boy (also hotel guests, with tickets showing £35 each). The boy was wearing the trappings of Toffeemen, 2005-06. This was strange, as it had been emphasized to us how keen the club was on safety and segregation. This was the only ground with separate tunnels for the teams, to avoid contact – before a 'contact sport' fixture. Our view was mouth-watering – sun-soaked hills outside, gantries and cantilevers within; also just behind us was one of the in-house cameras for filming of audience rather than contenders, we had been informed on the tour. It was a colourful vista: Wanderers all in white, Everton all in blue and the pitch a vivid green apart from the patch below us in dark shadow throughout.

The main highlight was the scoreboard, easier to see than the game itself, which proceeded languorously far below us. Between play I was trying to comprehend how it worked. Too often electronic scoreboards serve to irritate, as they seem designed primarily to boost income, alongside conveying a modicum of information, like the score and time, whether using a real clock, time elapsed since kick-off or what remained of the current 45 minutes. At Ewood it was the last of these. The Bolton game score was represented only by what was probably the coat of arms of the home team (above) and away team (below). No names. In between was the tally of each, i.e. the score of the game we were here for. The space allocated to this was less than a third of the board, the remainder being dedicated to a plethora of commercial activities. There was an impressive range of these in a complex arrangement. The board was modified at half-time to vary the bits, no doubt to capitalize on fans' need to absorb something other than pitch activity during the break. Interval messages on a narrow strip were more of a diversion in presenting personal notices. Round numbers were the thing – 50th birthday, 50th anniversary, 40th birthday. The bottom panel featured a circuit of upwards of a dozen advertizers, several of which could be accessed in the ground or online at home, e.g. new home and away kits and even the programme for the game. (In hindsight that might have proved helpful in view of the length to which I had to go at other grounds to obtain a programme.) It was interesting to note how many 'official' attachments the club had, from radio through smart card to, simply, partner, which was the main sponsor. There was also a special attraction widely displayed: Donny Osmond, 'everyone's favourite', was to appear there on Saturday 17 September.

Unsurprisingly the match programme was fully attuned to selling opportunities. It comprised 84 pages of which about 20 were purely commercial (Blackburn had 64, but in a larger format, with 15 of advertizing). Both programmes were £3. I'm sure I didn't have to spend more than £2.50 in 2004-05 at Premiership games: 20% was a big jump. Furthermore, it occurred to me that we had witnessed a large percentage of overseas players out of upwards of 50 on the pitches on two afternoons. Why don't clubs how country of origin after names on the programme team page?

After the diversion of scoreboard analysis, Everton gave the game a boost a few minutes into the second half, scoring the only goal, against the run of play, provoking muted applause from Man and Boy and joyous celebration from the bank of Toffee people to our right. Meanwhile the hotel dining room, clearly visible above them and laid for a repast (all in white with blue glasses), was empty.

That was interesting as it was a protected area within the hotel, whose business was mainly around the Brasserie and bar on the next level down. Was there no take-up? After the goal the away fans lost their inhibitions. The taunt 'you've never won fuck all' was telling, but rather sad in view of the close relationship these clubs have had, Everton doing better in the final analysis, including this time (the reverse fixture was perverse: 0-4 to the Trotters). We were looking forward to the antics of their character player, Duncan Ferguson, and were rewarded, once, with an entertaining set-to with Bolton's keeper in the second half. Paul Cookson, Poet-in-Residence at the National Football Museum, wrote of him in *Introducing Some of the Team*:

Big Lee Merick

*A tower of strength I each game*
*A powerful gigantic frame*
*Mean, moody, colossal*
*Of menace and muscle*
*A triumph of brawn over brain.*

With about 20 minutes remaining there was some activity round us. Boy had left his seat for a wander. A steward escorted him back and insisted that Man and Boy be re-seated in the away end (close but still quite a journey with not much of the game left) as the part of the ground we were in was a designated home area. Man argued that they had been admitted at the turnstile, so why was it not mentioned then, and these tickets had been given them by the hotel, although he had said they were away supporters. The steward prevailed. Off they trundled reluctantly. Five minutes after their exodus, they returned, stewardless, for the remainder of the game. Man said the officials had seen sense in the end but they 'took a bit of persuading'. The final whistle was nigh.

We took advantage of our hotel-reservation cards to return by the swing doors and enjoy a civilized pot of tea while the masses outside abated. There was thankfully no queue at the tea counter. We bypassed the ever-lengthening line to the bar.

I drove Wakey the five miles to Bolton where there was a total absence of signs to the station, just like many football grounds, but I was now free from crowds and commercialism, kicking off with Massive Attack on minidisk and a packet of extra-strong mints. I mused on Burnden Park and those restorative pints at the Sweet Green Tavern, my mind's eye shifting to the recent Reebok event and Whites shortbread, then contemplating the new showpieces to come.

83 achieved, 9 in line.

*24 August*

*Tiptoes has taken on the project of Sunderland v Birmingham City (to start with, Brummagem connections – Blues fans who don't want to take up their allocation) on 26 November, a weekend on Wearside with various younger generation in attendance on a jolly from Durham University. Actually I'd rather be a home fan at the Stadium of Light. Already press and punters are adjusting to disappointing sales in the Premiership. The days of ticket trepidation may be on the wane in some quarters.*

*The weekend's best result was Sunderland's 0-2 win in the derby at Middlesbrough. This followed West Brom robbing the Black Cats of their first win in the final few seconds last week. The stadium, however, was not full. The debate continues about Premiership attendances. Apparently there were 62,000 empty seats at the nine Premiership matches played. The point was made that up to four or five games i.e. half of them, are now scheduled at times other than Saturday at 3pm, discouraging away supporters. However, nothing will change as the commercial corners of the Premier League and Sky perceive the market as unthreatened after a sequence of previous years' success, the Cup Final being a good example of a record-breaking televised event. Even so, following early-season gate dips the FA Premier League has set up a working party to investigate the issue.*

*Exciting result from an FA Cup Preliminary Round replay: Tunbridge Wells 2 Littlehampton Town 2, Tunbridge Wells won 16-15 on penalties. The 40 spot kicks established a new record for the longest shoot-out in a senior cup match.*

*28 August*

*The paper carries the League Cup Round 2 draw. Sunderland v Cheltenham and Wigan v Bournemouth: I quickly chose the latter for the shorter hike, and plans seem promising for the Stadium of Light in November. Being midweek there may well be an availability problem as most potential companions were in work.*

*(Cup draw information seems somewhat erratic. The biggest – the FA Cup Third Round – is fanfared on TV. Meanwhile the Fourth Qualifying Round draw in 2006 was pre-ordained as being announced at 'noon' on the appointed day. However the information curiously deposited itself on the website some time earlier. Exeter City had drawn AFC Wimbledon. It promised much, not least that the Grecians should make it to the second most exciting draw, the First Round Proper, having been bundled out by 'Satanage' the previous time. And it promised to attract a big gate. The real Wimbledon boasted an immense following and City were the best-supported non-League team in 2005-06, though overtaken by Oxford United, early leaders, the next year – bigger city, bigger stadium, surprising relegation.)*

*30 August*

*Arrangements initiated for Swansea v Hartlepool on Saturday 21 January. Shame it won't count for the away team too, though actually I'm looking forward to Victoria Park for the prospect of the grim North Sea. Tallulah will host in Penarth after the New Stadium, but won't do footy. Robin, our mutual friend, will drive, with or without his hound. Tallulah has imposed a dog ban.*

*8 September*
*Northern Ireland 1 England 0. What a waste of money on all those prima donnas.
But the Ulstermen were well served by two Villa players: scant compensation.*

*10 September*
*The biggest result of the day was Swansea 7 Bristol City 1. Manager Brian Tinnion
out (Gary Johnson took over and steered City from table bottom to near play-off
qualification at the end of the season). What's happening? I've just seen a reference
to the Swans' new ground in Landore as the 'White Rock Stadium'. Was this a
failed deal?*
 *Wigan trip sorted out. I've failed with six contenders, all unavailable, they
said, but Graham, that doughty Millwall enthusiast, is willing to take the afternoon
off and leave at lunchtime. I shall drive – no change there – and we will meet
Stedders there for a pint and the match as he's already in the area pushing his four
new volumes, especially the Premiership one which includes Wigan.*

*15 September*
*Manchester United, aiming for success abroad, scrambled to a 0-0 draw versus
Villarreal at Old Trafford, with ten men, Wayne Rooney having been dismissed on
65 minutes. Following a yellow card, he sarcastically clapped his hands at the referee.
This is our new star, about to replace David Beckham (if you believe quite a lot of the
press), thought to be in decline for England and being upstaged on the fashion front
by new, younger images. The Rooney red mist/red card issue has sparked off articles
with angles ranging from his need for support and cuddles to the urgency for discipline
and coercion, to him in particular, and in general to bad boys. The responsibility
expected of people in the public eye and in receipt of unimaginable remuneration has
been mentioned.*

*17 September*
*More sensation as Chelsea have set a new Premiership record, with 100% points
after seven league games and no goals conceded. Declining attendances are
now a keen discussion point. This – in the Premiership but not Championship
and League 1, which are rising – has been attributed variously to excessive Sky
coverage, high prices (I have read that Arsenal's top price is now £85; £16 at
Bristol Rovers the previous week in the bottom division) and the uninspiring
character of game plans. Everton have just been criticized after their recent game
at Highbury, for playing a dull, containing game and still letting in two goals.
Was there to be a spectator drift towards the lower divisions? Negative opinion
has also been expressed about Chelsea's game. Not exciting it is said. Even less
thrilling is the foregone conclusion for this season, reached before the cricket
season is over, that Chelsea will top the final table in a stride.*

## Wigan Athletic 1 Bournemouth 0
## League Cup Round 2, 20/9/05

Who in their right mind would do a 12-hour-plus trip, spending substantially more than half of it on the journey, and necessarily downing cups of tea and latte (Graham) at a motorway service station to stay awake? For years I have applied a quiet ruling that to justify a journey you should have a longer period at the destination. Otherwise it wears you out. You end up feeling suicidal and looking like a motorway.

Well, this was the only such venture in the countdown, and Graham and I did do a lot of catching up and putting the world (especially of football) to rights.

We eventually attuned to the niceties of Wigan's one-way system and sighted the Anvil, to become Stedders' 'Premiership pub of the year, as voted by the readers 2006-07' and his 'personal pub of the year', and we indeed found him there as arranged. We recovered with pints and halves (Graham) including Hydes Anvil Ale, no less. Graham regaled us with anecdotes from his lifelong Millwall affiliation. Stedders was on the subject of his countrywide knowledge for the guides; also proof-reading. That's something we all had in common with varying degrees of professionalism.

The ground was easy to find and parking was free. However, the car park served all the temples of delight in the complex, including a multiplex cinema. The multitude of venues served by the car park did not bode well for the exodus at the end of the game.

It was a ticketless turnstile event at the JJB Stadium, which opened for business in 1999 at a cost of £30m. We paid £10 admission and, being in good time, had the choice of the whole stand. Eventually a mere 3,346 watched the game. At the other extreme the record crowd, of 25,023, was established when Liverpool visited in February 2006. Alongside a board exhorting bets on the tie was a line of punters awaiting their turn to make donations to Ladbroke's.

The first half was tentative; most of the promising play coming from the visitors, one of the 'Cherries'. We agreed the number.8, Brian Stock, who had been with the club for seven years (said the programme), was pivotal and had the run of midfield. At half-time among the scores from other games was Wycombe 3 Villa 1. I was preparing my stomach for a similar churning to that endured the previous week when they let in 4 goals at West Ham: soft ones, I heard from Tiptoes who suffered the spectacle in person. And West Ham finished a lowly sixth in the Championship last year with 15 defeats and 73 points (Sunderland 94 and Wigan 87). It's all the fault of the play-offs!

Back to reality and the second half. Bournemouth never looked like scoring, and it was left to Latics big guns Jason Roberts (of the follicly inclined girlfriend as revealed when with Bristol Rovers) and David Connolly, introduced as substitutes up front soon after the interval, to develop more penetration. The game took off, but as the scoreboard clocked up 80 minutes, extra time loomed, not a welcome prospect in view of the return journey, even if the travel/activity time ratio would be improved. At last Mr Roberts overcame staunch defending and earned the trip to the hat for

Round 3. The final few minutes – time added on had been announced as two minutes – seemed to be focused on trickery near Bournemouth's corner by Roberts and full-back Steve McMillan over the milling defenders. Most deft i'faith in earning several consecutive throw-ins through nimble footwork, thus obviating a final thrust from Bournemouth. I probably labour this because it was right below us and proved compulsive viewing. The time-added board was raised aloft at precisely the end of each half. I now

believe that there is an understanding that there will always be at least one minute, as that is what we got in the first half, which I'm sure suffered no interruptions at all. Or have I misunderstood the rules? It's strange that meanwhile the Man of the Match award is habitually announced some minutes before the end, which could produce crucial and influential contributions from players other than the lucky nominee.

P.S. The programme was £2, but comprised only 20 pages with no League tables. In Cup games, I submit, there should be included the table of the division of each party, to set the scene. The other trivium is that the cover was very shiny and the squads were listed on the back. Should you wish to mark such information as the result, goal scorer and substitute information, the surface would make this difficult. I don't usually carry marker pens about my football garb.

Throughout the game the stalwart band of Cherries fans produced tribal chants, and a purposeful drum, for their team; Wigan's only response, for a short time only, was the smug 'Who the fucking hell are you?' The stadium had a good ethos, helped by three styles of white-painted roofs round a ground with the full complement of four, neatly enclosing the ground. The seats were in blue, white and red, the initials 'JJB' forming a large part of the central seats. What was to happen when Chairman David Whelan and his interests depart from the club? The scoreboard itself was wide enough to present the entire name of the teams, though thankfully AFC Bournemouth was shown without the prefix. Most clearly we were given 'time elapsed' and 'real time', and no promotional stuff, except the ubiquitous JJB. Not even the rugby team. On entering the metropolitan borough you are informed that it is the home of Wigan Athletic and Wigan Warriors. In the ground you are not made aware of the cohabitants.

Departure took a while. I wonder how much longer when Chelsea, or the neighbouring Lancashire teams, visit. They were Category A in the programme and it was quite flattering that Villa were among those for which the top-price ticket was £25, against £20 for Category B. It was suddenly easier to understand this interpretation when the Wycombe v Villa result came through. The result was 3-8. Villa had netted seven times in the second half! What was the story there? Were David O'Leary's mellifluous tones working a marvel?

Sequels followed this evening for Winning Wigan all the way to the final, their first big one.

84 complete, eight more.

*27 September*
*I suffered an unpleasant jolt when I read about Bournemouth's 'new £5.5m stadium'. Was this another stadium move which had slipped past me quietly? Not Dean Court, upgraded?*

*Fears were allayed soon enough when I discovered that Fitness First is the new Dean Court, improved to the tune of £5.5m. Can you have a double exposure to the physical – saunas then corners? You'd have thought that the team would have acclimatized at Wigan – very obviously situated adjacent to the stadium was a sign saying 'Fitness First'. Home (away) from home.*

*4 October*
*My favourite result in the Second Qualifying Round of the FA Vase was Glasshoughton Welfare 7 Rossington Main 1. This served as a Yorkshire derby, too. We can only guess how many patrons the encounter attracted. The Welfare had beaten Chester-le-Street Town 2-0 in QR 1.*

*By the way the Vase was created in 1974 to replace the Amateur Cup, thus providing for professionalism.*

*And in the Welsh Cup Second Round Lex XI 4 Connah's Quay Nomads 2. I'm still awaiting Rhyl Nil.*

*16 October*
*By the way England also came good – 2-1 against Poland and they've qualified for the World Cup finals. What a relief, whichever stance you take, and mine is very sceptical, i.e. may we please have a rest for a while? How droll that Mr Beckham was sent off. Two yellows maketh one red, David.*

*24 October*
*David Beckham sent off during Real Madrid v Valencia for sarcastically applauding referee. Aping Wayne? The result: 1-2. The public has been given to understand that our two stars don't like each other. Is the boy now a role model in toys-out-of-prams prima donna doings? It was only a month ago that D was putting his arms round W's shoulders, after a display of volatility. He offered a*

*therapeutic, perhaps avuncular, contribution to the errant lad's future, or a hot tip concerning gambling.*

*There is another development. Des Kelly wrote in the* Mail: *'not that Rooney is short of a wannabe shrink. An even more preposterous Samaritan than Beckham has announced he is on hand to "help"…none other than convicted rapist and paranoid ear-biting psychopath Mike Tyson…embarking on a UK speaking tour and planning to build a role for himself in youth development… Since it was Rooney's 20th birthday yesterday, I'll give him some advice for free. Should Beckham or Tyson call with tips on "how to cope" tell them to mind their own business, as only you can.'*

*Finally, Becks is still schoolboys' idol choice, according to a survey this month.*

## Milton Keynes Dons 1 Rotherham United 1
### League 1 (3), 29/10/05

his was an adventure months in the planning. The party convened organically: Ruthie as driving half of us, not in her peripatetic van (unwittingly in Blackpool colours), less her, but the car. Can't remember the make and model and she's since embarked pon a worldwide year out and hasn't been heard of for yonks. Rutz was recounting arns, posing the riddle:

> *Long and thin,*
> *Covered in skin,*
> *Red in parts,*
> *Goes in tarts.*

We built up anticipation for the forthcoming fun in a pub in Stony Stratford ormer quaint country town, now absorbed into MK, by then nearly 39 years old), he pub chosen as a *Good Beer Guide* entry. We were joined at the last minute by the uch-mobiling Rand (strange that, as he's since developed an almost total avoidance f the item, representing, as it does, modern life), who had endured untold torment ircumnavigating the capital. Thence to the prepaid Travelodge and thither to a nearby oadhouse, MK Boulevard style – that is, part of a chain. It served our purpose – we ould enjoy a drink, washing down the microwaved casseroles recently devoured, on he metal seats on the terrace.

Approaching 3pm we crossed the boulevard to the landmark. All this was easy nd unencumbered by traffic. The group was immediately complete, as we caught sight f Wakey and Goatwoman darting from under stray branches. They were breathless. he three cars were now conjoined in the Travelodge car park, thankfully dead opposite he National Hockey Stadium, on a sunny autumn afternoon. Milton Keynes is blessed ith an abundance of trees, at that time mostly retaining golden foliage. The stadium, land and unatmospheric within, was set in an almost idyllic scene. We were token way supporters – no-one likes the former Wimbledon, certainly not us, and Wakey hailed from 'Rovrum'. 'Goatwoman', Goatums for short, was a somewhat theoretical appellation as she didn't own one, but was merely obsessed with the beasts. I imagine she would not welcome the idea of 'the central Asian sport of Kok-Boru – or goat grabbing', to illustrate which the *Guardian* featured a double-page action shot: 'The Kyrgyz team take on the Kazakh team…Players on horseback must throw a goat carcass into the opponents' goal.' One keen on improving her word power, Goatums applied the approving adjective 'cimarrian' to a particularly delicious chocolate pudding. At one time, in fairly recent memory, she professed a long-term interest in Leeds United, since revised radically to Doncaster Rovers – she lived within a bus journey of the forthcoming Keepmoat Stadium.

The two sides on display spent the whole of 2005-06 in the relegation zone. United disappointed this time, worth maximum points but uncommitted when

going forward. The whole experience was friendly, laid back. I hope it to prove an encouragement for the novices and spasmodic footy attenders in our group to try another game sometime in the future.

The self-ordained package led next to recovery over the road (tea and results), followed by the customarily mounting urgency to find space in a downtown eating house with limited pre-curtain-up time. It was duly achieved in some chain restaurant or other (instantly forgotten) – whence to part two of the Main Event: Matthew Bourne's all-male production of Tchaikovsky's ballet *Swan Lake*. This proved to be magnificent – there was much more enthusiasm for a repeat visit to the very same production than for another League 1 football game. It was an eerie contrast of expressions of male athleticism and skill that a score of blokes turned it on for a macho football game and another such group did it in the name of high art. Well, this weekend had been chosen for the curious combination of the Dons and Millers and men in tights. Ruthie had a more heartfelt take on the episode, concerned at the terrifying cacophony of men chanting, emitting primevally, their worst characteristics of aggression and competitiveness rearing themselves when a ball was being kicked around. The other side of that coin revealed itself to her in the vigour and beauty of the dance. Black, white.

A night (extra hour as we fell into clock-winter), coffee-shop breakfast and gallery visit later, we sheltered from persistent rain in a tavern in Bradwell Village, a suburb (formerly a charming backwater), for traditional Sunday fare. Later the omission occurred to me. We had failed to track down MK's famous permanent Cattle exhibit. Did this mean a return visit – cows perhaps by then adorning the completed Denbigh stadium?

> *From south-east, north and west the tale begins,*
> *Rotherham's fans increased by six for this,*
> *The well-hatched plan, a day and night of bliss,*
> *The destination Central Milton Keynes.*
> *And on the way four tried two pubs, which means*
> *The other two delayed, their car amiss,*
> *Our nosh and noggin nice but hit and miss,*
> *Dons' local bar too quiet for footy scenes.*

> *Turnstiles were oiled and passed us through apace,*
> *Wimbledon distant from this hockey ground,*
> *With time in hand we made to look around*
> *The Millmoor end to find a row of space,*
> *The stadium quaint, no build-up in this place,*
> *Then came our late arrivals, safe and sound,*
> *The whistle blown, the cue for boys to bound.*
> *Two of us, new to football, said their grace.*

> *Monkhouse scored first for red and black and us*
> *Bovril time next, leaves fell, scant atmosphere, no fuss*
> *Then MKD came good, a single time, to draw.*
> *All done, the new guys wanted something more.*

> *At night we glimpsed the Dons' forthcoming home;*
> *Football for real or multi-function dome?*

And in the event the Dons went down, the Millers didn't but went into administration. They were saddled with a ten-point penalty with which to open 2006-07. They rallied for a while, but in the end were relegated to join the Dons, who were fated to turn another corner, alongside the prospect of their very own stadium.

85 turnstiles passed, seven left.

*2 November*
*Choice results from The FA Vase First Round Proper: Glossop North End 6*
*Romulus 4; Friar Lane & Epworth 5 Shirebrook Town 1. Glasshoughton Welfare*
*marched on up at Alnwick Town: 1-3. Up the Welfare!*

## Coventry City 1 Stoke City 2
## Championship (2), 2/11/05

There were daily revisions to the pre-match plan, as I was now on foot in Birmingham a few days on from 'Wimbledon'. Landy was working at home and Loz coming down from his new job in Manchester. It was finally resolved, but without Loz who couldn't find a way of making the trip work. After years of wanton and drunken irresponsibility

and debauchery (i.e. couldn't afford to go to footy games, let alone his adopted team, a certain Sky Blue lot) the youth suddenly became a responsible adult and found himself unable to get away from

work in time for the kick-off. He missed the lovely Ricoh Arena and Landy forewent £21 ('better stadium than game' he was to adjudge). There could be no refund as the ground was by no means full – a mere 16,617 turned out, albeit on a foul night. We found the ground easily enough, gleaming through the gloom, and decided to search for a pub serving food on the way into the city, its pulsating heart all of four miles away. It was certainly a prime example of footy without its own nomenclature: the name 'Coventry City' has become something of a misnomer in this place so remote from the fair city itself. We tried Foleshill, the nearest named place, without success, the options apparently all Asian. Landy decided his digestion wouldn't be able to cope. At length, after a tour of one-way systems, bus lanes and wrong turns, we happened upon the Old Stag, in Lamb Street, Coventry. An animal event then. The driver tried the corned beef hash. Our pragmatic route to the ground assumed a wide arc via signs to Warwick and Leamington in completely the wrong direction. It had looked so easy on the map, but instructions were obscured in the teeming rain. Having reached the Ricoh, resplendent and reflective through the deluge, the car park nearest the ground urned out to be for the superstore, not football, and would have carried what mounted to a £25 fine for more than two hours' occupancy. We readdressed the motor to Car Park C, which we could only guess was for football purposes. Up to the roundabout and back again, and a filter to a blancmange of yellow-coated stewards, one of whom expressed surprise that we weren't members, and then charged £10 or slot N4. I'm not surprised he was surprised. We heard later that a more sensible option is a £5 park on the other side of the ground (not indicated on the road) or Park and Ride. All this doesn't help a newcomer in this kind of weather. The 2006 supporters' guide I had purchased for ground information, including this, the virgin stadium announced blithely '2,000 spaces available at the ground'. The Ricoh had been scheduled to stage the first 2005-06 fixture versus Norwich. That one was switched to Carrow Road, the delay in part attributed to an arson attack on pallets, damaging seats back in January.

Directions were clear to our seats and we were in good time. Later on it would have been necessary to go up to each bay to note the number, as they were painted in white on the space itself. After the game a plastic bag adhered to the windscreen contained a sodden piece of paper. It read:

*Please Check your Bay and Row Number*
*This is Row N Bay 4*
*Thanks*
*Car Park Attendant*
*(Squiggled signature)*

Fortunately no further action was indicated, like an instant penalty, or summons. I guess all those staff have to find something to occupy them after the mad rush before the game.

We had left the ticket, saying 'N4', inside the windscreen quite patently. Petty officialdom like this does not help, and is symptomatic of the self-importance which accompanies football clubs and their acolytes in new stadia.

It was good to escape, though the worrying mixture of cars eager to leave, on green lights, and pedestrians eager to get to their cars, was perilously close to producing squashed fans on the road.

Landy and I agreed that the spanking new stadium was appealing with another mixture, seductive this time, of rain in the air and omnipresent sky blue and brash new white, on breezeblock walls, evocative of a Greek island. This was emphasized by, on the pitch perimeter, a promotional Canaries property hoarding in brilliant sky blue, as was Coca Cola, instead of the familiar red. A peculiarity was the Jewson South Stand, the only one inscribed with 'SKY BLUES' but designated as away end. Over 900 Potters fans were present, leaving '—Y B—ES' for all to see in the under-populated bits. They had more to enthuse about, their team recovering from an early home goal just below them to equalize in the 37th minute and take the lead on 55 minutes. A single-goal deficit was how the score stayed, though there was some horseplay in the second half, all the more enjoyable as, despite being near the top in row MM, we had clear sightlines and felt involved with the action. The programme (£3 for 60 pages) featured Old Potter Adrian Heath, now Assistant Manager for Coventry. The article filled some of the gaps in time since he thrilled many, including me, as a young forward at the Victoria Ground. In it he concurre with my view that the Britannia Stadium doesn't compare with the Victoria Ground. He 'would have liked the club to have stayed on that site and developed it', like Preston.

Speaking of clubs with more past than present, the Championship, i.e. Second Division in old money, does offer an impressive array: those mentioned plus Wolves and the Sheffields, Leeds and Burnley. Also the East Midlands duo, Derby and Leicester. Alas their rival, Forest, were languishing even further down the hierarchy. 'Twas ever thus, of course. Soccer is making its own history as we speak. Every club certainly has its ups and downs. At half-time we met David and Polly, who had completed not only the 92 but the 42 Scottish League grounds as well. Tha is dedication. I'm on 10 up to Rugby Park, Kilmarnock and it's going to take years, maybe scores of them.

Another page announced the delay of the electronic scoreboard. I had been a mite apprehensive of a repetition of the ghastly experience at the Reebok and no scoreboard at all was certainly better than a Reebok repeat. It was reported that Coventry was the first football club in the country to install an electronic scoreboar in 1964, and the new hi-tech version would be amongst the best in the country. It's enough to discourage a further Ricoh episode. It was reported a mere 17 days later that 'a large video screen type scoreboard' has been installed in one corner. A narrow escape, methinks.

86 visited, six on the list.


*7 November*
*FA Cup Round 1: Bournemouth 1 Tamworth 2. Not only a shock but perhaps significant for the Cherries whose mountainous debts have been publicized recentl It could be receivership or administration at the end of this week. Unfortunately i a story of a failed community-controlled football club.*


*12 November*
*England jangle our sensibilities in making it 3-2 against Argentina in injury tim That was thanks to Michael (though not much longer for our team). The popular hope is that this will help their ranking on the World Cup seedings front.*

*I've discovered that Swansea's new ground is now to be the 'Liberty Stadium' for a few years. They've been breaking attendance records game after gam – Tranmere then Nottingham Forest. Will there be a good crowd for the Hartlepo game, in January?*

## Sunderland 0 Birmingham City 1
### Premiership, 26/11/05

There was plenty to enjoy in the City of Sunderland (only since 1991 and thankfully the association football club resisted adding 'City' to their name, sufficiently sonorous already; Swansea converted to 'City' after the town's enhancement), the first source of relief being the weather. Snow was threatened after a week of frosts. As it turned out the weekend was wet and cold, but not blighted, the utter atmospheric bleakness being of wondrous effect in a Sunday morning wind battle along Roker seafront, close to that vanished shrine and a far cry from the memory of the Roker Pie Shop, which sported a red and white striped awning.

Waves were pounding, the elements fierce and all was a pervasive grey, except for a few Roker-red pebbles. We failed to patronize the Bungalow café on the seafront, the subject of a nearby signpost, which also pointed to Germany, over the turbulent North Sea. As it turned out a splendid two days' weekend break terminated on a steeply rising graph with pints in three contrasting and all meritorious pubs, the Saltmarsh also providing the best three-course Sunday lunch in my memory. That broth: Yummm! Almost a rival to Aggborough stew.

From now on I shall proclaim the merits of Sunderland. The mission can replace that perpetrated for decades for Brum, which I feel no longer needs any help from me. A woman next to me in the train back to the Midlands was doing a day's shopping trip from Derby to Birmingham. She used to go to Nottingham. We did the *Guardian* quick crossword together. This occurred during a sequence of anagrams whose answer was a football club. That day's was Plymouth Argyle. By the way, another publication to note is *A Love Supreme*, fanzine extraordinaire and winner of the north-east magazine of the year.

The best thing, it is my privilege to report, was the Stadium of Light, home of Mick McCarthy's Red and White Army, the Black Cats. There were tom and queen cat mascots in purposeful gait, but only up to kick-off, alas, as they cut a decorative air. The prelude to the action was the famed Prokofiev's *Cinderella* sequence booming round the enclave, lasting longer than I expected and all the better for that. My niece, Clemmie, whose first football game this was, loved everything, and so said all five of us. As far as the occasion went it has to be one of the hardest acts to follow. It's a loud stadium. The scoreboards (two) were admirable with the score clean cut:

SUNDERLAND   0
BIRMINGHAM   0 (for most of the game)

The clock time below left; time played below right. To the left and right were demure panels promoting Metro Radio.

Even the corridors were, rare for a modern construction, adorned with exhibits to please the eye: banners, photos of former heroes, not much blank concrete, and, the acid test – a triumphant chicken balti pie. Even with tomato ketchup Clemmie reported favourably.

Not so Tiptoes, whose round it was, comprising three Bovrils, a coffee, a Yorkie and the pie. He was charged £8.50 by the male minion.

A supervisor intervened, asking 'What did you have?'

On his response she did a quick sum: 'Yes, it's right.'

'Still bloody expensive.'

'I know – it just didn't sound enough.'

The morsels of the game worth reporting, to mitigate complete despondency, were: Sunderland's (young) goalkeeper Kelvin Davis managed a few good saves, and his team dominated for a while in the first half, not by then totally inept. It has been very evident, however, that these Red and Whites (or 'SAFC' as the £3 programme irritatingly insisted on referring to them. Does the 'A' make all the difference? Though brief it comes across as impersonal) tended to fade away in the second half. This afternoon they were abject. As the Blues started the afternoon with six points from 12 games, the Black Cats with five from 13, both with a single win, away, my earnest hope was that a draw (the highest aspiration, a win unthinkable) could be achieved by the team in whose ranks we were numbered. Their previous two home games had resulted in defeats, 1-4 to Portsmouth, 1-3 to Villa, both of whom were underperforming in lowly positions, but with potential, given a couple of wins at this stage of the season. City showed some spirit with David Dunn getting around a bit up to his injury substitution at 65 minutes. Andy Gray came on and scored the only goal after a sequence of moves soon after.

The Blues chanted 'Keep right on to the end of the road' and, not being blessed with a lot of imagination or relevance, 'Shit on the Villa.' Thereafter it was desperate, dreadful stuff. The programme unfortunately allocated a double page to Nyron Nosworthy (number 12), whose reply to the question 'What's the biggest mistake you've ever made?"'was 'Not paying his parking fines.' He used to ignore them and that was a big mistake. Well, yes, Nyron, and his performance that afternoon was, more or less, a big mistake. Why can't players (not just top-level but any being paid for the job and therefore professing a degree of quality) achieve accurate passes?

Being in Row D just above the dugout and well placed to observe to the right the gesticulations of Messrs McCarthy (wearing a black Lonsdale number and 'Reg Vardy') and Bruce (Steve – black Lonsdale; 'flybe') and to the left a 'Stockton-on-Tees Mackems' flag sogging in the drear, we were also in the precipitation firing line. The term 'Mackem' was to be awarded an entry in the *Oxford English Dictionary* in 2006, written evidence having been proved of its absorption into the tongue by way of an appearance in a football fanzine. It may be newer than the equivalent 'Geordie' up the road, but is an essential matter of pride in referring to the football fraternity and Sunderland's industrial heritage.

For ten first-half minutes the heavens opened with a hailstorm. Quite exciting really. Later on seagulls and crows circled in the heavens. Many more performances like this and the players will expire, to herald a vulture influx.

With the defeat written in tabloid ink Sunderland were starkly adrift from the pack – by four points. It was tragic to have to wonder where any more points were to come from. Mick McCarthy was admirably plain-speaking afterwards, to the effect that the players were not good enough for this level. Very strange that they were outstanding in the Championship the previous year (29 wins, 94 points). In the current table their promotion companions Wigan were still fourth after two defeats running, and West Ham ninth.

32,442 attended this game, and were polite to their hapless contingent. This was except for a thug in a Tyneside restaurant that night, who, recognizing a cosy foursome nearby, assaulted chairman Bob Murray: Mick McCarthy to the rescue. This was an entertaining report in a national newspaper. I wonder who pulled the plug on such dignified local celebrities pursuing their customary evening out. On their way to their second Championship championship in three seasons in April 2007, the Mackems' controversial new manager, Roy Keane, led the team to a 2-1 victory over Wolves, whither McCarthy had immigrated. It was reported thus: 'Roy Keane puts one over on Mick McCarthy. The once sworn enemies have finally made up thanks to a private phone call and exchanged not just a cordial handshake but a brief, albeit slightly awkward, embrace – initiated by Keane – at the final whistle here. Both must have been inwardly desperate to come out on top of the promotion tussle.' (Wolves went on to lose to WBA in the play-offs.) This laid the ghost of the 'well documented, appallingly acrimonious fallout in Saigon…and Keane's subsequent storm out. Both men insist the events surrounding the 2002 World Cup are now consigned to history.'

There were 39,707 for the Villa game a week before, in fact the best this season. There's no danger of the 48,300 capacity being achieved for a while, so my earlier concern about obtaining tickets was again misplaced. This was my last Premier League ground. Good ground, bad teams. As a matter of interest the Stadium of Light was now licensed for civil marriage and announced its intention to stage Civil Partnership ceremonies, the new law coming into force in December 2005.

Next to Lincoln (again).

87 dealt with, five remaining.


*26 November*
*George Best is dead. I've never heard an absolute demise prediction before but television reporters were quite certain that his death would occur later that day. And it did.*

*The other recent departure was the much delayed walkout from Manchester by Roy Keane.*

*Birmingham City, should they be granted a regional casino licence, are to be helped by Las Vegas Sands to erect a 55,000 capacity stadium. (In due course it went to the NEC, close to where the national football stadium should have been, may I moot.) Casinos are also being considered by Sheffield United, MU, Newcastle etc. etc. How I look forward to leaving all this bigness behind next year.*

*And at last I've heard it: 'Rhyl Nil,' in the Welsh Premier League, articulated on the wireless.*

*Georgie has been honoured far and wide, especially at Upton Park where speeches preceded the WHU v MU game. He once said: 'When I was 17 or 18, I used to love being recognized... Later on I would have given anything to be anonymous.'*

*FA Vase Round 2: Glasshoughton Welfare 1 Squires Gate 2, I'm hesitant to report. On awhile to August 2007 and the Welfare redressed a half-time deficit to earn an FA Cup extra preliminary round replay against Liversedge. A popular favourite, Bruce Grobbelaar, 49, proved himself 'a great motivator' in an interval word or two, by invitation, following those of the manager. The forerunner to this was that Bruce turned out for Glasshoughton in the 2006-07 2-1 win over Maltby Main. Fast forward again and the team succumbed to Liversedge in the replay, 4-3. Bruce wasn't there to inspire the lads that afternoon.*

*In London's Victoria Palace theatre Billy Elliot has been thrilling many, the setting the former Durham coalfield for which Sunderland was the local team. One of the characters, a schoolmate of the hero's, gets a football strip for Christmas. He swaps it for a 'Sadie the Nurse' costume. We'd already enjoyed a scene where the two of them dress us in his mother's clothes. A good show, though there's no direct reference to the Rokerites, rather like the Stoke-free 'Zigger Zagger', Peter Terson's play, born of the Potteries.*

## 4 December

*Bolton's home record is now won seven, lost one, which latter item was the home defeat by Everton, whose away record until now was similarly gruesome. How lucky were we to see a freak result? I ask ironically and rhetorically.*

*The Hartlepool trip will have to be a League game as the Lambs of Tamworth beat them away in the FA Cup Second Round. The boat was missed there as I had it in mind to sample a couple of Cup games in this countrywide trudge.*

## 8 December

*There's been plenty for headlines recently: now Mr. Gascoigne has added his bit, ousted from Kettering in a very different vein, but with eerie echoes of George's lifestyle. Gazza lasted 39 days. Imraan Ladak, the Poppies' Chairman, saying there had been 37 disciplinary incidents, relating to drink, over the period, and has reinstated the previous manager. The now-ex-manager has stated his intention of buying the club.*

*Manchester United bombed out of Europe – not even UEFA knockout eligibility as compensation, though I've always wondered why losing teams are awarded even more. Surely they, and we, have had enough? Now the Traffs only have the FA Cup to concern them, versus Burton Albion for starters.*

*The other crisis is at the City Ground, Nottingham. As Forest play in League 1, they are qualified for two extra rounds of the FA Cup. They met this challenge first by being held by Weymouth (former local rivals of Yeovil, who strangely are now one of Forest's peers, beating them recently). Having survived the replay in the Second Round, Forest lost 3-0 at Chester, possibly overawed by the ground, a bit of a comedown from what they're used to (roll on the 2 January excursion to Bumpers Lane – now decided upon).*

*Not since 1951 has the biggest Cup draw of all lacked Nottingham Forest FC. At least that year Notts County were in the Second Division (proper) and proceeded to lose 3-4 to Southampton in the Third Round.*


## Lincoln City 3 Chester City 1
## League 2 (4), 10/12/05

The frustration at failing to see the Red Imps in 1998 was followed this time by getting the date wrong for the Lincoln Christmas Market, which was intended as part of this weekend's fun and games. As it turned out we missed a wash-out by all accounts. The weekly market, through which we strolled on the Saturday morning, had little to excite and much to infuriate, in the crowds under the gushing heavens, with Yuletide on their minds. Having witnessed Lincoln's historic centre this Saturday night, most notable for the ubiquitous raucous, scantily clad youth, replicating city centres anywhere, it was easy to imagine how unpleasant it must have been a weekend earlier.

So we'd made it to Sincil! It had endured for long as a quest in itself and, once here, occurred as a lightweight achievement. The weather on both failure and success days was sunny and fresh, and the city sported just the right atmosphere for a birthday weekend, for it was Wakey's, as well as being a mood promoter for the festive season, which for him started on the 12th: birthday first, then Rudolph and Jingle Bells. I was glad to have been born in June.

Sincil Bank is a drain, rather important to the basic functions of the biggest centre of population for many miles around. The place is all landmarks: the Minster/Cathedral (look up an ecclesiastical dictionary) is an utterly stunning Early English wonder; as a building its peers are Wells and Salisbury Cathedrals, over 800 years old. What a shame that such urban design is unthought-of in the plethora of contemporary projects that disappoint. This comment has to be contradicted without drawing breath is the recently opened Collection, nearby, a most effective seductively shaped building of timeless stone and glass, presented, alongside permanent displays, 'Wunderkammer, the Artificial Kingdom, a major exhibition of 38 leading contemporary artists'. The idiosyncratic display varied wildly from a Korean songstress dubbed in German to a backdrop of cudding cattle to a ten-foot-tall steel cylinder carved and decorated in scarlet flock wallpaper, and this was just below the cathedral. Meanwhile down steep Hill and the Strait followed the most unusual High Street, pursuing a route immediately out of town, in fact past various water channels and Sincil Bank, which lay a street away to the east. The football ground serves as a monument backed by hills, a reminder that this is a comparatively underpopulated part of the world. The most striking landmark is on the way, the Ritz, sometime a cinema, now a Wetherspoon pub and dubious late-night venue, neoned in brash blue and pink at night, to be observed from the old city up the road.

Obtaining a ticket was easy. The practice of lower prices for prior purchase is clearly on the increase. We paid £16 (extra for plastic) – it would have been £15 for cash, but we were fresh out of that. It would have cost even more at the turnstiles (in other words the standard price). It doesn't seem much of an incentive, particularly as *The Imp*, the programme, explicitly enunciated that the 'Early Bird philosophy' was aimed at reducing cash and improving turnstile flow. I should note this for future action (four games remaining in this quest, for a start). After all it mounts up, especially when you're giving a friend a birthday treat. The programme was £2.50 and half-time draw £1. We chose the Co-op (local spelling Coop) Stand for easy post-match egress to the results in a nearby pub. The Coop turned out to be the luxury stand. We could have saved £2 in the (home) Stacey West Stand, erected in place of an old terrace in 1990 – and perhaps named after a local slapper or footballer's wife or girlfriend? It was later to emerge that this was a tasteless conjecture as the name was actually chosen in memory of Bill Stacey and Jim West, Lincoln supporters who perished horribly in the Valley Parade fire in 1985.

Having indulged in a hearty breakfast at our lodgings, the need for nosh didn't become a priority until the aroma of 'full meat pie' and 'Lincolnshire sausages' wafted towards our chosen seats. The serving boy, kitted out in striped team colours, was clueless when I quoted the latter option, indelibly displayed overhead. 'You mean hot dog' he retorted. A bit of a comedown, but still tastier than many. The full meat pie was well endowed with meat, I was informed. Plus Bovril. In the gents was a guy from Derby who had been making the journey to Lincoln for 23 years from the age of six. He was so depressed (he said 'I'm so depressed') and they weren't even losing. 'They've had been more terrible in recent months than for years' he added. I wished I could have seen his reaction after their (fairly) convincing victory – happy chappie on the return journey or just a terminally miserable football supporter?

I had to overcome my hostility towards both teams in view of their previous reluctance to get their fixtures real enough to see them off my list (in that long-distant world before the list). My affiliation was with the home side; in Sunderland colours (see last time) as this was a pleasant experience already, both city and ground. The same cannot be expected for the Deva, more than once bracketed with Scunthorpe and Walsall in the 'devoid' category of new football grounds. I was looking forward to hearing the chant 'Come on you Deviants (or Devoids)'. But it was not to be, as Chester's address was listed in *The Imp* as 'Saunders Honda Stadium, Bumpers Lane', no longer Deva. What does the self-respecting fan do with that? The best I could come up with is 'Ye Hons', which somehow lacked resonance. The city of Chester did have a fleeting acquaintance with northern European tribes I seem to remember. This was to have further ramifications on the next stage of the quest. The decision has been made to adopt the Oxford U's for the Chester day (see below).

Sympathy was due to the home side anyway: languishing under threat of Conference duty next year, they hadn't won for six games. Chester were fourth, which can't be right. Their away record was better than Lincoln's at home.

There was a minute's silence for local lad Tony Emery who had died aged 78. He made 424 appearances from 1946 to 1959. Quite a contrast from George Best to whom we had paid respects at Sunderland.

The Red Imps weren't too impressive, but the fans could at least rebuke Justin Walker, former Imp, who made it to Chester via Exeter. Lincoln usually picked up after Christmas, it said in the programme. After the meat session at half-time, Chester put on the pressure and netted, the perpetrator being Sincil reject Marcus Richardson. Lincoln were soon down to ten men and the 'improve after Xmas' prophecy, in fact requirement, appeared to be vindicated. It couldn't get much worse and Xmas was only 15 days away. But no, they got their act into focus and built up to equalize on 68 minutes, followed by a penalty conversion soon after. Tom Curtis, Chester's number 11, entertained us with a manful tackle with a sequel, under the referee's instruction, of dropping two pairs of shorts on the touchline. Most people would be mooning good and proper at these removals but Tom had a trick up his sleeve, or on his nether regions – a third, dinky, covering lurked beneath, deftly to be augmented by re-application of another pair of standard-issue white shorts. One can only deduce that there was a clash between black and white.

The ref contributed a further diversion later on in banishing Bumpers' manager Keith Curle to the stand for altercationary utterances. Mr Curle did argue, for a long time, for what? To set a suitable example to his team? (They were losing by then, of course. Oh, the pride of players turned managers! He was out of a job a few months later, and in 2007 oversaw another of his charges, Torquay United, sinking to the Conference, rock bottom.) The Red Imp brigade were enjoying themselves: 'Marcus, Marcus, what's the score?' Chester's threat evaporated (Can't give them a nickname. It's listed as 'City', dull enough anyway, and I can recall when they were just 'Chester', up to 1983, so what was their tag then? Oh yes, 'The Blues'.) Lincoln's supremacy was complete when the most energetic Derek Asamoah coolly stabbed into an open goal in injury time.

The grand sum of 3,563 witnessed this game which turned out to be the most entertaining of this final batch – most goals that is. Uniquely up to now the away contingent tally was also announced: 211, also listed in the programme stats, both figures a little lower than for another Cheshire side, Macclesfield, the previous visitors.

Subsequent bibulousness in Lincoln proved a rewarding pursuit – many atmospheric pubs available without intrusion from the unclothed brigade, whose presence was paradoxically mainly in evidence on the streets, exposed to the elements. On upper part of the High Street was the prizewinner: the Treaty of Commerce, which deserves note if only for its name. It offered several other rewards, however: Bateman's beers from a few miles down the road, a jukebox – five for £1 and lots of 1960/70s stuff; best of all, the sparky landlady of mature years, who charged Wakey £10 for the second round (I was fairly treated), revising it under query to £4.80, the change from a tenner initially being £5.19…,he wuz robbed. Her banter was what was needed after the World Cup draw on telly earlier, complete with a German soap bimbo and overkill commentary from the Motson while the facts were being broadcast along with the action in English. My birthday activity was already being planned, hung on England v Trinidad and Tobago.

The mixed memory of last time in Lincoln was comprehensively annulled by this weekend.

88 in the store, four more.

*14 December*
*The hype surrounding the World Cup draw – Sweden again, wonderful, at least pretty colours – can be ignored for now, what with FA Cup excitement. Northwich Victoria, most unfortunate victims of misguided bureaucratic regulations in ending up in Conference North this season, will be at the Stadium of Light for the Third Round. Sunderland want to maximize attendance, so want ticket prices at £5 and £3, while The Vics are naturally pushing for higher prices, for a bigger cut, as that is what travelling supporters would expect when visiting a Premiership ground – like a £20 tag. I think they're right. Exeter City, said the report, made £1m from their encounters with the Traffs last season.*

*Bolton are through, along with Middlesbrough, to the knockout last-32 phase in the UEFA Cup. Three cheers! It's so good to see less fashionable sides getting a bit of the limelight.*

*A word about ground names, after the 'Saunders Honda' discovery. As I have this week seen the Fitness First Stadium (at Boscombe aka Bournemouth – I have to be specific as who knows how many other FF stadia will seep through as the plot thickens) referred to as 'Dean Court', its uninspired but familiar name; there is at least confusion as to nomenclature. Is the time nigh when you are advised to have knowledge of a whole range of commercial names applied to clubs' playing places?*

*Naughtiness at ground number 90. Swansea City's Ijah Anderson has been suspended pending a cocaine hearing, under threat of being fired if found guilty.*

*19 December*
*Harry Redknapp, many shenanigans behind him, is back at Portsmouth. They deliver their first home win, 1-0 v WBA.*

*Reverse-fixture days for the first of the Last Ten: Bolton trounce Everton 0-4 at Goodison, a wee bit more impressive than the display observed at home in August. Meanwhile Fulham got revenge against Blackburn (2-1).*

*The point has been made that the ethos of the FA Cup is about such ties as Sunderland v Northwich Vics being possible. It is misguided for the latter's chairman to claim that his team are a draw justifying £25 ticket prices, while I've read that the tickets have now been priced at £10 and £5. Last year's equivalent produced a crowd of 17,536 for Crystal Palace's visit (2-1 the outcome). Remember all that way back, Sunderland the Championship challengers against a Premiership team? Yes, they swapped divisions in May 2005. Cup games simply do not attract the same volume of support as League fixtures. (In the event 19,323 watched Sunderland win 3-0; 32,442 had watched the Birmingham City League game.)*

New Wembley is scheduled to be handed over on 31 March. This would appear unlikely (understatement), so will the Millennium Stadium again host the FA Cup Final? In any case Robbie Williams is booked at the new place in September, necessitating a new pitch, as with the Cardiff palace, whose turf is changed every time the discipline switches between rugby and soccer.

## 24 December

Niall Quinn makes interesting points in his Guardian column: 12 points between Manchester in second place and Newcastle in tenth, 10 between Charlton ($11^{th}$) and Birmingham ($19^{th}$), with Chelsea miles ahead at the top and Sunderland adrift at the bottom. Hands up for Wigan too, who are still there, rallying with a 3-0 victory over Charlton last weekend after a bad patch. '...not only are they proving me and everyone else wrong, they are doing it with a smile. At first they got by on adrenalin, but gradually they have also shown steel. Paul Jewell has been great. Their team focus reminds me of Chelsea's.' And they're in the League Cup semi-finals. That 1-0 win we witnessed over Bournemouth in their first appearance seems so long ago.

The managers of Torquay and Stockport, $91^{st}$ and $92^{nd}$ at present, were interviewed on the radio, with identical stories: the best job in the world is playing football, the second best is football management, though your career decision involves loss of Christmas. They both expected to escape the drop, and they both did: Torquay $88^{th}$ and Stockport $90^{th}$.

## 29 December

It's been bitterly cold but you'd expect Premiership clubs to get their pitch preparations together, wouldn't you? However, the Reebok Stadium and Ewood Park were not fit for play. Why not install a proper, checked and maintained surface-heating system? My heart bleeds for Sam Allardyce who's worried about fixture pile-up. Perhaps he should have made sure the heating system worked. Newcastle called their game off too, with snow still falling - owing to conditions outside the ground, plus the minor influence of road traffic accidents. So the authorities weren't prepared, and panicked. This is exacerbated by the fact that their opponents were to have been Charlton, whose fans had already made one of their longest journeys. One fan interviewed left home at 9am and got back at 4am. Questions have been asked:

i) Why schedule such midweek games at this period: four in eight days – is there no other suitable week, like the week leading up to Christmas, if the months to come have no free weeks?

ii) Could the computer not identify more geographically convenient fixtures at times when it is predicted that the weather may be at its worst?

Harking back to the primitive days before a computer could be blamed, there were huge treks to be suffered on consecutive days after Christmas. Exeter had to travel to Bradford (Park Avenue that was, in 1969) the day after entertaining Newport, and before the M5 was available. The same day Plymouth were bound for Birkenhead, fresh from a 6-0 destruction of their neighbours, the Gulls, on Boxing Day. Consulting the grid of season's results B(PA) won 2-1 and Tranmere 3-1. Oh well! I don't know whether either was postponed, the weather always seeming to be at its worst just after Christmas.

## Chester City 0 Oxford United 1
## League 2 (4), 2/1/06

Chester again! Done it at last, six years, four months and two days after the previous time I braved Bumpers Lane and all of 23 days since the thrill of their comeuppance at Sincil Bank. With Fredders as pilot, we had enjoyed a sufficiency in the glorious city centre – two pubs, a few pints, the prize going to Spitting Feather bitter at the Ship Victory: not just for the names or the pub's obvious prowess as an oasis of calm after the debacle of finding somewhere to park in the congested road system on the New Year Bank Holiday. We rambled up and along part of the Rows, Chester's special black and white showpiece, and would have attempted a canal had we been blessed with more immediate knowledge of the layout, as there were recommended pubs thereupon. However, we then fell victim to this very phenomenon. Ancient cities appear to be the worst places at dealing with contemporary traffic. Crawling towards signs to Sealand Road, site of the dismal dead eponymous Chester ground, the minutes ticked away.

It was reassuring to see pylon floodlights, of all things at an identikit stadium, emerging from the already fading light. And there it was, the edifice, with the bonus of a pavement just beside it, where we parked safely, as seemed to be the custom. The Saunders Honda Stadium was already defying resigned forebodings. It turned out to be a pretty good experience, and a fair imitation of an old-fashioned football ground, more appealing than the likes of Glanford Park, Scunthorpe. Its location right at the end of the extensive pre-fabricated units provided advantages. From the away end among the 'U' contingent there was a field of cattle in direct view from our terrace, which was pleasingly covered with a shallow, anachronistic roof arranged in blue and white corrugated stripes. And escape was easy afterwards except that, in his enthusiasm, comrade Fredders turned into the road to Wales in an attempt to avoid the 5pm curfew for shoppers in the retail parks in a citywards direction. So we went foreign, briefly, despite which the whole episode was to go down as a good day out, with even the right result as we were away tokenists for the afternoon.

It hadn't looked like that for 65 minutes. CC defenders had kept the U's penned back whose shouting mainstays had slagged off 'Gippo' Ben Davies (number 14), sporting an inventive hairstyle. There was a noticeable piece of ball control at the feet of Eric Sabin, followed nine minutes later by a proper cross. City won a corner reply. But the game was to go to the Ox Blacks, sorry Yellows, as Steve Basham gratefully converted the spinning ball, also yellow, as was the referee, landing at his feet into a goal. Basham later left Oxford to play for Exeter.

'Walking along, singing a song, Walking in a Basham Wonderland' quoth the season-sensitive away contingent. Fredders noted that Chester were dressed identically to Brighton, his team, for what it's worth, as they were in the bottom three, two divisions higher, much to his dismay. Chester, sinking fast too, were destined to hit the table foot before a late rally to finish 15th. The travellers also sang to the prowess of the valiant custodian, Chris Tardiff (according to the club).

Thirteen pounds having been handed over at the well-oiled turnstile, no ticket issued, which these days suggests fraud potential as much as old-fashioned informality, so suspicious have we become. Arriving late led to a programme search, eventually yielding a £2.50 40-pager at half time. This was not very good value, carrying two identical team photos, from the summer it appeared, one wishing us all Happy New Year, the other doing the same, courtesy of Asda.

It was full of spelling mistakes: 'Tardif/f' had two small 'f's' twice and one once, if you follow me, and we were treated to a report of one of Chester's finest hours, the Classic Encounter in the 'F.A. Challnge Cup' Second Round, 9 December 2000. CC 3 OU 2. The spell-check facility picked it up here, so why not on the programme-producing machine? I shall pursue the nitpicking with 'quiz one'. Twenty questions, six mistakes at least (not sure about 'Georghe Hagi' – of Romania). My favourite was 'Wnger', Wenger to many. The quiz was quite fun, really, between bites of the steak and kidney pie (not bad at all: Wakey liked his pasty too, though Fredders was suffering from chronic Yuletide excess and declined the opportunity for Wales View Fodder). Examples of quiz questions:

9. Which club did Mark Atkins join on leaving Blackburn Rovers?
A: Woverhampton [sic] Wanderers.
20. Which team does Cardinal Basil Hulme [sic] support?
A: Newcastle United.

Educational, you see.

The steward near us had been recruited from arch-rivals Macclesfield. The New Year's Eve game there, another 0-1 for Chester, had been afflicted by ill temper and had 12 minutes added on after the 45 The steward also shared the general glee at Macc's 6-0 recent annihilation of Stockport, then at the bottom of the table. He remembered the protracted arrival of the Silkmen into the League, as they had to qualify for League status twice, ground improvements being implemented in between. Then, as often happens with new sides, they raced up another division (1997-98), only to crash down again the next year.

Chester were in their second year back in the League, having endured four years of banishment to the Conference. Meanwhile the next adventure in this region will be to Stalybridge Celtic, – yes, please, especially for the famed pub on the station platform, but still in Conference South, at least in 2008-09.

9 in the bag, three outstanding.

## Swansea City 1 Hartlepool United 1
## League 1 (3), 21/1/06

The Vetch (= cattle fodder) Field visit was always named thus – my single visit was on 8/8/98, the first-day fixture that year, to see Swansea City 2 Exeter City 0 in Div III (4). If I'd known how close the ground was to the ocean I would have gone prepared for a dip. It was wonderful to renew acquaintance with footy in the sunshine. Shame about the result.

The visitors' toilets were singled out for comment:

Male: 'What is there then?' 'Nothing' came the reply. 'Just three walls and a little grate.' And natural air conditioning and ventilation (i.e. no roof).

Female: '…in the end it was no contest. The female MATITLA (Most Awful Toilet in the League Award) goes to Swansea City. Neither loo was flushing, one door wouldn't shut and both cubicles stank. But it was the large puddle, littered with coke cans and sweet wrappers, which really clinched it.'

'Take me to the Vetch Field way down by the sea, where I will follow Swansea, Swansea City.'

Already Swansea's new home has had four different names conferred upon it. Even before 'New Stadium' it had been 'Morfa', after the fringe area of Swansea in which it rests, then 'White Rock' for a while. Finally it produced computerized match tickets as 'Liberty Stadium'. It was a relief to confirm all this through actual attendance.

But at last a benefit was to be derived from a new ground. The stadium was all of four miles out of town, so we were able to patronize a village pub at lunchtime near the M4 and on the way in. Also, unlike the Ricoh and Reebok, those formidable Rs, we found a space in a back street up the road, round a corner or two and under a railway bridge, near pubs called Station and Railway – overkill? After the match this meant a scramble up a sodden bank between newly planted treelets and through a somewhat inefficacious fence. Why do they never get this kind of thing right? The escape routes were hopelessly inadequate for upwards of 13,000 escapees after the denouement. This was a purpose-built ground only a few months old.

My other grievance surrounds an unlikely problem – the pursuit of a programme:

1. Our party traversed round more than half the ground and saw no programme sellers; entered the haven where I was told by one of a posse of officials that a ruling was in force not to sell programmes inside the ground. (Other contentious issues were: no smoking, parking provision and the long distance from the city centre.) I was lent assistance by a splendidly pink-tufted steward called Christopher, who uttered the observations above. What a shame he wasn't more overtly indigenous in name, e.g. 'Geraint'. He admitted to being a Jack Army member, i.e. Swansea City fan. He proudly flourished the tattoo on his forearm to prove it, such being the local supporters' label. It's obvious once you know! And he called me 'gentleman', many times. There were banners around the ground attesting to 'Jackarmy Carmarthen', 'Merthyr Jacks' and others. But all this emerged from our conversation while touring the perimeter, with the concession (rarely granted after kick-off) of being released from the enclave to search for a programme. No purveyor in sight, the game having started, we tried the club shop, which proved to be closed until after the game. On readmittance to the ground and further discourse with sundry people in yellow and orange, the conclusion was reached that the shop was the only resort – buy one when it was all over.

As well as nourishment:

2. Towards the end of half-time, of uncertain formality as there was a distinct lack of announcements of any kind, we decided to queue for a hot drink, mistakenly judging that this would be a brief interlude. In fact a full quarter of an hour passed before we managed an order, of Kenco coffee and Suchard chocolate. NO BOVRIL! The first such experience ever. I couldn't quite bring myself to try a tea, remembering Wigan, where I had decided never to compromise standards again as it had been foul. Deserved a warning. It was good of Robin to accompany me in the current venture, affording convivial musings. I missed a chunk of the game on these pursuits, but thankfully caught both goals.

The confrontation itself was just a bit frustrating. It pitched two clubs together which had themselves enjoyed name changes in memory: city status was conferred on Swansea in 1970. The Swans followed. Hartlepools United became simply 'Hartlepool' in 1968, reintroducing the suffix in 1977. Mere name change wasn't enough for them. Their address was upgraded from Victoria Ground to 'Park' in 1995.

The various Jack Army groups had enjoyed a good season up to then. Promoted from League 2 in 2005 they had been consistently near the top. Hartlepool were sinking, in 19th position before the game. Complacency may explain the failure to convert their superiority into goals. Under a cirrus-clouded sky, the Swans looked the better team and went ahead on 20 minutes. For Hartlepool this was the longest journey of the season, explaining the paucity of away-end attendance. Needless to say, they scored deep into injury time. They had been industrious in defence (Robin's phrase), something to which they had become accustomed given their humble League position. This away point was a triumph. Colchester were to end the day at the top of the table. Colchester, with the most meagre attendances in the division? Whatever next? (In due course they rose to their first-ever second-level membership, while Hartlepool went down.)

It was a picturesque event. The stadium won my companions' approval. Robin, whose last outing to a football game had been to Villa Park for John Gregory's debut eight years earlier, considered the ground to be light and airy, more roomy than on the terraces. We certainly had a clear, close view, though the Vetch Field, home for so long and conveniently between the centre of town and the sea, was much lamented. The setting reminded me of the Walkers Stadium, Leicester, including the nearby Morrisons. After the match my pursuit of a programme bore fruit through the single open door at the shop (congestion ensued) while Robin hurried back to the vehicle, having discovered that he had mislaid his wallet. It turned out to be in full view on the driver's seat, still. Duly settled into steering-wheel mode, he assessed what we had witnessed as anodyne and sanitary, a low level of football – perhaps in comparison with Villa v Liverpool that fresh Gregory day, and his memory of quality play at the Hawthorns while a regular there.

The programme-selling system was flawed. The system comprised an unnecessary separate queue and a lack of change. It was £3, for, I submit, an unsuitable artefact, up to 2008 only beaten at a League fixture by Bristol Rovers, whose final (old) Memorial Stadium £3.50 item was an 80-page souvenir number. Called *The Swan* the Liberty one was more evocative of Swan Lake than Swansea, viz Jack armies; reminiscent of the kind of catalogue you get encouraging you to invest in capital bonds and properties in far-off locations. It was laminated and in too large a format to fit in my football programmes mushroom box. All alone it was to reside on the top, out of synch.

More appealing was the mascot, Cyril the Swan, who has had his moments, like revealing an affiliation with the floodlights. In heraldry birds have no threat from animals, so Cyril can glean comfort regarding the various lions chosen as mascots by other clubs. He's a sharpshooter, as evidenced at the first 'Battle of the Mascots' at Shrewsbury on April Fool's Day 2001. Elvis J Eel (aka The King) reported: 'The match…itself was terrific, with the two mascots' teams roared on by a crowd of 3,000 – more than come to watch Shrewsbury Town sometimes! The flesh-and-blood character Alex the Greek from Exeter City and Swansea's Cyril both ran riot, scoring goals creating others, and generally exploiting the soggy defence and shambolic goalkeeping of my side. Around thirty mascots turned up, with many of us being shown a red card, but we nobbled the ref a few times to get our own back…The match finished 8-3… There's talk of an England v Scotland match next (who will Swansea's Cyril play for?)

hat will see serious fur flying!' (*Mascots, football's furry friends* by Rick Minter.)

It was weird to observe the elegant North, away, Stand almost devoid of ccupants with the lower tier smartly displaying 'OSPREYS' (adopted name of Neath-wansea Rugby Union Club – headquarters here as co-tenants) in black on white haded with a tasteful dove grey. Our view, where at Chester there had been a pastoral cene, was a dual carriageway bound for city centre and M4, with ever-brightening raffic as the light faded. A rare announcement informed us of the attendance: 13,916. he average for the season so far had been 14,632, far more than had been the case at he old Vetch. I was told that supporters were continuing use of the old name. Perhaps n response to audience reaction, the stadium's next name should be 'New Vetch', like New Den?

Yeovil Town had achieved a personal first in their third year of League nembership. They were the visitors for the Liberty's record gate of 19,288, not at ll bad for the third level of Leaguedom, where average gates this season have been round the 6k mark. It's Swansea's new-ground honeymoon, the Vetch Field playing o 8,458 in its last year, in itself an improvement of 1,800 on 2003-04. This has some ssociation with their form. They were promoted in 2005 and had been top for a spell his year. Meanwhile Yeovil's Huish Park was in flux on the record attendances front. Leeds visited on 25 April 2008, confirming their League 1 (3) play-off place with a 0-1 ictory in front of 9,527 enthusiasts, a new record.

After the game came the ungainly scramble in full sight of the required universal retail stuff. This was the last new stadium on the list. Scrambles are part of he tradition of the walk to the game. At a new ground it took on a self-conscious quality, being inappropriate in a setting intended for out-of-town shopping and amily gatherings.

I just hope that completing the new grounds list means that I don't ever have o look a Frankie & Benny's in the face again in my entire existence (not wishing to over-egg the pudding at all. Perhaps their desserts are of outstanding merit.)

Onward to Tallulah, but without Robin, owing to the dog embargo.

Ninety down, two to do.

*22 January*

*Theodore Walcott, 16-year-old prodigy and great nephew of West Indian batsman Clyde, has been hyped up as a must-catch by the big clubs from the Southampton paylist. Arsenal beat Chelsea to the contract, initially for £5m, rising to a maximum of £12m. Theo eventually entered a professional contract worth a (reported) £1m p.a. through to Summer 2008. I've heard of hype and I've also heard of burning out, and 'potential not achieved'. And Sven picked him for potential heroism status in the World Cup squad. History was made quickly: Theo was literally a waste of space, being omitted entirely from public performance, exacerbated by England's shameful dismissal following unintelligent penalty execution. It was unsurprising to read the progress report in January 2008. 'At the moment he is not where I expected him to be,' said Arsène Wenger. But the very next month he saved their bacon at St Andrews in scoring both goals in their 2-2 draw with Birmingham City. And, come the Spring of 2008, another page was turned as he was picked by new England boss Fabio for his friendly squad, and many columns written after his spectacular hat-trick against Croatia in September.*

*Anagram of David and Victoria Beckham: 'Bravo, a victim and dickhead'. Tallulah unearthed that snippet in a Sunday paper the morning after the Swansea event, having just informed us that the water was off, all over Penarth. She compensated with a vengeance, her blender producing an unctuous concoction, employing any number of fruits.*

*26 January*
*Gary Neville has been charged by the FA with improper conduct following his gleeful and aggressive response in rushing a full 60 yards to pump fists and kiss his Trafford badge in front of the Liverpool fans after Manchester's late winning goal. He expressed his surprise at this treatment, citing previous complaints about the lack of player passion. You are 30 years old, Gary (less excuse than for a teenager) and can't wear that nice red jersey without the baggage that goes with it.*

*Sven will be out of his England job after the World Cup tournament in June, following his blurtings to a pressperson under cover (of robes) in the Middle East. His successor will be chosen in time for some empirical grooming in Deutschland.*

*Wigan, who must be accorded 'big achiever' status this season whatever the final Premiership table (top half, a huge achievement), have reached the League Cup Final, to face the Traffs. They beat the Arse 2-2 on away goals. Their first appearance in October (see above) has now reached the status of 'nostalgia'.*

*29 January*
*Notable match involved the two remaining clubs in the quest clashing at Victoria Park. It's only the 'Pools' now in this quest and 'Black' vanquished 'Hartle' 3-0.*

## Hartlepool United 1 Chesterfield 0
## League 1 (3), 10/2/06

The journey took me on an East Coast-line train bound for Newcastle, which, already crowded, it being Friday afternoon, was bursting at the seams after the 'Quiet' carriage, F, was evacuated following the malfunction of a door. The one cavernous restroom (US usage as it seems curiously appropriate), singular in the whole vehicle because the other one was out of order, was fortunately outside its limits. I had made the mistake of drinking tea all morning and a send-off pint as I, rarely, had some spare minutes at Birmingham New Street.

Perhaps regular train users have clocked the policy of minimum toilets with maximum space (for wheelchairs) and avoid such ingestion. Let it be a lesson to me, as it was not comfortable awaiting the facility to become available, for an interminable duration. The route the system determined for me to this County Durham outpost involved an easy change at Darlington (the station a considerable improvement on the Williamson Stadium, at least fit for purpose). Then 40 minutes at Thornaby (-on-Tees), where I espied a haven, Dubliners, a beacon in the gloom still decorated with Santa's sleigh and reindeer capping the entrance. The Guinness there seemed right, even if not in any way noteworthy, and I had the reassurance that only Billingham (-on-Tees) and Seaton Carew now blocked the trail to the destination. On time in Hartlepool Station, the first thing encountered turned out to be the best: an old North East rail network map on the wall by Platform 1. Not even retro but the real thing. I was informed there were only three of these masterpieces extant.

At the game the mascot, H'Angus Monkey, was the highlight, or rather the story behind its choice. Briefly, local fishermen during the Napoleonic Wars captured a monkey, taking it for a French spy, called it 'Pierre' and hung it. Hence 'H'Angus'! The blue and white stripes brought out its fur a treat. Those from the headland, as opposed to West Hartlepool ('East H.' would be awash) are known as 'Codheads', another fishing reference, with smelly overtones. And, don't forget the spectre of the nuclear power station. And, predictably Hartlepool folk as a whole are 'Hartlepudlians'. Later on I discovered another H'Angus on display in a pub in Brentford plus a photo of the team (1956-57). I guess Hartlepool is a good place to escape from to take up licensed premises elsewhere.

The ground, sorry 'Park', was centrally sited next to an endless Morrisons establishment. I had hoped much from reading in Simon Inglis's 1983 book *The Football Grounds of England and Wales* that Hartlepool was the least favourite ground with players because of its facilities, a verdict enhanced by remoteness, surely. I had also heard that ocean-bound craft could be seen from one of the home stands, the source grimacing when I said the intention was to enjoy the visit from an away point of view, by reports even more bleak and exposed, but facing the wrong way. In reality the whole place was enclosed and covered, I have to admit comfortingly on a bitterly cold evening. It was still disappointing not to endure the anticipated hardship of exposure, uneven steps and intense competition for the crusty urinals. I haven't undergone this footy lark for so long without developing masochistic tendencies. There were telling reminders to note: excellent floodlights through which the cold moon became a photographic subject and bits of old terracing adjacent to the end of the stand where the dimensions betrayed a lack of tape measure, or was the stand a recycle from a failing local industry – ship building maybe? As Blackpool's was reputedly an upgrade job, after all Bloomfield was on 'Seasiders Way' now – the ground's situation became most ominous for those with old-fashioned inclinations. So there must remain another tempter – to find crappy terraces down in the feeder leagues and below. I've always fancied Welton Rovers. It could well soon be time to try them out.

The programme was £2.50, back to a sensible price tag, and thoroughly average, a relief after the pretension of Swansea City. 'Stuart Drummond… the Mayor's View' claimed 'Friday night games are always enjoyable. We actually win a lot more than we lose and the atmosphere is usually far better than a Saturday afternoon.'

Exactly. 'In 2002 the team's mascot "H'Angus the Monkey", aka Stuart Drummond, was elected mayor of Hartlepool as an independent, under the slogan "free bananas for schoolchildren", even though his candidacy was just a publicity stunt. Stuart has since been re-elected after throwing off his comedy image and identifying himself increasingly with the Labour group on the council.' (Wikipedia had this one.)

The mayor's opinion on Friday nights was borne out on this occasion with the Pool leaping six places out of the bottom four on the back of this surprise, but deserved, win. Chesterfield may have been suffering from Mayor's syndrome in producing a lacklustre, or absent, game plan, losing to the Pool's industry, Matty Robson the scorer, breaking his duck in the process. As temporary Spireites in the roomy ranks of the Rink End, it was disappointing to see a team in Liverpool-style outfits belie their position just below the play-offs, there by virtue of a meritorious away record: 6-6-4, against the home team's 3-6-6 at the Vic. A home victory was due, I suppose. We were probably cast in the role of 'temporary talismen', having witnessed their surprise draw in Wales.

My long-term memory of this club is as perennial strugglers, eternal re-election applicants. They were fortunate not to go the way of Gateshead, voted out in 1960, though finishing in 22nd position in the basement division, the Pools finishing bottom. As a remote outpost you have to wonder how they managed to survive. The mid-Noughties can be considered a golden era – up and down, and up again in 2008-09.

In generous spirit I will not mention the town centre, sampled the next morning, but instead the sole pub pinpointed after the game, inevitably called Jackson' Arms. Ralph Ward Jackson was very busy here doing much for the town in the Nineteenth Century, his name living on in the Historic Quay Museum of Hartlepool: Jackson's Landing and Dock. The pub was busy with all generations, Magnet Ale (our nectar) and, now and again, favourite sounds on the juke box suggestive of the days of the hopeless Hartlepools United of the rundown Victoria Ground up the road. What does become of the broken-hearted?

And now a breather until the final game, a flurry in Blackpool.

91 done, one undone.


*12 February*
*Another week on and Middlesbrough beat Chelsea 3-0, Jose Mourinho's worst-ever score while at the helm. A bit suspicious that – complacency? Burst bubble? Or are they just displaying a streak of human weakness to which we are unaccustomed? Still, they went on to see off the challengers and win back-to-back titles.*

*Early April*
*A few days before the final game it has been announced that Wembley will not be ready this year. On the other hand, the FA Cup semi-finals will be played in a week's time at Villa Park and Old Trafford. I was afraid that the Millennium turf, far from yielding such provender to the regions, would enfold yet more bits, like*

*the Conference play-off final. That is destined for Upton Park, somewhere in east London. And, the day after the euphoric happening below, the Villa at last rose to the occasion of a home derby with the Blues and impressed with a 3-1 win. It was their first double over their rivals for 25 years and may well have helped to consign Small Heath to relegation 13 days later. Had it gone the other way the tussle with Pompey and the Baggies might have drawn Villa in as further sufferers. By then Sunderland were already down.*

## Blackpool 1 Swansea City 0
## League 1 (3), 15/4/06

This was the end of the line and of a series of coincidences: Chester away, then home; Hartlepool the same; Swansea home, then away on this ultimate outing. Prediction: 1-1 draw – that was the trajectory.

The streets were attuned to travellers' needs, of course, in sight of Blackpool's South Beach and the Tower. Swansea fans were ubiquitous, clad in startling black and white pantomimic costumes, in evidence in the area all around the ground, in fact far more than Tangerine people. The dominant Swans' presence may have been a matter of timing, as we arrived early. Perhaps the local fans either get there late or avoid the brash tourism of Lytham Road, where there was no shortage of activity to pass the time. Chip meals were in abundance. The evening saw the Blackpool of the mind's eye: many gaggles of hen revellers. One batch, uniformed in puce and jet black, staggered before us, their cognomens at eye level. Wakey unofficially chose 'Big Bird' and I picked out 'Juicy Melons' as preferences just as they disappeared into a cavernous void off the pavement. Another option would have been 'GB', which we interpreted variously as Gigantic Boobs and Generous Breasts. The problem was lack of opportunity to conduct much empirical observation as we only had a back view.

I had written an imploring letter to chairman Karl Oyston for tickets for the game to mark the occasion of the 92nd ground. He very kindly obliged – we were honoured with seats in the Pricebusters West Stand. We went to the wrong section to start with – it was soon clear that it was a season ticket enclave.

I successfully purchased a programme, having scoured the swarming perimeter before the turnstile search to avoid a repetition of the Swansea problem where they were only available *outside*. Bizarrely they were only available *inside* Bloomfield Road and I didn't miss any of the action this time. It was £2.50, 68 pages and indelibly shiny like the Wigan one. A table of facts near the back told us of totals of away fans in a column headed 'Trav'. The Seasiders had been supported by between 220 at Swindon and 971 at Huddersfield. The latter, 8.1% of the total gate (it had been a majestic 14.8% at Oldham), saw a 0-2 triumph. The best away following to Bloomfield Road, surprise, surprise, was from Nottingham. Forest brought 1,858 (22.1%) and their average home gate was 19,288, easily the highest in the division. Swansea came next with 13,940. What would happen there next year when the novelty of the Liberty had worn off?

The programme offered many tempting statistics – one more to mention was 'Current form' – the last six games. Forest topped that too, with 14 points out of 18. Blackpool, battling against relegation, were ninth, and MK Dons were 24th, bottom both in the last six and all 41 games. Inside the back cover was the squad check, answering my prayer expressed at Bolton in August, in that national flags were entered adjacent to each player. Alongside this was 'at a glance' – the up-to-date table giving games played, goal difference and points. All the clubs had five left to play, most tidy and workable. Blackpool were two places above the relegation places and under serious threat of the drop. The Swans, black today, were 5th, in combative mode. Plenty for both to play for. Perhaps the preoccupation with tabulations went too far, as on page 63, along with 'Current form', were the Coca-Cola League 1 standings, several playing days older than 'at a glance', giving more, but outdated, detail, the teams having played 39 or 40 games. After 46 games, Swansea finished sixth only to fail in the play-offs; Blackpool managed 19th, safe by three points.

In a season coinciding with celebrations for Lord Nelson's Trafalgar triumph, let us pay homage to his ghost, which haunts the Bloomfield Road boardroom. The reason is that wood from his flagships was recycled as panels therein. In the part where spectators are allowed, only the north and west (ours) sides were covered, the south being closed and awaiting the next stage of building. The east was the away side and bulging with the pied.

The ground's capacity was 11,295 and average gate 5,584 (6,709 today), and the atmosphere was keen and vocal, most contribution, coming from the North Stand, an echo chamber and the Tangerine hotbed, flanked by boards on the corrugated frame offering carpets, laminates, vinyls, karndean (what is that?), rugs, beds and quickstep (a bit anomalous?). This was interesting, and helped to give the place a tatty, dated ethos. Somehow the Swansea flags, recalled from the game there in January, representing Jack armies from Neath Valley, and also Barnsley and Harrogate; yes, really. Bloomfield Road was just what was needed – in essence an antiquated ground with the ingredients all in place for the ideal Saturday game of football. That is what transpired. The game was competitive, though when wishing to identify a home player for flair or transgression, the white name and number ere unclear against the rather insipid tangerine shirts, perhaps showing the effects of relentless boil-washing. Strange that the shirts worn by fans around us were a stronger orange, more like the Dutch look.

The Tangerines exercised a little wit in chanting 'we are going to Germany', unlike the opposition from over the border. Lee 'Magic Daps' Trundle, formerly at Rhyl (nil) and Wrexham (Dragons), was a notable presence for the Swans, but no goals were forthcoming, nor even chances. At half time there was grief to observe in the tangerine corridor's Hall of Fame. Among the photographic display featuring Jimmy Armfield et al. were blank photo frames, one carrying a newspaper article from February: '…thieves stole pictures of some of Blackpool's greatest players in a raid… during the non league clash between FC United and Blackpool Mechanics on Saturday 18 February.'

In the second half, Blackpool's Scottish front man, Keigan Parker, having shot high and wide earlier, got his eye in and scored the only, excellent, goal, just below us, on 59 minutes. The crowd was electric, complete with universal old-fashioned body contact. Simon Grayson's barmy army was echoing all round the ground, bouncing off the corrugated iron. The plucky Scotsman tried again a few minutes later without success, but one out of three attempts isn't bad when the effect is a home win against apparently superior opposition and the effect is to rise a place in the table, five points clear of Hartlepool in 21st place.

There was no scoreboard to announce this turn of events. At least, I eventually happened upon something, an apology for a display, blowing gently in the sea breeze under the exposed camera gantry mounted above the away bank. It comprised a series of illuminated red zeros, which I first noticed representing the remaining time when 11.54 appeared and continued to descend to 00.00 again. So, no real scoreboard to proclaim the Seasiders' achievement. In the 'minimum of three minutes' time added on' Swansea pressed mightily and missed a set-piece opportunity. The strange practice, often witnessed in these countdown games, of making substitutions with scant time left, was exercised here, several fresh players joining the fray in injury time. This had no influence on the observation that the average Swansea player was several inches taller than the Blackpool boys.

The final, final whistle blew. Evidence of widespread jubilation suggested this, though it was inaudible. The quest was over and I had my Blackpool FC mug (official merchandise) as a souvenir.

A single goal had been scored, essentially disappointing, but no matter, the occasion had been good. Maybe this was evidence of a growing immunity to a dearth of goals, after only 17 goals had been observed in the final trawl: of the ten games six had produced one goal, two a 1-1 draw, leaving a 1-2 and a 3-1. So Sincil Bank gets the venue award for entertainment value on the basis of output.

As an aftermath we went to a nearby hostelry for television results. Blank screens. A programme in Arabic ensued halfway through our pints in which it was inferred that it was a Lebanon v Kingdom of Saudi Arabia encounter. A fitting end to the pursuit of the 92, I reckoned.

## Chapter Nine
# Time Added On

## New Grounds after 2005-06

The quest for the 92 was concluded at Blackpool in April 2006. But football is all about the unexpected, the unpredictable, the unexpurgated, the rest. Here is the final chapter. Interspersed among the entries through the preceding pages are observations relating to life after Bloomfield Road.

The score in the pub after that game stood at LEB (Lebanon) 0 KSA (Kingdom of Saudi Arabia) 0 when we left, after about 20 minutes. The KSA jogs an irritation: how come (the Republic of) South Africa is abbreviated to 'RSA' on TV screens, as during their World Rugby prowess in 2007? Wouldn't 'SAF' be more consistent with other nations, the nature of whose constitution isn't otherwise emphasized?

Anyway, the focus of the evening was a suitably outrageous show at the Flying Handbag, perhaps serving to counter the aftermath anticlimax. The place was populated by obvious hen parties, and probably stags, too, not so clearly identified, among the substantial gay presence. Women seem to be better at this kind of display. And there were many other interestingly kitted-out punters.

More seasons passed, awash with further football, culminating with the denouement of the spring of 2008. It is bits of this story which follow.

## Arsenal Supplementary
### Emirates Stadium Tour, 26/11/07

Arsenal FC has more than a million members. The stadium holds a paltry 60,432. In my phone call to the ticket office I was told that games were always sold out in advance. Red members, of whom there were over 80,000, had booking priority a month before the fixture. Rarely, for less popular international matches, were there a few residual seats left for public sale. I stood even less chance than at the New Den, with a slightly different scenario of getting in. I tried a friend whom I knew to be a long standing season-ticket holder, but he was pursuing an 'adventure year' in New York, so even an illicit borrowing was impossible. Anyway the photo-match system at the turnstile would have foiled me, I'm sure, as I don't look anything like someone with Turkish Cypriot origins. 'Send the stadium my love,' he emailed. Good luck, Anatol. He had made a commanding Charles the Wrestler in *As You Like It*.

So I accessed the website for information about stadium tours, having read an alarming reference to them in a Sunday paper, to the effect that they cost £36. However, an exhausting internet ramble found me the true options: Standard £12, Legend £35 (museum included in both) and Museum £6. The legends involved the presence of a choice of Arsenal's former finest. I think I would have plumped for Kenny Sansom, '1987 League Cup winning captain' and on the detailed page 'often referred to as Arsenal's greatest left-back'. But £35? Not even the most wonderful captain ever, Dennis Mortimer, would have enticed me at that price – I was after information and observation, not the somewhat dubious performance of a hero manqué. Rand and I were duly booked for the appointed tour at 12 noon, and Anatol had recommended a hostelry wherein to mull over the experience afterwards. All set.

The day arrived. Rand and I hotfooted it up the Piccadilly Line. Turning left outside Arsenal station we were assaulted by sky-stretching cranes, doing their bit for the new housing project on the site of the extinct 'Highbury', address Avenell Road. It was worth the wander round two sides of the plot to peer at the Art Deco East Stand, lurking behind scaffolding, and snap an amalgam of metal and faded paint, grey, red and white. Elsewhere was the buzz of a muddy building melée. Back at the equally 1930s underground entrance a more recent sign directed us rightwards to Arsenal football ground. Far from presenting the expected A to Z challenge negotiating railway embankments, the first Emirates tempter stood immediately before us in an unpalatably strong turquoise – the retail outlet (one of the club's four), which made a valiant attempt to ply us with wares, such as 'Arsenal sweets' (sherbet lemons, rhubarb and custard), a match programme (£3, the top price I encountered in 2007-08, though you don't have to go to a prestigious club to pay that much – try Swindon Town), the current season Handbook (£5), dog bowl (£8), for kiddies the £8 Gunnersaurus bag or, even more damaging to the credit card, Mini Gunner at £13. This was a kind of garment for people too small to appreciate it. Or was it really for the doting parent? I still haven't found a basic greetings card in any football club shop, let alone one I'd like to invest in.

At length a party of 44 gaggled in the entrance to the Directors' Room, by entrance S, the final stage in the alphabetical sequence round the stadium. We were regaled by tour guide Paul, with Ramina in support, who admitted she was able to fill in when necessary, she'd heard it all so many times before. Naturally, the route to the directors' box was via the cocktail lounge adorned with a floral display on match days in the colours of the visiting team. Wigan had recently occupied that pointless (pun intended) task but I saw no subtle hyacinths or delicate white snowdrops, the weather having been such as to expect native winter flowers. Upon reflection I'm sure exotic blooms would have been imported from the southern hemisphere to impress the guests. It's not all a matter of giveaways, however. Guests, including that much-maligned sector of society, the Press, have to pay for their spirits. The directors' seats were yielding enough for a quick kip, but Paul was a clear presenter, having possibly attended the same college of oratory as Thatcher, or at any rate Sir Beckham. Having enjoyed Wembley (new) purely as a turnstile negotiator, it was illuminating to hear of the advances in thinking underlying the design of a 60k-seater stadium. It opened on time and within budget. Say no more. Also Arsène Wenger, implicitly exercising Strasbourgeois efficiency, facilitated such touches as the contours of the home dressing room (number 1 of 4): curves, which he imagined inculcated a positive attitude in the players. Never a sharp angle. The away dressing (not 'changing', oh no) room we had it on Paul's authority to be rectangular and square, the most ominous shape of all.

The Arse's home record spoke for itself – the last defeat so far back mere mortals can't remember when. They were in pole position in the Premiership and seemingly invincible. However, it has to be reported that two days after this tour they came a cropper in Seville, upstaged 3-1. Their League form went a bit tepid, too, declining to a mere third place. What was that about mere mortals? Gary Jacob wrote in *The Times*: 'accustomed to overwhelming teams with their exhilarating pace, Arsenal got a taste of their own medicine as they were infested by a rampant Seville last night. Not only did the Spanish side end Arsenal's unbeaten run of 28 matches in all competitions, dating back to last season, but they also scored the first Champions League goals against the North London club this season…'.

Among our co-tourers, who also marvelled at how the away allocation barrier could be adjusted vertically all the way up the stand to execute capacity requirements on the day, was a couple from Italy, Inter Milan supporters on holiday. No doubt they were looking forward to a chance for their team to emulate Seville. This wasn't likely for a while for another couple, from Japan. They professed their English team to be Leeds United, who for the first time on the coming Saturday (1/12/07) were not even due to grace Round 2 of the FA Cup (removed by Hereford in the first round). No chance of an Emirates baptism for them just yet. We all admired the stadium. The pitch, seats, all-embracing white roof and the ten pitch-warming sunlamps (idea from PSV Eindhoven), also white, which shone in the bright conditions, though the sun was somewhere out of sight. That's worth noting. As at Wembley (new), the elements were almost entirely absent, so space-age machines had been introduced to make good what Nature is precluded from – very unlike Swindon where it was so wet for the Forest Green Rovers Cup match that The Dude and I were surprised the tie was still on. And my shoes leaked that afternoon. The Swindon second half was thrilling, though. The sequence of goals was 1-0, early on (the Green's keeper blinded in a rare ray of low sun, we reckoned), 1-1, 1-2, 2-2, 3-2 in added time, in true Roy of the Rovers Cup-tie fashion. That's the action for this entry.

The home team ablution room got the biggest gasp from the 44. (We could, you might imagine, have conjoined in two full-scale encounters on the pitch, with Paul and Ramina as 'first officials'). The wet room seemed to hark back to the ethos of lads-together camaraderie in an enticing spacious pool. What a bath! Aquamarine in tone, with an exotic array of accoutrements. The whole recovery and relaxation suite would have graced the most exclusive health spa. Those massage couches! Away teams only have boring old (new) showers.

The bloke from Stevenage was mightily impressed. A local long-term season-ticket holder, but not here, he could remember Alex James, 'old baggy shorts', one of whose quotes, in the museum close to the north side of the ground, was 'ye canne play fitba, if the ball's in the air.' I made a comment about the displayed photos, featuring the man, who made 261 appearances between 1929 and 1937, scoring 27 goals, being historic. He replied: 'Well, I'm historic.'

A much younger Arsenal fan was from Worcester, on the tour with his family – a party of four. He hadn't been bothered about football, let alone Arsenal, until persuaded by his wife to join the throng. The time had come, this season, when he tried to acquire tickets for the Gunners' League fixture at Villa Park, also on the coming Saturday. The requirement was five vouchers from Emirates games attended. He only had four, so didn't qualify – too early in the season. Catch 22 in a way, as it was famously difficult to get to see the Gunners live at all. Paul informed us of the 185k members, whether silver or red, and 44k season-ticket holders. The latter included Harpenden-based supporters on the tour – it panned out at £35 per game, the head of the family told me. But you do have to commit yourself. Right! This didn't apply quite so much to a Swedish footballer, on vacation, with weekend case on tow. He and his two friends were curious, said Rand, who enjoyed an exchange with them.

This virtue applied to many visitors. Rand had opened an unwitting interview with Paul with the question 'Why do people want to do this tour?' The guide was discreetly speechless but recovered valiantly with a peppering from his arsenal of information. There was one misgiving: Highbury had been more intimate, the seats closer to the pitch – you felt more in touch with the play.

This is on the list of sights of the UK's capital. Some go to Wembley (new) and the Emirates, even on the same day. When will a shuttle system be introduced between the two? This 12 noon tour may have comprised a typical spread – a wide age, nationality and interest span; by no means all affiliated to the club. I reckon we were all pretty impressed by the end, when we were let loose in the retail outlet.

We had been warned about the Highbury clock. It had been erected, but on the south-east corner of the EXTERIOR. It was not proving a success and, as we sadly witnessed with our parting glance at this momentous structure, was obscured by scaffolding. If clocks could express themselves, I'd say it was grieving for being sited away from a view of the pitch, thus lacking much purpose. This was on the way down from the museum, displayed in two sections, right and left. The former displayed 'landmarks…matches…moments which shaped the club's reputation both at home and abroad'.

The timing was right for this piece of exhibitionism. Arsenal attracted, several times a day, a motley bunch of fee payers, within the fraternity and outside it, just to see their ground. I recognized a mounting burning sensation in my bosom and interpreted it as an urgent need of a venture to the north end of Preston to the National Football Museum. I have, I repeat, a tendency towards collecting, perhaps now also of football museums.

## Wembley Stadium (new) – I:
## Exeter City 1 Morecambe 2
## Conference Play-off Final, 20/5/07

This was the third-ever domestic competition at the new place. A week earlier Stevenage had beaten Kidderminster 3-2 in the FA Trophy Final, and in the Cup Final the previous afternoon, Chelsea had got their own back, a little bit, against new champions Man U by squeezing one in. Of course I had been forced to suffer the last Cup Final under the twin towers in 2000 from a public house. That had been just as feeble a game and Chelsea beat Villa 1-0. Good old David James, who late in 2006-07 assumed the mantle of most Premiership clean sheets. What a shame that he'd taken an extra 100 games to achieve this than the previous top geezer, David Seaman. I suppose if you hang around long enough…or are there just not enough old goalkeepers? But I shouldn't carp about 'Calamity James' (for myself as a Villa fan, and Wakey, who also suffered him at Manchester City) in view of his new found popularity as renewed England top choice in 2008. He discovered a new lease of goalkeeping life at Pompey, a real presence in the second level of the Premiership, also breaking the top-four domination of the FA Cup in May 2008.

What a happenchance was this event! The Grecians had finished in fifth position and then came through impressively against Oxford United to earn their Wembley debut. Then came a ticket challenge as gruelling as any for Millwall admission. I spent days on the phone to the St James' Park ticket hotline and electronically to the TicketZone dedicated website. On my steaming handset when I, rarely, got an answer, the messages fizzled gradually to a doom-laden 'Sorry, sir, there will be a few more released at 3.30pm but that's all.' And that was on the Tuesday, with five days to go, the service to be terminated 'at 14.00 hrs on Wednesday. (Final despatch of tickets Wed 16th May).' On the TicketZone page at no time did I get anything but a greyed-out screen, thus precluding any chance of placing an order that way. Meanwhile the Gnetters (ECFC supporters) email system was awash with updates about the demand for tickets. Exeter supporters were growing into a glut. This was worrying. Plan B had evolved, which was to resurrect the New Den approach. New Den, new Wembley. With aplomb and nerves awry I ventured into alien territory – the Morecambe FC website. The Wolves-at-Millwall experiment was to be repeated. In fact, at about this time, three years after 1-2 at the New Den, a Molineux-led call centre took to sending me a number of mobile text messages with enticements for their Championship play-off against West Brom. They lost too. It's easy to sign up to a list, but there you stay.

After the grief so far suffered, it was pathetically easy to sign up with the shrimps – I thought it would have been 'Cockles', but no. There was no choice: £25 or nothing. I wasn't concerned, just mightily relieved that the tickets were booked. Then began the awful wait. Like Fuckin' Dave, who had managed to secure Bristol Rovers tickets at Wembley (new) – they went on to beat Shrewsbury in the Fourth Division went the following week – I wondered if that envelope would ever arrive. In, with hindsight, unwarranted apprehension about the ticket sending process, I'd subscribed to Special Delivery (£5.95). With the Administration Charge (£1.50) and Booking Fee (£5.62) this converted £75 for three tickets into £88.07. Rather a lot, methinks. When I book tickets with less pressure and more time, I send a cheque and s.a.e., usually avoiding these charges and feeling more secure. Not so when you're caught by the short and curlies, a victim of the whims of Wembley (new), and a computerized system. If anything, Special Delivery status served to delay actual delivery, being a more formal means of despatch. As it was, two whole days later, I was forced to attend the Post Office collection department, as the drop had been made while I was out and had to be signed for. Eventually, after securing the passports to pleasure, anyone I bumped into was treated to gushings of glee. I was going to 'Wemb-er-lee' (it said in the Morecambe FC fanzine, *Corpus Christie*).

On the day, our party arrived via the excellent Wembley Stadium Station on the Chiltern line, excellent mainly because of its existence. However, we were forced to stand all the way as the train was bursting with red and white, to which add red and green Leicester rugby fans, signed up for the Heineken Cup Final at Twickenham and, despite being favourites, defeat by Wasps (25-9), that famous outfit from High Wycombe. This visual cacophony may have been something of a one-off on the way to Marylebone and, perhaps, perplexing to the unwitting general public used to a quiet trip from stations such as Bicester North. Once on solid concrete I foolishly purchased a T-shirt and banner, and we waded through dense red and white pedestrian traffic into the first tavern espied, the Torch. A glance in the station, street, stalls, bars, garden revealed the ubiquitous twin colours, but mostly proclaiming 'Exeter City Conference Play Off Final 2007'. Grecian pint-holders in the bar presented a consistent baritone bellyful of 'Zyderrrrrh'!! There had been email exchanges about chants, including the suggestion of a reference to north-west Lancashire experiences with cockle beds. In the event I didn't hear 'Have you ever played Man U?' Or, for Sky viewers, 'Have you ever played Brazil?'

While a gently bucolic atmosphere wafted over the entire proceedings, not many attempts at linguistic dexterity were in evidence. I asked an amenable-looking fan on the next table to take our photo. She turned out to be from Bristol, her habitat Ashton Gate, but supporting Morecambe 'because my son lives there now.' She got it right with both his season. I should have taken her mobile number (much in evidence) for future Grand National tips.

There were ample photographic opportunities, like the Grecians sporting their manager's (Paul Tisdale) mask on the back of their heads and a yellow sign proclaiming 'Sunday market cancelled due to a stadium event'. Wakey posed by that rather modest obstacle, with the dramatic arch beyond. At '133 meters above the external concourse… the London Eye could fit between the top of the arch and the pitch' we learned from the programme (£5 – the Cup Final one £10). Within was a cornucopia of background detail; the pages weren't numbered but on the 17th, I counted, dedicated to 'Martin O'Neil' (sic), at the time a season into promising managership at the Villa, he related his experiences as a non-league manager at Wycombe, where the Chairboys shared their ground with Wasps. Bobby Moore's statue stood fresh and proud above Wembley Way, with an abundance of mounted police nearby. There were some country gentlemen, to judge from their plus fours, perhaps in the role of farming fans from Exonia, conversing in dignified passion near Bobby's effigy. As we passed, an urgent paparazzo was making a beeline for them.

Once past the shiny chrome turnstiles (thumbs up to those) we faced the 'Response Team', examining the contents of bags. Mine was approved by a charming member who conducted no more than a superficial assessment of my bag contents and a friendly 'Ok sir.' A Tottenham fan I surmised, as he sported a cockerel somewhere on his garb but I didn't have a chance to find out as he was onto the next contestant. Then came the notice 'Condiments', below which was a troughful of packets of stuff for your Pizza Baguette (£5.50 Meal Deal, £4.00 each) or Assorted Pies (£6.00, £4.50). We'd consumed our Boots Meal Deals (rather less expensive), purchased on the way to the station, which included three old-fashioned sandwiches. No Bovril offered here, as one might predict – down the road to Leyton for that – but chocolate (Pots £3.80, Bars £0.90). That's a new one to me. The choc bar should have been tried, being the cheapest item on offer. Beyond Condiments was the only Shrimp I'd seen, perched on a bloke's head. Wondrous. We had arrived. It really was the Morecambe section, away that day as they had lost the toss, forcing the players to don their all-blue away strip.

The seats were perplexingly commodious. I was able to spill my tea without ill effect. Row 31 in the front row of that section, a block up from the pitch, afforded a clear and reasonably close view in the south-east corner. The panorama was composed of swathes, with the Morecambe allocation in the foreground. Then the lush, and at that point, smooth and redivotted playing area, after its recent hacking. ('The wrong type of turf' – in the press. Can it be, with all that money and delay? Yes, it can. It then proceeded to lose £22m during its first year of operation.)

Beyond lay the massively dominant Exeter section, it's been reported 30k strong. These were surrounded and surmounted by another red – all those empty seats, contriving to break up Grecian rapport, giving me a brief surge of anger as I'm sure the Grecians' ticket provision problem was much to do with underestimating the interest generated. The Wembley authorities released tickets in a very slow and piecemeal way. Like politicians, stadium managers have no sense of the reality of a situation. Fifty-three thousand had piled into Wembley for the Trophy Final so why the recalcitrance this week?

The scoreboard was in a clear font and legible size. None of the Reebok-type sales pitches. And above, the sky. Judging by the size of the aperture, only some of the pitch and its occupants would have been affected by precipitation. Anyway it was a fine day. The occasion was fine too, up to the 42nd minute. City scored in the eighth (Lee Phillips), but as they had the best record of all

Conference sides for coming back from behind, and Morecambe had never beaten them in their eight meetings to date, the outcome was predictable. The ultimate kiss of doom was the fact that City were favourites, and as a club were primed for renewed League membership. They did lead for most of the first half, for longer than Morecambe whose second goal was frustratingly close to the end of normal time. I have thereby tried to glean a modicum of comfort. But it's no good. 'What a bummer,' transmitted Landy; and from Tiptoes 'Alas and alack!' Another friend, an actor treading the boards in Shakespeare and Ibsen productions in 2007, was as eloquent: 'Bstrd re Extr,' he texted. Pom asked 'What happened re Xtr.' I was too cut up to respond.

In the new season they were doomed to derbies with Turkey (= Torquay, geddit?), and to trips to Droylsden, Farsley Celtic, Histon and Salisbury City (at least kind of local), the complement newly promoted from Conference North and South. How utterly depressing! There would be more trivia questions about the number of teams with 'x' in their name in the Conference. We were to be saddled with the 'Blue Square Premier' from August.

But in a way Morecambe were the natural heirs to the League place vacated by Boston, an equivalent outpost with minimal population and modest support. The Shrimps' achievement was worthy as this was their third play-off year in five and they were established as a consistently good Conference team. That's as positive as I can muster.

I've always hated play-offs. Oxford really should have gone up automatically, as runners-up. But at least the promotion issue wasn't spoilt by irregularities committed by a mismanaged and desperate club, an increasing facet of the game. Meanwhile relegated Boston's position in the BSP had not by then been confirmed, following their 'in administration' status. Soon enough the powers decided to send them down a further level, to BS North. It was to be the first year of total virgin blood in the League since two teams have been promoted from the Conference, with Dagenham & Redbridge already promoted. I had projected a prayer to the Almighty that D'n'R dispense with such a witless appellation and either return to one of their constituent parts – I had 'Walthamstow Avenue' in mind – or concoct a totally new name. We were already to anticipate 'Ebbsfleet United', converted from Gravesend and Northfleet (and named after the new international train station hosting Eurostar vehicles) prompting vitriol from their fans in the *Non League* paper and all around that part of Kent. Still a bit of 'fleet', though, I suppose. (A big thrill to remain in 2007 was the Grecians' 1-3 win at Graves/Fleet in the Fourth Qualifying Round of the FA Cup, earning them a home tie with the troublesome Satanage, aka Stevenage – birthplace of 2008 Formula 1 champion Lewis Hamilton – in the First Round proper, in which they duly triumphed 4-0. Easy! Easy!!!).

Not content with a new identity, in November 2007 Ebbsfleet became the (guinea pig) Blue Square Premier club to be taken over by fans' community website MyFootballClub. 20,000 members paid £35 each to run the club. That is, each one may go online to register their preferences for team selection, transfers and management - Fantasy turned real life. And the team went on to win the FA Trophy the week before Exeter's triumph the following May.

The outcome, a fifth year in the fifth division, prompted a further source of foreboding: the Conference annually yielded a paltry two inmates up to the League, and there was an increasing number of former league clubs, with comparatively good facilities and long histories, languishing there. It might be some while before the Grecians' great escape. The authorities' conservatism in not recognizing that the Conference/Blue Square was, properly, the fifth division, with a four-up, four-down arrangement, had become a chronic frustration.

Just as in 1996, disconsolate, at the final whistle I sped to Wembley Park tube station, to meet fresh friends for some culture of a more certain nature. I alone was destined for some Smoke exposure. Think no more of unpredictable football and the chagrin it had induced yet again, but the arts, oral and visual.

Wembley Stadium (new) had proved to be a splendid thing and something of a relief: a showpiece to compete on the world sports map, and in a wider context, in parallel with the better examples of arts venues. It was worth the wait. But I had now been to the Wembleys six times, not once for a winning side.

## Morecambe 0 Darlington 0 (abandoned after 22 minutes – waterlogged pitch)
## League 2 (4), 8/12/07

### 1. Free of charge – The National Football Museum

It was happenstance to be able to drop into Deepdale so soon after the visit to the Emirates Museum. Compare and contrast. This turned out to be a fine institution, complete with an education programme and packs, 'Teachers Resource Material' and the 'Citizenship Trail' - which includes a reference to the 'Show Racism the Red Card' website. That was the worthy bit. There was such a plethora of absorbing goodies that I found myself in just the kind of situation I had aimed to avoid: the rush hour in the rain, and the final leg to Lancaster and Morecambe in prospect.

Erected as an extension to Preston's ground, on the first floor was an open view of the acting area, much improved onsite since my visit in 1994, though looking curiously irregular, the opposite side coming across as a blank space. This was reminiscent of Blackpool, which lacks a building on the side with the erratic scoreboard. And Blackpool FC were to visit the North End the next day, to return to Bloomfield Road with an away win. Preston weren't too proud up to that point in 2007-08. They seemed set on a downward trend, never having quite completed the thrust to the Premiership which had looked on the cards earlier in the decade.

In the museum, there was a vast amount of material, broken down into the

First Half', the 'Second Half 'and special exhibitions, on this occasion football poetry. One example was by John Hegley:

> *The Sub*
>
> *At school I used to play a lot of subbuteo*
> *(table football game)*
> *and they used to call me 'sub'*
> *and it was good to have a nickname*
> *until they told me it stood for 'sub-human'.*

The tone was set by a display of merchandise from various clubs, headed 'A fan's life': Brighton shower gel, a Villa radio, an eraser from Grimsby, a Tranmere pennant, an autograph book from Crewe. And Cyril the Swan, the mascot from that Welsh club.

Nearby was a 'modern seat', relinquished by the home club. The stadium through those concrete walls was bedecked with blue seats and white architecture. Later, being a turnstile obsessive, I was obliged by Ryan, bookshop operative and that day's superintendent. On hearing my inevitable enquiry, he led me to a back corridor where two beautiful original Wembley (old) turnstiles resided. Most ornate, very Art Deco. Strange to think that our former national stadium was erected at the same time as Belle Vue, Doncaster. And their dismantlement coincided, more or less. In the same decade, anyway. The design was similar, down to the counter and pedal-release mechanism. However, this one was painted a hue of cream, compared with Donny's vermilion. Also backstage was a pylon from the recently defunct Gay Meadow, Shrewsbury. But, as this was all, it was pertinent to express dismay at the loss of so much from dead stadia. Ryan saw the point.

The exhibits in the museum were comprehensively fascinating. The story of football from its earliest beginnings, the footballs painted in bright colours, composed of rags, which got heavier as a game progressed, and souvenirs down the ages: an image of the demise of Liverpool's Spion Kop, Stanley Matthews's Cup Final winning number 7 shirt, football stout brewed by Thomas and Evans. I was pleased with an exhibit on the subject of Arsenal's dubious promotion after the First World War. 'Chairman Henry Norris had spent heavily on the club and persuaded the league to promote Arsenal (who finished fifth in the last pre-war second division table). Arsenal have never been relegated since, but it took Barnsley (who finished third) 78 years to win promotion to the top division.' And then a 1897 painting depicting a game between the first great rivals, Aston Villa and Sunderland. I arrived at the story of the building of the former home of those turnstiles. Wembley (old) was built in 300 days in 1923 with a capacity of 126,500. Compare and contrast that, too. Also the posters advertising the 1926 and 1930 Cup Finals 'from any underground station'. And *Terrace Talk* fanzine, one of the first in 1981. 'It came out of a number of concerns by football supporters at York City regarding transport arrangements to away games.' A wry grin was apposite at the *Spitting Image* Terry Venables puppet, with an easy recollection that only a few weeks had passed since the visages of himself and Steve 'Ugly' (The Dude) McLaren were unappealingly displayed in dugout mode to millions during England's comeuppance by Croatia in the Euro 2008 qualification debacle.

It was time to move on to the Second Half: Poetry in Motion. One example:

*Sidney by Colin West*

*He ate up all the pies, did Sidney*
*Then, sadly, he EXPLODED, didn'e?*
*The pitch, no mistake,*
*Was spattered with steak,*
*And the stands were all covered with kidney.*

Games were on display, like a bagatelle board, which is how I would term it, but with the caption 'Pin Football', alongside wooden toy-footballer figures 'about 1895–1905'. 'When pressed, the trigger on the handle moves the leg of the player to kick the ball.' Chuckles were inadvertent at some of the personalties displayed – Kevin Keegan and Henry Cooper advertising Brut aftershave in 1980, the Beckhams posing with Elton and Lulu at a film premiere. And a photo of Roy Keane, the first player to earn £50k per week, in 1999 – in 1965, when he retired, Preston's Tom Finney had earned £20 per week plus £2 for a win and £1 for a draw. There was a Bovril advert, and one for fags, 'Player's Please'. Of one I still partook in many grounds; the other had become taboo. By arrangement you can practise your skills in 'GoalStriker' – £2.95 for three penalties.

After all this, nature called. The male toilet door was apposite, adorned with a poster carrying the image of a line of defenders cupping their relevant bits. To the poin I reckoned.


## 2. Free of charge – Christie Park
## (turned out to be a semi-refund, less postage)

Blame the weather, whose Wet department overindulged big-time all Saturday. Staying in a hotel on the Promenade in a room with a sea view, there was no such thing until the Sunday morning, when everything from Eric Morecambe's statue to the cut-out display on the Promenade were bathed in winter sunshine. This display identified the sights over the bay from sea level, Barrow to the far west and Helvellyn right at the top; all a matter of some interpretation.

As a prelude to the game, whose fruition was worryingly suspect given the small consideration of waterlogging, Wakey and I did the obvious (Tiptoes, after initial enthusiasm along the lines of trying a multi-starred restaurant up the coast a bit, had absented himself, for legal reasons, and I believe Rouge took advantage of that for some retail therapy – they overdo it, you know). We survivors tried the pubs, in the name of reviews for the *Stedders Football and Real Ale Guide* website. Morecambe FC were now in the League but publess in the list of 92. We changed that, contriving to unearth hidden refuges walkable from Christie Park. The outcome was an intriguing selection of three bars in Morecambe itself, the remaining two allocated to inns in Lancaster – shame about Lancaster City FC, which folded with a paucity of points (just one, in Conference North at the end of 2006-07. The pub provision is safe from such a fate, and they are close to transport.

So now you can say that Lancaster is the tourist centre, with an abundance of students, and history, Morecambe the football centre with a few shrimps, though the one shellfish outlet we identified through the gloom was closed. Chris Mason, the landlord of the Smuggler's Den, the one CAMRA member thereabouts and with a background in the Post Office and the Army, was content enough to welcome away fans, and it was fun to hear of the tunnel to the beach, through which nefarious deeds were perpetrated (smuggling-related) as well as a complement of ghosts in residence from times of yore. I tried a perry to start with. It was mellow, fruity, subtle and my starter before graduating to Hyde's Gold, a guest beer. These days perry providers don't seem to be confident in the name of their product. It's obvious enough, being made of pears, I'd say. But often it's sold as 'cider' with 'perry' underwritten discreetly. This is a misnomer as the *Concise Oxford Dictionary* defines cider as 'fermented drink from apple juice'. On the other hand the actual word 'cider' derives from the Hebrew 'shekar', a 'strong drink', and most ciders are extremely powerful. Too much can send you legless, blind and, earlier than most, deceased. So we've come full circle, in that a strong drink could include perry. But I don't want to suggest that we rewrite the dictionary, but keep the word 'perry' going by applying it to the alcoholic pear drink.

> There was an old woman in Ryde
> Who ate forty green apples and died.
> The apples fermented
> Inside the lamented,
> Made cider inside her inside.

I'm still looking out for a pear-based limerick.

Skipping on, we next imbibed in the York Hotel on the Lancaster Road, the base for the Shrimps' supporters' club. Note that 'Shrimps' is the correct nickname. They don't want to upset the Shrimpers of Southend by presenting competition. There were warnings to deter away colours: clearly a scare tactic, as there were some obvious Darlo people, brazenly sporting black and white garb, including a very well-got-up brace of matrons near us. Everards Beacon was my tipple. Wakey concurred. Smokers seemed content to light up on the balcony exposed to the relentless elements. We squelched to the Main Stand, forewarned that it offered the only access to the club's bar, so home fans we would be. The turnstiles were duly braved, and unnumbered tickets conveyed to our gloved hands, with a portentous comment from a retainer nearby who, having noted that we weren't from those parts, foresaw the lack of play.

We were in, swiftly finding what manager John Whittaker told me was correctly titled 'Morecambe Football Club Limited – Bell's Bar'. One of the directors also ran Bryson's Brewery, a local concern. Thank you, Peter Cross, for we guzzled pleasurably, through a power cut and the inevitable further soaking when a call of nature necessitated a visit to a (permanent) portacabin outside. I learned from John that League membership had meant a change in pre-match practice for hard core supporters in the terraced North Stand. They were now segregated from the Main Stand, by means of an ominous fence – no Hurricane Bitter for them.

Also it was inevitable that the club would move to a new stadium. It's a different ball game. Since their Wembley (new) success, far more people were interested in joining the Christie Park cohorts. Morecambe's average home gate for the previous ten games was 3,220; in the Conference it had been below 2,000, and of the visitors only Port Vale (League Cup – won on penalties – and FA Cup – lost) represented a higher division. Top-level clubs could now be expected from time to time, requiring bigger and better facilities than were currently provided.

At length Bell's Bar (named after the whisky distillery) emptied, and not only due to the power cut. We mounted the steps above and found seats with an open view of the sodden panorama. We could discern the car-wash facility opposite – and the eponymous terrace in the foreground. Yes, it's called 'Car Wash Terrace'. Also resplendent, picking up the floodlights in the gloom, were widespread puddles. They deadened play. The Darlo squad and faithful faced a mercifully short return journey. The game was abandoned on 22 minutes. Not even a quarter of it had been played. Quel horreur!

However, we had saved a treat, actually for half-time, but now would do: the famous Potts's pies (with mushy peas). A couple near us had been munching theirs provocatively but we hadn't identified the sales point on the way in. Between mouthfuls they put us right. It was discreetly sited within the fabric of the stand round the front where the fodder was delivered through a narrow window, sharing a wall with the bar behind. This must have afforded a view of the action on a good day. I doubt whether the new stadium would have such conducive facilities for your repast – food separate from drink: both good. So we rested under the canopy to devour our pies. This allowed more absorption of the compact ground, with extensive brown blotches among the patches of water. The next issue was that of the ticket refund. The queue to the office had abated by then, and after establishing that we couldn't avail ourselves of the offer to use the tickets for the rearranged game, I was given the address to use for a full refund. This was blissfully simple: 'Send them to Morecambe FC', with no embellishments of departments or floor numbers. I guess it's all in portacabins there – the office was probably in one. The next move had to be back to the Smuggler's for a consolation pint. This time, partly in anticipation of that final new, London, League member, Dag/Red, in the same category as Morecambe and yet to be sampled, I chose Fuller's London Pride. We tarried there a while and made it back to the hotel thoroughly damp – it took all night to dry my coat. But as a rarity after an afternoon of football, admittedly in bars for the most part, there was to be a full helping of BBC1's *Final Score*.

This is how the club handled the issue of the refund. Two phone calls and 59 days later (26 Jan), in fact 11 days after Darlington had eclipsed the newcomers 0-3 in the rearranged game, I received a letter enclosing a cheque dated 30 December. It was for £13.50, explained as follows:

'The refund that you will receive is in line with the Football Leagues own Customer Charter, and the very vast majority of all other Football League clubs, including that of our opponents Darlington.

Therefore the refund is based on the principal of 50% refund on the price that you paid.

[list of prices follows]

…Therefore the cheque for £14 less 50p that you have received equates to

| No | Area | Category |
|----|------|----------|
| 2 | Main Stand Seated | ADULT |

Thank you for your patience in this matter, as you can imagine it has been a new and difficult situation for all of us,

       Neil Marsdin

       Club Secretary.'

Thanks for the apology, Mr Marsdin — it must have been a challenge. In the end it provided yet another new experience – I shall forgive them for the delay, the low value of the remittance, even the errors in the letter for that. After all, I probably wouldn't have made the effort to visit Morecambe, and been exposed to its offerings quite so soon, without MFC's presence among the 92.

## Hereford United 1 Tranmere Rovers 0
## FA Cup Round 3 Replay, 16/1/08

I remembered the May 1985 Edgar Street jolly, as referee's pal, in serious rose-tinted mode. This time it was for real. The Toff hailed from the Wirral, being of the fraternity which believes that a football fan should be committed to a single club. He had no hesitation in suggesting the ominous journey to support the travelling Tranmere. He wanted a companion in his distress.

      The arguments against going were strong:

1) the elements (mid-January evening trip, the weather having been erratic at best, precipitant often and floods widespread);

2) I had a much-postponed dinner date that evening: to cancel this could prove terminal in the (not quite) friendship, similar to turning down job offers once too often from a particular employer, certainly in the arts;

3) the prospect of failure, nay embarrassment. After all Rovers had to come back twice from behind at Prenton Park (2-2 the result) and were at that time only 16 places above Hereford, notwithstanding the divisional separation. This was reinforced by the home club's reputation as doughty Cup fighters, i.e. giant-killers, as testified by Newcastle in the equivalent replay in 1972.

      The relative status of the clubs was in sharp contrast: Hereford, population 56k (third smallest town with a League club in 2007-08) and remote, a true outpost in the 92, members 1972-97 and now again for two seasons, versus Tranmere, original 1921 members of the Third Division (North). While not having achieved a lot in that time in terms of silverware, Rovers carried all the weight and character of a traditional League club in a 96-year-old ground.

Toff also undertook to obtain the tickets and drive. My bit related to the event itself, especially choice and detecton of a watering hole. I therefore agreed, to spend nine days of mounting anticipation. As things transpired, it was my car (his turn for Villa v Blackburn ten days later) and we eventually made it to a space close to Hereford Cathedral, but only after an inadvertent diversion to Abergavenny (distracted by football chat) and, once in Hereford, abuse from local youth – two of each – 'you knobhead', 'fucking prats' behind whom we trailed the length of a street from which cars were barred up to 4.30pm. It was approaching 6pm at that time.

Armed with recommendations for pubs for away fans, we managed to fail completely, having effectively run out of time. Fortunately Hereford is an old-fashioned market town, the hub for vast hectarage of farmland, bulls aplenty (though the wish to observe a specimen led round the pitch remained unfulfilled) and not many people. We were seduced into a refreshment prelude in the Courtyard 'Herefordshire's Centre for the Arts'. Fortunately Toff had prior experience of the venue, having interviewed the cricketing buff Jonathan Agnew (Aggers) there not long before. I had reckoned the latter's utterances the most exciting aspect of the endless 2007 Cricket World Cup in the West Indies, along with the performances of the brooding Sri Lankan record-breaking bowler Muttiah Muralitharan. On a lush couch at the Courtyard, Aggers had railed against *Test Match Special*'s changed obeisance from Radio 4 to 5 Live. We gained nourishment there in the form of Wye Valley Butty Bach bitter (me) – I won't mention Toff's choice – and a hot dish (one each and how he scoffed his Lasagne verde). The place was packed, for 'An Evening with the Stars of Country & Western', a few displaying the pied scarves of the Bulls.

Dead opposite, over Edgar Street itself, stood the Floors 2 Go Stand ('Oh, you mean the Len Weston Stand,' said a helpful local nearby when asked which entrance to use in a vast mass of corrugated iron obscured by fervent fans of all shades in the gloom). It appeared as the 'Len Weston', too, in *Football Grounds* by Simon Inglis (1983), where Hereford was listed in the South Wales and Borders section, 'named after the club president who had died just before seeing his dream of League football at Hereford come true. Edgar Street thus became the only non-First Division ground to have two cantilevered stands...'

The stand was remarkable. We clambered vertically above the lower terraced bank to choose seats at the back, which afforded an immediate, steep view of everything (including the delicately lit cathedral) except the touchline below us. The stand couldn't have been narrower, in complete contrast with the pitch, at 80 yards the widest in the League. I wondered what the distance was between the pitch and road. Not a lot. Stedders – a much-travelled Bristol Rovers fan – had claimed another rarity: the Gents in the Main Stand afforded a view of the game while tending to your needs. The other fascinating feature was the decaying Blackfriars Street End, divided midway between home and away supporters on this occasion, open for the Rovers contingent because of the large gate – 6,471 was the best so far in 2007-08, of whom 1,095 were

ounted as visitors. The Toff reckoned the rowdiness of some was due to the free coach
ravel offered at Prenton Park, encouraging an unsuitable element. The forestage of the
Blackfriars Street End was an open semicircular space, around which the exposed fans
oamed, sometimes in a manner perhaps designed to assume the mantle of the absent
ull. Above this was the scoreboard, with red lettering, as follows for most of the game:

HEREFORD    0

Tranmere     0

ut interspersed with, regularly, 'Many thanks to A4 OFFICE SUPPLIES for their
ontinued support'. Rovers dominated the first half without scoring, hampered no
loubt by their appalling kit suggesting untimely primroses or bananas, perhaps
oowdered scrambled egg, in reality possibly the result of a laundry accident.
Congolese number 8 Calvin Zola at least showed some wit in the singular choice of
ed boots, in which he danced to good effect. He was Man of the Match for both
of us, an accolade officially given to Toumani Diagouraga. Well, it was Hereford's
ground, and their evening. The loud vertical stripes of the Bulls (programme name:
*Bullseye*) was far more impressive. Our team's faithful (and, perhaps, some of the

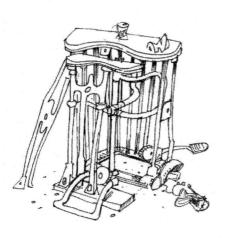

novices) gave voice to 'Tranmee'er',
a kind of chant in the circumstances,
perhaps lent potency in that 'Tranmere'
isn't a widely recognized place. Naturally
we heard a lot of 'Who the fucking hell
are you' from divers quarters.

The evening's other fixtures
began to assume prominence on the
scoreboard. After 14 minutes: 'Havant &
Waterlooville 1 Swansea 0', another replay.
The first corner we witnessed was on 24
minutes, by which time Waterlooville were
2-0 up, then 3-0. That would have been a
better choice for excitement: Blue Square
South (that's the 6th= Division) v top of the Third Division. There were times when
eyes were fixed expectantly on latest scores, rather than on the skirmish below. In the
econd half, interrupted by the euphoria when United scored at the other end, it went
o Havant & W 3 Swansea 2, then 4-2, which it stayed, representing a monumental act
of giant killing to rival Hereford's of the Tynesiders, back in 1972.

It's time for a limerick I was told, in honour of a native of that successful place
n Hampshire:

*There was a young fan of Havant*
*Whose conduct, I'd say, was gallant.*
*He slept with his dozens*
*Of nieces and cousins,*
*But always found time for his aunt.*

Another scoreline from League 2 had also become intriguing. From Chesterfield 0 Rochdale 2 at half-time, the home side drew level. It ended up 3-4 – and I recalled with a soft spot the Saltergate turnstiles. I hadn't read anything of the Spireites' projected move for some time. The Hereford turnstiles were patchy – some boring black ones and one seriously tatty, with filigree effects and peeling paint, tucked away after it had done its job for the evening. This was in such subdued light, though near the extravagantly massive floodlight pylons, that the only photographic facility I carried that evening, aka mobile phone, didn't register it to reveal more truth. No flash, you understand.

At the end we were informed: 'It is a criminal offence to encroach on the playing surface.' With Bulls and Bananas safely back in the changing rooms we manoeuvred back to the city centre, happening upon a pub from the list. The queue wasn't excessive but the beer choice unpalatable, the list being one of convenience rather than quality. The guide was proving to be more concerned with away-fan acceptance than what s/he would drink once through the doors. Fair enough. We settled for the famous Green Dragon Hotel for a different Wye Valley brew (and coke) as one for the road.

And I had a rescheduled restaurant engagement to look forward to.

## Accrington Stanley 0 Peterborough United 2
## League 2 (4), 1/9/07

Let the first be (almost) last in. In 2006 Accrington at last toppled the Arse from pole position in alphabetical lists of the 92.

This tale also involves Stedders, for the visit became an ingredient in a stay at his pub in Colne, as in 'Nelson & Colne' – and remember Colne Dynamos? The purpose of the tryst was the development of the pub guide, from Accrington to Yeovil, and of course hands-on testing was essential. So three of us, Graham (Priv) being the other, made for the lost horizon of Peel Park, where the team had played while a League member up to 1962. Priv, the Stockport County man, and I were enjoying a mutual novelty in having a day arranged for us (good on you, Stedders). I took some snaps of the municipal pitch in mid-use by a bunch of lads in yellow and blue, of a sign so faded on a red-brick hut that all I could make out was 'officials.... only' and another, clearer 'Erected by the supporters club 1937'. Stedders knew the way, which saved time, and we managed pints in the eponymous Peel Park Hotel, right next to the old place, followed by more, having parked near the Fraser Eagle Stadium (or 'Crown Ground'). This is an example of a club's new ground breaking with tradition. It's on the other side of town, with views of promising walking country from the Clayton Terrace where we took up our positions. When nourishment was needed the food counter predictably announced Stanley's Menu, red letters on white and the aprons were a red and white check.

The ground was small with a strongly local feel. The team wasn't doing well. Posh were tipped for success after close-season investment in players, while for Stanley this was to be the fourth goalless defeat on the trot (and Peterborough were to win the January return match 8-2). That they were in the league at all was remarkable. They managed a runaway success in the Conference in 2005-06, evidence of the idea that consistency is what gets a club promoted. They strung many good results together that season. Back in the League the next year they finished 20th. Having occupied one of the scant and valuable promotion places in the fifth division, you don't want a club to suffer a return there for a while. That would be a waste of a space. Therefore I'd like this red and white outfit to stay up for a while. And Hereford, Morecambe and Dag/Red.

We have to enjoy the 'Accrington Stanley, who are they?' story which brought the club into public consciousness through its name. During the oblivion of the Eighties, the question was posited in a milk advert by a pair of Scouse blokes, and repeated many times. And the 'Stanley' comes from an Accrington team called Stanley Villa, named for its base, the Stanley Arms. The new combined entity was to perform under the name we all know. And that was in the Nineteenth Century. The member of the original Football League in 1888 was plain 'Accrington', along with its neighbours Blackburn Rovers, Bolton Wanderers, Burnley and Preston North End.

This late-summer fix of soccer was the epitome of a 92 visit for all time, the better for the crumbling edifices and the sign declaring: 'This is Stanley, the club that wouldn't die.' During the game there was much to observe: the odd Union Jack hung above the top row of the Thwaites Stand. Not much support in numbers but many of the 1,484 present assaulted ears and eyes (an abundance of fans in uniform): more than at many places. The turnstiles were drab but there was an abundance of somewhat modest pylons, if you could count them all. It was too light for a switch-on, but this kind of quirkiness is what it's all about.

How strange that over the last few decades in the further reaches of north-west England clubs were lost to the :eague in what amounts to a trend: Accrington (1962), Barrow (1973), Workington (1978), Southport ('79), and of course Carlisle (2004), who then started the reverse process – up again the next year, followed by the new Accrington (2006) and Morecambe (2007). And for a brief few seasons you could have chosen Gretna, who used to operate just over the border from Carlisle. But that was no use in 2007-08 as they were sharing Fir Park, Motherwell – not far from Glasgow. That was the price of success, their ground not meeting Scottish Premier League criteria. Relegated in bottom place, they expired, to be replaced (in the Third Division) by Annan Athletic. Annan, situated between Dumfries and Carlisle, thus became the next fresh blood in southern Scotland. Meanwhile, observe Barrow's resurgence, extended through the 2008 play-offs to Blue Square Premiership membership.

⚽

## Dagenham & Redbridge 0 Stockport County 1
## League 2 (4), 2/2/08

Of course their address has helped. This is London overspill and Essex-girl territory (what is the difference between an Essex girl and Arsenal? Arsenal have never gone down). Meanwhile lesser football clubs (and no doubt at any level) within reach of action and the world at large, for which normally read the London area, have a built-in advantage when recruiting new players. Many footballers, whether fresh in fetlock or long in tooth, have decided against places of work in remote areas. Dag/Red is just one beneficiary of this tendency.

This was confirmed on the day. It was a small, featureless ground, whose sanction in joining the League was to augment seating from c1k to 2k, over two years. Conveying all the ethos of 'Non League' it could easily be missed on the trudge up Rainham Road, with its low stands and ineffectual floodlight uprights, all tucked away from the predictable industrial/urban landscape – dual carriageways, nondescript housing, road houses providing alcoholic and social nourishment. Here was the Victoria Road ground (posters called it that, so did the Stockport County website, not the 'Glyn Hopkin Stadium' nor the 'London Borough of Barking and Dagenham Stadium' as was proclaimed on the first bit of the ground we saw on entering the contiguous car park). An entity since 1992, then absorbing several clubs to replace Redbridge Forest FC in the Conference, the club had surged into the fourth division in 2007, but at our visit languished in 90th place after 28 games, under threat of an immediate return. Following this sorry display at which 'no hope' was the most appropriate response, along with 'Is this the team which romped away with the Conference last year?', the very same team rallied with a sequence of good results which propelled them up the table, only to do a lead-balloon impersonation all over again. Finally Mansfield and Wrexham were just too bad to let them drop. The Daggers finished in 20th position.

There were six in our party to pig out on the final, final ground in the quest. Much planning and enquiry went into the day trip. How about spending a day at the ninth Chelmsford Winter Beer Festival and staying there for the night? After all, Dagenham looked close on the map. The trouble was that, although only a few miles away from Essex's county town, it was a shift down, on the Southend, not the Colchester, railway line. That meant going in and out of London stations, negating the purpose of a stopover in Essex. In the event we stayed in the capital.

Having checked in at the hotel, Wakey, Priv and I set off for culture (Chelmsford Cathedral, where Priv espied and acquired a copy of Peter Lupson's book *Thank God for Football*) and empirical testing, in the form of many half pints (a favourite was Shalford Brewery's Levelly Black, a new stout, itself concocted a handful of miles away). The next morning was another sunny one. Shining on the righteous. I had noticed that week that the weather had adopted an alternate-days policy. Thursday was inundated, to the point of my train to London packing up altogether, at West Drayton, though the true blame was likely to lie with First ('Worst') Great Western. Again. So Saturday, fine and wintry all day, was a bonus.

Roddums and Bob joined us in Dirty Dick's, apparently the only pub offering real ale – an essential ingredient, open at weekends in the appropriate part of the City of London. Bob, the actor, a veteran, reckoned it would have been in 1947 when he went with his father to the pub. It was 'filled with every imaginable kind of stage-managed filth, dead creatures and all sorts. It looked like the inside of a vacuum cleaner bag!' Sixty-one years on he was shocked by its cleanliness, i.e. not 'dirty' at all! Priv placed Stockport County beer mats ('Act now! Buy bonds!') on the table and posed in his (rather small) top hat, which was to prove useful in identifying him in the ground – he was with the Stockport hard core on the Pondfield Road terrace – seats in the Barking Stand for the rest of us. We traversed the few streets to Fenchurch Street, armed with advice from Neil 'With Exeter City in my Heart' Le Milliere that the best approach to Dagenham East – not Dagenham Heathway, which might afford a Wetherspoon hostelry with that rare animal in those parts, proper beer, but meant something of a hike – was by rail to Barking, then the District Line (4 stops). From Liverpool Street, opposite the pub, it would have been 15.

On the tube we would have been captive observers, stopping at West Ham and Upton Park, among the many others. As it was we spent time gawping at the Lloyd's Building, then the Gherkin with a dwarfish, it seemed, church from a very different age nestling in its shadow. The prospect on an adjacent site was overwhelming. The embryonic perpendicular structure was big enough, yet another city tower under construction, but awesome was the vast, top-heavy mass above it, extending wildly beyond it on all sides. Hard-hat territory, certainly. Fenchurch Street Station was kind of cute after that, and a straightforward relief after the confused retail (with incidental transport) hell at Liverpool Street.

Rand was at our destination to meet us – our driver to cover the tracts of Dagenham between hostelries. He and I had already discounted the first port of call by mobile phone as it was loud and aleless. It became evident that those who had printed out the day-trip timetable (which I had emailed) had each done it on different coloured paper. Most decorous. And so we reached the lunch stop, the Eastbrook, providing all an adopted Stockport County supporter could wish, and a bonus, the Sky lunchtime performance overhead in several spots for our edification.

What has to be added is the bulletin hitting the headlines the next week announcing the aim of future Premiership games being played in the developing markets abroad, like China. Please not – the Alans on *Match of the Day* viewed such a scheme with disdain:

'How do the fans get to Beijing when they're working all week?'

'First class' came the riposte.

'The Premier product is absolutely massive,' said Mr Hansen, 'The system has to be workable. This is unworkable.'

Chairman Lineker terminated the exchanges: 'I'm sure they'll find some way to make it work.' Instant resignation that there's a grain of truth in that. Money talks, loudly and expensively. That was after Villa had taken top billing by beating Kevin Keegan's new (again) team Newcastle 4-1 with a hat trick from John Carew. The next day Manchester City completed the first double over the Traffs for many decades with a 1-2 result. Of course the home team were weary after recent exploits – the (successful despite fears of disruption) minute's silence for the Busby Babes 50 years on from that terrible air crash, and more happenings to promote the Manchester United brand. The world is their pitch.

Once in the ground our team turned out in the same shirts we had derided on Priv's back – a sort of satiny gold, shorts too. They looked better on our team, shining in the sun, then floodlights. The Daggers sported a curious combo: broad vertical blue and red stripes in front and all red backs. The shorts were stark white. Meanwhile two massive Stockport flags were erect behind the goal, 'like the Nuremberg rally,' commented Roddums, for whom, alas, there were no saveloys on sale. In fact Wakey got the range of pies wrong for our order (and, vacating our seats on 40 minutes, Roddums and I volunteered to do the honours, forsaking more dull play and no goals). We got to the front of the queue just on half-time for one steak-and-onion and three chicken-and-mushroom pies. And five Bovrils. Well, the 'beef-flavoured drinks' were approximately correct, but we emerged with the last three *steak-and-kidney* pies and a pasty (nothing else left, but Bob was happy as he thought the pasty was what he had ordered).

Our excellent 'Blues' had scored after six minutes (a fine strike from Leon McSweeney), flattering to deceive on the penetration front. There was precious little more for the rest of the game, a shame for the rare attenders: Roddums, who had previously only been to that single evening Villa game, Rand, who, in developing the vestige of an interest in football games as my good companion a few times in recent years, by now 'was looking for something special; there were so many lost opportunities, like corner kicking the same each time – why didn't they try something different?', and Bob, who at least enjoyed a Charlton game from time to time, taking advantage of a friend's spare season ticket. He lived a mere trot away from the Valley.

The gate was 1,834. (1,756 average in 2006-07 – I noted later that 3,436 attended St James' Park, Exeter, that afternoon). Of the small crowd a substantial number were on their travels, most sonorous, if repetitive, with a single drum and chants like 'Come on County.' They waxed slightly more adventurous when growing more confident of success with 'Shall we sing a song for you?', and at the poor Redbridge goalkeeper 'Roberts is a wanker.' On hearing one continuous refrain Roddums, when enlightened as to the lyrics, posited 'How do you get "Jimmy Gannon's Blue and White Army" out of that?'

Half-time was an oddly muted affair, rather Non League I felt. There was no articulation of added time that we could detect, but there were about 48 minutes in the first half as we could guess from the Pie Queue. It was perilously close to the Gents, causing some confusion. The outcome of the half-time '50-50 Draw For The Ground Development Fund' was a secret. Was 3435 the winning ticket? I shall never know.

After it was all over we had arranged to reunite with Priv in the Clubhouse.

his we enjoyed in the spacious and populous bar for, mostly, Guinness, the results
n the telly aloft, the best of which was Exeter's 4-0 annihilation of Satanage to
ise to a single point below the play-off positions. But we remained Privless. Rand
eparted to fetch the car – how munificent. I was last in the queue to leave, bumping

nto the hat man by the doorway. He and his friend Carol had been in the upstairs
ounge enjoying the comfortable seats. That was ok, as he had been standing for a
onsiderable time before that. We'd noticed the Sponsors' Lounge, and passed it by,
s there was a bouncer on duty. In so doing we failed to spot the stairs, which were
djacent but obscured. This was now rectified all too late. But Priv – after all, well-
nown in Hatters environs, introduced me to Norman Beverley, Chairman of the
ictorious Stockport County FC, and his wife, Linda. Great, and an appropriate final
ouch to mark the ultimate conclusion. In April 2006, at the end of the 92 quest, I
ad missed out on meeting Karl Oyston at Blackpool.

    The final touch, though, came later that evening, after we left a cross-legged
Bob to the mercy of the District Line – he had omitted to make a final piss-stop in
he Clubhouse. The survivors of the day's enterprise managed some numbers higher
han 0-1 after all. We underwent celluloid therapy and elected to watch the award-
vinning Romanian film on the subject of abortion: *4 months 3 weeks and 2 days*.
Dagenham had seemed bleak, yes, but Bucharest during the Ceausescu regime…?

Attila the Stockbroker provided the Foreword, and unwittingly has contributed almost the last gasp.

## Aldershot Town 2 Brighton & Hove Albion 6
## FA Cup Round 1, 18/11/00

Attila wrote: 'The FA Cup match at Aldershot was an absolute inspiration …Aldershot were expelled from the Football League due to 'financial irregularities' several years ago (1982), wound up, reconstituted and cast into the lower reaches of Ryman League football under a new name, Aldershot Town. It is an enormous credit to their several thousand fans, so unjustly and hideously betrayed by the custodians of their club, that they stayed loyal and swamped tiny amateur suburban grounds in numbers unseen in non-league history…

'How fitting that Aldershot's new crest is the phoenix. I look forward to the day when they regain their rightful Football League place.

*Making History*

*Packed in the stand, the rival choirs compete.*
*The pylons bathe the pitch in eerie light.*
*I feel the concrete hard beneath my feet.*
*It doesn't feel 'outdated'. It feels right.*

*Seconds till kick-off now. A long-lost sound:*
*Expectant hum. The acclamatory cheers!*
*Anticipation echoes round the ground.*
*I feel myself transported through the years.*

*This is the game I loved, the game I learned.*
*Not censored, sanitised for corporate gain.*
*Each watching eye ablaze, each penny earned.*
*We stand here singing in the pouring rain.*

*They tell us that such times are past and dead.*
*But Shots and Seagulls heard that talk before.*
*We stood together till the vultures fled.*
*Now damn them all, and hear the terrace roar!*

*The Shots reborn, the Albion on a roll.*
*Two sets of fans victorious in our strife.*
*We battles long and hard for football's soul.*

*Today we brought its spirit back to life.*

On 15/4/08 I witnessed Attila's wish-fulfilment. The Shots won promotion through the 1-1 draw at St James' Park, Exeter, that evening. They were reckoned to have prospered from a campaign well organized by manager Gary Waddock – a settled squad, attacking style and enviable consistency.

In the mixed (both play in red) pub pre-game patronage there was cheerful unanimity that it would be good to meet again next year. It was a good game, too (which the Grecians should have won).

Aldershot's home is one I would earmark for a revisit. Attila opined in 2000: 'the Recreation Ground has been left more or less exactly as it was twenty-five years ago when I went there for the first of several visits with the Albion. The atmosphere at this match was unbelievable and the memories came flooding back...'

My own previous visit there was to see them lose 0-1 to Cardiff City (Div III, 2/1/89) in front of 2,768 punters. The recollection is dim but Attila's principle is right by me. The (faint) hope had to be that the ground eulogistically assessed by Attila in 2000 had not been compromised significantly, given the combination of so many promotions and regulations in the seasons since.

## Wembley Stadium (new) – II:
## Cambridge United 0 Exeter City 1
## Conference Play-off Final, 18/5/08

The Grecians had caused hearts to flutter tantalizingly in reaching a play-off position, jockeying between sixth and fifth since beating, yes, Cambridge at the Abbey Stadium at the end of January. They saw Satanage drop out of the reckoning on 45 games and, in the 46th, in edge-of-armchair heart-string-stretching mode, nab a goal in the final, last minute of all to earn a 4-4 draw at rivals Burton to clinch fourth place, the best since August, and, a little inevitably, a two way tie with their neighbours from Torbay, ultimately third in the table.

On semi-final evening at St James' Park I made it to my front-row seat in the flybe/Doble/Cowshed – thanks to Neil (procurement) and Mike (availability, owing to wife's absence). All was in keeping with the occasion – a goal apiece with the signalled four minutes of added time to come. But...player of the season Matt Taylor delivered an all-too-casual back pass to goalkeeper Paul Jones, who was similarly underweight in his clearance, to gift an opportunity to the well-placed Zebroski: Torquay took the 1-2 advantage and odds-on favouritism back to Plainmoor.

This time the viewing venue was the Greyhound, a tavern convenient to me and fit for purpose, where in January I had successfully beseeched the barmaid to switch the telly to Setanta for Exeter's 2-0 defeat of Oxford. It has developed as a rarity to find a pub willing to show Conference games. Obviously Setanta's revenues do not depend upon anything so trivial. So, more in hope than expectation, on the morning of the second leg, following a worthy walk as token exercise, Wakey and I were full of greasy breakfast and in need of a pint (good in the Greyhound). I approached the barman with the selfsame request. He very kindly replaced Surrey v Kent with the Devon debacle. The two of us and a couple of geezers in corners watched the unravelling drama.

After some Gem bitter and (quickly reported) a goal – from the United lot – the task seemed beyond the team: a two-goal deficit and the clock ticking away towards a paltry 20 remaining minutes. Fatalistically I surmised that I really would be making the journey in the new season to a (non-cricketing that day) part of Kent with Rand and try out Ebbsfleet next year for a League match, alas not Gillingham, where he lived. They had recently been relegated to the fourth division (funny that, Ebbsfleet going on to beat TU in the Trophy Final).

But there followed 'the most exciting turnaround I can remember' as one of our companion blokes put it. He, the day before, had witnessed Bristol City's three goals, not before time. Exeter totally turned it on. Wakey and I leapt out of our seats gleeing repeatedly as they scored first ONE (Ryan Harley) – exultation! – then TWO, a sweet penalty converted by Ben Watson – to draw level; THREE top scorer Richard Logan, oh my God, to take that precious lead and, just in time from the foot of Wayne Carlisle, to reinforce and rejoice, FOUR (for the eighth time in the season), to emerge two goals clear – a fabulous 5-3 on aggregate. What eye candy on the screen, together with the beautiful 14, for manager Paul Tisdale had shown shrewd judgement in his substitution choices and timing. We were treated to an entertaining interview (the star was a loquacious and linguistically-uninhibited defender, Steve Tully). On the way out I apologized for the excessive emotion, but the chaps (and barman) were smiling indulgently. Wembley rivals-to-be Cambridge were a bit more nonchalant on the following day each time: 2-2 at Burton, 2-1 at home.

For Wembley (new) this time ticket acquisition was straightforward, not least owing to my membership of the Supporters Trust. Neil ran this initiative: I was teaming up with the doughty Wakey again and we elected to sit on the side (Toff always does that for the fullest view of Tranmere Rovers – he didn't like the Big Bank at St James' Park, despite the view of the cathedral), having been on a cusplike corner for the Morecambe debacle.

The wasp-coloured U's fans bounced up and down in the 'home' end – the lower tiers were full. 42,511 were there and vociferous (the upper level empty), up a bit from the 40,043 last time, and a transformation from the 2006 Play-off Final when 15,499 saw Hereford beat Halifax at Leicester. Still more seats could productively have been made available I'm sure. It is 'Wembley', after all.

The experience, while rendering us shitless, you might say, was kind of familiar, you might add. Actually incredibly tense, and not helped by our boys taking the lead, courtesy of the splendid 33-year-old Rob Edwards (with only a quarter of the game gone). What joy! Flags a-flying, fans (the red ones) leaping in ecstasy, embracing, emoting. However, I – and I can't have been alone – couldn't help recalling the previous occasion, when City had also been 1-0 up at 22 minutes. But this bunch were good. They were intent, and, it proved, undaunted. From manager Tisdale, right through the

atfit, 'The Pride of Devon', had learned from experience. They'd even foregone the
kits which served to overawe the team on the Morecambe occasion.

'You're not bouncing any more' came the call. No, we were doing that. We'd
already heard 'You only win at the boat race' on the way to the stadium and I'd enjoyed
a comforting exchange on the tube with a woman who, observing my tasteful red and
white scarf, told us that she had been there for (FA Cup winners) Pompey the day
before and wished the best for Exeter. Not to mention the chat in the Railway with
Mercy, from Peckham out of Kenya. She was an Arsenal fan, 'and I like Manchester,
Chelsea, Liverpool.'

Past the turnstiles, still silky smooth in their bright perfection, in the
nourishment and relief zone we found ourselves entwined within the ubiquitous buzz,
observing that prices had jumped up in the intervening year. No longer was there a
cheap chocolate option, though there was more congestion around the condiments,
including a smattering of battle-ready Grecians where there had been a single Shrimp
in dedicated uniform representing Morecambe in 2007. And so many smiles, for many
after so much 'Zyderrrghhh!' Of course ticket prices had been hiked up too. Inflation,
much publicized of late, couldn't be that much. Yet.

'WE ARE Exeter, We are EX-ET-ER.!' There were chances at both ends in
the dying minutes. Hearts were athrob as Matt Taylor cleared off the line (thankfully a
better reaction than the Torquay episode) and at the other end a thrusting move by our
man Dean Moxey was thwarted by the advancing keeper, Danny Potter – the thought
balloon of a two-goal cushion banished in an instant.

But 'We are going up' was to come true. Tears, hugs, unbelief, astonishment.
The League, after five long years in exile! The League Cup, Port Vale to come, no more
Rushden, no more bloody Setanta with its imperious approach to fixture manipulation
all of these flickered through my mightily challenged brain. The world-stopping
ramifications of the achievement were finally confirmed on the scoreboards which
had been singularly uninformative during the match: 'Congratulations to Exeter
City, promoted to the Football League.' Our red, and white (mostly – they'd chosen
the third strip), squad mounted those eternal steps to receive and display the trophy,
skipper Danny Seaborne in pole position.

And so it was. Seventh time lucky for me at a Wembley, and a record-breaking
absorption of the environs. This team had appeared there twice in the stadium's 53
weeks of operations – never at Wembley (old): 1923-2000. We were lost in all the
trappings of success – fireworks, our waving heroes' tour of the pitch and evocative
songs like 'Hi Ho Silver Lining' to which for once many there contributed. I realized
what I had missed on all those previous, failed occasions, and by no means only at this
venue. One by one we applied lips to the bear mascot proffered by a diehard in the
row behind, my visage (and empathically coloured polka-dot hanky) by then as soggy
as during the most maudlin bits of *The Sound of Music*. To add my faithful cohort,
Jakey, who impressed in his adoption of Devon's best.

Wending our weary way down to the promenade outside we were met with
'We are going to Shrewsb'ry', a closely harmonized epithet. More fun: 'There's only one

team in Devon' with a much repeated alternative, 'the Exeter is wonderful', through the melée of all those punters. Somehow the defeated hordes had evaporated, no doubt to resurface somewhere in East Anglia. Again the erstwhile ignominy was evoked.

A small personal reward was in store a short hike away: the first victory pints, of Itchen Valley Pure Gold. And to round things off there soon emerged another prospect, to quote the June 2008 issue of *What's Brewing*: 'An Exeter cider producer struck gold in CAMRA's National Championship at the Reading Beer Festival. New champion Green Valley Farmhouse Vintage Cyder was described by judges as having "a lovely, proper cider aroma, like an autumn morning."' Zyyduurrrrgghhhhh!!!

## THE END

# Appendices

## Appendix I
# Table of Grounds and Fixtures Attended

| Club | Ground name when visited | Opponent | Match status note i | Score | Date |
|---|---|---|---|---|---|
| **League Members 2005-09** | | | | | |
| Accrington Stanley | Fraser Eagle Stadium | Peterborough | League 2 (4) | 0-2 | 1/9/0 |
| Aldershot (Town) note ii | Recreation Ground | Cardiff | Division III | 0-1 | 2/1/8 |
| Arsenal | Highbury | Nottingham F | Division I | 1-3 | 11/3/8 |
| Aston Villa | Villa Park | Southampton | Division I | 2-1 | 28/3/8 |
| Barnet | Underhill | Doncaster | Division III (4) | 1-1 | 4/11/9 |
| Barnsley | Oakwell | Bolton | Division II | 3-1 | 5/3/8 |
| Birmingham City | St Andrews | Exeter | League Cup 3 | 1-2 | 26/9/7 |
| Blackburn Rovers | Ewood Park | Fulham | Premier | 2-1 | 20/08/0 |
| Blackpool | Bloomfield Road | Swansea | League 1 (3) | 1-0 | 15/4/0 |
| Bolton Wanderers | Reebok Stadium | Everton | Premier | 0-1 | 21/08/0 |
| Boston United | York Street | Cheltenham | Division III (4) | 4-1 | 11/10/0 |
| Bournemouth | Dean Court | Exeter | Division II (3) | 1-3 | 6/3/9 |
| Bradford City | Valley Parade | Coventry | Premier | 2-1 | 2/12/0 |
| Brentford | Griffin Park | Exeter | Division IV | 5-0 | 31/10/7 |
| Brighton & Hove Albion | Withdean Stadium | Darlington | Division III (4) | 1-1 | 29/1/0 |
| Bristol City | Ashton Gate | Southend | Division III | 0-2 | 14/11/8 |
| Bristol Rovers | Memorial Stadium | Oxford | League 2 (4) | 1-1 | 13/9/0 |
| Burnley | Turf Moor | Millwall | Division II (3) | 4-3 | 22/4/0 |
| Bury | Gigg Lane | Notts County | Division III | 0-1 | 9/4/8 |
| Cardiff City | Ninian Park | Reading | Division III | 1-2 | 8/10/8 |
| Carlisle United | Brunton Park | Doncaster | Division III (4) | 0-0 | 29/3/9 |
| Charlton Athletic | The Valley | Bradford City | Premier | 2-0 | 4/11/0 |
| Chelsea | Stamford Bridge | Aston Villa | Premier | 1-0 | 21/8/9 |
| Cheltenham Town | Whaddon Road | Blackpool | Division III (4) | 0-1 | 28/10/0 |
| Chester City | Saunders Honda Stadium | Oxford | League 2 (4) | 0-1 | 2/1/0 |
| Chesterfield | Saltergate | Aston Villa | Division III | 0-4 | 19/4/7 |
| Colchester United | Layer Road | Millwall | Division II (3) | 0-0 | 28/11/9 |
| Coventry City | Ricoh Arena | Stoke | Champ (2) | 1-2 | 2/11/0 |
| Crewe Alexandra | Gresty Road | Sunderland | Champ (2) | 0-1 | 12/3/0 |
| Crystal Palace | Selhurst Park | Stoke | Division II | 1-0 | 9/5/8 |
| Dagenham & Redbridge | Glyn Hopkin Stadium | Stockport | League 2 (4) | 0-1 | 2/2/0 |
| Darlington | Williamson Stadium | Macclesfield | Division II (4) | 3-1 | 3/1/0 |
| Derby County | Pride Park | Leeds | Premier | 2-2 | 31/10/9 |
| Doncaster Rovers | Belle Vue | Bristol Rovers | Division III (4) | 5-1 | 4/10/0 |
| Everton | Goodison Park | Stoke | Division I | 3-0 | 11/9/7 |
| Exeter City | St James' Park | Rochdale | Division IV | 5-0 | 24/3/9 |
| Fulham | Craven Cottage | Aston Villa | Division III | 0-2 | 28/11/7 |
| Gillingham | Priestfield Stadium | Notts County | Division III | 3-1 | 22/11/8 |
| Grimsby Town | Blundell Park | Watford | Division I (2) | 2-1 | 14/4/0 |
| Hartlepool United | Victoria Park | Chesterfield | League 1 (3) | 1-0 | 10/2/0 |
| Hereford United | Edgar Street | Tranmere | FA Cup 3 replay | 1-0 | 16/1/0 |
| Huddersfield Town | Macalpine Stadium | Cheltenham | Division II (3) | 3-3 | 15/2/0 |
| Hull City | KC Stadium | Huddersfield | Division I (2) | 2-1 | 1/1/0 |

| Club | Ground name when visited | Opponent | Match status note i | Score | Date |
|---|---|---|---|---|---|
| Ipswich Town | Portman Road | Norwich | Division I (2) | 5-0 | 21/2/98 |
| Leeds United | Elland Road | Sheffield Utd | Division I | 1-0 | 22/1/72 |
| Leicester City | Walkers Stadium | Wigan | Champ (2) | 0-2 | 16/4/05 |
| Leyton Orient | Brisbane Road | Scunthorpe | Division IV | 4-1 | 13/5/89 |
| Lincoln City | Sincil Bank | Chester | League 2 (4) | 3-1 | 10/12/05 |
| Liverpool | Anfield | Stoke | Division I | 2-0 | 23/2/85 |
| Luton Town | Kenilworth Road | Aston Villa | Division I | 1-0 | 1/10/83 |
| Macclesfield Town | Moss Rose | Southend | Division III (4) | 2-1 | 1/3/05 |
| Manchester City | City of Manchester Stadium | Newcastle | Premier | 1-1 | 2/2/05 |
| Manchester United | Old Trafford | Aston Villa | Division I | 4-1 | 6/2/82 |
| Mansfield Town | Field Mill | Blackburn | Division III | 1-0 | 12/2/72 |
| Middlesbrough | Riverside Stadium | Coventry | Premier | 4-0 | 7/9/96 |
| Millwall | New Den | Wolverhampton | Champ (2) | 1-2 | 22/1/05 |
| Milton Keynes Dons | National Hockey Stadium | Rotherham | League 1 (3) | 1-1 | 29/10/05 |
| Morecambe | Christie Park | Darlington | League 2 (4) | 0-0 aban | 8/12/07 |
| Newcastle United | St James' Park | Barnsley | Division I (2) | 6-0 | 7/4/93 |
| Northampton Town | Sixfields Stadium | Barnet | Division III (4) | 2-0 | 28/12/96 |
| Norwich City | Carrow Road | Newcastle | Premier | 2-1 | 31/12/94 |
| Nottingham Forest | City Ground | West Ham | Division I | 1-0 | 21/8/71 |
| Notts County | Meadow Lane | Halifax | Division III | 3-1 | 12/3/72 |
| Oldham Athletic | Boundary Park | Blackpool | Division II (3) | 2-3 | 23/8/03 |
| Oxford United | Kassam Stadium | Leyton Orient | League 2 (4) | 2-2 | 28/3/05 |
| Peterborough United | London Road | Cardiff | Division III (4) | 2-0 | 13/4/98 |
| Plymouth Argyle | Home Park | Millwall | Division II | 3-2 | 17/11/90 |
| Portsmouth | Fratton Park | Millwall | Division III | 2-1 | 18/4/81 |
| Port Vale | Vale Park | Northampton | Division IV | 5-0 | 15/9/79 |
| Preston North End | Deepdale | Exeter | Division III (4) | 0-1 | 29/10/94 |
| Queens Park Rangers | Loftus Road | Tranmere | Division I (2) | 0-0 | 17/1/98 |
| Reading | Madejski Stadium | Millwall | Division II (3) | 2-0 | 1/5/99 |
| Rochdale | Spotland | Colchester | Division III (4) | 1-0 | 20/9/96 |
| Rotherham United | Millmoor | Northampton | Division II (3) | 1-0 | 16/4/01 |
| Rushden & Diamonds | Nene Park | Exeter | Division III (4) | 1-0 | 29/3/03 |
| Scunthorpe United | Glanford Park | Rochdale | Division III (4) | 2-2 | 10/4/04 |
| Sheffield United | Bramall Lane | Birmingham | Division II | 3-0 | 17/4/71 |
| Sheffield Wednesday | Hillsborough | Norwich | Premier | 0-0 | 31/8/94 |
| Shrewsbury Town | Gay Meadow | Plymouth | League Cup 1, 1 | 1-1 | 20/8/91 |
| Southampton | St Mary's | Colchester | League Cup 3 | 3-2 | 27/10/04 |
| Southend United | Roots Hall | Newcastle | Division II | 4-0 | 1/1/92 |
| Stockport County | Edgeley Park | Ipswich | Division I (2) | 0-1 | 14/3/98 |
| Stoke City | Britannia Stadium | Wolverhampton | Division I (2) | 3-0 | 8/11/97 |
| Sunderland | Stadium of Light | Birmingham | Premier | 0-1 | 26/11/05 |
| Swansea City | Liberty Stadium | Hartlepool | League 1 (3) | 1-1 | 21/1/06 |
| Swindon Town | County Ground | Chelsea | Division II | 1-1 | 9/10/88 |
| Torquay United | Plainmoor | Wigan | Division III (4) | 1-1 | 26/11/95 |

| Club | Ground name when visited | Opponent | Match status note i | Score | Date |
|---|---|---|---|---|---|
| Tottenham Hotspur | White Hart Lane | Manchester C | Premier | 2-1 | 19/3/05 |
| Tranmere Rovers | Prenton Park | Sunderland | Division I (2) | 4-1 | 13/11/93 |
| Walsall | Bescot Stadium | Carlisle | League Cup 1 | 2-1 | 12/8/03 |
| Watford | Vicarage Road | Aston Villa | Division I | 2-1 | 26/2/83 |
| West Bromwich Albion | The Hawthorns | Aston Villa | Division I | 0-0 | 8/11/80 |
| West Ham United | Upton Park | Aston Villa | Premier | 1-1 | 15/1/00 |
| Wigan Athletic | JJB Stadium | Bournemouth | League Cup 2 | 1-0 | 20/9/05 |
| Wolverhampton Wanderers | Molineux | Charlton | Division I (2) | 2-3 | 11/1/00 |
| Wrexham | Racecourse Ground | Bristol Rovers | Division II (3) | 1-0 | 3/4/99 |
| Wycombe Wanderers | Causeway Stadium | Bury | Division II (3) | 0-1 | 27/8/96 |
| Yeovil Town | Huish Park | Bury | Division III (4) | 2-1 | 17/4/04 |

## Former Grounds
### New from 2006*

| Club | Ground name when visited | Opponent | Match status | Score | Date |
|---|---|---|---|---|---|
| Arsenal | Emirates Stadium* | note iii | n/a | n/a | 26/11/07 |
| Bolton Wanderers | Burnden Park | Mansfield | FA Cup 2 | 2-0 | 10/12/83 |
| Brighton &Hove Albion | Goldstone Ground | Exeter | Division IV | 1-2 | 26/12/63 |
| Bristol Rovers | Eastville Stadium | Exeter | Division III | 2-3 | 9/2/82 |
| Bristol Rovers | Twerton Park | Blackburn | Division II | 3-0 | 7/3/92 |
| Coventry City | Highfield Road | Aston Villa | Division I | 0-0 | 6/11/82 |
| Derby County | Baseball Ground | Huddersfield | Division I | 3-0 | 15/4/72 |
| Doncaster Rovers | Keepmoat Stadium* | Huddersfield | League 1 (3) | 2-0 | 14/10/07 |
| Leicester City | Filbert Street | Bristol City | Division II | 2-1 | 7/9/91 |
| Manchester City | Maine Road | Everton | Division I | 3-0 | 21/2/76 |
| Middlesbrough | Ayresome Park | note iv | n/a | n/a | 22/7/78 |
| Millwall | The Den | Manchester U | Division I | 0-0 | 8/4/89 |
| Oxford United | Manor Ground | Wolverhampton | League Cup 1 | 2-3 | 5/9/00 |
| Reading | Elm Park | Bolton | Division I (2) | 3-2 | 8/2/97 |
| Shrewsbury Town | New Meadow* | Wycombe | League 2 (4) | 0-1 | 29/12/07 |
| Southampton | The Dell | Watford | Division I | 1-2 | 26/12/84 |
| Stoke City | Victoria Ground | Wolverhampton | Division I | 2-2 | 20/8/75 |
| Sunderland | Roker Park | Nottingham F | Division I | 1-1 | 18/2/84 |
| Swansea City | Vetch Field | Exeter | Division III (4) | 2-0 | 8/8/98 |
| Walsall | Fellows Park | Port Vale | FA Cup 2 | 1-1 | 17/12/77 |
| Wigan Athletic | Springfield Park | Stoke | Division III | 1-0 | 15/2/92 |
| Wimbledon | Plough Lane | Manchester C | Division I | 0-0 | 24/1/87 |

## Beyond the 92, or the pale

| Club | Ground name when visited | Opponent | Match status | Score | Date |
|---|---|---|---|---|---|
| Castleford Tigers | Wheldon Road | Salford Sharks | Super League | 22-24 | 13/4/01 |
| England - playing | Wembley Stadium (old) | note v | Euro 96 | 0-0, 5-6 pens | 26/6/96 |
| England - renting out I | Wembley Stadium (new) - I | note vi | Conference Play-off | 1-2 | 20/5/07 |
| England - renting out II | Wembley Stadium (new) - II | note vii | Conference Play-off | 0-1 | 18/5/08 |
| Kidderminster Harriers | Aggborough | Cardiff | League Cup 1 | 1-1, 4-5 pens | 24/8/04 |

## Notes

**note i** Throughout the text each League game carries its level within the four divisions in brackets, if necessary, for clarification, e.g. from 2004-05, if a 'Championship' game is covered, the suffix (2) is added; **note ii** The club was called 'Aldershot' at the time of the visit; **note iii** Stadium tour; **note iv** Cleveland Jazz Festival; **note v** England v Germany; **note vi** Exeter v Morecambe; **note vii** Cambridge v Exeter

# Appendix II
# League Structure from 1958-59
# and League Cup from 1960-61

## League Structure

| From | To | Structure - names of divisions |
|---|---|---|
| 1958-59 | 1991-92 | Divisions 1 to 4 |
| 1992-93 | 1992-93 | Premier Division; Leagues 1 to 3 (2,3,4) |
| 1993-94 | 1993-94 | FA Premier League; Barclays Divisions 1 to 3 |
| 1994-95 | 1994-95 | FA Carling Premier Division; Endsleigh League Divisions 1 to 3 |
| 1995-96 | 2001-02 | FA Carling Premier Division; Nationwide League Divisions 1 to 3 |
| 2002-03 | 2003-04 | FA Barclaycard Premier Division; Nationwide Divisions 1 to 3 |
| 2004-05 | | FA Barclays Premier League; Coca-Cola Championship (2) Coca-Cola Leagues 1 & 2 (3,4) |

## League Cup

| From | To | Official Name |
|---|---|---|
| 1960-61 | 1981-82 | Football League Cup |
| 1982-83 | 1985-86 | Milk Cup |
| 1986-87 | 1989-90 | Littlewoods Cup |
| 1990-91 | 1991-92 | Rumbelows Cup |
| 1992-93 | 1997-98 | Coca-Cola Cup |
| 1998-99 | 2002-03 | Worthington Cup |
| 2003-04 | | Carling Cup |

## Appendix III
# Towards a Fifth Division (Non League top tier)

| INTO AND OUT OF THE LEAGUE from 1919 to 1960 | OUT OF THE LEAGUE | Consecutive League Seasons |
|---|---|---|
| 1919-20 (two divisions of 22 clubs each) | Glossop | 19 |
| | Leeds City | 14 |
| 1920-21 Third Division - 22 clubs | | |
| 1921-22 Third Division (North) 20 clubs | | |
| 1923-24 Third Division (North) from 20 to 22 | | |
| 1927-28 | Aberdare Athletic | 6 |
| 1928-29 | Durham City | 7 |
| 1929-30 | Ashington | 8 |
| 1930-31 | Merthyr Town | 10 |
| | South Shields | 11 |
| 1931-32 | Nelson | 10 |
| | Wigan Borough (resigned) | 10 |
| 1932-33 | Thames | 2 |
| 1938-39 | Gillingham | 18 |
| 1950-51 | | |
| 1951-52 | New Brighton | 28 |

1958-59: Third and Fourth Divisions
introduced to replace Third Division North and South

## INTO THE LEAGUE

| | |
|---|---|
| 1919-20<br>(two divisions of 22<br>clubs each) | **Coventry City**<br>**Port Vale**<br>**Rotherham County**<br>**South Shields**<br>**Stoke City**<br>**West Ham United** |
| 1920-21<br>Third Division - 22 clubs | |
| 1921-22<br>Third Division (North) - 20<br>clubs | |
| 1923-24<br>Third Division (North) from<br>20 to 22 | **Doncaster Rovers**<br>**New Brighton** |
| 1927-28 | **Torquay United** |
| 1928-29 | **Carlisle United** |
| 1929-30 | **York City** |
| 1930-31 | **Thames**<br>**Gateshead** |
| 1931-32 | **Chester** |
| 1932-33 | **Aldershot**<br>**Mansfield Town** |
| 1938-39 | **Ipswich Town** |
| 1950-51<br>increase from 88 to 92 clubs | **Colchester United**<br>**Gillingham**<br>**Scunthorpe & Lindsey United**<br>**Shrewsbury Town** |
| 1951-52 | **Workington** |

-

| IN AND OUT OF THE LEAGUE from 1961 to 1979 | OUT OF THE LEAGUE | Consecutive League seasons |
|---|---|---|
| 1960-61 | Gateshead | 30 |
| 1961-62 | Accrington Stanley (resigned) | 41 |
| 1962-63 | | |
| 1963-64 | | |
| 1964-65 | | |
| 1965-66 | | |
| 1966-67 | | |
| 1967-68 | | |
| 1968-69 | | |
| 1969-70 | | |
| 1970-71 | Bradford (Park Avenue) | 62 |
| 1971-72 | | |
| 1972-73 | Barrow | 51 |
| 1973-74 | | |
| 1974-75 | | |
| 1975-76 | | |
| 1976-77 | | |
| 1977-78 | Workington | 26 |
| 1978-79 | Southport | 57 |

## FIFTH DIVISION

**Alliance Premier League**

| 1979-80 | | |
|---|---|---|
| 1980-81 | | |
| 1981-82 | | |
| 1982-83 | | |
| 1983-84 | | |
| 1984-85 | | |
| 1985-86 | | |

**Gola League**

| 1986-87 | Lincoln City | 74 |
|---|---|---|
| 1987-88 | | |
| **GM Vauxhall Conference** | Newport County | 67 |
| 1988-89 | Darlington | 67 |
| 1989-90 | Colchester United | 39 |
| 1990-91 | Aldershot (bankrupt) | 59 |
| 1991-92 | Maidstone United (bankrupt) | 4 |
| 1992-93 | Halifax Town | 71 |
| 1993-94 | | |

**Vauxhall Conference**

## INTO THE LEAGUE

| Year | Club | | Champions but not Promoted |
|------|------|---|---|
| 1960-61 | Peterborough United | | |
| 1961-62 | | | |
| 1962-63 | Oxford United | | |
| 1963-64 | | | |
| 1964-65 | | | |
| 1965-66 | | | |
| 1966-67 | | | |
| 1967-68 | | | |
| 1968-69 | | | |
| 1969-70 | | | |
| 1970-71 | Cambridge United | | |
| 1971-72 | | | |
| 1972-73 | Hereford United | | |
| 1973-74 | | | |
| 1974-75 | | | |
| 1975-76 | | | |
| 1976-77 | | | |
| 1977-78 | Wimbledon | | |
| 1978-79 | Wigan Athletic | | |

**Alliance Premier League**

| Year | Club | | Champions but not Promoted |
|------|------|---|---|
| 1979-80 | | | |
| 1980-81 | | | |
| 1981-82 | | | Altrincham |
| 1982-83 | | | Runcorn |
| 1983-84 | | | Enfield |
| 1984-85 | | | Maidstone United |
| 1985-86 | | | |

**Gola League**

| Year | Club | | Champions but not Promoted |
|------|------|---|---|
| | | | Wealdstone |
| 1986-87 | Scarborough | | Enfield |
| 1987-88 | | | |

**GM Vauxhall Conference**

| Year | Club | | |
|------|------|---|---|
| | Lincoln City | 1 year out | |
| 1988-89 | Maidstone United | | |
| 1989-90 | Darlington | 1 year out | |
| 1990-91 | Barnet | 93rd club | |
| 1991-92 | Colchester United | 2 years out | |
| 1992-93 | Wycombe Wanderers | | |
| 1993-94 | | | |

**Vauxhall Conference**

| Year | Club | | Champions but not Promoted |
|------|------|---|---|
| | | | Kidderminster Harriers |

| FIFTH DIVISION (cont) | OUT OF THE LEAGUE | Consecutive League Seasons | Bottom, but not Relegated | Consecutive League Seasons |
|---|---|---|---|---|
| 1994-95 | | | Exeter City | |
| 1995-96 | | | Torquay United | |
| 1996-97 | Hereford United | 24 | | |
| 1997-98 | Doncaster Rovers | 74 | | |
| 1998-99 | Scarborough | 12 | | |
| 1999-2000 | | | | |
| **Nationwide Conference** | Chester City | 68 | | |
| 2000-01 | Barnet | 10 | | |
| 2001-02 | Halifax Town | 4 | | |

| INTRODUCTION OF TWO UP, TWO DOWN | 92nd | | 91st | |
|---|---|---|---|---|
| 2002-03 | Shrewsbury Town | 52 | Exeter City | 83 |
| 2003-04 | York City | 74 | Carlisle United | 75 |
| 2004-05 | Cambridge United | 34 | Kidderminster Harriers | 5 |
| 2005-06 | Rushden & Diamonds | 5 | Oxford United | 44 |
| 2006-07 | Torquay United | 79 | Boston United | 6 |
| 2007-08 | | | | |
| **Blue Square Premier** | Wrexham | 87 | Mansfield Town | 77 |

## INTO THE LEAGUE

| | | |
|---|---|---|
| 1994-95 | | Macclesfield Town |
| 1995-96 | | Stevenage Borough |
| 1996-97 | | |
| 1997-98 | Macclesfield Town | |
| 1998-99 | Halifax Town | |
| 1999-2000 | Cheltenham Town | |
| **Nationwide Conference** | | |
| 2000-01 | Kidderminster Harriers | |
| 2001-02 | Rushden & Diamonds | |
| 2002-3 | Boston United | |

| | 1st | Years out | PLAY-OFFS (Position) | Years out | RUNNERS-UP (If not promoted) |
|---|---|---|---|---|---|
| 2002-03 | Yeovil Town | | Doncaster Rovers (3) | 4 | Morecambe |
| 2003-04 | Chester City | 4 | Shrewsbury Town (3) | 1 | Hereford United |
| 2004-05 | Barnet | 4 | Carlisle United (3) | 1 | Hereford United |
| 2005-06 | Accrington Sranley | 44 | Hereford United (2) | 10 | |
| 2006-07 | Dagenham & Redbridge | | Morecambe (3) | | Oxford United |
| 2007-08 | | | | | |
| **Blue Square Premier** | Aldershot Town | 16 | Exeter City (4) | 5 | Cambridge United |

# Appendix IV

# Populations (Census 2001)
## Highest: Non League/Lowest: League

### Top 20 Populations without a League Club

| | 2005-06 League Membership | Notes | pop: '000 | | 2008-09 Membership | Notes | pop: '000 |
|---|---|---|---|---|---|---|---|
| 1 | Aldershot | i, iv | 243 | 1 | Crawley | | 180 |
| 2 | Crawley | i | 180 | 2 | Warrington | vi | 158 |
| 3 | Warrington | i | 158 | 3 | Mansfield | iv, vi | 158 |
| 4 | Poole | vii | 145 | 4 | Poole | | 145 |
| 5 | Slough | i | 142 | 5 | Oxford | ii | 143 |
| 6 | Newport (Gwent) | i | 139 | 6 | Slough | | 142 |
| 7 | Telford | i | 138 | 7 | Newport (Gwent) | | 139 |
| 8 | York | | 138 | 8 | Telford | | 138 |
| 9 | Gloucester | i | 136 | 9 | York | | 138 |
| 10 | Nuneaton | i | 132 | 10 | Gloucester | | 136 |
| 11 | Cambridge | i | 131 | 11 | Nuneaton | | 132 |
| 12 | Hastings | | 127 | 12 | Cambridge | | 131 |
| 13 | Thanet | i | 119 | 13 | Hastings | | 127 |
| 14 | Southport | | 116 | 14 | Thanet | | 119 |
| 15 | St Albans/Hatfield | | 115 | 15 | Southport | | 116 |
| 16 | Exeter | iv | 107 | 16 | St Albans/Hatfield | | 115 |
| 17 | Eastbourne | | 107 | 17 | Torquay (Torbay) | iii | 110 |
| 18 | Bedford/Kempston | | 102 | 18 | Eastbourne | | 107 |
| 19 | Basildon/North Benfleet | | 101 | 19 | Bedford/Kempston | | 102 |
| 20 | Chelmsford | | 100 | 20 | Basildon/North Benfleet | | 101 |

### Bottom 10 Populations with a League Club

| | | Notes | pop | | | Notes | pop |
|---|---|---|---|---|---|---|---|
| 1 | Boston | iii | 35 | 1 | Yeovil | | 42 |
| 2 | Rushden | ii | 38 | 2 | Macclesfield | | 51 |
| 3 | Yeovil | | 42 | 3 | Hereford | ii | 56 |
| 4 | Macclesfield | | 51 | 4 | Shrewsbury | | 67 |
| 5 | Wrexham | iv | 63 | 5 | Crewe | | 68 |
| 6 | Shrewsbury | | 67 | 6 | Accrington | ii | 71 |
| 7 | Crewe | | 68 | 7 | Carlisle | | 72 |
| 8 | Carlisle | | 72 | 8 | Scunthorpe | | 73 |
| 9 | Scunthorpe | | 73 | 9 | Hartlepool | | 86 |
| 10 | Hartlepool | v | 86 | 10 | Darlington | | 86 |

| Notes | pop: '000 |
|---|---|

i  These are 'urban areas', closely-related towns which are aggregated for the purpose of population figures; e.g. Thanet, whose main town is Margate (59k).
Metropolitan boroughs are excluded

| | |
|---|---|
| ii  League swap in 2006-07 | |
| Accrington in | 71 |
| Hereford in | 56 |
| Oxford out | 143 |
| Rushden out | 38 |
| (ground location, Irthlingborough:6k) | |

| | |
|---|---|
| iii  League swap in 2007-08 | |
| Dagenham & Redbridge in | 241 |
| Morecambe in | 96 |
| Boston out | 35 |
| Torquay out | 110 |

P.S.: Morecambe/Lancaster (96k) was the 22nd most populous place without a League club in 2005-06 (Worthing was 21st with 97k).

| | |
|---|---|
| iv  League swap in 2008-09 | |
| Aldershot in | 58 |
| Exeter in | 107 |
| Mansfield out | 158 |
| Wrexham out | 63 |

| | |
|---|---|
| v  County Durham photofinish 2005-06 | |
| Hartlepool | 86,075 |
| Darlington | 86,082 |

| | |
|---|---|
| vi  Big towns 'runners-up photofinish' 2008-09 | |
| Warrington | 158,195 |
| Mansfield | 158,114 |

vii  Poole is part of Bournemouth Urban Area but historically was an independent Dorset entity, Bournemouth having been transferred from Hampshire.

| | |
|---|---|
| viii  Out of interest, Burnley is well known for its small population compared with the football club's achievements. | |
| Total population of Burnley/Nelson, | 150 |
| of which Burnley itself (absent from list above, for the sake of consistency) | 73 |

*Winter pageant crisp*

*Rattling sharp odd Saturdays*

*Iced turf hacks to bruise*

# INDEX

## Teams

## Grounds

# Football People and Others

# MAPS OF LEAGUE GROUNDS IN ENGLAND AND WALES

LEAGUE MEMBERSHIP 2005-2009

# North West

Carlisle United

1

Morecambe

Blackpool

Preston North End

Burnley

Blackburn Rovers

Accrington Stanley

Bury

Rochdale

Wigan Athletic

Bolton Wanderers

Oldham Athletic

Everton

Liverpool

Manchester United

Manchester City

Tranmere Rovers

Stockport County

2

Newcastle
United
Sunderland
Hartlepool
United
Darlington
Middlesbrough

Bradford
City
Leeds United
Castleford RFC
Hull City
Huddersfield
Town
Barnsley
Doncaster Rovers
Scunthorpe United
Grimsby
Town
Sheffield
United
Rotherham United
Sheffield Wednesday
Chesterfield

3

Macclesfield Town

Chester City

Crewe Alexandra

Wrexham

Port Vale

Stoke City

Shrewsbury Town

Wolverhampton
Wanderers

Walsall

Aston
Villa

West Bromwich Albion

Kidderminster Harriers

Birmingham City

Hereford United

Cheltenham Town

Swansea City

Cardiff City

4

● Lincoln City

● Mansfield Town
● Notts County
● Nottingham Forest
● Boston United

● Derby County

● Leicester City

Norwich City ●

● Peterborough United

●
Coventry
City

● Rushden and Diamonds

● Northampton Town

Ipswich
Town ●

● Milton keynes Dons

● Luton Town

Colchester ●
United

● Oxford United

329

5

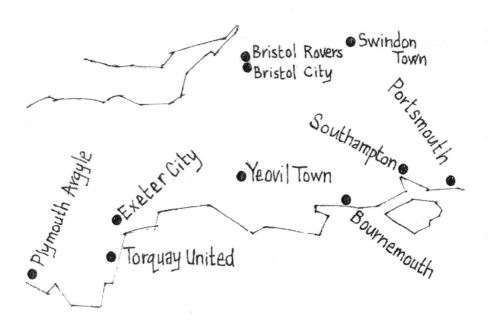

Bristol Rovers
Bristol City
Swindon Town
Portsmouth
Southampton
Plymouth Argyle
Exeter City
Yeovil Town
Bournemouth
Torquay United

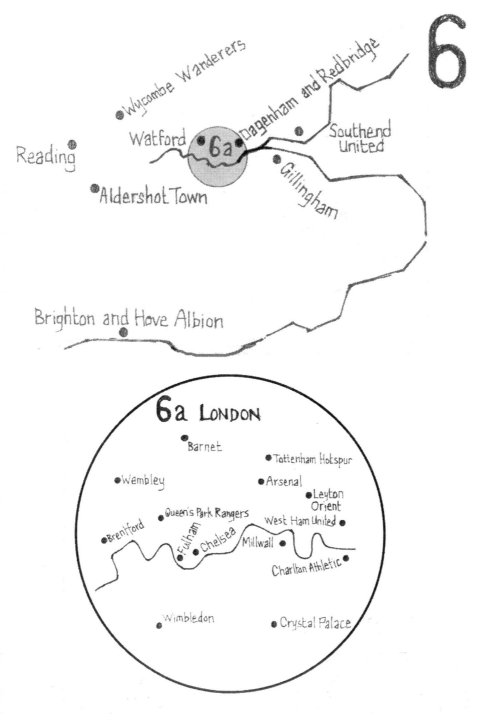

**6**

Wycombe Wanderers

Dagenham and Redbridge

Watford **6a**

Southend United

Reading

Gillingham

Aldershot Town

Brighton and Hove Albion

**6a London**

Barnet

Tottenham Hotspur

Wembley

Arsenal

Leyton Orient

Queen's Park Rangers

West Ham United

Brentford

Fulham Chelsea Millwall

Charlton Athletic

Wimbledon

Crystal Palace

# Notes

# Notes